APPLIED BEHAVIOR
ANALYSIS IN EDUCATION

APPLIED BEHAVIOR ANALYSIS IN EDUCATION
A Structured Teaching Approach

WILLIAM R. JENSON
University of Utah

HOWARD N. SLOANE
University of Utah

K. RICHARD YOUNG
Utah State University

Prentice Hall, Englewood Cliffs, New Jersey 07632

Library of Congress Cataloging-in-Publication Data

Jenson, William R.
 Applied behavior analysis in education.

  Bibliography
  Includes index.
  1. Teaching. 2. Behavior modification. 3. Learning,
 Psychology of. 4. Classroom management. I. Sloane,
 Howard Norman (date). II. Young, K. Richard (date).
 III. Title.
 LB1025.2.J46 1988   371.1'024   87-14327
 ISBN 0-13-039561-7

Editorial/production supervision and interior design: *Marjorie Borden Shustak*
Cover design: *20/20 Services, Inc.*
Manufacturing buyer: *Margaret Rizzi*

 ©1988, 1979 by Prentice Hall
A Division of Simon & Schuster
Englewood Cliffs, New Jersey 07632

Previously published under the title *Structured Teaching.*

Printed in the United States of America

10 9 8 7 6 5 4 3 2 1

ISBN 0-13-039561-7   01

Prentice-Hall International (UK) Limited, *London*
Prentice-Hall of Australia Pty. Limited, *Sydney*
Prentice-Hall Canada Inc., *Toronto*
Prentice-Hall Hispanoamericana, S.A., *Mexico*
Prentice-Hall of India Private Limited, *New Delhi*
Prentice-Hall of Japan, Inc., *Tokyo*
Simon & Schuster Asia Pte. Ltd., *Singapore*
Editora Prentice-Hall do Brasil, Ltda., *Rio de Janeiro*

Contents

Preface

There is no shortage of available texts on teaching and classroom management. There is also no lack of books telling elementary, secondary, and special education teachers, or would-be teachers, about behavior modification in the classroom. These are available to school psychologists, school counselors, and other support personnel. Why write another?

We, along with many of our colleagues, feel that most "methods" texts and other classroom teaching volumes omit one critical ingredient: what the teacher actually does! Many books explain how to set up activity areas or interest centers for a specific topic or detail the goals, philosophy, or considerations of some particular approach to teaching; but most of these texts stop short of describing what the teacher has to do to use the centers or activities effectively or to implement the goals or philosophy to work effectively with children. Support personnel similarly lack useful guidance in working with teachers. Knowing how to prepare materials and set up various types of work areas is important, as is understanding the philosophy or goals of an approach. But what comes after the knowledge and understanding—what does the teacher do to implement these things? Exactly what can support personnel suggest? This text attempts to describe for teachers, would-be teachers, and other staff one approach to the problem of what to do.

Some how-to-do-it approaches sound good until they are tried in the classroom. Frequently, this is because they do not cover all that is actually important in carrying out a teaching procedure. It is not enough to detail the tactics for an individualized one-to-one reading program; such a program must be scheduled to fit 30 children, and methods of maintaining fruitful and useful activities for 29 students while working individually with one must be described. How can reinforcement procedures be integrated in a total classroom plan? Earlier chapters in this text discuss specific tactics and procedures; later chapters present logistics, strategies, and procedures for accomplishing these more difficult tasks.

This text presents an overall approach called structured teaching, based upon applied behavior analysis (behavior modification). Applied behavior analysis is the application of principles derived from the learning laboratory to real educational and social problems. These procedures have much to recommend them. For a start, the procedures are based upon an integrated set of principles validated carefully in the laboratory. This consistency helps a teacher make decisions in novel situations and avoid working at cross-purposes from moment to moment. These basic principles have been the subject of intensive "real-life" research oriented around adapting them to the actual situations confronted in teaching. The integrated set of principles is in effect a theory, but the reason teachers and support personnel should be interested in it is quite practical; wisely used, the procedures derived from these principles have been shown to produce beneficial effects in children in the school setting. Teaching based upon such a set of principles of this sort has two additional advantages. The guidelines derived for classroom design or intervention are not ambiguous; given a set of goals, these guidelines suggest specific actions or procedures rather than general precepts or philosophies. At the same time, a consistent theory gives a basis on which to make decisions, reach new goals, or meet unexpected situations. One reason for this is that the principles relate mainly to how people learn and change, rather than what they should learn. One might say that the principles themselves are "value-free," although this is obviously not true of individual practitioners, including ourselves.

We have called the integrated behavior analysis approach presented in this text "structured teaching" because it includes an overall model for classroom design and teaching, as well as specific tactics for specific problems. We feel the approach is flexible and creative rather than rigid, without being haphazard or chaotic. A thorough reading of the text should reveal that the authors' biases are towards the use of a set of consistent principles to develop a classroom that is highly individualized and as unrestricted as possible, yet at the same time efficient and effective.

Many texts which present behavior analysis procedures for teachers (also called precision teaching, behavior modification, a reinforcement approach, a behavioral model, a social learning approach, etc.) stress classroom management without describing how the approach can be used to improve student learning. Can these two goals be integrated? We think so. Are there ways to take particular procedures or concepts from a behavioral approach and synthesize them into an overall approach to the classroom? Again, we think so. Do these approaches indicate how to actually conduct large-group, small-group, or individual instruction? Once again, we think so.

A common question raised about a behavioral approach is whether it can be used to teach more complex subjects or to develop socially approved but rarely taught goals, such as independence and problem solving. These issues are discussed in Chapter 9 on social skills training.

Who This Book Is for

This book is designed primarily for beginning and experienced elementary, secondary regular education teachers. However, it can also be used by special education teachers and support personnel who work with teachers. It does not assume that the reader is already familiar with the basic concepts of behavior analysis. These are presented in the early chapters, in a manner easily applicable to the classroom. In all chapters, we have tried to emphasize applying concepts in the classroom rather than merely learning abstractions for their own sake. Our objective is that after reading this text, the beginning teacher will have concrete ideas about overall strategies and logistics for structuring a classroom and about specific tactics for instruction, presentations, and classroom management. We hope that experienced teachers will be able to integrate these ideas with their experience to develop new and beneficial classroom procedures. Support personnel should have an expanded repertoire for dealing with pupil and classroom problems.

How to Use This Book

Each of the chapters in the book have a set format and structure. At the beginning of each is a set of objectives that the reader will accomplish by completing the chapter. Following the objectives section is an overview section, which is a survey of the basic information presented in the chapter. The major divisions of each chapter reflect the objectives stated at the beginning of the chapter. At the end of each major chapter division is an Example, Exercise and Feedback section. The Example section is designed to give the reader a concrete educational example of the concepts presented in the major chapter division. The Exercise is designed to give the reader experience in working with a concept or skill from the major chapter division. The Feedback section is constructed to give the reader immediate information about the correctness of their answers on the exercise. At the end of each chapter is a Cumulative Exercise and Feedback section which covers the whole chapter. In addition, a Fast Track section at the end of the chapter reviews all the major concepts presented in the chapter.

A student who first reviews the objectives and overview will understand the basic structure of the chapter and what information is presented. By working through the Examples, Exercises, and Feedback sections, a student will gain experience with the basic concepts and skills presented in the chapter. By reading the Fast Track section, the student will receive one more review of all the important material presented in the chapter. The Fast Track can also be used as a pretest.

A Final Word

We have avoided talking down or pandering to popular preconceptions which suggest that persons in the field of education like "cute" language and "clever" gimmicks. Teaching is fun, or can be, and a wise teacher makes learning fun for students. However, there is rarely any way to teach effectively without hard work. A teacher, school psychologist, or school counselor who is doing a competent job is probably one of our most overworked and underpaid citizens. Good teaching or teacher support is not a casual occupation to be treated lightly. It is a serious, difficult, professional career based upon our best knowledge of children. Like most serious, difficult undertakings, there can be a lot of joy in doing it well! We have no quick and easy suggestions about how to do this. We hope you will find the challenges worth the effort.

APPLIED BEHAVIOR
ANALYSIS IN EDUCATION

ONE

An Introduction
for Teachers

TARGET OBJECTIVES

After completing this chapter, you will be able to describe how applied behavior analysis can lead to effective schools and effective teaching. To do this you will learn to:

1. Describe the characteristics of effective schools and effective teaching identified by research.
2. Describe the history and assumptions of behavior analysis, and how they meet the requirements for effective teaching and effective schools.

Effective teaching must be based on an understanding of what teachers want, what the community wants, and what research has shown works for schools and for individual teachers. What characterizes effective schools? What differentiates successful from unsuccessful teachers? How can effective teaching and school procedures be integrated into an overall approach to education?

What Teachers Want

Some teachers enjoy their careers and are effective with students; they manage their classrooms smoothly and prepare interesting and appropriate tasks. Their students are well behaved and work hard. Other teachers are also committed to their work, but find teaching drudgery. Their students are disruptive, have learning problems, and appear uninterested. For these unfortunate teachers, the classroom is an unfulfilling and punishing place to work. What are the differences between these two kinds of teachers? What exactly do good teachers want in the classroom?

Effective teachers can describe student behaviors that are valued as contributing to a good classroom, as well as maladaptive and disruptive behaviors. Clear specification of the difference between appropriate and inappropriate behaviors is a first step in designing and conducting an effective classroom program, and prevents the ambiguity which confuses both teacher and students.

Walker (1980) asked regular-education and special-education teachers to rate the importance of adaptive classroom skills and competencies in children, and to indicate which behaviors were considered maladaptive. Although they found some differences in teacher expectations, there also were many consistent findings.

Most teachers indicated that appropriate compliance, such as working independently on academics and attending to assigned tasks when requested, contribute significantly to classroom order (see Table 1–1). Of particular im-

TABLE 1-1   Adaptive and Maladaptive Benefits as Judged by Teachers

Adaptive Behaviors	Maladaptive Behaviors
1. Follows classroom rules	1. Talks out of turn
2. Complies with teacher demands	2. Gets out of seat
3. Takes turn	3. Whines
4. Listens to teacher instructions	4. Disturbs others
5. Makes assistance needs known	5. Disrupts the class
6. Produces work of acceptable quality	6. Defies the teacher
7. Attends to assigned tasks	7. Does not complete assigned tasks
8. Volunteers	

From H. Walker, "Adaptive and Maladaptive Behaviors," unpublished. Used with permission.

portance was responding positively and promptly to teacher requests. When children follow directions, the teacher has time to *teach* instead of reprimanding and redirecting.

Noncompliant behaviors, such as rule breaking, talking out of turn, being out of seat, and not completing assignments, were considered maladaptive. Behaviors rated as even more difficult by teachers involved defiance, stealing, tantrums, and physical aggression.

Some teachers and schools are extremely effective. Others seem overwhelmed and unable to focus on effective teaching. What separates these effective and ineffective schools? What are the differences between effective and ineffective teachers? Recent research has identified specifics that answer these questions.

Behavior analysis, an approach to understanding and changing behavior, lends itself easily to classroom application. In addition, its assumptions and procedures are congruent with the characteristics of effective schools and effective teaching.

EFFECTIVE SCHOOLS AND EFFECTIVE TEACHING

A recent development in educational research has been the "effective schools" movement, in which schools are studied to determine what makes some schools effective and others failures (Purkey & Smith, 1983; Rutter et al., 1979). Findings from this research have shown that although family background and school location are important variables, equally important are the teaching styles and the structure of the neighborhood school. Schools in the same locations drawing students from the same types of families can have greatly different teaching effectiveness (Rutter et al., 1979). What makes the difference are the teachers and other school personnel. The effective teachers and effective schools have been found to contain the following qualities:

1. The school and teacher recognized, publicly honored, and encouraged academic success. This required some type of measurement and feedback data collection system.
2. The school and teacher maximized the students' learning time. Simply stated, students had to spend more time in learning activities, which required a classroom that was well controlled and free of distractions. Some type of classroom control or behavior management system was thus a necessity.
3. The school and teacher had clear goals and high expectations for the students. Even if students came from limited backgrounds, the teachers had to maintain expectations for achievement and behavior. Again, this requires some type of data collection and measurement system and objectively defined goals.
4. The school and teacher had a system that maintained order and discipline. It only makes sense that a child will have difficulty learning in a noisy, distracting, disordered classroom. But order on a classroom or school level requires student compliance, which in turn requires a consistent system for managing behavior.

These four points reflect only some of the teacher and school competencies outlined in the literature on effective schools. Other points include strong principal leadership, emphasis on basic academics, and parent involvement (see Table 1–2). However, the four basic points just listed are at the core of teacher effectiveness. Effective teaching does not happen by mistake. It requires systematic, planned teaching techniques. Such a planned system is found in applied behavior analysis techniques for teaching.

The Bottom Line: Educational Responsibility

Confusion over the lawfulness of behavior and acceptance of pseudoexplanations often serve as excuses for educational failure or reasons for success. However, recent poor showings in national achievement tests have

TABLE 1–2   Qualities of Effective Schools

1. There is school-wide recognition of academic success.
2. Basic academic subjects are emphasized.
3. Clear goals and high expectations are maintained for *all* students.
4. There is a school-wide sense of order and discipline.
5. Teachers reward, praise, and recognize student performance.
6. The school principal provides strong leadership, which filters down through the teaching staff to the students.
7. The principal supports and encourages the staff.
8. The school has a monitoring system that reports student progress.
9. Teachers, principals, and parents are kept aware of pupils' progress relative to school objectives.
10. The amount of time students spend on engaged academic tasks is high (minimum 70%).
11. Teachers set the stage for learning at the beginning of the school year.
12. Teachers prepare students for independent inquiry and study.
13. There is widespread support from the school staff, parents, and students regarding school norms for behavior.
14. Teachers use a variety of discipline strategies for managing disruptive behavior.
15. Teachers create an environment that *models* high learning expectations.
16. Teachers are able to motivate children.
17. Teachers use a classroom system of rules.
18. Teachers optimize learning time.
19. Teachers move around the room, are aware of what is going on, and use a system of spot checking.
20. Teachers handle disruptive behavior in a low-key manner.

Partially abstracted from: Colorado Department of Education, School Improvement and Leadership Services Unit (1982). "Indicators of Quality Schools" (unpublished paper); A. MacKay (1982). "Project Quest: Teaching strategies and pupil achievement." Occasional Papers Series, Centre for Research in Teaching, University of Alberta; S.C. Purkey and M. S. Smith (1983). Effective schools: A review. *Elementary School Journal, 83,* 427–52.

placed more of the educational responsibility on teachers themselves and on the universities that prepare them to teach (National Commission on Excellence in Education, 1983). This trend will continue, with the public expecting more for their tax dollars from both schools and teachers. It is easy, however, to mislead oneself and offer excuses. One statement of several years ago on this topic still, unfortunately, seems applicable (Sloane & Jackson, 1974, pp. 52–57):

> Teachers rarely assume responsibility for what they do, whether it is good or bad. An elementary child is doing poorly, according to his teacher, because of "emotional problems" or because he is "unmotivated" or even, sometimes because he is "not too bright." A student does very well because "his family encourages academics" or he is "very motivated" or is "bright." A college professor says that a student did very well "because of his enthusiasm," and another says a student did poorly because he was "lazy." Students, it appears, never do well because their instructor did a good job. And they never do poorly due to bad teaching. It appears that the role of the instructor is merely to select and hand out materials, give tests, and assign grades. Whether or not students learn has nothing to do with the teacher.
>
> However, if student motivation is interpreted within a reinforcement framework, we get a different picture. Student motivation, and thus student progress, seems to be a function of environmental events which, after all, can be modified, rather than internal factors, which are rather hard to get at. Teachers do have control over the content of the materials they select, over the feedback they provide to students, over the relationship between student performance and student grade, over their personal interactions with students, over the way materials are sequenced, over all the other things that make up a course. So who is responsible for student motivation? Is the fact that Johnny does have home problems a sufficient excuse for his not learning in class? Is it satisfactory to state that students sleep during lecture because they do not "appreciate" the topic?
>
> In many of the activities which comprise our society, such as manufacturing, lack of satisfactory productivity eventually leads to dismissal. If teachers are supposed to produce learning, who is responsible for the product? Lawyers who always lose cases also lose clients. But what happens to teachers who do not teach?
>
> *Answer:* They may not be teaching in the future.

EXAMPLE

Ms. Jones is recognized by her peers as an effective teacher who tries to deliver the best possible educational services to her students. As a result, her students are among the best-behaved and most academically accomplished in the school. Ms. Jones requires her students to produce work of acceptable quality, to keep on task, and to respond to her requests. She has been very effective in dealing with problem behaviors, yet her classroom is extremely positive. When asked about her success, Ms. Jones indicates that she tries to encourage and recognize students who work hard. In addition, she maximizes her students' on-task learning time, which she feels has produced the notable academic gains in her classroom. Ms. Jones says that she isn't a "hard" teacher, but she does have high expectations and she maintains order in her classroom.

Exercises

1. What are Ms. Jones's effective teaching qualities? (List four.)
2. Which behaviors are most wanted by teachers in the classroom? Least wanted?

Feedback

1. The effective teaching characteristics of Ms. Jones are the following:
   a. She understands her students and has clear goals and high expectations for them.
   b. She publicly honors and encourages hard work in her classroom.
   c. She maximizes her students' on-task learning time.
   d. She maintains order in her classroom in a positive fashion.
2. Teachers want children who follow classroom rules, comply with requests, takes turns, listen, make assistance needs known, produce work of acceptable quality, attend to assigned tasks, and volunteer.
   Teachers do not want children who talk out of turn, get out of their seats, whine, disturb others, disrupt the class, defy the teacher, and do not complete assignments.

BEHAVIOR ANALYSIS AND EFFECTIVE TEACHING

Applied behavior analysis was derived from the experimental laboratory work of several researchers, including I. Pavlov, R. L. Thorndike, J. Watson, and B. F. Skinner. Thorndike based his early work on his laboratory studies of the problem-solving ability of cats placed in puzzle boxes. He developed a set of laws of learning that were essential to early applied behavior analysis. Thorndike's most important law was the law of effect, which stated that satisfying results following a behavior would tend to "stamp in" that behavior, or to make it more likely to occur. If a behavior were followed by an annoying consequence or result, however, then the behavior would tend to fade out, or be less likely to occur. In other words, if a child receives candy for being good, she will act the same way the next time the situation arises. If the child is spanked, on the other hand, she will tend not to repeat the behavior in a similar situation.

Watson (1924), who coined the term *behavioral* psychology, was mainly concerned with reflex behavior. Reflexes in dogs had been studied by Ivan Pavlov (1927) and were found to occur automatically when elicited by stimulation. The knee-jerk reflex is an example: When the knee is tapped in a certain spot, the leg automatically jumps. Reflex behaviors are not affected

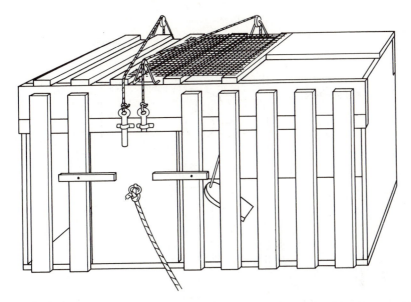

Figure 1-1 Example of a puzzle box developed by Thorndike. The door would open if the cat learned to open a latch mounted inside the box.

by either their consequences or effects that follow the behavior. A person who is punished for a knee-jerk reflex will continue to jerk when the knee is tapped even though he may try to stop the behavior. Watson incorrectly assumed that much or all behavior was basically reflexive; it is now known that this is not the case. The lower an animal is on the evolutionary scale, the more its behavior is likely to be controlled by reflexes. As animals become more advanced and complex and are higher on the evolutionary scale, reflexes play an increasingly less important role. Watson's interest was limited to reflex behavior, and most behavior of interest in educational settings is not reflexive; therefore, his direct contribution to educational issues is minimal.

This early work in learning interested many persons, however, the best known of whom is probably B. F. Skinner. Much of Skinner's work was done with rats and pigeons in a "Skinner Box," in which the animal's behavioral responses (lever pulls or key pecks) were recorded and automatically rewarded. His research, speculations, and concern with social problems resulted in several influential books. In *Science and Human Behavior* (1953) Skinner summarized current laboratory data on learning and attempted to explain many of the implications of these findings, including implications for education. However, applications in education were slow to start.

The history of published work on applying behavior analysis to classroom education is recent. In 1954, Skinner published "The Science of Learning and the Art of Teaching." This theoretical paper discussed reinforcement

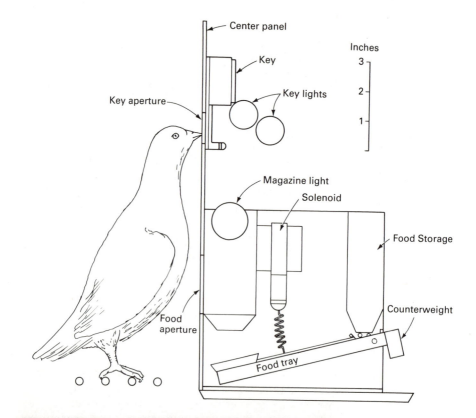

Figure 1-2   Examples of operant conditioning chambers developed by B. F. Skinner for pigeons and rats.

principles that could be applied in the classroom. (The precise meaning of the term *reinforcement* will be developed in Chapter 2. For purposes of this chapter, it is approximately synonymous with *reward*, although, as will be seen later, the equivalence is not exact). Although there was an extensive section on teaching machines (automated teaching by machines), there were no concrete applications to classroom teaching.

Eight years later, Zimmerman and Zimmerman (1962) reported on modifying the classroom behavior of two emotionally disturbed boys in a residential hospital setting. A year later, Bijou and Baer summarized their work and that of their colleagues in using systematic social reinforcement methods such as praise, approval, or attention to improve the behavior of individual children in a laboratory preschool setting. It was not until 1967 that Becker and his coworkers reported the application of such procedures to an entire classroom. However, in "What Psychology Has to Offer Education—Now" (1970), Bijou described the many ways in which applied behavior analysis had progressed in ten years in meeting the real needs of education, including classroom teaching. *Education: Behavior Analysis, 1971* included a full range of topics, including behavior management and academics in settings for both regular- and special-education children. In 1977, *American Psychologist* reported that the *Journal of Applied Behavior Analysis (JABA)* ranked third of 57 leading social science journals on mean citations per article (White & White, 1977). In the late 1970s through the 1980s, behavioral researchers developed an extensive body of scientific literature documenting the effectiveness of behavioral technology. However, behavioral approaches remain controversial, and debates among educators continue (Greer, 1982; Brophy, 1983; Skinner, 1984).

THE SHAME OF AMERICAN EDUCATION

On a morning in October 1957, Americans were awakened by the beeping of a satellite. It was a Russian satellite, Sputnik. Why was it not American? Was something wrong with American education? Evidently so, and money was quickly voted to improve American schools. Now we are being awakened by the beeping of Japanese cars, Japanese radios, phonographs, and television sets, and Japanese wristwatch alarms, and again questions are being asked about American education, especially in science and mathematics."

So begins B. F. Skinner's classic article (1984) in which he examined the failure of American education while leading the world in effective teaching research.

But research and effective behavioral technology are not enough to ensure that educators will adopt the practices that are known to work. We tend to resist new approaches, even when their effectiveness is demonstrated. In this article, for example, B. F. Skinner quotes Frederick Mosteller's comment (1981) on scurvy, a vitamin C–deficiency disease that commonly afflicted sailors on long voyages. The cure for scurvy was discovered in the year 1601,

(continued)

but more than 190 years passed before the British Navy began to use it regularly to stop the disease. Established systems, such as the British Navy, a college, or a school system, are resistant to effective techniques when they are first introduced. Applied behavior analysis techniques in education have been in use for approximately 35 years. Surely they should have been accepted by now; when compared to scurvy, however, these techniques are still in their infancy.

Innovative new approaches need a shock, like Sputnik, and time, like scurvy, to be adopted into organized systems that are slow to change. The techniques are effective. B. F. Skinner points to research demonstrating that an eighth grade class can go through an entire algebra class in half a year using teaching machines based on behavioral principles. Some of these principles are particularly effective when used in conjunction with teaching machines.

Be clear about what is to be taught. The subject matter must be presented to students in terms of skills that can be mastered using a step-by-step approach. A curriculum subject is not some "special ability" or "mental faculty;" rather, it is a skill that can be taught in steps.

Teach first things first. The fundamental, basic steps to a skill must be taught to mastery before proceeding. One cannot teach a final product without first establishing an adequate base. For example, according to Skinner, creativity as an ultimate goal is useless. A student must first understand basic skills and techniques, and can then multiply these skills into new variations, which is creativity. "Eventually some students behave in creative ways, but they must have something to be creative with and that must be taught first. They can then be taught to be creative by multiplying the variations which give rise to new and interesting forms of behavior."

Stop making all students advance at the same rate. In American schools, students are expected to move from grade to grade and concept to concept at the same rate of progress. Skinner states that the educational system could double its efficiency if each student were allowed to progress at his own pace. Teaching technologies and instruments (teaching machines or computers) must allow teachers to teach students at optimal and individual rates.

Program the subject matter. Learning through natural discovery and curiosity are fine concepts, but today's students must learn too much and the discovery process is too slow for this to be an effective teaching method. Thus, subject matter must be "programmed." Skinner suggests that subject matter be broken into basic steps that build on one another, that teaching be individualized so that students can progress at their own rates, and that the program should guarantee success, which is naturally reinforcing.

What is Applied Behavior Analysis?

Applied behavior analysis comprises interventions "derived from the principles of behavior analysis designed to change behavior in a precisely measurable and accountable manner; restricted to those interventions that include an experimental design to assess treatment effects" (Sulzer-Azaroff & Mayer, 1977, p. 511).

Assumptions

The behavior analysis approach begins with the assumption that behavior and learning are not due to chance, but rather can be described by general scientific laws. It is generally believed that with scientific research we can understand much of human behavior. This does not mean that today we even approach this high level of understanding, nor does it mean that anyone will even "know" all there is to know about a single individual. There is a tremendous gap between what might be known in theory and what is know in actual practice. Theory states that even if all the laws describing human behavior were known, complete understanding would require a person to know every detail of his genetic background, every detail of every event that had ever occurred in his life, and every current world event that affected him. This is impossible, and it is hard to imagine anyone even attempting such an endeavor. Given the practical limits on observation and measurement, such an attempt would surely fail.

Applied behavior analysis does not assume that the child's biological constitution, developmental history, or past learning experiences are unimportant. However, instead of having these factors set narrow limits within which behaviors can be changed, the applied behavior analysis model assumes that these factors set broad limits. Many behaviors that fall within these limits can be changed by systematic learning–based procedures. For example, behaviors associated with conditions such as chronic bedwetting (Doleys, 1977), seizures (Mostofsky & Balaschak, 1977); mental retardation (Beck, 1983), hyperactivity (Ross & Ross, 1982), and infantile autism (De-Myer, Hingten, & Jackson, 1981), all of which have biologically or developmentally based causes, can be greatly improved with applied behaviors analysis techniques. Although a mentally retarded or autistic child can never be "cured" by these techniques, he can be trained to live a functional life in the community. The problems of regular-education children are easier to deal with than the more severe cases just cited.

Applied behavior analysis is a scientifically based technology of behavior change which emphasizes learning as a cause of behavior. Terms that have been used synonymously include *behavior modification, behavior therapy,* and *learning-* or *conditioning-based therapies.* The defining assumption of applied behavior analysis is the emphasis on learning as a major cause of behavior. Operant, or instrumental, learning (as studied by Skinner and Thorndike), which is voluntary and nonautomatic, is considered important, particularly for educational purposes.

A central assumption of applied behavior analysis is that behavior is lawful and that both normal and abnormal behavior follow the same basic laws. The same learning-based principles govern both types of behavior in lawful ways. Disordered behavior is changed using essentially the same applied behavior analysis principles as are used to change average behavior. The only difference is that the principles have to be applied in a more consistent and structured manner for the behaviorally disordered child.

If behavior is governed by lawful principles, then the best way for applied behavior analysis practitioners to discover these principles is through the *scientific method*. With today's research findings and advances, applied behavior analysis and teaching should be far more scientifically based than artfully based. The scientific method requires four basic steps. First, the behaviors to be studied have to be defined so that they can be objectively measured and observed. Assumed theoretical or underlying causes of behavior that are impossible to measure directly are deemphasized. Second is the generation of hypotheses, which generally involve a "functional analysis"—a cause-and-effect relationship between an environmental variable and a behavior. For example, what is the relationship between praise (the environmental event) and improvement in children's academic work (the behavior)? Does it improve because of the praise? Or does it worsen when the praise is given in front of peers? Third, data have to be objectively collected with a sound scientific research design, and the results must be openly and objectively evaluated. (This last step generally leads to publication of the research results if there is a positive finding that is educationally meaningful.)

Using the scientific method to discover the lawful relationships of behavior sounds reasonable to most teachers. However, what sounds reasonable is not necessarily the same as actual educational practice. Educational products are frequently marketed with beautiful packaging, but with little or no scientific research behind their development. Similarly, educational techniques and procedures are often faddish, with their effectiveness attested to by their promoters but with little scientific validation. Teachers have a professional obligation to "scientifically kick the tires" on the educational products and techniques they use in the classroom.

Behavior analysis assumes that behavioral laws continue to operate to produce results whether or not a person intends to produce that result. This is somewhat of a difficult assumption to understand, particularly for our culture and legal system, which emphasize intention for behavior change. An example might help. If attention from parents will reinforce a child's behavior, the parents might intentionally plan to improve their daughter's table manners by providing attention (praise) when she eats correctly. However, this "law" will also operate when the parents do not intend it to. For instance, if the parents attend to the child when she is "naughty," this, too may increase such behavior. Behavioral laws are "in effect" 24 hours a day, regardless of whether anyone has planned to produce some behavior change.

The assumptions of applied behavior analysis makes it a scientifically based technology for behavior change. This is an important distinction; as a technology, applied behavior analysis does not have inherent values. It is simply a highly efficient set of procedures and techniques for changing behavior. This technology assumption, however, is no different from other scientific

TABLE 1-3 Assumptions of Applied Behavior Analysis

1. Most of the behavior exhibited by humans is learned through classical and operant conditioning procedures.

2. Behaviors that are observable and measurable are the targets for change, rather than assumed underlying causes, that are difficult or impossible to measure.

3. Genetic and physiological variables and past history set certain limits on what behaviors can be changed and how much. However, many behaviors occur within these limits, and they are controlled by the principles of learning and by environmental contingencies.

4. Behavior is lawful, and both normal and abnormal behaviors follow the same laws of nature.

5. The best way to understand and discover the laws of behavior is through the scientific method.

6. The principles of behavior change discovered through the scientific method form a technology of behavior change.

7. A technology of behavior change includes no inherent values. Values have to be supplied by the people who use the technology in order to ensure that it is not misused.

technologies such as physics, medicine, or applied chemistry. It means that unless those who use applied behavior analysis technology hold a positive set of values, the technology will be misused. The basic criticisms of applied behavior analysis (or any technology) result from practitioners having poorly applied the techology because of inappropriate values.

The basic principles of effective teaching practices (as described in the previous section) and applied behavior analysis have much in common. For example, both approaches emphasize well-defined behaviors and goals, with a measurement and feedback data collection system for students. Many of the characteristics of effective teaching, such as encouraging academic success, setting high academic and behavioral expectations, motivating students, and maintaining order and discipline in the classroom, can be best realized through the technology of applied behavior analysis. The rest of this book is designed to show students how effective teaching goals can be reached through applied behavior analysis.

EXAMPLE

An effective applied behavior analysis program for the regular-education classroom assumes that behavior is primarily learned and is controlled by contingencies within the environment. The child's response to these contingencies is lawful and can be understood by studying well-defined behaviors through the scientific method. The outcome of such scientific applied behavior analysis studies is an effective technology of behavior change that can be used by any well-trained teacher to maximize a children's academic and social success.

Exercise

1. Applied behavior analysis, as outlined in this chapter, has eight basic assumptions. What are they?
2. What is the definition of applied behavior analysis?

Feedback

1. The assumptions of applied behavior analysis are the following:
   a. Most human behavior is learned.
   b. Biological, developmental, and historical variables place a broad limit on behavior change.
   c. Applied behavior analysis is most interested in the functional relationships between precisely measured behavior and environmental variables.
   d. These relationships are best discovered through the scientific method.
   e. The relationships are the same for both normal and abnormal behavior.
   f. These relationships are independent of intention.
   g. These relationships form a technology of behavior change.
   h. The values to govern this technology are not inherent in the technology and must be supplied by people.
2. Applied behavior analysis is a set of interventions "derived from the principles of behavior analysis designed to change behavior in a precisely measurable and accountable manner; restricted to those interventions that include an experimental design to assess treatment effects" (Sulzer-Azaroff & Mayer, 1977, p. 511).

FAST TRACK

REVIEW

Teachers want orderly classrooms with compliant children who make them feel successful as teachers. They have difficulty with disruptive behaviors, such as defiance, rule breaking, aggression, arguing, and throwing tantrums. It is difficult for many new teachers to gain an understanding of why inappropriate behaviors occur and how to effectively control them.

A number of theories have been advanced to explain the causes of certain behaviors. Some of these theories include developmental explanations, biological explanations, or environmental causes such as family background and socioeconomic level. There are even pseudoexplanations that purport to explain a behavior by naming it and then using the name in a circular manner to explain the behavior. For teachers, however, many of these explanations do little good to actually change behavior in the classroom. Concrete explanations that show a clear relationship between the behavior and an environmental variable are the most useful for teachers because many environmental variables can be changed. The recently researched area of "effective teaching" has demonstrated that many adverse variables can be overcome by a set of consistently applied educational practices.

Researchers in the field of applied behavior analysis attempt to establish functional relationships between the occurrence of behavior and environmental events. These functional relationships were developed from the early works of Pavlov, Skinner, Watson, and Thorndike.

The area of applied behavior analysis forms a scientifically based technology of behavior change. This technology is based on a number of assumptions: (1) A child's biological constitution, development, and history place broad limits on the extent to which behaviors can be changed. These are broad limits, however, and much behavior occurs within these limits. (2) The majority of human behavior is learned, and most of the behaviors relevant to educators is learning-based. (3) It is important to research the functional relationships between precisely measured behavior and environmental variables. (4) Behavior is lawful, and the same principles of behavior change apply to both normal and abnormal behavior. (5) The functional relationships between behavior and the environment are best discovered through the scientific method. (6) The principles of behavior change operate whether a person intends for them to operate or not. (7) The principles that are derived from applied behavior analysis can be used to establish a practical technology of behavior change. (8) This technology has no inherent values, however; they must be supplied by the practitioner.

Applied behavior analysis is not without its critics. Much of the criticism is based on a general lack of understanding of the basic assumptions of applied behavior analysis. These criticisms include (1) the statement that applied behavior analysis will attempt to make all people exactly alike; (2) the fear that applied behavior analysis will be used inappropriately to make children docile, quiet, and still; (3) the concern that applied behavior analysis denies, and will take away, basic individual freedom; (4) the criticism that applied behavior analysis ignores emotional or affective factors; and (5) the concern that applied behavior analysis reduces human creativity. The values in using the techniques, as with any technology, have to be supplied by people.

CUMULATIVE EXAMPLE

A brief example of applied behavior analysis in action may clarify many of these introductory topics. One of the authors consulted with a teacher who had an exceptionally aggressive group of children. Could the teacher possibly be encouraging their aggressive behavior? On the surface it did not seem probable. She was not a violent or aggressive person, and she made it clear to the children that she disapproved of their continual fighting and disruption. The initial feeling was that either the children had learned their aggressive behaviors from their parents or peers, or they had genetic, chemical, or biological imbalances that spurred them to aggression. These were some of the explanations that seemed reasonable until one day an intriguing pattern of interaction in the classroom was observed. The teacher would generally *attend* to the children when they were misbehaving, but would usually ignore them when they were working quietly or otherwise cooperating. Her attention to misbehavior was not positive; in fact, it was often threatening or punishing. Nevertheless, it was attention following a misbehavior. The more negative attention she gave to the inappropriate behavior, the more frequent the behavior became. Could it be that the teacher's attention was really promoting disruptive behavior? Was the teacher unknowingly creating the problems?

In the language of behavior analysis, the teacher was *positively rein-forcing* aggressive behavior. A **positive reinforcer** is an environmental consequence that, over time, increases the behavior or behaviors that closely preceded it. When behavior is followed on many occasions by a consequence that increases the rate of the behavior in the future, the consequence is called a positive reinforcer. When the aggressive children were disruptive, they generally received immediate attention from the teacher. If this attention were a positive reinforcer, the rate of aggressive behavior should have increased. It did. It appeared that the teacher was indeed inadvertently promoting these unwanted behaviors. It is important to realize that although the teacher may have thought her attention was *aversive* (threatening and punishing), it was actually positive because the rate of aggression increased. The children's behavior rate actually defines what is a positive reinforcer, not the teacher's perceptions.

The problem thus became one of designing a set of procedures that would both eliminate most aggressive behavior in the children and substitute more functional academic and social behaviors. To this end, two basic rules were formulated: (1) When a regularly occurring behavior is harmful to learning, locate the classroom events that closely follow the unwanted behavior and determine whether they function as a reinforcer. Then prevent those events from following occurrences of the unwanted behavior. (2) At the same time, begin to reinforce more desirable behaviors that are incompatible with the unwanted behavior.

In the case of the aggressive children, this two-pronged strategy was implemented by training the teacher to ignore the misbehaving children as much as possible and to attend to children when they were working or otherwise cooperating. In addition, when the children were behaving properly, they were given social praise and small plastic tokens (see Chapter 8) which could be periodically exchanged for desirable activities and materials.

The result was that behavior quickly diminished to a tolerable and, finally, to a satisfactory level, and cooperative behavior increased. By the end of the 15-week experiment, these children appeared to be normal school children to a casual observer. It seems that the teacher's assumed aversive attention was indeed reinforcing disruptive behavior. When her reinforcing attention was no longer given for disruptive behavior but was instead reserved for cooperative behavior, disruptions were reduced and cooperation increased dramatically.

The origins of the aggressive behavior should be considered for a moment. It is unfair to claim that the teacher was the cause of the children's aggressiveness. It is possible for a teacher to train passive children to be aggressive through systematic reinforcement of aggression, but these children were aggressive when they started school that year. They had long histories of extreme aggression and had probably learned to be aggressive long before they arrived in this teacher's classroom. When they tried this well-learned behavior at school, they found that aggression earned attention and other reinforcers. They received attention from the teacher whenever they "acted up." So they continued to be aggressive when their aggressive behavior continued to reap rewards. When this reward pattern was altered, however, their behavior altered accordingly.

TWO

Behavioral Analysis: Basic Procedures

OBJECTIVES

After completing this chapter, you will be able to define, describe, and identify procedures used to strengthen or weaken behavior. To do this you will learn to:

1. Define and discriminate between operant and respondent behaviors.
2. Describe and label reinforcement and punishment procedures.
3. Describe and label procedures that strengthen or weaken behavior by changing what have been the typical consequences.
4. Describe and identify factors that modify the effectiveness of response-strengthening and response-weakening procedures.
5. Describe and identify procedures for starting new behavior.

Like all practitioners of scientific disciplines, behavior analysts have their own set of terms to accurately describe the concepts they develop and the complicated processes they study. Learning the proper use of scientific language is always important, but it is especially so when it comes to behavior analysis. Incorrect use of terminology by people outside the field has been the bane of behavior analysis, for misuse of terminology has been the source of a great deal of confusion and misunderstanding of just exactly what behavior analysts do and what their views of the individual and his environment are. This chapter discusses the concepts needed to analyze behavior and to design procedures to modify behavior. It provides the background necessary to read the professional literature in the field.

1. OPERANT VS. RESPONDENT BEHAVIOR

Behavioral Control

The concept of "control," as it is used in behavior analysis, is often misunderstood. When a behavior analyst says that something "controls" behavior, all that is meant is that it has some reliable effect upon an individual's behavior. For example, for many people, rain clouds control the behavior of carrying an umbrella. If there are clouds in the sky in the morning, this behavior is much more likely to occur than if there are no clouds. Similarly, Johnny is more likely to say "Albany" when the teacher asks him what the capital of New York State is than when she does not ask him this question. If Johnny has learned this fact, the teacher's statement controls his saying "Albany"; before learning occurs, the control does not exist. If Maxine regularly raises her hand in class and is nearly always called upon, she will probably raise her hand more and more often. However, if the teacher decides not to call on Maxine for a few days, the likelihood that Maxine will raise her hand will probably decrease. Being called upon controls Maxine's hand raising.

Consider the events that might control each of these behaviors:

1. A particular child in class talks when he is supposed to be silent.
2. The teacher gives a class an assignment or seatwork.
3. The teacher praises a child in class.
4. The teacher reprimands a child in class.

The following circumstances might control a student's talking out: another child talking to him, the fact that children have laughed in the past when he talked out, inability to read the book given him, and being unable to hear the teacher when she is making a presentation. Because all these circumstances make talking out more likely, they all exert some control over that behavior.

The following circumstances might control a teacher's giving a class homework or seatwork: noting that the class has completed the reading that precedes a written exercise in the text, finding that students have performed poorly on a test or exercise on a unit, having a written assignment available, not having any other activity prepared for that time, and having noted improvement after written assignments in the past. Because all these circumstances make giving such an assignment more likely, it is said that they all control the behavior of giving such an assignment.

Many circumstances might control the behavior of praising a child. A few of the more obvious are the child's giving a correct answer, the child's working hard when other children are being distracting, the child's helping another child, the teacher's having noted in the past that children worked harder after being praised, and a statement in an inservice training program about the value of giving praise.

Some factors that might control the behavior of reprimanding a student include the child's talking during a quiet work period, the child's not working when he has been told to do so, the teacher's having missed a night of sleep, and the teacher's having noted in the past that children become quiet after being reprimanded.

Objective Descriptions

As is probably clear by now, behavior analysis deals with objective descriptions of both behaviors and environmental events. A prerequisite to changing classroom behavior is developing a clear and objective description of it and the environmental events that support (control) it. Things that cannot be seen or observed in any way cannot be changed by the teacher. If an event is described in a manner so vague or subjective that people cannot agree on what actually occurs, it is difficult to reliably detect, produce, or prevent the occurrence of that event in the future. Some rules for clear descriptions follow.

Physical.   A behavior or event should be described in terms of its physical characteristics, which should be visible to any skilled observer. Objective, rather than subjective, adjectives should be used.

It is far less ambiguous to say "Marvin shouted, yelled, and punched Terry" than to say "Marvin lost his temper." The second statement might mean different things to different people, while the first is unlikely to. The first statement tells exactly what Marvin did, while the second does not. If we heard that "the teacher praised Eugenia and smiled at her," we have a fairly definite idea of what transpired; however, we might not know precisely what happened if we heard that "the teacher made Eugenia feel good." Similarly, "Mary wants to open the door" scarcely tells what happened, while "Mary asked if she could open the door" is much more communicative.

Nonjudgmental.   It is difficult to reach agreement on judgmental descriptions. Who knows what Harry did when he is described as "incompetent" or "immature" or "not up to par" at recess? If an observer describes crying, fighting, standing in a corner, or staying with the teacher, on the other hand, we have clarification. More subtle judgmental descriptions are statements such as that a child is "babyish" or "does not do a good job." These tell us about the speaker's opinion of the child rather than describing the child.

Quantitative. When an indication of "how much" is necessary, quantitative statements are better than judgmental ones. What is "a little" to one person may be "average" to another. That Alex only did 50 percent of his problems is much less open to interpretation than the statement that he did only "a little."

Respondent Behaviors

For reflex, or respondent, behaviors, control is often fairly automatic. For example, in a healthy person, a tap on the correct spot on the knee will elicit a knee jerk, regardless of other factors. Rene Descartes (1596–1650), the French philosopher, labeled "involuntary" behavior we now call **respondent behavior.** Involuntary behavior was seen by Descartes as completely automatic and entirely dependent on the antecedent (preceding) physical environment. Thus, if a hand is placed on a burning surface, the physical heat or pain will automatically elicit withdrawal of the hand. A tap on the correct place on the knee will automatically elicit a knee jerk.

EARLY IDEAS ABOUT RESPONDENT BEHAVIOR

Descartes believed that all animal behavior, and some human behavior, was involuntary. Some human behavior was influenced by the will or the mind, however, and Descartes called this *voluntary behavior.* Thus, he classified behavior as voluntary or involuntary according to the stimuli initiating the behavior rather than the form of the action or the part of the body involved. Involuntary behaviors quickly became known as *reflex,* or *respondent,* behaviors. Several famous researchers—Bell (1774–1842), Magendie (1783–1835), Sechenov (1829–1905), Sherrington (*The Integrative Action of the Nervous System,* 1906), Pavlov (1849–1936), and Watson (1924)—studied the nature of reflexive behavior.

Nearly all behaviors of concern in the classroom, however, are not reflexive. Talking, walking, socializing, moving about, solving problems, writing, reading, and so forth are not reflexes. The control of these nonreflex behaviors is not automatic; many different kinds of events usually exert some control over any one of them.

Operant Behaviors

Behaviors that can be controlled by consequences are called **operant behaviors.** They roughly correspond to Descartes's *voluntary* behaviors. All behaviors subject to behavioral control are operant behaviors if their frequency of occurrence in the future can be controlled by consequences—that is, by events that follow them.

Earlier in this chapter it was suggested that a child's talking out in class might be controlled by the fact that the talking had produced laughter in other children, that a teacher's giving assignments might be controlled by the academic improvement this has produced in the past, that a teacher's praise might be controlled by the children's resultant diligence, and that a teacher's reprimands might be controlled by the fact that children in the past had become temporarily quiet when scolded. Such behaviors are called **operants** because they cause their environment to produce consequences that, in turn, control them. An operant may also be controlled by things other than consequences, but if the future frequency of a behavior is at all controlled by consequent events, the behavior is an operant. Some other examples of operant behaviors and controlling consequences are pressing the button on the water fountain and getting a drink, reading the newspaper and finding the football scores, reading a book and receiving a teacher's praise, and wearing the proper gym clothes and avoiding the gym teacher's angry remarks.

Everyday language concerning operant behaviors often tends to ascribe the behavior to mentalistic and purposive factors. Thus, if a child misbehaves in class and this behavior is controlled by his classmates' laughter and attention, we might say that the child clowns "in order to get attention." Such language suggests that his behavior is controlled by events that have not yet occurred—that attention in the future controls misbehaving in the present. This description is not really accurate. It is difficult to understand how events in the future can work backwards to influence present behavior. Clearly, the likelihood of further occurrences of an operant behavior are controlled by the consequences that follow current behavior. But these consequences do not affect the behavior already emitted. Behavior is controlled not by what might occur in the future nor by the "expectation" of future events, but by what has happened in the past.

Expectation is a shorthand way of describing the effect of current or past consequences on future behavior. Its use as an explanation leaves unanswered what "expectation" is and how it arises. Thus, the statement that a child expects attention or acts in order to get attention describes the observation that attention has followed that behavior in the past and seems to have strengthened the behavior. The fact that the child, when asked, may say that he does something "to get attention" merely shows that children can learn to note the consequences of their behavior and to use the same verbal metaphors as adults.

EXAMPLE

When Frank saw the strange yellow flower, he walked toward it. The sight of the flower controlled his walking. He smelled it and sneezed from the pollen (a *respondent*). The pollen controlled sneezing. He picked the flower and gave it to Maria when he saw her a few minutes later. She shared her ice cream with him (a *consequence*). The next day he saw another bright flower and gave it to Maria, an operant strengthened by the ice cream he received after having given her a flower in the past.

Exercise

1. What controls saying "hello" when you see a friend?
2. Name two things that might control doing a homework assignment.
3. Why is the following description inadequate? "During school today John made aggressive and stupid remarks to bug Jack."
4. State whether or not the following behaviors are operants or respondents, based only on the descriptions provided.
   a. The doctor hit his knee with a hammer and the knee jerked.
   b. Carl studied his lesson, which he usually did not do, and was later able to answer three questions during class discussion. He studied again the next night.
   c. Francine walked to the water cooler.

Feedback

1. The sight of the friend controls saying "hello."
2. Past grades, the teacher's handing out the assignment, parents' comments, and seeing that the clock says 7:00 PM (regular homework time) are among things that might control doing a homework assignment.
3. The description is inadequate because it is subjective, not physical or objective, it is judgmental, and it is not quantified.
4. (*a*) is a respondent; (*b*) is an operant; and for (*c*), no information is given upon which to base a decision.

2. STRENGTHENING AND WEAKENING BEHAVIOR THROUGH REINFORCEMENT AND PUNISHMENT

Reinforcement and Punishment

Presenting a consequence (usually called a *stimulus*) after a behavior or response can have three effects on the likelihood of that behavior occurring again:

1. It can make the response occur more frequently in the future.
2. It can make the response occur less frequently in the future.
3. It can have no effect on future response frequency.

For instance, suppose that Miguel rarely asks questions in class. The teacher decides to increase his rate of question asking. The teacher goes out of his way to praise Miguel every time he asks a question. After a week of this, the teacher notices that Miguel is asking questions quite frequently. Praise (a stimulus) following each response (asking a question) has increased the frequency of that behavior.

James, on the other hand, talks excessively. The teacher decides that each time James talks, he will shorten his recess period by five minutes. After a week of this, James rarely talks in class. The teacher has decreased the frequency of this behavior by taking something away each time the behavior occurs. Flushed with success, the teacher tries praising Mary each time she works (which is rare). After a week of this, there is no noticeable change. Mary still hardly works at all. The teacher has had no effect on the frequency of this behavior. (You can't win them all.)

THORNDIKE AND THE "LAW OF EFFECT"

Thorndike (1898) studied the ways in which animals learned to escape from puzzle boxes—that is, boxes in which the animal had to learn to operate a latch or escape mechanism to obtain freedom and/or food. In early trials the animals were very inefficient, running and scrambling and emitting a large number of responses until the latch was opened. With more and more trials the animals' behavior became more and more efficient, smoother, and more rapid. Thorndike (1911) summarized his studies by formulating the law of effect:

> The Law of Effect is that: Of several responses made to the same situation, those which are accompanied or closely followed by satisfaction to the animal will, other things being equal, be more firmly connected to the situation, so that, when it recurs, they will be more likely to recur; those which are accompanied or closely followed by discomfort to the animal will, other things being equal, have their connections with that situation weakened, so that, when it recurs, they will be less likely to occur. (p. 244)

Procedures that increase the frequency of behavior by presenting or removing consequences after the behavior are called **reinforcement**. Reinforcement always increases the frequency of behavior, unless the behavior is already so frequent that the reinforcement merely maintains it. Procedures

TABLE 2-1   Reinforcement and Punishment*

	Response Frequency Increases	Response Frequency Decreases	Response Frequency Doesn't Change
Stimulus is presented	positive reinforcement	punishment	——
Stimulus is removed	negative reinforcement	punishment by response cost	——

*The contemporary formulation of these concepts is usually associated with Skinner (1938).

that decrease the frequency of behavior by presenting or removing consequences after the behavior are called **punishment.** Punishment always decreases the frequency of behavior, unless it is already very low. Procedures that involve the presentation or removal of stimuli (consequences) after behavior and have no effect on the frequency of the behavior do not have a particular designation.

Mother gives Jane a piece of candy each time she cries, and Jane tends to cry more and more often. The procedure in this case is *reinforcement,* because a consequence increases the frequency of the behavior. If Mother takes off Jane's galoshes each time she cries and as a result Jane cries more, what is the procedure? Once again, it is *reinforcement,* because the behavior increases in frequency. If Father spanks Henry each time he screams, and as a result Henry screams less, the procedure is *punishment,* because the frequency of the behavior (screaming) decreases. If Father takes a penny from Henry's piggy bank each time Henry screams, and Henry screams less and less, the procedure again is *punishment,* because the behavior becomes less frequent.

Both reinforcement and punishment can involve either the presentation of a stimulus or the removal of a stimulus relatively soon after some behavior. This gives rise to two different kinds of reinforcement and two different kinds of punishment, which are summarized in Table 2–1. These concepts give rise to the definitions of the four basic reinforcement and punishment procedures.

1. *Positive reinforcement.* If a stimulus is presented after a response, with a resulting increase in future response frequency, the procedure is called **positive reinforcement.** For example, when Miguel was praised each time he asked a question, he asked more questions. The stimulus is called a *positive reinforcer.* (The positive reinforcer was "praise.")

2. *Negative reinforcement.* If a stimulus is removed after a response, with a resulting increase in the future frequency of the response, the procedure is called **negative reinforcement.** For example, Jane's crying was strengthened by the

---

SKINNER

In *The Behavior of Organisms* (1938), Skinner proposed a different sort of approach based upon an experimental analysis of stimuli and responses. Skinner's formulations stressed observable consequences and antecedents and avoided speculation about nonobservables, such as drive reduction, satisfaction, or learning relations. The basic concepts presented in this book are essentially the development, elaboration, and refinement of these concepts. Skinner's concept of reinforcement and punishment is basically a restatement of Thorndike's law of effect in terms of observables (Skinner, 1953):

> Events which are found to be reinforcing are of two sorts. Some reinforcements consist of presenting stimuli, of adding something—for example, food, water, sexual contact—to the situation. These we call positive reinforcers. Others consist of removing something—for example, a loud noise, a very bright light, extreme cold or heat, or electric shock—from the situation. These we call negative reinforcers. In both cases the effect of reinforcement is the same—the probability of response is increased. (p. 73)

The procedures correspond to Thorndike's concept of satisfaction. Punishment (removing positive reinforcers or presenting negative reinforcers), which is similar to Thorndike's "discomfort," weakens behavior. Obviously, the list of possible positive or negative reinforcers is more complex (but still objective) for people than for animals.

---

    removal of her galoshes each time she cried. The stimulus is called a *negative reinforcer.* (The negative reinforcers were "galoshes.")

3. *Punishment.* If a stimulus is presented after a response, with a resulting decrease in future response frequency, the procedure is called **punishment.** For example, because Father spanked Henry each time Henry screamed, Henry learned to scream less often. The stimulus presented is a *negative reinforcer.* (The negative reinforcer was "spanks.")

4. *Response cost.* If the removal of a stimulus after a response leads to a decrease in the future frequency of that response, the procedure is called **punishment by response cost,** or just **response cost.** For example, Father fined Henry a penny each time Henry screamed, and Henry learned to scream less often. The stimulus removed is a *positive reinforcer.* (The positive reinforcers were "pennies.")

These definitions are based only upon what is done and what then happens, not on subjective evaluations. For instance, if the teacher gives a student a penny each time he answers in class, and as a result he answers less and less, the procedure is punishment. (The behavior becomes less frequent.) In this case the pennies are negative reinforcers.

It may be helpful to note that words ending in *ment*, such as *reinforcement* and *punishment*, are the names of procedures, while terms ending in *er*, such as *positive reinforcer* and *negative reinforcer*, are the names of stimuli.

Two ways to strengthen behavior. From the previous discussion, it is clear that there are two ways to strengthen responses. Behaviors that produce positive reinforcers or remove negative reinforcers will be strengthened (increased in frequency) through the procedures labeled *positive reinforcement* and *negative reinforcement*, respectively.

Two ways to weaken behavior. Behavior can also be weakened or decreased either by the presentation of negative reinforcers or by the termination or removal of positive reinforcers after the behavior. The two associated procedures are labeled *punishment* and *response cost*, respectively.

EXAMPLES

On Pepe's first day of school, the teacher listed the rules on the board. The first was to work steadily during seatwork periods. In the first few days, whenever Pepe worked, the teacher praised him. Soon he worked continuously, until his assignments were complete—an example of positive reinforcement, with praise as the positive reinforcer.

In Nola's class, the teacher told everyone to work steadily. When Nola worked during the first day, little happened, but when she stopped the teacher came over and nagged her. When she started working, the teacher stopped nagging her, so she, like Pepe, also worked. In this case, negative reinforcement was used. Nagging was a negative reinforcer for Nola's working.

In Randy's class, talking without permission during work periods was prohibited. When Randy talked to his neighbor, the teacher yelled "be quiet!" at him, and soon he sat silently. Punishment had worked. The yell was a negative reinforcer for Randy.

Sarah's teacher gave all the students a cup of paper clips to keep on their desks. Everyone with enough paper clips at the end of a period could choose a play activity to engage in for 5 minutes. Each time Sarah talked when she was not supposed to, the teacher took a paper clip from her cup. She talked less frequently during quiet times—an example of response cost at work. The paper clips were positive reinforcers.

Exercises

Complete the following brief exercise. After you have written the answers, read ahead and see whether you were correct. If you miss any, reread the section "Procedures and Kinds of Consequences" and the two sections on strengthening and weakening behavior, and try again.

1. Mary occasionally "clowned" in class. Pete, a new student, then joined the class. Pete always laughed hysterically when Mary clowned. Mary clowned more and more frequently.
   a. The procedure brought into effect by Randy was _____.
   b. The stimulus that affected the rate of Mary's clowning behavior was _____, and it was a _____.
2. Ms. Spicer gave children "fun money" when they worked well. They could use the "fun money" to purchase extra recess time. Julio constantly pulled the hair of the girl who sat in front of him. Ms. Spicer then started taking away one "fun money" dollar each time Julio pulled hair. Julio stopped pulling hair in a few weeks.
   a. The procedure Ms. Spicer used is called _____.
   b. The stimulus that affected Julio's hair pulling behavior was _____, and it was a _____.
3. Marvin continually interrupted his parents when they spoke at the dinner table. Finally, his father started hitting him each time he interrupted. Interrupting became less frequent.
   a. The procedure used by Marvin's father is _____.
   b. The stimulus that changed the frequency of Marvin's interrupting was _____ and is called a _____.
4. Elery bent James's arm up behind him and told James that he would not let go until James said "uncle." James said "uncle" after a while, and Elery let go. This occurred quite often. It was noted that, with time, James said "uncle" much more often, rather than resisting.
   a. The procedure used by Elery to get James to say "uncle" is called _____.
   b. The stimulus that controlled James's saying "uncle" was _____ and is called a _____.

Feedback

1. a. positive reinforcement
   b. laughter, positive reinforcer
2. a. response cost
   b. fun money, positive reinforcer
3. a. punishment
   b. being hit, negative reinforcer
4. a. negative reinforcement
   b. bent arm, negative reinforcer

3. EFFECTS OF CHANGING THE TYPICAL CONSEQUENCES

Discontinuing Reinforcement: Extinction

If an operant behavior has been strengthened and becomes frequent due to repeated reinforcement, what will happen if the reinforcement no longer occurs? Specifically, what will happen if the response occurs, perhaps many times, and is no longer followed by positive reinforcers (or the termination of negative reinforcers)? The answer is that the response will decrease in strength to its original level; that is, the response will be performed as frequently as it was before the reinforcement began. This reduction in the strength or frequency of a behavior when reinforcement is discontinued following a history of reinforcement is called **extinction.**

Extinction is a third way to weaken behavior. When extinction is used, reinforcers the individual already has are not removed or taken away, as they are when response cost is used. Instead, reinforcement simply does not follow the response, as it previously had. Thus, during extinction there is no longer a stimulus change after such behaviors, although there had been before.

An experienced kindergarten teacher once gave a student teacher advice that was based on using extinction and avoiding positive reinforcement. Early in the autumn, a number of the children had been crying fairly frequently. The teacher commented to the student teacher, "Don't pay any attention to it any more. Otherwise you'll have a whole lot of it." The apprentice followed the suggestion and was surprised to find that the crying soon disappeared.

In another instance, a teacher had allowed his students to earn points that counted toward additional recess time by completing extra math, reading, or science assignments. After a while, he noted that the students were spending all their time doing extra science but were not doing any reading or math. He then changed the rule so that points were no longer given for extra science. The students were soon doing a lot less science and more math and reading.

From the teacher's point of view, the extinction procedure is what is frequently known as "ignoring" when the reinforcer has been attention. However, extinction can involve reinforcers other than attention, as in the previous example in which points were discontinued for science work and it declined. Extinction is an important procedure that is different from positive and negative reinforcement and punishment.

Although there is little mention of it in the educational literature, extinction also occurs if negative reinforcement is terminated. If negative reinforcers whose removal has been maintaining a behavior are no longer removed after the behavior, the behavior will become weaker. Similarly, if punishment or response cost cease, the behavior will "recover" to its prepunishment level. This effect is called *recovery*. Unlike extinction, it leads to an increase in behavior due to changing procedures.

Sometimes positive or negative reinforcers are terminated, and no extinction or recovery are noted; the behavior may not change even though the assumed major consequences are discontinued. This is often because something "new" has been added to the picture. For instance, John initially did reading assignments only because the teacher praised him. After a while, the teacher stopped praising John, but John kept reading. It is likely that, as John became a better reader and was able to understand the stories, events in the plot became reinforcers. Teacher praise was no longer the only reinforcer.

Time-Out From Positive Reinforcement

Another response-weakening procedure that has some characteristics of punishment and some of extinction is called **time-out from positive reinforcement**. When this procedure is used, all opportunities to earn reinforcers for any behavior are removed for a brief period following some misbehavior. Some teachers do this by sending a student who has just misbehaved to a corner of the room where he is isolated from all materials and from other children who are earning positive reinforcers. Others send the student to sit for a predetermined length of time behind a screen or to a special room in which there are not reinforcers. The location of the time-out area does not matter; what is important is that the period is a time-out from positive reinforcement. This means that in the regular classroom setting, there must be many opportunities to earn reinforcers so that the time-out period contrasts sharply with other times.

The difference between time-out from positive reinforcement and extinction are subtle but clear. When extinction is used to weaken a particular behavior, it is arranged that reinforcers do not follow the behavior. While that behavior is extinguished, however, other behaviors may still be reinforced. Thus, if the teacher decides to weaken John's behavior of shouting answers to questions, the teacher may ignore John for shouting but reinforce him immediately if he quietly raises his hand. When time-out from positive reinforcement is used, after the target behavior occurs, reinforcement is not given for any behavior for a brief period. If time-out were used for shouting, the teacher would not reinforce any behavior of John's for a brief period after he shouted. Thus, once John yelled (which the teacher ignored), for two minutes he might also be ignored if he raised his hand, he might not be able to earn points for seatwork, and he might not be able to use any class materials.

Because time-out requires that all behavior not be reinforced for a short period, it may often be easiest to implement the time-out by isolating the child. However, isolation and time-out are not synonymous. Time-out can sometimes be used without isolation, and all isolation is not a time-out. Isolation is time-out only when it is for a brief period contingent upon (depends upon and immediately follows) a specific behavior for the purpose of preventing reinforcement of all responses. Problems, abuses, and ethical issues concerning the use of time-out and other response-weakening procedures will be discussed in Chapter 4.

Time-out becomes important when simple extinction cannot be used. For instance, a child may misbehave because when she does, all the children in the room look at her and laugh or make approving or attending noises. It is difficult for a teacher to extinguish this; to do so would require changing the behavior of every child in the room. However, time-out may be possible; that is, the misbehaving child can be isolated from all opportunities for reinforcement following instances of inappropriate behavior.

Charlie was a 13-year-old student enrolled in a special program for "overactive" boys. According to his former teacher, students in Charlie's classes would rarely accomplish any work because Charlie was constantly talking, running around the room, or fighting with them. When Charlie was enrolled in a positive reinforcement program, however, his behavior improved considerably. He enjoyed the field trips, parties, games, and special privileges he earned in this class by behaving properly and completing his lessons. Occasionally, however, Charlie would engage in his old disruptive and aggressive patterns. If the aggression or disruptions were mild, the teacher would impose a small fine. (Mild and more serious misbehavior had been defined and agreed upon before the reinforcement system had begun. Some examples were minor fighting, stealing, shooting paper clips, tipping over chairs, marking textbooks, and throwing coats on the floor.) For more serious infractions, Charlie would be "timed-out" in the cloak room for 10 minutes. If he refused to go, he was reminded that he could not begin to earn points again until the completion of the time-out. This reminder was generally effective in eliminating any uncooperative behavior.

While he was "timed-out," Charlie could continue his work, but he would not be reinforced for it. This combination of substantial positive reinforcement with occasional fines and time-outs greatly increased Charlie's appropriate behavior and academic performance and virtually eliminated his disruptive, aggressive behavior within a 3-month period.

Overcorrection

This procedure for weakening behavior, originally described by Foxx and Azrin (1972), has two forms (Kazdin, 1984). The first, **positive-practice overcorrection,** requires the individual to repeatedly perform a "positive" incompatible behavior after emitting a targeted undesirable behavior. For example, the teacher might require 15 minutes of repeated chalkboard erasing from a child who had written obscene words on the board. The second overcorrection procedure, **restitutional overcorrection,** requires having the individual overcorrect the environmental effects of the targeted misbehavior. For instance, a child who threw food in the lunchroom might have to clean the entire lunchroom.

Foxx and Bechtel (1983), in a review of overcorrection procedures and research, cite the efficacy of this procedure compared with many alternative response-weakening procedures. Research by Gibbs and Luyben (1985), who showed that contingent positive-practice overcorrection was more effective than noncontingent positive practice, strongly suggests that the response-weakening effects are, in fact, a form of punishment, rather than due to the "educational" effects of the practice or restitution.

EXAMPLES

Tommy frequently made jokes and snide remarks while the teacher was talking. The teacher felt that this behavior was maintained by the attention and laughter of the other children. She was successful in getting the other children to ignore Tommy's remarks, and his inappropriate socializing decreased significantly as a result of extinction.

Linda often had violent temper tantrums in class, during which she screamed and threw things. Each time she had a tantrum, the teacher removed her to the time-out area for 5 minutes. There was nothing in the time-out area for Linda to do or play with; the area was a bare room measuring 2.5 by 3.0 meters. No reinforcement was available for any behavior. Linda's tantrums became very infrequent.

Bob often chewed his cuticles, to the point where they occasionally bled. Each time he was caught chewing, he was required to rub lotion into his fingertips for 15 minutes. His habit decreased significantly.

Exercises

Following are several briefly described situations. For each, indicate which of the following procedures is described:

positive reinforcement   time-out from positive reinforcement
negative reinforcement   extinction
punishment   overcorrection

1. Sally frequently used to look at her neighbor's paper while taking a test. Each time she did, her teacher took 5 points off her score; as a result, she now looks at her neighbor's paper less often.
2. Mr. Cherney nags his students when they do not work. If a student is not working, Mr. Cherney repeats "let's start working," and "don't just sit there," and similar remarks. When the student starts working, Mr. Cherney says nothing. As a result, many of his students have learned to work when he is in the room.
3. Archie used to get out of his seat every few minutes. Each time he got up, Ms. Perkins would say "sit down," but Archie continued to get up frequently. Finally, Ms. Perkins completely ignored Archie when he got up. He got up less and less frequently.
4. Mr. Lothrup, the principal, used to rant and rave every once in a while. He hired an attractive young secretary. When he would rant and rave, she would come into his office and say things like, "There, there, Mr. L., you mustn't let little things upset you." Now he rants and raves every day.
5. Clark frequently put his bubble gum in girls' hair. When this happened, the girl would scream, the boys would laugh and tell him he was "cool," and the teacher would yell. Finally, his teacher tried a new tactic. Each time Clark was seen putting gum on someone, he was immediately placed in the empty storage room for 6 minutes. He has not put gum on anyone for a month.
6. Brian used to hit himself in the head with such frequency and force that he was at risk for neurological damage. Under the new program, Brian

was required to do 500 arm-raising exercises each time he hit himself. His head-hitting rate decreased to nearly zero.

7. Randall frequently stated that he could not work because his stomach hurt. When he did this with his new teacher, Ms. Franklin, she would hug and kiss him and express sympathy. Within 2 weeks he stopped all complaining.

Feedback

1.	response cost	5.	time-out
2.	negative reinforcement	6.	overcorrection
3.	extinction	7.	punishment
4.	positive reinforcement		

4. FACTORS THAT MODIFY THE EFFECTIVENESS OF PROCEDURES

Immediacy, Repetition, and Schedules

Reinforcement is more effective when it is immediate: The shorter the delay between the behavior and the reinforcement, the more effect the reinforcement will have on the future frequency of the behavior. Especially with younger children, even a short delay may substantially decrease effectiveness. When a first or second grader volunteers a correct answer and the teacher immediately says, "You were really paying attention, Marilyn," attending and answering may be substantially strengthened. If the teacher waits until the end of the period to praise all children who volunteered, however, the reinforcement may have no effect. With preschool children, retarded children, or disturbed children, delays of a second or a fraction of a second between response and reinforcement are believed to significantly reduce any effects.

Immediate reinforcement also prevents the possibility of accidentally strengthening an undesired behavior that occurs after the desired behavior but before the consequence. The following situation is an example. Arnold had a tendency to bother his neighbors. One day, as his teacher was helping Juanita with her math, she happened to notice that Arnold was working. Because she was occupied with Juanita, however, she said nothing at that moment. A few seconds later, when Juanita began to work on her own, the teacher went over to Arnold and said, "I like the way you are behaving today, Arnold." Unknown to her, however, in the few seconds between her noting Arnold working and praising him, Arnold had thrown a spitball at Harry. This behavior was instantly followed by her praise (reinforcement) and was therefore likely to be strengthened! Immediate reinforcement could have prevented this undesirable outcome.

Course grades or grades on tests or papers usually have little effect upon the studying behavior of students. The long delay between studying and receiving a grade is a major reason. Having students grade their own papers or tests immediately after completion can help solve this problem. Self-instructional materials, which enable students to verify their answers immediately, and teacher-conducted small group instruction can also provide instant reinforcement for correct responses.

As might be expected, reinforcing a behavior twice (that is, reinforcing it when it occurs on two occasions) strengthens it more than does reinforcing it once, and reinforcing it ten or twenty times has even more effect. Repeated reinforcement of a response has two effects:

1. With a newly learned behavior, the response will become more frequent as it is reinforced more frequently, until it reaches some maximal level.
2. The more frequently a learned behavior is emitted and reinforced, the longer it will take to extinguish if reinforcement for some reason becomes unavailable for that response. Thus, a behavior that has occurred and has been reinforced many times will probably continue to be emitted for some time if it is not reinforced for a while. However, a newly learned behavior that has only occurred and been reinforced a few times will probably extinguish quickly if it is no longer reinforced.

When a response is reinforced every time it occurs, the schedule of reinforcement is **continuous.** When a response is sometimes reinforced and sometimes not, the schedule of reinforcement is **intermittent.** Because behavior that has a relatively long history of reinforcement will continue to occur for a time if it is not reinforced, well-learned behaviors will be maintained with only intermittent or occasional reinforcement. Obviously, in "real" life, most reinforcement is scheduled intermittently. Children in school are not called upon every time they raise their hands nor praised every time they work. Similarly, every effort of the teacher's is not reinforced with some positive result.

When a behavior has a long history of intermittent reinforcement, it becomes resistant to extinction. Gamblers continue to gamble even though the payoff (reinforcement) is very infrequent (intermittent). These, and the prior observations, lead to four guidelines which will help increase the effectiveness of reinforcement.

1. In teaching a new behavior, reinforce every instance of the behavior.
2. In maintaining a well-established behavior, reinforce intermittently.
3. Whenever possible, and particularly with new behaviors, reinforce as promptly as possible.
4. When teaching behaviors you wish students to repeat, use intermittent reinforcement once the behavior is initially well established.

Motivation

The word *motivation* has a long history in psychological and educational literature. Unfortunately, it has been used to explain everything and anything, and it has been given a variety of meanings. As used here, *motivation* refers to things that a teacher can do to render a reinforcer temporarily more effective or less effective. This corresponds loosely to the popular usage, wherein we say that a person is "motivated" for food, attention, sex, or money as a function of temporary conditions.

The two most common ways to affect motivation are through deprivation and satiation. A teacher who wishes to use candy as a positive reinforcer will restrict the availability of sweets at other times. Similarly, attention will be a more powerful reinforcer if an individual has been deprived of human interaction for a period. This is why, in spy novels, a period of isolation is frequently used before interrogating a prisoner. Conversely, if a child frequently interrupts class presentations and it appears that this behavior is reinforced by teacher attention, the teacher can weaken the behavior through satiation by giving excessive attention at times and for behaviors that are appropriate.

From a teaching point of view, the role of motivation suggests additional ways to temporarily strengthen or weaken behavior. If praise, attention, or other likely positive reinforcers are used to develop appropriate behavior, **deprivation** of these reinforcers outside the teaching situation will make them more effective in the teaching situation. Alternatively, if a reinforcer, such as attention, is strengthening an undesirable behavior, **satiation**—providing excessive attention which is not contingent on undesirable behavior—should temporarily weaken the behavior. However, neither deprivation nor satiation alone will produce a permanent behavior change; when the motivating condition "wears off," the behavior will be as strong or as weak as it originally was.

Pinpointing Behavior

Pinpointing behavior means defining it objectively and precisely. This is a first step toward changing behavior. Behaviors selected for modification must be clearly identified if behavior analysis principles are to be helpful in changing them. Goals for changing must be stated in objective terms that describe what the children actually do.

If target behaviors are not clearly expressed, teaching personnel cannot provide clean, consistent contingencies because they will be unable to reliably determine when a particular behavior has or has not occurred. As a result, behavior that is ignored today may be reinforced tomorrow and punished at some other time.

Goals for change that cannot be observed, specified, or measured are not appropriate classroom targets. Many commonly stated educational goals are not really useful in teaching. Goals such as developing "self-concept," "achievement motivation," and "intrinsic motivation" are too vague. They do not specify exactly what behavior should be strengthened or weakened or when positive or negative reinforcement should be delivered or removed. This is not to say that these terms do not refer to potentially important goals. To be useful, however, they must specify exactly the behaviors to which they refer.

Thus, instead of choosing "improved self-concept" as a goal, a teacher might analyze "improved self-concept" and identify actual behaviors that define self-concept. The behaviors, which should be observable so they can be taught and be reinforced, might include the following:

1. Will try new and difficult work.
2. Will not make remarks about how stupid he is, or how he cannot accomplish new and difficult work.
3. Will play or socially interact with children who are different from him in terms of grades and school accomplishment, racial or ethnic group, or social skills.
4. Will show his work to teachers, peers, and parents.
5. Will talk in an audible voice and look at the listener.

Teachers generally pinpoint two areas of behavior: social and academic. Social behaviors are the observable interactions that children have with other children, with their teachers, and with instructional and play materials. Academic behaviors are often pinpointed in terms of the products that result from work on instructional tasks. Some examples of pinpointed behaviors in the social and academic areas are given in Table 2–2.

TABLE 2-2 Pinpointed Social and Academic Behaviors

Social Behaviors	Academic Behaviors
Raise hand before answering or asking questions.	Score above 80 percent on arithmetic assignment.
Listen to directions as indicated by eyes on teacher.	Read at least one library book a week and write a report.
Tutor other children who need help.	Identity, record, and learn to spell at least 20 new words per week.
Select, during free work times, academic tasks that are appropriate in terms of diagnostic data—neither too difficult nor too easy.	Write at least one short story a week.
Arrive at school on time, by the time the bell rings.	Complete at least two social studies units a week.
Work at seat without disturbing others.	Recognize instances of quadratic equations in "word problems."
Clean up food after lunch.	

EXAMPLES

Mr. Carter usually checked all seatwork at the end of each day. Franklin completed the assignments about half the time. When Franklin completed an assignment, Mr. Carter would occasionally give him a small privilege the next morning. Franklin's work completion did not improve. Mr. Carter started giving Franklin a small privilege *immediately* after Franklin handed in a complete assignment. For a month, Mr. Carter did this *continually and repeatedly* every time Franklin handed in a completed assignment. After a month, Mr. Carter started doing this on an *intermittent schedule*, giving Franklin a privilege about 50 percent of the time he completed an assignment, and later only about 25 percent of the time. Franklin's work completion continued at a high level, demonstrating the efficiency of frequently, immediately reinforcing new behavior, and then switching to intermittent reinforcement to maintain it.

Mr. Carter also had trouble with Melissa, who kept asking the same questions over and over again even though she could give the correct answers when asked. Mr. Carter decided that his attention was reinforcing Melissa for asking unnecessary questions, so he began to give her a great deal of attention at times when she was not asking unnecessary questions, *satiating* her with his attention, and her question asking decreased.

Basil also had trouble completing his assignments. His parents suggested that Mr. Carter let Basil work on his railroad models for 10 minutes as a reinforcer for finishing his work. When Mr. Carter tried this, it did not work. However, when Basil's parents prohibited Basil from getting up early in the morning to work on his models before school, this small amount of *deprivation* made model building an effective classroom reinforcer.

Martin presented a different problem. Mr. Carter felt Martin lacked independence, and he started a program to make him less dependent. He tried to praise Martin when he acted independently. When no improvement was noted, Mr. Carter decided it was because *dependent* and *independent* were too vague. So he *pinpointed* three important "independent" classroom behaviors: starting work without being reminded, starting work without asking the teacher or other students to explain the assignment again, and selecting and starting a free-time activity within 4 minutes after the chosen activity period started. Whenever one of these three behaviors occurred, Mr. Carter praised Martin. All three behaviors increased significantly.

Exercises

A list of six words or phrases and six situations follow. All take place in a class for moderately to severely retarded children. Indicate which letter fits in which blank to suggest a reasonable behavior-improvement procedure.

a. immediate
b. frequently and repeatedly
c. intermittent schedule
d. deprivation
e. satiation
f. pinpoint

1. Carol's parents say "she loves candy." Attempts to improve her articulation using small candies as reinforcers have been unsuccessful, however, in spite of the use of a program known to be effective for children similar to Carol. One thing that might be tried is candy _____.

2. Staff members all feel that Ronald could do better if he were more confident, so they decide to try to increase his confidence. These efforts would probably be more successful if the staff would _____ goals.

3. James dresses himself very well if he receives constant attention but stops the minute he is ignored. He could probably become more independent if _____ were used.

4. Sarah is teaching Nancy colors using a program wherein Nancy receives a candy after she correctly names the colors of ten objects. Gains are small. Reinforcing _____ would probably accelerate her gains.

5. Jack is teaching Gordon to clean up the day room. Jack supervises several students in this activity. Jack manages to get around to praising Gordon after Gordon has completed his task, but usually not for some time after the job is done. Gordon does a mediocre job, but he would probably do better with more _____ reinforcement.

6. Emily always steals the brooms from the hall and puts them in her room. Betty collects all the brooms in the building (literally hundreds) and stacks them in Emily's room, in an attempt to weaken the behavior through _____.

Feedback

1.	d	4.	b
2.	f	5.	a
3.	c	6.	e

5. STARTING NEW BEHAVIOR AND LEARNING MORE THAN IS TAUGHT

How can a teacher start a new behavior? If a child is not already doing what the teacher wishes, however infrequently, the teacher cannot reinforce it. The teacher must take steps to start the new behavior so it can be reinforced. In addition, it seems impossible to teach every new behavior each child will need in order to function effectively. Can children be taught in such a way that they will learn more than is taught?

Shaping

One procedure to start new behavior is **shaping.** When shaping, the teacher reinforces better and better approximations to some desired behavior, perhaps starting with something that does not even resemble the target behavior, until eventually the objective is reached. Shaping depends upon two procedures.

Selective or differential reinforcement. No matter what a child is doing, there is probably some variability in his performance. It may be that Isaac never does his work, but what he *does* do is not always exactly the same. Sometimes he may sleep in class. Sometimes he may stare at the clock. Sometimes he may just flip the pages of his workbook. The teacher who uses **selective reinforcement** picks the variant of behavior that is closest to what is ultimately desired and temporarily reinforces it. In Isaac's case, flipping through his workbook is closer to working than are his other responses (since he does not work at all), so this behavior is selectively reinforced, and other behaviors are ignored (extinguished). With selective reinforcement, the best variation of behavior, no matter how undesirable, is selected for reinforcement, and other behavior is ignored. Of course, in theory, one can also selectively reinforce undesirable behavior.

Successive approximations. When one response is reinforced and other responses that occur in that setting are extinguished, the reinforced response will become more frequent and the extinguished responses will become less frequent. For example, if a powerful reinforcer were used Isaac could be expected to start flipping through his workbook more and sleeping and staring into space less. But children, like all living things, rarely do things exactly the same way more than once. Isaac's method of flipping through his workbook will probably vary each time he does it. Sometimes he will flip through pages without looking at them; sometimes he will read part of a page; sometimes he will go fast, sometimes slow. A newer and better variant is then chosen for selective reinforcement. Perhaps the teacher now reinforces Isaac only when he stops and reads a bit as he flips through the book. This response is thus strengthened, and other responses or variations of thumbing through his workbook are extinguished. Regularly switching to a new and better response variant—one that is a closer approximation to the ultimate desired target behavior—for successive reinforcement is called using **successive approximations.** Progressively better approximations are selected for differential reinforcement.

When successive approximations are used, one response variant at each stage receives selective reinforcement, while others are extinguished. When a stage is successful, a better approximation is then selected for reinforcement. By selective reinforcement of better and better successive approximations, the goal behavior is finally reached. This combination of procedures in which some behaviors are reinforced at each step while others are extinguished (selective reinforcement) and in which criteria for selective reinforcement are changed over time (successive approximations) is called **shaping.**

Ms. Jones required her sixth-grade children to identify 20 new words each week from outside reading and to record their meaning in a vocabulary

SUCCESSIVE APPROXIMATIONS FOR ISAAC

Step 1.   Reinforce any kind of flipping through the workbook, and ignore other behaviors that occur during seatwork time.

Step 2.   Reinforce Isaac only for stopping to read, even for a second, as he flips through the workbook.

Step 3.   Reinforce Isaac only when he reads for about 3 seconds.

Step 4.   Reinforce Isaac only when he reads for about 3 seconds in the assigned unit.

Step 5.   Reinforce Isaac only when he reads for 3 seconds in the assigned unit and has his pencil in his hand.

Step 6.   Reinforce Isaac only when he reads for 3 seconds in the assigned unit and makes some mark in the workbook.

Step 7.   Reinforce Issac only when he completes any fill-in or writes any answer, correct or incorrect, in his workbook in the correct unit.

Step 8.   Gradually increase the amount of work required, until Isaac completes (correctly or incorrectly) all the problems or blanks.

Step 9.   Reinforce Isaac only when he completes all the problems with at least one correct.

Step 10. Gradually increase the percentage of correct answers required until Isaac reaches the level that diagnostic work indicated was appropriate for him.

notebook. Most of the children submitted a list of at least 20 new words each Monday, but Jimmy rarely had even 1 new word listed. Ms. Jones tried a simple shaping procedure. On Monday, Jimmy was reinforced if he had identified and defined at least 1 new word. Words that other children had located were then reviewed, and Jimmy could copy one of them if he wished. He was also given the chance to do supplementary reading during the day. He had to identify 3 new words the following week, and then 5 the next week. The minimum number remained at 5 for the next week, but then Jimmy was required to identify and define words on his own before coming to school on Monday. The minimum number was then gradually increased on a weekly basis until Jimmy was finally able to record a list of 20 new words every Monday.

Jane was a kindergartener who was isolated from the other children. She never talked or otherwise interacted with her classmates. Instead, she would sit by herself in the corner of the room or beside the teacher's desk. Jane's teacher was concerned about Jane's apparent inability to interact with the other children. In order to build social behavior, the teacher decided to shape more elementary behaviors that together would lead toward interaction. The following successive approximations were differentially reinforced, one at a time, in sequence over several weeks:

1. Sitting somewhere between the teacher's desk and the other children.
2. Sitting at a table with other children.
3. Sitting next to another child.
4. Attending to the interaction of other children (appearing to watch and listen).
5. Interacting with other children (talking, smiling, touching).

QUESTIONS TO BE ANSWERED IN A SHAPING PROCEDURE

1. *When should I use it?* The shaping process is not as efficient a way to get behavior going as instruction, prompting, or imitation. If a child will not follow instructions or imitate, however, shaping procedures must be used.
2. *What excessive approximation should I select for reinforcement at each step?* Experience, observation of children in general, and observation of the target child are the best guides. A series of very small steps is better than a few large steps. Each new approximation must be only slightly different from the last one and should be a variant of what the child had previously been doing.
3. *How fast should I move?* If the teacher moves too fast, the new behavior and its variants will not be well established and the whole set of behaviors will extinguish. If the teacher moves too slowly, the process may take forever, or it will at least be very inefficient.
4. *When should I move back?* If a child fails to succeed with a new approximation, the teacher should move back to the old one. With further reinforcement the change may be attempted again. The approximation selected might not have been a good one, and a move to a different one should be attempted.

Shaping has the same effects whether it is used intentionally or unintentionally. Most teachers use shaping procedures even when they don't realize they are doing so. Understanding the rationale and steps for shaping allows intelligent planning of its use in the classroom, which usually makes the process more efficient.

Unfortunately, the shaping process can also inadvertently produce undesirable results. Mr. Smith had a student who would occasionally ask him to repeat instructions or to explain things a second time. Sometimes she asked in a quiet, pleasant manner; sometimes she asked in a loud, demanding manner. In the beginning of the school year, Mr. Smith replied to all these requests politely, but as the year progressed and Mr. Smith had less time, he stopped responding to all such requests. When the student was loud or demanding, however, Mr. Smith did reply, without noticing that he was selectively reinforcing only loud demands. Soon the student regularly voiced noisy, obnoxious requests. Mr. Smith then became annoyed and decided to ignore such questions, but sometimes the student was so obnoxious that he replied anyway (new successive approximation). Not surprisingly, this student became a problem in the classroom. She had inadvertently been taught, through a shaping procedure, to be unpleasant!

Prompting

Prompts are methods of getting behavior started when some antecedent stimuli that control part of the appropriate behavior are already available. The most common type of prompt is an instruction: The teacher may say, "Sometimes when we see the letters "*ei*, we make the "long *a*" sound, as in the word *neighbor*." In this case, the children can already say the "long *a*" sound and are under control of the simple instructions given—they can understand the instructions—so using instructions (prompts) is the most efficient way to start the new behavior. Teaching prompts must eventually be "faded," as they will not be present under typical out-of-classroom conditions. Other types of prompts, all of which involve using stimuli that already control behavior, are not always called instructions.

The following are some common examples of prompts:

1. The teacher takes the child's hand and guides his pencil around the curves of the letter *s*.
2. Arrows are used under letters to remind children to read from left to right.
3. A teacher exaggerates the position of her mouth for the letter *m* as she asks a child to make a sound.
4. The teacher raises her hand to model how children are to raise their hands before asking or answering questions.
5. Children are reminded that *i* comes before *e*, except after *c*.
6. The teacher writes on the board, "Stalagmites come up from the ground, and stalactites hang down from the ceiling."
7. The teacher says, "At the battle of Gettysburg . . . "

Prompting is used to get the new behavior going. Eventually, however, the child must be able to perform without the prompt. The teacher wants students to learn how to pronounce *ei* words correctly without her instructions, and children must learn to write correctly without guidance of their hands and without arrows to remind them to write from left to right. The prompt is used to exert temporary control over the behavior so it can occur correctly and be reinforced.

The typical stimuli in the situation should eventually control the correct behavior, so the prompt will have to be faded out. For instance, in the *ei* word situation, the teacher may repeat the rule a few times, then she may remind the children that *ei* is often pronounced like the long sound of some vowel, then she may merely say that *ei* is often not pronounced the way it looks like it should be, and then she may discontinue all prompts completely. In teaching children how to make the *m* sound, the teacher may exaggerate the position of her mouth less and less with each illustration.

Imitation (Modeling)

Another way to get new behavior going is to use **imitation,** or **modeling,** which is a special form of prompting. Children who have been reinforced for imitating others in the past are likely to imitate new behavior when requested. This is particularly true if they see someone else being reinforced for performing that behavior. Many teachers have discovered that they can use modeling techniques effectively to teach children, particularly to start new behavior. Instead of scolding disruptive or inattentive children, for example, many teachers have found it more effective to positively reinforce cooperative or attentive children (that is, good models) in full view of the other children. This procedure has several advantages:

1. The cooperative and attentive children receive direct, positive reinforcement for their behavior; hence, their good behavior is maintained.
2. The other children are provided with clear models to imitate.
3. The teacher avoids the risk of unintentionally reinforcing unwanted behavior with attention while trying to punish it.

A third-grader, Tyrone, had difficulty concentrating on his seatwork assignment when the teacher was occupied with a reading group in a far corner of the room. Instead of completing and reviewing his lesson, Tyrone would roam around the room and bother other children or sit idly in his chair and stare out of the window. The teacher first tried to eliminate these nonproductive behaviors by making frequent requests for him to "get to work" and by giving warnings that he'd better "shape up." When this strategy failed to produce a change, the teacher began to ignore Tyrone's nonworking behavior while frequently praising students who were working diligently in their seats. "That's good, Fred," the teacher would say. "I like the way you are working quietly at your seat. I wish all the boys and girls would work as hard and quietly as you do because they would learn better and enjoy school more."

Tyrone continued to procrastinate and disrupt for several days after the new procedure was put into effect, but then one day he sat down at his desk after the assignment was given and began to work. "Good for you, Tyrone," the teacher immediately exclaimed. "I like the way you got right to work." On the following days, the teacher continued to compliment Tyrone for his improved work habits. Modeling had paid off for Tyrone and for his teacher.

Generative Learning

With **generative learning,** after direct teaching of a skill with certain materials or certain response forms, students are able to make correct responses with similar, but novel, materials or responses. For instance, in an early study by Guess and colleagues (1968), a retarded girl who originally used no plural noun forms was taught to correctly use singular and plural forms to label a number of objects. Training used prompting, modeling, and reinforcement procedures. After training on a sufficient number of objects, the girl began using the correct singular and plural forms with new items that had not been included in the training.

In another study of generative learning, Glover and colleagues (1980) showed that college students trained to identify the "main idea" or "semantic base" of written passages could identify the semantic base of new passages with which they had had no training. Similarly, Endo and Sloane (1982) showed that children could be taught to use personified verbs or phrases with inanimate objects through modeling and reinforcement. After sufficient training using appropriate procedures, children used new personified forms with words that had not been used in training.

These studies, which are representative of a much larger sample, show that with the right type of training, generalization of the skill to new stimuli is possible, as is generalization to new but correct responses. With sufficient training on a large enough sample of materials, responding starts occurring to novel, untrained instances and can include responses that are similar in some abstract way but different from those used in the initial training. Thus, training or teaching can change behaviors that go beyond those directly involved in the training. With generative learning, a student can learn more than is taught.

Stimulus Classes

If we can teach children some behavior with respect to certain stimuli, and if they will then perform adequately with equivalent stimuli but without additional learning, we can again say that the children learn more than is directly taught. For instance, children just entering school have already learned a great amount of behavior in response to oral language. If you ask a child whether a cat is an animal, a piece of furniture, or a vegetable, most will answer correctly. If we can teach them to match written words to oral language (to sound out or memorize words), they will know whether the word *cat* (perhaps on a flashcard) is an animal, a piece of furniture, or a vegetable, without additional teaching. Once they have learned that the spoken word *cat* is equivalent to the written word *cat*, a wide range of behavior already exists with respect to the written word.

Items are members of a common **stimulus class** if an individual will respond in an equivalent way to all of them. Some development of stimulus classes occurs merely because of classical stimulus generalization—the fact that a response learned to one stimulus will occur for physically similar stimuli. But this does not explain some of the similar responding we often see to physically dissimilar objects; not only are the spoken word *cat* and the written word *cat* dissimilar, but they are also in different modalities (auditory and visual). Roller skates are not physically similar to a submarine, but both might be labeled *transportation*.

Sidman and his colleagues (1982, 1985) have studied the experimental production of stimulus classes in monkeys, atypical children, and other human subjects. They have found that stimuli become equivalent, and thus members of the same class, as a function of rather specific learning experiences.

The development of stimulus classes, especially if these procedures extend to even more complex learning, suggests that much of what children do may be learned, though apparently untaught. Like generative processes, the indirect development of stimulus classes indicates that children can learn, as a function of experience, much more than we directly teach them. Many behaviors that appear to be inherited or to stem directly from biological structure, because they appear untaught, may actually be due to experience. As we learn more about these procedures and their applications to education, we may be able to design instruction that will teach a great deal more in much less time.

EXAMPLES

Shaping. Originally, Helen praised Jill if Jill wrote anything that even vaguely resembled her name. Her handwriting slowly improved, and Helen praised Jill only for fairly legible *Jills.* As Jill's performance improved, praise was contingent upon getting every letter form correct.

Prompting. Mr. Miller was teaching his class to use a digital multimeter. First he said, "Use this dial to set the DMM for the maximum likely current. If you apply a current that exceeds the range you have set, you can burn out the meter."

Modeling. David was trying to teach Pete how to "tuck" correctly in a dive. He finally said to Pete, "Watch me." He then demonstrated the correct form, and had Pete try it.

Generative learning. Ms. Camille was teaching her class to conjugate the present tense of regular *-ar* Spanish verbs. She had them copy the forms for *hablar* from their text and then copy a second *-ar* verb from the text. She then gave them one to do without a model, but the error level was high. She had them copy four more. Then she gave them some new *-ar* verbs, and the error level was nearly zero.

Stimulus classes. In his study, Peter first taught his class to say aloud the correct sounds when he presented common phonetic symbols. Peter then taught his class to write phonetic symbols corresponding to Cyrillic characters. He never taught his class to say aloud sounds corresponding to the Russian letters. After they learned the sounds for the phonetic symbols and the phonetic symbol–Cyrillic character equivalences, however, they could pronounce the Russian letters.

Exercises

Indicate whether each of the following descriptions is an example of

a. shaping,
b. prompting,
c. modeling,
d. generative learning, or
e. stimulus class development.

1. James was initially unable to stack any of the toys in such a way that they did not fall. James's mother helped him learn how to stack the small plastic blocks. She then helped him learn how to stack the circular washers. Then she taught him to balance the plastic logs in a tall pile. He then placed six trucks on top of each other in a column.

2. Patricia saw Murph hit Carl and then take his candy. Patricia then went up to Bill, smacked him, and took his ice cream.

3. Frederick, whose native language was German, could read English fluently, but knew no Hindi. He read a Hindi language text in English, and then translated a brief poem from Hindi to German.

4. When Xavier caused the car to stall when he tried to start moving, Candia said "Let the clutch out more slowly." Next time, Xavier let the clutch out slowly and the car began to move.

5. Millie told Sam to take a few swings. After the first she said, "Keep your left shoulder a bit forward." He did, and she said "good." He did it again, this time even a bit better, and she said, "Great; try again." He did, and the sequence was repeated several times, with Sam improving each time.

Feedback

1. d   4. b
2. c   5. a
3. e

FAST TRACK

REVIEW

When changes or variations in any stimulus event are functionally related to changes in a specific behavior, we say the stimulus "controls" behavior. All *control* means is that some specific change in the environment is related to some specific behavior change.

Terminology used to describe behavior must be objective (physical), nonjudgmental, and capable of being quantified. When ambiguous language is used, it is possible neither to apply contingencies consistently, nor to evaluate the effects of educational interventions.

Behavior whose occurrence is controlled mainly by antecedent stimuli is called *respondent*. Respondent behaviors are referred to as *reflexes* in some of the traditional literature. Behavior whose rate of occurrence is mainly controlled by the consequences which have followed the behavior in the past is called *operant*. Operant behavior has been referred to as *voluntary* in the traditional literature.

Consequences can change the future rate of occurrence of operant behavior in two ways—by either increasing or decreasing the rate. Procedures that increase the rate through consequences are called *reinforcement,* and procedures that use consequences to decrease rate are called *punishment.*

Positive reinforcement increases the rate of a behavior due to consequences presented after the behavior. Consequences that have this effect are called *positive reinforcers.* *Negative reinforcement* strengthens behavior due to the removal of consequences after the behavior. Consequences that have this effect are called *negative reinforcers.*

Punishment is used for weakening behavior by presenting stimuli after it. The stimuli presented are, as in negative reinforcement, also called *negative reinforcers.* This is because it has been found that the same consequences that weaken behavior when presented after it, strengthen behavior when removed after it. Weakening behavior by removing stimuli after occurrences of the behavior is called *response cost.* The stimuli removed are found to be *positive reinforcers,* as they also strengthen behavior when they follow it.

Behavior that has been strengthened through positive or negative reinforcement will become weaker if the reinforcement is then discontinued. This process is called *extinction,* Behavior that has been punished or weakened through response-cost will recover prior strength if the response-weakening procedures cease.

A behavior can also be dramatically weakened if *time-out* from reinforcement is made contingent on the target behavior being emitted. With time-out, all opportunities for reinforcement of any behavior are unavailable for a specified period following occurrences of the target behavior. Most commonly, this is done using isolation in a barren room or area.

Another procedure for weakening behavior is *overcorrection.* With overcorrection, after instances of an undesired behavior, repeated performance of a desirable and incompatible behavior is required (*positive practice* overcorrection), or the individual is required to "overcorrect" the environmental effects of the undesired behavior (*restitutional* overcorrection).

Reinforcers presented or removed after instances of behavior strengthen or weaken the behavior more if they immediately follow the behavior. With young or impaired children, even delays of less than a second between a response and its reinforcement can dramatically alter effectiveness. Frequent, repeated reinforcement is necessary to develop response strength. Once behavior is developed, it will be more persistent and resistant to extinction if reinforced on an intermittent schedule.

The likelihood of behavior occurring can also be changed by changing *motivational* factors—that is, by making the reinforcer temporarily more or less effective. Reinforcer deprivation and reinforcer satiation are the most common motivating operations.

Pinpointing behavior means specifying it exactly. Much more consistent contingencies result when behavior is well pinpointed than when it is ambiguously defined.

Shaping can be used to start new behavior. Shaping involves differentially reinforcing existing responses that more closely resemble the ultimate goal, while extinguishing more dissimilar variants; criteria for reinforcement become more rigorous over time through successive approximations.

Prompting is another way to start new behavior. It involves using stimuli that already control behavior, such as verbal instructions or physical guidance. *Modeling,* or imitation, can also be used to start new behavior. Learning to model behavior is based upon the reinforcement history for imitating, and may be controlled by consequences the model is observed to obtain.

Generative learning occurs when an individual generalizes a repertoire learned in certain situations to unlearned situations. When behavior learned with respect to one stimulus occurs with other physically dissimilar stimuli, we say the stimuli are members of the same *stimulus class*. Procedures exist to help ensure generative learning and the development of stimulus classes. These procedures enable an individual to *learn more than is taught*.

EXAMPLES

Each time sweets are placed in Paula's mouth, she salivates. Salivation, controlled by an antecedent stimulus, is a *respondent*. Paula has also learned to yell "candy," as this is frequently followed by an adult giving her some. The yelling is an *operant*. The yelling has been developed through *positive reinforcement*, and the candies are *positive reinforcers*.

Gerald's older brother, Tom, often hits him until Gerald yells "uncle!" Then Tom stops. Gerald learned to say "uncle" quickly, through *negative reinforcement*. The "hits" are *negative reinforcers*.

Gerald's mother notes the fighting and hitting, and spanks Tom each time Tom hits Gerald. Tom stops hitting Gerald, an example of the effectiveness of *punishment* and of the fact that "spanks" are *negative reinforcers*.

Gerald, however, also has his faults. A major one is his undesirable language. His father notes that most of this relates to his overusing two words, and takes 10 cents from Gerald's bank each time he says either word. Gerald's language cleans up, due to the *response cost* procedure, evidencing that, for Gerald, the dimes are *positive reinforcers*.

With Gerald and Tom, behavior improved quickly due to the *immediate and repeated* consequences. Delayed consequences, such as waiting for Tom's father to come home at night and spank him for fighting, would probably be less effective.

Paula's mother could not understand why Paula continued to yell for candy for weeks after she had stopped giving Paula candy when she yelled. It was probably because the behavior had originally been under an *intermittent schedule* of reinforcement, as Paula's mother was frequently busy or had no candy when Paula yelled. After a long enough period of *extinction*, however, the yelling for candy became infrequent.

Tom caught Gerald once when no adults were around and started hitting him again. Gerald yelled "uncle" but Tom did not stop hitting him; he kept it up for what seemed like forever. Gerald kept yelling "uncle" for a while, but when it had no effect, the behavior eventually *extinguished*.

Tom's parents, thinking the boys had "learned their lesson," discontinued the spankings for fighting and the fines for swearing. Soon, fighting and swearing increased again, demonstrating *recovery* when the punishment was discontinued.

The fighting became so bad that the parents put Tom in the spare room for 5 minutes each time he hit Gerald. Everything had been removed from the room. This *time-out* dramatically reduced the fighting.

A new technique was tried with Gerald for swearing. Each time he said these words, he had to say "I'm sorry for being rude" 200 times. This *overcorrection* procedure reduced his swearing.

Paula's mother was still having trouble with her yelling for candy. As she had little interest in or knowledge of health matters, she decided to use a *motivational* approach—that is, to *satiate* Paula with candy each day. So for breakfast Paula received three bags of candy along with her cereal. She yelled for candy a lot less as a result.

Gerald continued to swear until a motivational approach was used with him. His allowance was cut in half, and the *deprivation* made the dimes (and the loss of them) more effective reinforcers.

As a result of all this work, Gerald and Tom's parents decided they needed some new hobbies to brighten up their lives. Mother chose karate. Her teacher tried to teach her a punch; each time she improved a little, he praised her. The use of *shaping* procedures quickly turned her into a lethal expert.

Her husband decided to learn to play pool. In his first lesson, his teacher demonstrated a triple bank shot and then told him to do it, a probably ineffective use of *modeling*. When he was unable to make the shot, his teacher verbally *prompted* him to "shoot at this spot."

Paula's mother wanted her to speak in sentences. When Paula said "candy," Paula's mother said, "Say 'Me want candy.'" When Paula said the whole phrase, she gave Paula a candy bar. She also bought her a new toy when Paula imitated "Me want toy" instead of just yelling "toy" in the store. After several similar experiences in which Paula's mother modeled noun-verb-object sequences, prompted Paula to say them, and reinforced Paula when she did, Paula began to use these phrases spontaneously. *Generative learning* produced a change in her language. In addition, when her mother told her that new items were "toys," she started asking for them the same way at once, due to the formation of the *stimulus class* "toys."

CUMULATIVE EXERCISE

I. Following are eight suggestions based upon the procedures discussed in this chapter. Indicate which suggestions best fit the situations by writing the appropriate letter in each blank.
    a. Use continuous reinforcement.
    b. Use intermittent reinforcement.
    c. Reinforce more promptly.
    d. Reinforce for a longer time.
    e. Use shaping.
    f. Use prompting.
    g. Use modeling.
    h. Pinpoint more accurately.

1. Ms. Rivera has been trying to teach her students to raise their hands before speaking. For two weeks, each time a child raised his hand, she called on him and thanked him. This Wednesday she stopped reinforcing hand raising and, to her chagrin, by lunchtime students started yelling out instead of raising their hands. To get them to persist longer in raising their hands, she should _____.

2. Mr. Carter gave Henry a candy bar twice when Henry was working, which Henry did occasionally but not regularly. During the following week, however, Henry still did not work regularly. Mr. Carter should _____.

3. If Henry hardly ever worked in spite of being told to do so, Mr. Carter might have been wise to _____ or _____.

4. Perry never, or hardly ever, spoke in class. For unknown reasons, he spoke on five occasions on Tuesday. On two of these occasions Ms. Randolph praised him, but the praise did not have much effect. Ms. Randolph should _____ if Perry starts talking again.

5. Ms. Withrow has told her students that they could earn privileges by being good in class. However, her class seems about the same after several weeks. It would probably help if she would _____.

6. Ms. Betty gives her kindergarteners who pay attention during music a candy at the end of the session. It does not seem to do much good, however, and the behavior of few children has even begun to worsen. Ms. Betty might _____.

7. Mr. Peterson's class is having trouble remembering the locations of the states. A good program to help them memorize this would probably _____ as well as provide appropriate reinforcement.

II. A brief list of situations and a list of terms follow. Match them correctly by writing the correct letter in each blank.

a. Use objective terminology	k. Increase motivation through deprivation
b. Behavioral control	
c. Respondent	l. Decrease motivation through satiation
d. Operant	
e. Punishment	m. Time-out
f. Response cost	n. Positive-practice overcorrection
g. Positive reinforcement	
h. Positive reinforcers	o. Restitutional overcorrection
i. Negative reinforcement	p. Extinction
j. Negative reinforcers	q. Generative learning
	r. Stimulus classes

1. He ate spaghetti before going out so he would order less in the restaurant. ____

2. The more people insulted him, the more he did it. ____

3. "Improve your self-image." _____
4. After training, the child would imitate anything. _____
5. She laughed so hard every time he said it, he stopped. _____
6. When it rained, he often wore galoshes. _____
7. He went to the store more often after they hired the attractive woman. _____
8. Each time he made an error, they took one of his trading cards, and soon he was always correct. _____
9. He never sold anything to Miller Manufacturing, so he stopped calling on them. _____
10. He already had a good oral vocabulary, so once he could sound out the words, he could define them. _____
11. The judge made him do 100 hours of community service when he was convicted of vandalism. _____
12. When he returned from basic training, he dated every night. _____
13. The doctor tapped his knee and it jerked. _____
14. He would do anything for money. _____
15. He always agreed once she called him a thug or a bully, as that was the only way to get her to stop. _____
16. What are the words "thug" and "bully" in the previous situation? _____
17. He was sent to his room for yelling. _____
18. If he used what his mother called "grease" on his hair, she made him wash it ten times in a row. _____

III. A list of terms follows. For each term, you should be prepared to do the following:
   a. Define it.
   b. Use it in a sentence in which you give an illustration from the classroom. Do not use illustrations from the text.
   c. Be able to identify it in a classroom illustration given by someone else.

Control	Extinction
Operant	Time-out from positive reinforcement
Reflex (respondent)	Continuous reinforcement
Response	Intermittent reinforcement
Stimulus	Immediate reinforcement
Positive reinforcement	Reinforcing for enough time, or
Positive reinforcer	enough responses
Negative Reinforcement	Shaping
Negative Reinforcer	Prompting
Punishment	Modeling
Response cost	Pinpointing behavior

Feedback

Part I

1.	b	5.	h
2.	d	6.	c
3.	e,g	7.	f
4.	a		

Part II

1.	l	10.	r
2.	g	11.	o
3.	a	12.	k
4.	q	13.	c
5.	e	14.	h
6.	b	15.	i
7.	d	16.	j
8.	f	17.	m
9.	p	18.	n

Part III

Do this part with another student.

THREE

Using Positive Reinforcement to Improve Student Behavior and Academic Performance

OBJECTIVES

After you have completed this chapter, you will be able to use the principles of positive reinforcement to improve both the school behavior and academic performance of your students. To do this you will learn to

1. Define the term *positive reinforcement* and describe five types of positive reinforcers.
2. Select the appropriate type of reinforcer to use in a specific situation.
3. Use reinforcers effectively.

Everything you do has a consequence. Some consequences may seem trivial, others traumatic, but they all have some effect on our behavior. If you enter a dark room and you want light, you flip a light switch. The consequence is usually light. If the light doesn't go on, you will probably emit other behaviors—turn on a flashlight, light a candle, replace a light bulb. If you watch a television program rather than studying for an exam, you may do poorly on the exam. Whether the consequences are positive or aversive, they do occur and they do influence our behavior.

When consequences are pleasant or satisfying, they usually influence us to behave the same way in future similar situations; thus, our behavior is likely to produce more positive consequences. This process has been referred to as the **principle of reinforcement.** Aversive events tend to decrease the probability that we will behave the same way in similar situations. Psychologists have referred to this process as **punishment** (the principle of punishment and its effect on behavior will be discussed in Chapter 4). These principles are continually shaping our behavior, whether we are aware of them or not. As a teacher, your being unaware of these principles may influence the development of undesirable behaviors. If you understand and use the principle of reinforcement correctly, however, you can teach your students constructive, beneficial social behaviors and help them improve their academic performance.

This chapter defines positive reinforcement and explains how the process affects students' behavior. Five types of reinforcers are discussed: social, activity, token, tangible or material, and edible. Strategies for identifying potential reinforcers are explained, including watch-and-see, ask the children, ask other teachers, try-and-see, and marketing strategies. Guidelines are provided for using reinforcement effectively and increasing the use of positive reinforcement.

I. "POSITIVE REINFORCEMENT" AND TYPES OF REINFORCERS

Reinforcement always increases the frequency of behavior unless the behavior is already so frequent that the reinforcement merely maintains it. Thus, a stimulus (an object or event) is defined as a positive reinforcer if it follows the occurrence of a behavior and increases or maintains the frequency of that behavior in the future. Paying a child for cutting the lawn is probably reinforcing; we will know for sure if he continues to cut the lawn in the future.

Types of Reinforcers

Social reinforcers. **Social reinforcers** are stimuli which come from other individuals, including attention, praise, and hugs. Positive attention, such as compliments, smiles, and pats on the back, may function as a positive social reinforcer, strengthening the behavior it follows. The accompanying box lists examples of potential social reinforcers. Critical attention—threats, reprimands, and criticism—can also act as a positive reinforcer, increasing the future occurrence of the behavior it follows.

SOCIAL REINFORCEMENT COMMENTS AND STATEMENTS

Phrase

Excellent	I like that	Beautiful
Commendable	Exciting	Complete
Perfect	Right on	A-1
Keep going	Super	Wow
Fantastic	Outstanding	For display
Of course	Absolutely right	Bravo
Great	Yeah	Improved
Correct	Fine answer	Yes
Good response	Super	Nice work
Marvelous	Good job	Nice try
Creative	Clever idea	Unbelievable

Thanks for getting your eyes up front so fast.

That's a good way to make friends.

Good working quietly while you waited for me to help you.

I'm glad I can depend on you to come in and take your seats.

I like to read what you have written. That's very imaginative.

Now you're really trying.

I appreciate your attention.

I admire you when you work like that.

You learned that very quickly; you must have been listening well.

It was nice of you to loan her your _____.

Will you please show me and the class how you did that?

That's a good point.

Let's put this somewhere special.

I'm happy your desk is so straight and organized.

Show this good work to your parents.

Your working so quietly helps the whole group.

Physical Expression of Social Reinforcement

Grinning	Cheering	Walking among students
Winking	Shaking hands	Smiling
Laughing	Thumbs up	Patting shoulder
Whistling	Signaling OK	Nudging
Nodding	Sitting near students	Ruffling hair
Patting back	Patting head	Hugging
Applause	"High five"	Hand slaps

Any time two people interact, one person will probably have some influence over the behavior of the other. This is especially true in the classroom. Almost everything the teacher does or says makes certain student behaviors more or less probable. A teacher can never say, "I do not want to influence my students all the time. Now I am teaching, and what I do will affect the children. But five minutes ago, I wasn't teaching. What I did then won't affect them." Such thinking simply deludes the teacher and results in inconsistent, noncontingent, or unplanned social attention, which is ineffective and may actually be destructive.

Social reinforcement is the most natural and frequently used type of reinforcement. Opportunities to administer social reinforcement happen hundreds of times each day. It is easy for a classroom teacher to socially reinforce students without interfering with normal classroom activities. A teacher may be conducting a reading group in a corner of the room and still verbally comment on the good behavior of other students in the room without interrupting the reading group.

Social reinforcement can be either positive or critical. Unfortunately, many of us have learned to react negatively to behaviors we don't like, but we often fail to react positively to appropriate behavior. We seem eager to criticize but slow to praise. One group of researchers (Madsen et al., 1970) who studied a large group of teachers found that 77 percent of their interactions were socially negative and only 23 percent were socially positive. White (1975) examined the rate of 104 teachers' approval and disapproval statements (grades 1 through 12) and found that students received more teacher disapproval than approval. Thomas and colleagues (1978) replicated White's study with junior high school teachers and found similar results. Walker and Buckley (1973) reported that 89 percent of the interactions between problem children and their teachers were a result of the teacher's attending to negative behavior. These studies demonstrate that there is a much higher probability of teacher disapproval of inappropriate behavior than praise for appropriate behavior.

A negative approach is generally met with a negative response and can actually strengthen the behaviors that triggered the criticism (Madsen et al., 1968). When a teacher is constantly warning, scolding, lecturing, and even spanking children, the children often become uncooperative or hostile, or they withdraw from the interaction. The teacher then reacts even more negatively, and the undesirable patterns are further reinforced. Fortunately, a positive approach to children, with precise praise for well-defined behaviors and only occasional criticism, leads to positive, productive behavior.

Activity reinforcers.   One very powerful kind of reinforcer used in classroom programs is the **activity reinforcer;** examples are extra recess, leading the flag salute, or being able to choose which desk to sit in. Activity reinforcers are usually available in the classroom at no cost and are fairly easily administered. Common activities used for reinforcement are free time or social time, games, art activities, taking notes to the principal's office, calling home, gym play, passing out papers, being first in line, and working at the teacher's desk. Other potential activity reinforcers are listed in Table 3–1.

TABLE 3–1 Potential Activity Reinforcers, Privileges, and Special Activities

Free time	Pass out paper, scissors, etc.
Extra turn in a game	Read comics
Carry library books upstairs	Sit in easy chair
Computer games	Put up feet and relax
Teacher eating in the cafeteria with a student	Leader in line
	Listen to radio with earphones
Play a popular record	Make a phone call home
Ten minutes for a game	Listen to own voice on tape recorder
Fifteen minutes in library	Push adult around in swivel chair
Choose a story	Wear special hats
Movies	Walk in high heels
Get a drink	Answer the office phone
Make shadow pictures using a flashlight	Blow soap bubbles
Watch short film, viewmaster, filmstrip.	Select game or object for recess
Help custodian	Work jigsaw puzzle for ten minutes
Look out the window	Take a good work note to the principal
Play with squirt gun	Dance
Discuss something with teacher for five minutes	Visit another class
	Crafts
Extend class recess for __ minutes	Time in science library
Play marbles	Choose activity for the class
Listen to cassettes	Field trips (subject matter)
Help other children	Model with clay, putty
Exempt a test	Put blinds up or down
Look at projected slide	Participate in group organizations (music, speech, athletics, etc.)
Pick a story for teacher to read to class	
Early dismissal from class period	Plan daily schedules
Cut with scissors	Outside supervising (patrols, directing parking, ushering)
Take class pet home on weekends	
Turn off lights	Climb ladder
Outdoor lessons	Extra five minutes at lunch
Show and tell (any level)	"Senior sluff day"
Musical chairs	Attend assemblies
Use extra art materials	Play short game: tic-tac-toe, easy puzzles, connect-the-dots
Operate jack-in-the-box	
Comb and brush own or adult's hair	Represent group in school activities
Solve codes and other puzzles	Decorate classroom
Sharpen pencils	Be a line monitor
Select seat or desk next to friend or in a chosen place in classroom	Feed fish for a week
	Display student's work (any subject matter)
Extra time at recess (for self, class, with a friend)	
	Straighten up for teacher
Play instrument: drum, whistle, piano	Ride elevator
Be tickled	Put away materials

(continued)

TABLE 3-1 *(continued)*

Run in hall with truck for two minutes	Lead discussions
Buy extra straws	Construct school materials
Do ceramic project	Answer questions
Draw and color pictures, paint at easel	Get milk at break
Perform before a group: sing a song; tell a poem or riddle; do a dance or trick	An extra cookie at break
	Sit on adult's lap
Present talent shows, skits, puppet shows	Go to museum, fire station, courthouse, etc.
Captain of team at recess	
Write on blackboard: white or colored chalk	Compete with other classes
	Work problems on the board
Study with a friend	Dusting, erasing, cleaning, arranging chairs, etc.
Prepare for holidays (Christmas, Thanksgiving, Easter)	
	Go home five minutes early
Parties	Jump down from a high place into arms of adult
Make a game of subject matter	
Talk periods	Watch TV
Read to the principal	First for drink at recess
Carry purse, briefcase	Omit specific assignment
Build up, knock down blocks	Throw ball, bean bag
Have teacher wear funny hat for fifteen minutes	Read library books
	Chew gum during class
Take a message	Read to class
Pop balloon, paper, bag, milk carton	Extra swim period
First up to bat at recess	Have teacher get student's tray and food in cafeteria
Pull other person in wagon	
Play with magnet	Be turned around in swivel chair
Water plants	Blow out match
Lead the flag salute	Use playground equipment: slide, swings, seesaw
Roll wheeled toy	
Take care of calendar by the week	Look in mirror
Show filmstrip	Be pulled in wagon
String beads	Ten minutes for game at milk break
Listen to a song	Watch train go around track
Help with audio/visual equipment	Listen to short recording
Sit at teacher's desk for reading	Mark papers
Paint with water on blackboard	Run errands
Be pushed on swing	Run other equipment, such as string pull toys, light switch
Field trip (available once every two weeks)	
Helping collect displays, etc. for units	Be swung around
Blow up a balloon and let it go	Pull down screen
Use typewriter	Be student teacher

Token reinforcers. **Token reinforcers** become desirable to children and function as reinforcers because they can be exchanged for other reinforcers, such as activities or tangible articles. Money is the most common example of a token reinforcer. Its power as a reinforcer lies in what it can buy. Money substitutes, such as play money, chips, or other small objects, are usually used as tokens in the classroom. Points, which can be earned and then exchanged for privileges, are another frequently used token system. The use of token reinforcers is discussed in detail in Chapter 6.

Tangible or material reinforcers. A few students will not respond favorably to social or even activity reinforcers. They may have learned through past school experience that classrooms and teachers mean failure and punishment. They don't trust teacher praise because they have been praised so seldom. Some students need strong, obvious, immediate reinforcers. Objects such as toys, games, and personal goods have been widely used as reinforcers in a variety of programs. The specific items used vary with the population; for example, balloons and trinkets are more effective with preschool children, while phonograph records are more effective with older youths. Tangible or material reinforcers should always be paired with social reinforcers, so that the child begins to respond to social reinforcement, which is what he is most likely to meet outside the classroom. Table 3–2 lists some potential tangible reinforcers.

TABLE 3-2   Potential Tangible or Material Reinforcers*

Computer disks	Marbles
Jumpropes	Stickers
Hairbrushes, combs	Fans
Address books	Tape recorders
Silly Putty	Flowers
Bookmarkers	Dolls
Jacks	Notebooks
Notes home	Coupons
Playground equipment	Tickets to activities (movies, games, etc.)
Stuffed animals	Badges
Ribbons	Pins
Personalized pencils	Pencil holder
Coloring books	Boats
Pictures from magazines	Books
Toy musical instruments	Stationery
Pennies, foreign coins, play money	Makeup kits
Miniature cars	Blocks
Snakes	Seasonal cards (Valentines, birthday)
Comics	Chalk
Toy watches	Dollhouses
Pickup sticks	Balls
Birthday hats	Toy jewelry
Commercial games	Play dough, clay
Class pictures	Marbles
Collage materials	Puzzles
Counting beads	Compasses
Subject matter accessories	Purses
Yo-yo's	Calendars
Paint brushes, paints	Kaleidoscopes

(continued)

TABLE 3-2   *(continued)*

Bean bags	Beads
Grab bag gifts	Buttons
Cowboy hats	Flashlight
Toy guns	Plastic toys (animals, Indians, soldiers)
Bats	Household items(pots, spoons, all sizes of
Whistles	containers)
Pins	Papier-mâché
Headdress	Jumping beans
Book covers	Bubble blowing kit
Pencils and pens	Stamps
Crayons	Model kits
Perfume	Surprise box with candy, toys, etc.
Key chains	Wax lips and teeth
Good citizenship award certificate	Masks
Rings	Balloons
Scarves	Flash cards
Elastic bands	Banks
Striped straws	Kickball
Magnifying glasses	Pets
Cars	Colored paper
Cassettes	Pencil sharpeners, erasers

*Children may either purchase items themselves or purchase the right to use them without owning them.

Edible reinforcers.   In practice, edible reinforcers are not often used outside of preschool, early elementary classes, or special-education classes. Nevertheless, candy and other "goodies" are mentioned immediately when behavior modification is discussed by laymen. Much of the early work in the field was done with emotionally disturbed or mentally retarded persons, especially children, for whom there are few effective reinforcers other than edibles. In the regular classroom, however, although the proverbial M&M is occasionally used, much more reliance is placed upon other types of reinforcers.

EXAMPLE

The Saga of Izzie Able*

Consider the following situation: It's the first day of school and, armed with a resolution to be more positive and loving toward her students this year, Ms. Izzie Able awaits her class. The students rush into the room and choose

*"The Saga of Izzie Able" was originally written by L. S. Keleman, M. E. West, and K. R. Young and published in K. R. Young and L. S. Keleman (1975), *Classroom Management Systems*, Chapter III—Social Reinforcement, Salt Lake: BET Inc. It has been revised and reprinted here with permission of the authors.

their desks. One student in particular catches her eye. He wants the desk that another child has already taken. Ms. Able, putting her arm around him, asks his name. "Willie Maket," he yells as he pushes over the desk. Ms. Able keeps her temper, suggests that Willie might like the desk close to hers, and then helps the other student pick up the tipped-over desk. Willie stomps up to his new desk and tips it over. Ms. Able's resolution wavers and she grabs Willie and firmly places him into a nearby chair, where he sits docilely waiting for Ms. Able to start class. Izzie, without realizing it, is on the way to becoming entangled in another year of frustration and confusion.

With some training in the use of social reinforcement, Ms. Izzie Able might be more effective in managing the behavior of her class, although Willie may need more than praise. Let's give Izzie a second chance at a more successful first day back at school.

Izzie Able is standing by the classroom door as the bell rings, and 26 eager fourth-grade students rush into the room. She smiles and notices that one girl has quickly and quietly taken a seat in the front row. Izzie compliments her and asks her name. Izzie then repeats the praise statement so all can hear, "Susan came in and sat so quietly. Isn't that great?" Six other students scurry for seats and Izzie praises them. One student in particular catches her eye. He wants the desk another student has already taken. Ms. Able asks his name. "Willie Maket," he yells, as he pushes over the desk. Izzie ignores him and praises the student next to Willie. "You're sitting quietly. What's your name?" Willie, puzzled by the teacher's lack of attention, tries again. After shoving Mona Lott out of the way, he plops down at her desk. Izzie's self-restraint is wavering, but she continues greeting and complimenting the other 25 students who are now all seated and watching intently. Willie, determined to win this battle, jumps up and orders another student to trade desks. Ms. Able grabs Willie and firmly places him back in his seat. She regains her composure and praises 2 nearby students. The class is now attending to Ms. Able and is ready for instruction.

Exercises

1. Define the term *positive reinforcement.*
2. List and give examples of each of the five types of positive reinforcement discussed in this chapter.

Feedback

1. Positive reinforcement is a procedure that increases or maintains the rate at which a behavior occurs by contingently following the behavior with the presentation of a stimulus object or event (a positive reinforcer).
2. a. *Social reinforcement*—Complimenting a student for sitting quietly in a school assembly.
   b. *Activity reinforcers*—Watching a special videotaped movie after all class members have reached their individual goals for math.
   c. *Token reinforcers*—Having students earn points for completing math assignments and later exchanging the points for extra recess time.

> d. *Tangible reinforcers*—Putting a smiley-face sticker on a student's English composition, showing approval for good work.
> e. *Edible reinforcers*—Providing a popcorn party for the class on Friday afternoon for following the classroom rules all week.

2. SELECTING THE APPROPRIATE TYPE OF REINFORCER FOR A SPECIFIC SITUATION

As you learned in the last section, teachers have a large arsenal of positive reinforcers available to them. However, not all reinforcers work equally well in all situations. There are advantages and disadvantages to each type of reinforcer, depending on the target group and the overall school situation. Within a specific group, some reinforcers work better than others; your students may prefer extra recess to art activities, for example, so art activities will not be effective reinforcers. Finally, individual differences among students determine how effective a particular reinforcer will be with each student. In addition to understanding the advantages and disadvantages of the different types of reinforcers, it is important to be aware of some helpful strategies teachers can use in selecting reinforcers for their students.

Disadvantages and Advantages of Types of Reinforcers

When considering the appropriate type of reinforcer for a particular situation, you need to look at several general criteria: the type of student group for which the reinforcer is usually effective, how quickly students typically satiate on that reinforcer, how easy it is to administer the reinforcer, and any potential legal or ethical problems.

Social reinforcers.   Social reinforcers are a natural part of human interaction, and they are potentially effective for any student group at any age. To be part of an effective behavioral analysis program, however, social reinforcers must be response-contingent—that is, they must be given in response to appropriate behavior that deserves reinforcement. Random, noncontingent reinforcement is ineffective, confusing to students, and potentially damaging because it may reinforce inappropriate behavior.

Social reinforcers are so easy and natural that it is sometimes difficult for a teacher to remember to deliver them in a precise, contingent manner. Changing from random reinforcement to the systematic use of social reinforcers usually involves altering existing habitual behavior and can be very challenging.

Systematic use of appropriate social reinforcers can work well with all types of students. However, some students must be taught to respond to social reinforcers such as praise and attention. Students with a history of failure in school are not used to being praised and usually do not respond to positive social reinforcers like praise from the teacher. They can be taught to respond to social reinforcers by pairing the positive attention with tangible reinforcers. Social reinforcers are not always powerful enough to change the behavior of children who are handicapped or asocial. This is often the case with children in self-contained special education classes or with some handicapped pupils in mainstream classes. The ineffectiveness of social reinforcers with these children may be partially due to the way in which the reinforcers are delivered. Many teachers have found that an apparently asocial child who does not respond to the teacher's random praise and approval responds well to consistent social reinforcement for precisely defined behaviors.

After you have identified target behaviors to reinforce and worked out a plan to systematically reinforce your students, social reinforcers are easy to administer. They are natural, easy to deliver, immediately available, and do not interrupt classroom activities. A teacher can praise a child from any place in the room at the moment when the desired behavior occurs. Students do not usually tire of teacher praise and attention, and praise is free.

In our society, praising a child does not raise moral or legal issues. The only social reinforcer that might involve legal problems is touching. The human touch is a powerful reinforcer for many people, but it must be used carefully. Teachers should not touch students who do not like to be touched. Students who do respond well should be touched only on the back or shoulders, in a caring but clearly nonsensual manner.

Activity reinforcers. Other than social reinforcers, activity reinforcers are probably the most often used in regular elementary and secondary classrooms. Most people respond well to activity reinforcers, although there is the occasional student who would rather sit and eat than play a game. Activity reinforcers work especially well with groups that are self-directed and can accept a delay between behavior and reinforcement. However, appropriate activity reinforcers can be devised for almost any group of students.

Children usually do not satiate quickly or for very long on activities. Whereas candy may lose its reinforcing function if a child has eaten some chocolate before school, this is not likely to happen with activity reinforcers. Activities need not involve extra expense. Extra recess, choosing a special reading book, leading the flag salute, or a 5-minute period of talking do not require a financial expenditure by the staff or school.

Any social, work, or play activity that students engage in voluntarily when they have free time and opportunity can be used as a reinforcer. Such reinforcers are usually abundantly available in the school setting. However, administration of activity reinforcers can be a problem. They usually cannot be delivered immediately after an appropriate behavior has been emitted. In addition, it is usually not appropriate to reinforce a single specific behavior with an entire activity. For these reasons, activity reinforcers are frequently used in conjunction with a token or point system. Activities take time to perform; thus, activity reinforcers can interrupt academic work unless they are used as part of a system that sets aside special periods for the delivery of delayed activity reinforcers (token systems) or a system whereby students earn time they can spend in special reinforcement areas of the classroom.

The ethical and legal restrictions that apply to the use of activities as reinforcers are not clear. It seems apparent that students cannot be restricted or prohibited from engaging in regularly scheduled school activities that are part of the normal curriculum. Thus, academic classes, physical education, and recess probably cannot be withheld legally because these are educational experiences in which children have a right to engage. Less clear is whether or not extracurricular activities, which are not part of the program in which all students engage, can be withheld. Certainly, activities such as playing on the football team are withheld from many students on the basis of lack of ability or low grades. But it is not clear whether a student can legally lose a privilege, such as a special assembly or a club meeting, held during regular school hours. If such a question arises, the teacher should consult the local school district.

Token reinforcers.   Token reinforcers have been effectively used with almost all populations of children and adults. Token systems have been used in regular elementary and secondary classes, and in programs for handicapped persons, college students, predelinquents and delinquents, and adult offenders (Kazdin, 1977). Canter and Canter (1982) recommend a token system, using marbles, as part of their assertive discipline program for regular education classes. When the students are following the class rules and working, the teacher drops a marble in a jar. Marbles are exchanged for free time, class parties, or other activities. Token reinforcers can be as versatile as a creative teacher desires. Chapter 6 discusses the use of tokens in more detail.

A major advantage of token reinforcers is that students rarely satiate on the tokens because they can purchase many different reinforcers. For example, most individuals—with the possible exception of a few millionaires—never tire of receiving money because they never run out of things to buy. Another advantage is that the token can be given to the student immediately after he has emitted the target behavior without disruption of the class routine. The management of a token system can be quite involved, however. Having a variety of activities and/or tangible reinforcers available for purchase, establishing prices, making exchanges, and keeping records all take time. The use of tangible and/or edible reinforcers in exchange for tokens can become costly. The teacher will have to compare the needs of the students, the potential benefits, and the time, effort, and costs involved in order to decide whether a token system should be used. A token system may be simple or complex but should always be well planned and consistently administered.

A properly planned and administered token system would be conducted without legal or ethical problems. However, Martin (1975) points out three potential problems that must be avoided. The first concern is the possible abuse of the system and students. Martin states:

I have observed classrooms in which point sheets were turned in by students eagerly working to earn rewards and the sheets were destroyed by aides who did not like a particular child. We have also heard of situations in mental institutions in which staff were supposed to give tokens for communicative speech and ignore babbling, but they instead simply rewarded patients they liked and ignored patients they did not want to interact with. (p. 83)

The second concern deals with effectiveness. When token systems (and other procedures) are not effective in producing the desired results, teachers should change the program. Students have the right to an appropriate, effective education.

The third and strongest objection is the use of a token system that denies students' basic rights and requires them to purchase the "rights" with points. Token systems can require students to purchase privileges, but not rights. For example, lunch cannot be withheld, but a child might pay points to go to lunch 5 minutes early or to be first in line.

Tangible reinforcers. Children typically like tangible reinforcers and respond well to them. For this reason it is easy to overuse them, thus creating children who expect and demand tangible rewards for everything they do, rather than responding to praise or free time. In general, tangible reinforcers should be the reinforcer of choice only when social and activity reinforcers are not effective.

Children for whom social attention or activities may not be reinforcing often respond to material objects. Children who are deprived of material goods, toys, and personal items in their daily lives are often those for whom these items have the most reinforcing function. Thus, tangible reinforcers are particularly effective with nonsocial, handicapped, or economically deprived children. Children may satiate on particular tangible reinforcers. However, a different reinforcer may be just as effective as the first one. Some form of tangible reinforcement will probably always be effective.

Time can be a factor when tangible reinforcers are used. A teacher must take time to deliver the reinforcer, which could be easy or difficult depending on the item. If the object is highly reinforcing, the child is likely to play with it or otherwise interact with it upon delivery. Delivering the object immediately when earned may interfere with class activities. For this reason, tangible reinforcers are typically used in token reinforcement systems, and the token can be earned immediately and exchanged later for a tangible reinforcer.

The use of material reinforcers for an entire class can become a sizable expense, and purchase and storage can also become a chore. Instead of providing for the entire class, a teacher should consider having a few small tangible reinforcers which can be selected from a variety of other options, including activities and edibles.

The legal and ethical issues related to edible reinforcers apply to tangible reinforcers as well (see next section). Since very few items are usually given to students in a typical school program, most tangible reinforcers can be considered special privileges rather than rights. Obviously, this would not be the case if school textbooks, supplies, or other items regularly supplied by the school were restricted.

Edible reinforcers.   In general, the younger and less competent the child, the more appropriate it is to use edible reinforcers. The more control the teacher has over the child's environment, the more effective edible reinforcers will be. With young or handicapped children, candy, sugar-coated cereals, bits of fruit, sips of juice, and other edibles are likely to be powerful reinforcers, while social attention, things, or activities may be weak. Most children like candy and "goodies," and for these children such items are good reinforcers. However, many teachers and school administrators believe that the use of edibles with older, nonhandicapped students is inappropriate, so teachers should check with the school administration before using them. Edibles are more likely to be used with moderately and severely handicapped children than with nonhandicapped children in a public school or day-care setting.

Children often satiate quickly on candy and other snacks. When choosing an edible as a reinforcer, the teacher should make sure it can be given in small enough bits so that satiation is delayed. Edible reinforcers can be given immediately after the desired behavior occurs, or they can be delayed or even exchanged for tokens, depending on the students. Some teachers find the delivery of small candies or bits of cereal simple and direct; that is, it is mechanically easy. Others find using edible reinforcers "messy." Even when delivering small edibles is a brief procedure, some children, particularly young ones, can spend an inordinate amount of time consuming the edible— time spent at the expense of learning activities. Also, the use of edible reinforcers can become a sizable expense when used for an entire class. Purchase and storage can become a bother, especially when edibles are the only or the major reinforcer used. As mentioned in the last section, edible reinforcers are often useful as one item out of many from which children may choose. Some parents object to using edibles as reinforcers because of medical, dental, and meal-planning considerations. This often depends on the particular reinforcers and the amount used.

Teachers should be aware of violating ethical standards or children's legal rights when using edible reinforcers. When edibles are used as reinforcers, it means that receiving the edibles is contingent on some behavior. Thus, children who do not meet the criteria may at various times not obtain that particular edible. It is obvious that ethical standards are violated when students are not allowed healthy meals or access to water. But legal questions may also be raised by less severe restrictions if students are restricted from edibles that are considered rights rather than privileges (see discussion of Wyatt *vs.* Stickney and Morales *vs.* Turman, in Martin, 1975). This may be the case with foods that are normally available to all students as part of a school lunch, such as desserts. Teaching procedures to solve student behavior problems without resorting to restrictive procedures, such as the deprivation of edibles, should always be tried before instituting a program of restriction. A teacher with questions as to the legality or ethics of a procedure should consult the local school district. Teachers should note that legal and ethical restraints apply to all procedures used in a classroom, not merely to programs based upon behavior modification.

IDENTIFYING POTENTIAL REINFORCERS FOR GROUPS OR INDIVIDUALS

All the reinforcers discussed in the previous section can be used effectively in the right circumstances. When instituting a program of positive reinforcement, however, the teacher cannot simply choose possible reinforcers from a list and assume that they will be effective reinforcers for a particular group or a particular individual. The true test of a reinforcer is its ability to strengthen preceding behavior. One can never be certain that an event is a reinforcer for a particular child until its effect upon that child's behavior has been tested. This does not mean, however, that a teacher must use a completely random trial-and-error process to identify potential reinforcers. There are several general strategies a teacher can use to identify consequences that have a high probability of being positive reinforcers for any particular child or for most children.

The Watch-and-see Strategy

The first, and in many ways the most popular, strategy for identifying effective positive reinforcers is the watch-and-see strategy. In its most basic form, this strategy calls for the teacher to carefully observe the children's self-selected activities in a variety of situations (on the playground, in the hall, during free time) and to list the activities they choose for themselves without specific direction from the teacher or other persons in authority. The teacher can also plan periods when the children have free time to do "anything they want"—within reason, of course. The teacher then observes and records what the children choose to do on their own.

The psychologist David Premack (1959) demonstrated that any activity occurring at a high rate under free-choice conditions can be used to reinforce a lower-rate activity (this is known as the Premack principle). Thus, observation of what children do when they are relatively unrestricted is a good way to identify reinforcers.

Using this information, the teacher can utilize the preferred activities as reinforcing consequences that must be earned and can assess their effectiveness as reinforcers. For example, one teacher observed that students liked to congregate during recess to trade cards and pictures. She decided to allow them to have an additional trading time after they finished their arithmetic lesson. The total arithmetic period was 40 minutes long. After 20 minutes, any student who finished the assignment could go to a special area of the room and quietly trade cards or otherwise interact with friends. The longer they took to complete the lesson, the less time they had to trade. The procedure worked well for these children. They started working on the assignment much more quickly, and there were fewer delays and disruptions during the work period. Several children worked too quickly and sloppily, however, until the teacher added the requirement that the problems worked incorrectly on the previous day had to be corrected before a child could go to the trading area.

The "watch-and-see" strategy is not complete after a single observation, or even several. Preferred activities may change during the year, and the teacher should constantly be aware of new preferences. For example, playing marbles or jacks might be preferred activities in the fall, but by spring the children may prefer kickball and tag. Satiation will occur if a reinforcer is overused.

The teacher must remember that nearly any consequence will be more reinforcing for one child than for another. It is almost impossible to identify one event that will serve equally well as a positive reinforcer for all children. The "watch-and-see" strategy should make room for the child's individual preferences, particularly the more difficult ones who may require idiosyncratic reinforcers. In the case of one overly active boy, the only thing that seemed to work was the chance to stay after school and help the teacher clean up. The boy worked hard every day to earn this privilege. None of the other children wanted to stay, but this boy enjoyed staying to help the teacher above all else.

Ask-the-children Strategy

Asking children what they like is an obvious way to find out about potential reinforcers. There are good reasons for allowing children to participate in decisions about their education. There is evidence that involvement and participation are important ingredients in the quality and rate of work and learning. Also, the more practice children have in self-determination, the more skilled they are likely to become in managing their own behavior. In addition, children are an excellent source of information about the success and failure of a curriculum and about the instructional process. Children can also identify reinforcers, although they may require some training and experience in selecting consequences that are both reasonable and positive.

Children's participation in the identification and selection of reinforcers can take several forms. Individual children may make suggestions for free-time activities or special privileges they like to earn. Teachers who purchase items to be used as reinforcers may take a group of students to the store to help select reinforcers. The children may elect a group of their peers to make all decisions about reinforcers or to advise the teacher on possible reinforcers. Child and adolescent reinforcement survey forms can also be used to assess potential reinforcers (Cautela et al., 1982).

When asking children to suggest possible reinforcers, the teacher should encourage them to consider a wide range of possibilities. If children suggest no activities but restrict themselves to material things, the teacher might suggest a few activities for consideration and ask them to name others. The teacher should add suggestions for any type of reinforcer that the children don't mention. Also, children may get "hung up" on either "big" or "little" reinforcers. If all the activities they suggest are rather grandiose privileges—the kind of privileges a student could only earn on rare occasions and would require much behavior to earn—the teacher should suggest some more reasonable activities. The goal is to get a wide range, both in magnitude and in variety.

The teacher should also make sure that all children have a chance to express preferences, particularly "problem" children or children who are "different" in some way. Children may suggest reinforcers that are not attainable for classroom use, and even those that are potentially usable may not be available when needed. In addition, some children frequently may not meet the requirements to earn a specific reinforcer. To maintain credibility, the teacher must clearly state, in advance, that not all suggested reinforcers will be available. The children should be told that they are making suggestions, some of which may be used. Of course, the teacher should respond to all the children's suggestions politely.

In addition to asking the children before selecting reinforcers, the teacher must carefully observe the children's reactions when they earn the reinforcers. If the children do not appear to be interested in the reinforcer, even if they have chosen it, or if it does not affect behavior, alternative reinforcers should be tried. It is also important to remember that preferences change over time, so the teacher should continue to "ask the children."

The Ask-other-teachers Strategy

As a third strategy for identifying potential reinforcers, the teacher can investigate the successful positive consequences other teachers have used. This strategy provides at least two kinds of information. First, it gives a teacher specific suggestions about consequences to use as positive reinforcers. Second, looking at reinforcers that others have used can suggest the range of events that can be used as reinforcers. For example, when a teacher heard from a colleague that children liked to earn the right to pass out and collect papers, she reasoned that the children would also like to periodically purchase the first seat in the row, because the student sitting in that location is often given the job of passing and collecting papers. Another teacher learned that the class next door earned the privilege of seeing a weekly movie. She observed the movie period and noted that children scrambled and even fought to capture preferred seats. She then offered the children in her class the privilege of seeing a movie each week, but also the chance to earn the better seats.

The Try-and-see Strategy

Even if the children don't suggest a reinforcer or naturally seek it or other teachers don't recommend it, an activity or item may still be highly reinforcing. The fourth strategy draws on the teacher's teaching experience and childhood memories to identify and select reinforcers and to try any new reinforcers she has a "hunch" about. Careful observation will soon reveal whether her invention is functioning as a positive reinforcer—that is, whether it is strengthening the behavior that precedes it.

A slightly different variation of the try-and-see strategy is reinforcer sampling (Ayllon & Azrin, 1968). The reinforcer sampling rule states, "Before using an event or stimulus as a reinforcer, require sampling of the reinforcer in the situation in which it is to be used" (p. 91). For example, the teacher may have the entire class participate in a game at recess or during a brief break. Initially, all students participate and if there is a positive response— that is, the students indicate that they enjoy the game—the teacher may decide to put the game on his list of reinforcers. In the future, when students want to play the game, they will have to earn it by completing their work and earning points.

Reinforcer exposure is similar to reinforcer sampling except that the teacher allows the children to choose the reinforcers rather than presenting a particular activity to the entire class. A teacher may display on a table a variety of games, art projects, or other activities that could be potential reinforcers. During some free period, the students may have access to any of these games or activities; the teacher then notes any item that is highly sought after by the students, and that item becomes a reinforcer in the classroom reinforcement program.

"Marketing" Strategies and Miscellaneous Procedures

Another strategy for selecting or enhancing the effectiveness of known reinforcers is advertising. As we are all well aware, advertising plays a major role in our society in the sale of products and services. The teacher may take advantage of this cultural phenomenon by preparing special advertising procedures for the reinforcers in her classroom. The teacher may develop a poster to place on the board advertising an upcoming game, activity, or field trip or make (or obtain from a local advertising agency) pictures of movies that may be shown to the class as a reinforcer. The key to effective advertising is the teacher's creativity. If the teacher can make the potential reinforcer appear to be fun and exciting, the students are much more likely to want to work for the reinforcer. Activities that may not be functional reinforcers may obtain reinforcing qualities when a teacher promotes the activity through creative advertising.

Another marketing strategy is "packaging." The business world spends a great deal of time and money to package products in a way that is appealing to consumers. This same principle can be used with classroom reinforcers. There may be ways to dress up potential reinforcers or activities that have not been reinforcing so that they become more desirable for students. For example, a teacher may allow students to earn the opportunity to perform some classroom tasks, such as handing out papers, erasing the blackboard, getting and passing out milk during lunch time, or feeding the classroom pets. If these activities lose their reinforcement effectiveness or were not particularly reinforcing to begin with, the teacher may enhance their reinforcement value by preparing articles of clothing associated with each job. The student getting the milk may wear a milk deliverer's hat, those erasing the blackboard may wear the blackboard supervisor's apron, and so on. Sometimes dressing up a job, a task, or an activity may make it more appealing to students, particularly at the preschool and elementary levels.

At the secondary level, this idea has been capitalized on by developing a "mystery box." The box is decorated with a question mark, and a reinforcer that the class can earn is secretly placed inside the box. The reinforcer may be a radio for the class to listen to, a cassette tape or a record, or a poster of a video that the class may earn the right to watch. All these things may have some reinforcing value in and of themselves, but the mysterious aspect of not knowing for sure what is coming up sometimes enhances student motivation. Another idea at the secondary level is to develop a wheel of fortune. A large, decorative poster with a hand that spins around is made. A number of different reinforcing activities are listed on the wheel of fortune; those that are less desirable are listed more than once, while the most desirable ones are listed only once, and maybe in a very narrow area, on the wheel of fortune. When the class or individual student has earned the right to participate in a reinforcing activity, the hand on the wheel is spun to determine which activity has been earned.

Auctions sometimes enhance the effectiveness of reinforcers. Teachers have reported that reinforcers that were not particularly effective when placed on a menu and earned individually became desirable when students had to bid for them as part of a class auction. Teachers should be aware that a reinforcement system is in many ways like our own economy, in that the desirability of reinforcers makes the cost or the price (in terms of points) vary.

In summary, teachers should remember that, except for a few basic items such as food and water, no item or activity can be positively identified as a reinforcer before it has been tried and shown to work—that is, to modify the behavior it immediately follows. Children can satiate on any reinforcer that is overused, so even the most powerful reinforcer will lose its strength. It is better to have many reinforcers that are rotated in use than to have only a few reinforcers that are used too often.

Teachers must remember that what is highly reinforcing for one child may not appeal to another; therefore, a variety of reinforcers must be provided to satisfy the individual preferences of all children. Many teachers provide a "cafeteria" of reinforcers for their students, and a variety of reinforcing items or activities are available on any particular day. The total "menu" of reinforcers changes from time to time to prevent satiation.

The job of observing the effect of existing reinforcers and searching for new reinforcers is never complete. An effective reinforcement system is an ever-changing blend of established reinforcers with potential but untried reinforcers. The teacher should be careful not to think of reinforcers only in terms of candy or other material items that have to be purchased. There are many activities and privileges that are as good, if not better than, material items. Some teachers prefer to use material reinforcers initially to be certain of powerful consequences, but most have found that nonmaterial reinforcers can quickly be substituted.

EXAMPLE

Ms. Izzie Able has been successful in keeping most students on task, but she's been asking other teachers for ideas on finding better reinforcers for Willie. She has also learned about the watch-and-see strategy.

Returning to her class after lunch armed with a lot of new reinforcement ideas, Izzie finds that all the students are in their seats, even Willie. Willie, however, has his feet up on his desk and is reading a comic book. Izzie wants the class to start an assignment, but she feels uneasy telling Willie to begin work. What if he throws a tantrum? She tries praising the students around Willie for being ready to work, but Willie seems oblivious to these indirect reminders of expected classroom behavior.

Suddenly, Izzie thinks of another approach. She walks up to Willie, puts a hand on his shoulder, and announces to the class that if everyone starts their work right away, then as soon as they finish an assignment, they can put their feet on their desks and read whatever they want for 5 minutes before starting the next assignment. Willie puts away his comic book and starts working. Izzie makes a mental note to have a stock of comic books on hand to use as reinforcers in the future.

Exercises

1. Give an example of how the Premack principle could be used to solve a problem of students not completing their math assignments.
2. List and explain five strategies for identifying reinforcers for a group of students.

Feedback

1. A teacher who has students who do not complete their math assignments carefully and accurately can try the following strategy. Completion of the daily math lesson in a reasonable amount of time and with a high degree of accuracy could be considered an underdeveloped behavior that needs to be strengthened. An arrangement for free time to follow the math period would allow the teacher to try this experiment: Time spent at extra recess during this free period can be made contingent on meeting

some reasonable performance criteria on the math assignment. For example, children may be required to complete the assignment at 80 percent accuracy in 30 minutes if they are to earn extra recess time.

If some of the children are significantly better or worse in math than the others, different amounts of work may be assigned. Those who fail to meet their criterion levels may either miss the extra recess period entirely or be required to complete and/or correct their work before they can be released for extra recess, thus losing time in this valuable activity. Some children may not enjoy the recess period, so some other high-rate activity reinforcers could be provided for them. For example, they may earn the right to talk with a friend, do some additional reading, or have free time to do whatever they wish, within limits.

2. Five strategies for identifying reinforcers are
    a. *Watch-and-see*—Observe what children do and play with during free time; their preferred activities and toys can be used contingently as reinforcers.
    b. *Ask the children*—Simply ask students what reinforcers they would like to work for; you may have to guide their choices.
    c. *Ask other teachers*—Other teachers may share their ideas about reinforcers that have worked with their students.
    d. *Try-and-see*—Expose students to activities, materials, edibles, and so on that may be reinforcing and watch how they respond; select preferred activities and items as reinforcers.
    e. *Marketing strategies*—Advertise, package the reinforcer, or make it mysterious.

3. USING REINFORCERS EFFECTIVELY

In learning to use reinforcers effectively, it is helpful to understand some of the common objections to the use of positive reinforcement and the tendency of teachers to get trapped into a negative reinforcement cycle. This section briefly discusses these concerns and then focuses on methods to increase the effective, consistent use of positive reinforcement.

Common Objections to the Use of Positive Reinforcement

There are several reasons that many teachers do not use enough positive reinforcement. Some people find it awkward or "phony" to praise or compliment frequently. Many teachers feel that they are playing a role, that they aren't being genuine when they first begin to praise children frequently. There is nothing wrong with this feeling; it is to be expected and is only temporary. As the teacher uses more social reinforcement and makes it contingent on specific behavior, the children will start performing better. When this occurs, the teacher will, in turn, be reinforced. When this has occurred often enough, most teachers find that the increased use of praise and approval becomes spontaneous. It seems awkward and strange only until the results have made themselves felt; then it becomes spontaneous and natural.

Some people feel that positive reinforcement, especially tokens and tangible reinforcers, is "bribery." Reinforcement is not bribery, however, because (1) the reward comes after a good behavior is performed and thus earned, and (2) the reward is for legal, appropriate behavior, not for detrimental behavior, which is implied in the term bribery. The bribery objection can also be countered by using reinforcers that are natural to educational settings, such as activity reinforcers, grades, praise, positive feedback, and accomplishments.

The opinion that students should "learn for the love of learning" is also frequently expressed. In fact, some academic tasks are exciting and enjoyable and therefore act as their own reinforcers. However, the process of acquiring a new skill is often difficult and not reinforcing. When a child is having difficulty learning to read, reading is usually not reinforcing. As the child learns to read fluently, correctly reading the words and comprehending the meaning, reading may become reinforcing (Baer, 1981) and the student may read for personal enjoyment. Before this transition takes place, though, the teacher may have to use other reinforcers to maintain academic performance.

Another concern is the reinforcing of undesirable behavior. Unfortunately, some teachers have learned to attend to negative rather than positive behaviors. It does seem natural to ask a nonworking child what the problem is, or to try to calm or reprimand the disruptive student. It is hard for many teachers to realize that attention in the form of warnings, lectures, reprimands, and scolding may reinforce unwanted behaviors in their children. However, there is much evidence to suggest that such attention to unproductive behavior accelerates it—that attention, even a reprimand, is often a reinforcer in such situations (Madsen et al., 1970; Whitley & Sulzer, 1970). The experiences of many educators (Sloane, 1976; Williams, 1959) have shown that when this attention is withdrawn from deviant classroom behaviors, these behaviors are gradually extinguished, particularly if positive attention, praise, and/or tokens are used simultaneously to reinforce alternative desirable behaviors.

The criticism trap.   It should be easy, some people say, to establish a more positive relationship between teachers and students. All that is necessary is to give more praise and attention to desired behaviors and to pay less attention to the unwanted behaviors. Unfortunately, it usually isn't quite that simple. Over a period of many years, most people have learned to attend to negative rather than positive behaviors, and changing this pattern is difficult.

One reason that change is difficult is that teachers are often reinforced by an immediate decrease in disruptive behaviors when they direct their attention (warnings, scolding, lectures, reprimands) at an offending child. The child stops his undesirable behavior at that moment, but the change is usually temporary, and he quickly returns to the disruptive behavior that the social reinforcement (attention) strengthened. The teacher then reapplies the negative attention, producing another temporary suppression but a long-term increase in the bothersome behavior. This pattern can have disastrous long-term consequences for classroom behavior.

Some investigators have referred to this unproductive pattern as the "criticism trap" (Becker, 1971; Patterson, 1971). Negative attention produces a temporary positive change in children, but in the long run, the unwanted behavior is strengthened by the teacher's attention (O'Leary & Becker, 1967). The teacher receives immediate reinforcement from the quick, though temporary, reduction in the disruptive behavior that follows criticism or punishment (Gambrill, 1975). The temporary improvement reinforces the teacher for attending to undesirable behavior more than the long-range increase in undesirable student behavior punishes the teacher because immediate consequences have more effect on behavior than delayed consequences. Thus, the teacher is "trapped" into behaving in a way that in the long run produces results counter to the teacher's goals.

USING REINFORCEMENT EFFECTIVELY

The use of reinforcement can be improved easily by keeping a few simple "rules" in mind. First, it is important to have clear target behaviors in mind for each child and clear, acceptable approximations that can be reinforced along the way. The teacher must know in advance which specific behavior to reinforce. Second, he must watch for and reinforce the behavior immediately, or as soon as possible. Third, in establishing a new behavior, the teacher should reinforce every instance. Once the behavior is well established, he can reinforce intermittently. Reinforcement must be consistent and contingent on appropriate behavior.

Reinforcing Approximations

Rarely will a child suddenly reverse a problem behavior. Behavior usually changes gradually. It is important that the teacher recognize and praise the improvements in the behavior of children who are steadily improving but are still below par. These children probably do not obtain as much reinforcement from teachers for their academic efforts or from peers or parents for their social accomplishments as more competent children do; thus more reinforcement is necessary if they are to continue to improve. The teacher should not let a day pass without reinforcing the positive behavior of a problem child, even if his undesirable behavior is not yet extinguished.

Reinforcing Alternative Behaviors

One way a teacher can escape the criticism trap is to make each inappropriate act a cue to look for behavior worthy of praise. If a child is disrupting the class rather than working, the teacher should ignore her but watch closely for the first sign of working. Then, the moment she looks at her work, the teacher should offer praise.

Another effective way to combat undesirable behavior is to reinforce another child who is behaving desirably. This technique gives the teacher a concrete alternative to criticism. Instead of scolding or criticizing a misbehaving child, the teacher can use this unwanted behavior as a reminder to reinforce children who are behaving appropriately. If Mary is talking to her neighbor when she should be working quietly, the teacher simply looks for a quiet worker and says, "*Jane* is really working hard and quietly today," in a voice Mary is sure to hear. This procedure supplements the reinforcement of good behavior by enabling each child to observe another child being reinforced for desirable behavior.

Because modeling is one of the fundamental means by which new behaviors are acquired and existing behaviors are modified, reinforcement of the student who is modeling the correct behavior enhances the effectiveness of the process (Bandura, 1969). Thus, by reinforcing one child, the teacher produces positive effects in the behavior of other children because this reinforcement acts as a cue to others that they, too, can earn reinforcement if they behave similarly. Of course, some reinforcement must later be forthcoming to those who have patterned their behavior after that of the exemplar if they are to continue to emit the desired behavior.

Students with a history of attention-getting behavior may not respond to the reinforcement of other students modeling appropriate behavior. Even ignoring and positive reinforcement by the teacher may not counteract the attention the student receives from his peers for his loud, aggressive, disruptive behavior. The teacher may need to reprimand or punish the student, but without increasing the likelihood that his negative behavior will be strengthened by her attention. Classroom research indicates that a reinforcement (praise)/criticism ratio of 4 to 1 is most effective in establishing a positive learning environment (Brown, 1972). Thus, if a teacher must reprimand a student, she must also find four behaviors to reinforce in order to establish the 4 to 1 ratio. Remembering to reinforce a child four times for each time she attends to his inappropriate behavior may be difficult for the teacher at first, but reprimands without reinforcement will likely result in the teacher being caught in the criticism trap.

Distributing Reinforcement Equitably

Reinforcing students who are modeling correct behavior and maintaining a 4 to 1 reinforcement/criticism ratio may result in some students being reinforced at a high rate and others not at all. When teachers focus their attention on problem students and perhaps on exceptionally good students, the average students may inadvertently be neglected. In addition, some teachers occasionally take good behavior "for granted" once it is established. The student who works well and quietly is often ignored.

The teacher can avoid the possibility of extinguishing such behavior by distributing reinforcement to all children who are behaving appropriately. If a particular student is off task, the teacher "tracks" (or watches) the student until she is back on task and then reinforces her. Effective teachers continually "scan" the classroom, praising and reinforcing students who are following class rules and tracking those who are not. While some students may need more reinforcement than others, it is important that the teacher reinforce appropriate behavior of all students.

One reason many teachers attend to some students more than others is that behavioral principles also apply to teachers. Most teachers are not reinforced by asking for an answer and getting the wrong one. Thus, the teacher "learns" to call on those children who give correct answers. Teachers are also not reinforced for asking for an assignment to show the class and receiving an assignment that is messy and incorrect. They learn to call on the better pupils, and the "best" students learn to volunteer because they get reinforced so often, just as problem students learn that they get attention by misbehaving. Slowly, the student who is not good but is also not disruptive fades into the background until the teacher doesn't see or hear him at all.

What can be done to correct this? One answer is to place the teacher's behavior under control of something other than the immediate consequences. Some teachers make sure they attend to and call on all students by randomly calling names from their class list. When a student is called upon, praised, asked a question, or otherwise receives attention, a check is placed on the list, and future selections are made from students with fewest checks, assuming they are behaving appropriately at the moment.

Another system is to list each student's name on a card, stack the cards, and go through them systematically. The teacher waits until the child whose name is on top is performing appropriately, reinforces that child, and then turns up the next card. Children sometimes learn the order, or learn that they will not be attended to twice in succession, but frequent shuffling or having each child's name on several cards will avoid this problem. Systems of this sort are useful to establish equitable reinforcement; after a week or two most teachers learn to distribute reinforcements without cards, and the system can be discontinued.

Increasing Your Rate of Reinforcement

For reinforcement to be effective, it must occur frequently and consistently. As mentioned earlier, most teachers do not reinforce students very often (Madsen et al., 1970; White, 1975). Teachers who need to increase their frequency of delivering reinforcers should consider one of the following procedures.

Cards. One way a teacher can improve the rate of delivering reinforcers is to write each child's name on a card. After the child's name, several target behaviors or approximations to be strengthened are listed. The teacher carries the cards and, while teaching, turns one of the cards over every few minutes. If the child whose name comes up is engaging in the desired listed behavior, the teacher reinforces the behavior by saying, "I like the way you are working on your English assignment," or some other specific comment. The comment can be made about the student's academic work or social behavior. Or, if the teacher is near the child, a pat, a touch, or a wink might do. The teacher may need to deliver tokens along with the praise statements.

Signs and audio prompts. Posting signs as reminders to frequently reinforce children's behavior is another help in getting started. Alternatively, a kitchen timer might be set for variable time segments. When the timer sounds, the teacher is reminded to look around and praise good workers. Students can be taught to recognize and reinforce their own efforts when the timer goes off. An audio cassette tape with a tone sounding at various timed intervals can be used in the same manner.

Recording and graphing. The teacher may find it very effective to count praise statements daily and record the results on a graph. He can subsequently try to improve performance and reinforce himself for improvement. Using counters, such as golf score counters, is an inexpensive and convenient method for counting. Another counting method is to put a piece of masking tape on one's wrist and write tallies on it. An alternative approach is to assign the recording to children; the teacher can ask several children to keep a tally of the "nice" or "complimentary" things said by the teacher. Obviously, counting and graphing can be combined with cards or signs.

Teachers who increase their rate of delivering reinforcers will be reinforced by their students' improved classroom behavior and better academic performance.

EXAMPLE

The Saga Continues

A reinforcer strengthens the behavior it immediately follows. This simple principle could get poor Izzie into all kinds of trouble. Willie's appropriate behavior, sitting quietly in his seat, is probably a reinforcer and a pleasant occurrence for Izzie. When Izzie punishes Willie and consequently he sits very quietly, her punishing behavior is reinforced. She is likely to reprimand him the next time he misbehaves. When teachers punish, they are more immediately reinforced by seeing a quick change of behavior than they would be by the slower changes produced using principles of reinforcement. It is easy, therefore, to get in the habit of using punishment procedures. If Izzie can train herself to reinforce positive behavior frequently, she will be reinforced by both improved student behavior and her own good feelings about being a positive person. Ms. Able decides to put a sign on her desk that says:

"Ignore Disruptions, Reinforce Good Behavior, 4 to 1"

Izzie has survived the first few weeks of school and she is determined to establish a 4 to 1 praise/criticism ratio with Willie. She is praising more often but she begins to feel like a parrot saying "good raising your hand," "good sitting quietly in your seat," "I like the way you are sharing materials." Willie is still waging war, but when he misbehaves, Izzie quickly reinforces other students. The rest of the class seems to be responding well to the praise, and Izzie certainly feels happier about her interactions with them, but she needs more ammunition to help Willie.

Izzie has learned that the principle of reinforcement works because her class is behaving and working hard. She decides she needs more powerful reinforcers for Willie. Little Mona Lott also needs help completing her assignments. Izzie starts to make a list of activity reinforcers but wonders how to use them.

School is going quite well for Izzie Able. So is her social life, as evidenced by her Friday night dinner date with Alan, whom she has been trying to get to ask her out for weeks. While she looks over the dinner menu, her mind wanders back to her classroom and little Mona Lott, whom she has not been able to motivate. Suddenly, Izzie hits upon an idea. What if she prepared a reinforcement menu and let Mona and Willie choose an activity from the menu after they had earned points for working? That way Izzie could suggest things that followed the reinforcement rules—things that could be easily, quickly, and immediately administered. She plans to involve all the students and have them make a menu for a class art project the very next day.

Alan is a little disturbed that Izzie isn't giving him her undivided attention. When he asks what she is thinking about, Izzie apologizes and explains her new plan. Alan suggests that Izzie could take pictures of students and mount the pictures on the menu. Izzie agrees that this is a great idea. Not only will the menu be reinforcing for the students, but her devotion to work is reinforced because Alan sets up a date to come to school and help her. Alan is reinforced because he once again has Izzie's undivided attention. The point system will have to wait until tomorrow.

Exercises

1. Explain how a teacher could avoid falling into the criticism trap.

2. Ms. Klein has each student's name on cards. Children who are poor at answering oral social studies questions have their names on four cards, children who are average have their names on three cards, excellent workers have their names on two cards. Each card is marked "excellent," "average," or "poor" to indicate the child's level of performance on question answering. Categories are changed regularly when children improve.

   During each question period, Ms. Klein shuffles the cards. The difficulty of the question she asks depends on the child's skill level. If the child responds correctly, she reinforces the child for a correct answer. If a child talks to his neighbor, she praises others for attending and praises that child for attending at some later time. Describe the principles of effective reinforcement she incorporates in her procedure.

Feedback

1. By establishing the praise/criticism ratio of 4 to 1, using methods to increase the frequency of praise, and by monitoring student performance to ensure that students are receiving more praise than criticism, teachers will be less likely to fall into the criticism trap.

2. By assigning students to different groups, based on skills and asking questions appropriate to skill level, Ms. Klein provides herself the opportunity to *reinforce approximations.* By using cards to call on children, she avoids the tendency to call on the "good" children preferentially and ensures that reinforcement is *distributed equitably.* By calling on children every minute, she has *increased her rate of reinforcement* by providing more behavior to reinforce. By praising on-task children when another misbehaves, she *reinforces alternatives.*

FAST TRACK

REVIEW

Positive reinforcers are events or stimuli that follow a behavior and increase the probability that the behavior will be repeated in the future under similar circumstances. If an event or stimulus immediately follows a behavior and does not serve to increase or maintain that behavior, the event or stimulus is not functioning as a positive reinforcer.

Teachers cannot know whether a particular stimulus will be reinforcing for a child until the effect of the stimulus on the behavior is observed. Although everyone is reinforced by some stimuli, not all children respond to purely social reinforcement like praise and pats on the head. Effective teachers identify a large variety of potential reinforcers so that all their students can be positively reinforced.

Most reinforcers can be separated into one of five categories: social, activity, token, tangible, and edible. Each category has advantages and disadvantages. For most teachers, *social reinforcement* is essential for effective teaching because praise is a powerful reinforcer for most children. *Activity reinforcers* are also helpful in school situations. For some handicapped or more difficult students, *token, edible, and/or tangible reinforcers* may also be necessary in order to help the students progress educationally and meet the objectives of their individualized education programs.

Genuine praise and sincere compliments are powerful tools for modifying students' behavior. For most children, praise is an effective reinforcer. In order for a reinforcement program to be effective, the teacher must identify a large variety of potential reinforcers. Strategies that are helpful for selecting potential reinforcers, or for enhancing the effectiveness of existing reinforcers, include watch-and-see, ask-the-children, ask-other-teachers, try-and-see, and marketing.

A classroom in which social reinforcement is used as a primary method for motivating students is much more pleasant for both teacher and students than a classroom that focuses on criticism and reprimands. Some teachers find it difficult to praise and compliment students. The best method for increasing the frequency of praise statements and the quality and genuineness of praise is to *do* it. There are a number of procedures that teachers can use to help remind them to use praise in the classroom, including signs posted in the room, cassette tapes, and involving students in the process.

Teachers should be careful to avoid reinforcing undesirable behavior. It is common for teachers to attend much more to students' negative behavior and to spend more time reprimanding students than praising and complimenting. It is easy for a teacher to get caught in the *criticism trap.* When an adult attends to a child's negative behavior with reprimands or criticism, there is usually an immediate suppression of the child's negative behavior. Since negative attention can serve as a reinforcer, children may engage in that aversive or inappropriate behavior more frequently in the future. Therefore, a cycle is produced in which children behave inappropriately more often, and the adult criticizes or reprimands more often. The cycle of the criticism trap is broken when the adult ignores the disruptive behavior and gives positive attention for appropriate behavior. It is helpful to establish a 4 to 1 ratio of praise to criticism.

In the area of behavior change progress is often gradual. Reinforcing approximations will greatly facilitate progress toward the final objective in an academic or social behavior change program. Teachers must also make sure that they consistently reinforce all the students in the classroom for appropriate behavior, instead of concentrating on the very good or the very bad.

The principles of behavior are always in effect, whether we are consciously aware of them or not. It is more desirable for the teacher to plan and systematically use the principles of reinforcement to teach and shape desirable behavior than to allow negative and inappropriate behaviors to be formed by chance. The praise of an enthusiastic, sincere, and genuine teacher can greatly enhance the academic performance and social behavior of all students in the classroom.

CUMULATIVE EXERCISE

List five types of reinforcers that might be used in the classroom. For each type, give an example of an appropriate use, and describe one procedure that would make it effective.

Feedback

Your answers may vary from those presented here, but the principles mentioned should be covered.

1. *Social reinforcers.* Use verbal praise for being on task for seatwork. It is easy to deliver when monitoring a group. Systematically scan every student, perhaps by scanning one row at a time, in order to avoid ignoring poor workers and thus distributing reinforcement inequitably.

2. *Activity reinforcers.* Use a 5-minute period of free quiet talk (in the back of the room) for those who complete all their problems (in a junior high

school class). The teacher does not need to dispense the activity, and it reinforces systematic work completion rather than dawdling. Talking is a high-rate behavior at this age and may be an effective reinforcer (Premack Principle).

3. *Tokens.* Use points to reinforce each child who completes an individually prescribed assignment. Because each assignment is tailored to the child, approximations can easily be reinforced.

4. *Edibles.* With a group of three mentally retarded children of equal skill level, do repetitive, quickly paced choral drills on number facts, and dispense candy for correct responses. This type of reinforcer is nearly always effective with young handicapped children, and the rapid pacing of choral responding allows for a very high rate of reinforcement.

5. *Tangibles.* Individually contract for homework with a class of third graders, letting each earn one part of an individually selected crossword puzzle for each assignment completed. This affordable, noncontroversial tangible can be individualized.

FOUR

Response-Weakening Procedures

OBJECTIVES

After completing this chapter, you will be able to use response-weakening procedures. To do this you will learn to:

1. Decide when it is appropriate to use response-weakening procedures.
2. Explain the use of extinction, and specify appropriate target behaviors and advantages and disadvantages.
3. Explain the use of response-cost, and specify appropriate target behaviors and advantages and disadvantages.
4. Explain the use of time-out from positive reinforcement without isolation and with isolation, and specify appropriate target behaviors and advantages and disadvantages.
5. Explain the use of punishment, and specify appropriate target behaviors and advantages and disadvantages.
6. Explain the use of overcorrection, and specify appropriate target behaviors and advantages and disadvantages.
7. Apply response-weakening procedures in ways congruent with ethical and legal considerations.

Strengthening desirable behavior through effective, positive teaching should precede the use of response-weakening procedures. Desirable behavior competes with, and prevents the development of, undesirable behavior. A variety of ethical, procedural, and legal safeguards should document the need for and appropriateness of response-weakening procedures.

There are a number of ways to weaken undesirable or inappropriate behavior in the classroom. These include extinction, response-cost, time-out from positive reinforcement, punishment, and overcorrection. Each has certain advantages and disadvantages, and each introduces different ethical and legal questions.

1. WHEN TO USE RESPONSE-WEAKENING PROCEDURES

Chapter 2 introduced procedures for strengthening and weakening behavior. The chapter emphasized the basic behavioral philosophy that the best way to reduce undesired behavior in the classroom is to make desirable behavior so reinforcing that it successfully competes with undesired behavior. The implications of this approach for teaching are extremely important.

Possibly the most important implication is that the skills needed to implement response-weakening procedures are, relatively speaking, less significant than the skills necessary to teach new behaviors or maintain desirable behaviors. If a student is not doing something, a response-weakening procedure will not teach how to do it. For example, punishing "not carrying" in an addition problem will not teach the student to carry. Further, punishing the student for not doing something will not assure the teacher that the student will then engage in some alternative desired behavior. The student might simply move on to an equally inappropriate behavior.

When problems with student behavior arise, therefore, there are many steps to go through before implementing one or more of the response-weakening procedures that will be discussed later in this chapter. These steps essentially provide an analysis of the teaching–learning environment and clarify whether the use of response-weakening procedures is appropriate, whether more basic changes should be made in the instructional setting, or whether both approaches should be used. (See also Chapter 1.)

The analysis of the instructional setting should address the following questions:

1. Are activities in the curriculum the most effective and motivating ones available? Are the activities well organized and well sequenced? Do they relate to the stated objectives, or are they merely time-fillers and busy work? (See Chapter 5.)
2. Is the classroom organization such that it allows the teacher to work with individuals, small groups, and the whole class as necessary?
3. Are pupils grouped according to their skill levels and learning rates?
4. Are groups flexible enough to permit frequent and easy regrouping for different subjects?

5. Do the teacher, school district, and parents feel that the subjects being taught are important, and have pupils expressed an interest in them?
6. Are easier, more favored activities alternated with more difficult or less popular activities?
7. Does the physical environment of the classroom make it possible for the teacher to monitor individuals and groups in all parts of the room? Can the students and the teacher move easily about the room?
8. Is the teacher's pacing of presentation of materials adequate to hold attention? Is the transition from one activity to another accomplished quickly, with a minimum of wasted time and energy on the part of both the teacher and pupils?
9. Does the teacher use positive social reinforcement for desired behavior (is desired behavior rewarded in some way) and withhold attention for undesired behavior?

If the answer to any of the above questions is no, that aspect of the classroom environment should be improved before (or while) designing and implementing an explicit behavior management program to encourage pupils to become more on-task and prosocial, and less disruptive (see Chapter 11). The classroom environment may be one that promotes confusion and off-task behavior, is simply boring and not meaningful to students, or does not include procedures to individualize for students' skill levels, learning rates, or interests. If that is the case, simply getting students to be more compliant should not be the issue. If students are to be on task and responsive to the teacher's desires, the teacher should attempt to enhance the opportunity for learning necessary and important skills, whether they be academic or social.

Even if a teacher's classroom is a reasonable vehicle for promoting learning, problems will probably remain. This is not unusual, especially in the initial stages of a new program or the beginning of a class. It is quite likely that even in the most well-organized, positive, and best-run classrooms, the teacher will occasionally have behavior problems. Thus, even master teachers will occasionally need to use response-weakening procedures. An example might help to illustrate this.

The team-taught sixth grade was characterized by a a great deal of disruptive behavior, including talking at inappropriate times, undesirable language, fighting and teasing, taking others' belongings, and unacceptable wandering around. The teachers were tempted to immediately start a variety of response-weakening procedures. It was decided to first evaluate the classroom environment. The process was long and difficult, but indicated that in a number of subject areas many students were working on material that was too difficult or too easy. Because scheduling and physical organization had not been thought through in advance, changing students from one reading group to another was difficult and rarely done, so groups contained too wide a range of skill levels. In addition, in an attempt to provide an "open" environment, the class was physically arranged in ways that made it difficult to monitor students and move from one activity to another. Boring activities were clustered after lunch. Finally, some teachers, in attempting to handle the great heterogeneity of students, presented so slowly that 80 percent of the students were bored. Over several months a number of changes were made to correct these problems, and most disruptive behavior disappeared or reached acceptable levels. Response-weakening procedures were then implemented for the few remaining problems.

Exercise

Think of a class with which you are familiar and in which a lot of disruptive behavior occurs. Go through the list of questions that must be addressed before response-weakening procedures are started. List and describe the specifics of each aspect that applies to the class in question. What would you do first?

Feedback

You will have to judge this exercise. Would changes suggested by the exercise be likely to solve a substantial number of the problems?

---

2. USING EXTINCTION

Most behavior is learned and then maintained by positive or negative reinforcers that at least occasionally follow the behavior. If an individual engages in some behavior relatively frequently, it is usually safe to assume that the behavior produces some reinforcer (or removes or avoids a negative reinforcer), even though it may not be obvious what this reinforcer is.

What happens to already-existing behavior if conditions change so that reinforcement does not occur after the behavior? In other words, if the positive reinforcer that has been maintaining a behavior is prevented from occurring, what will happen to the future rate of the behavior? Similarly, if a certain behavior has been maintained by the removal of some negative reinforcer following it (such as seatwork which has been reinforced by the termination of nagging), what will happen to the future frequency of that behavior if this consequence no longer occurs? In Chapter 2, this switch from reinforcement after a behavior to no reinforcement after the behavior was called *extinction* and it was noted that its effect is to reduce the rate of the behavior. Thus, extinction is one procedure that can be used to weaken a behavior.

The procedure of extinction takes nothing away from the individual. Instead, reinforcers that used to occur (or terminate) after the behavior no longer do. For instance, suppose Johnny used to raise his hand wildly every time the teacher said or asked something. The teacher frequently called upon Johnny, thus reinforcing his wild hand moving. Finally, the teacher decided to extinguish this excessive hand raising by not calling on Johnny when he raised his hand. When Johnny raised his hand, the teacher no longer provided any consequence for hand raising. In time, the behavior extinguished—that is, got weaker—and Johnny stopped raising his hand all the time. Nothing was taken away from Johnny each time he raised his hand during the extinction procedure; he merely did not receive what had been the reinforcer (being called on) in the past.

The concept of extinction applies to behavior maintained by any reinforcer. In frontier days, a trapper may have ceased trapping in a certain area because game had become scarce. Trapping was no longer reinforced by finding game. Sam may stop playing the pinball machine if it no longer pays off in free games. Maria may stop giggling in class if people no longer pay attention to her. All of these are examples of extinction: A reinforcer that used to occur after instances of a behavior is no longer available after that behavior, and the behavior gets weaker.

Extinction has been successfully used both alone and in combination with other procedures for a variety of behavior problems. Neisworth and Moore (1972) taught parents to ignore asthmatic coughing responses in their child while allowing the child to earn money for decreasing the time spent coughing before going to bed. Coughing time was dramatically reduced.

In a program designed to decrease the amount of time a woman patient spent in the nurse's office, Ayllon and Michael (1959) taught the staff in the office to ignore the woman when she entered. (It was felt that she spent so much time in the office that she interfered with the nurses' work.) She had previously been given verbal instructions to leave and not to enter, and had even been led by the hand out of the office. Before the treatment program began, the patient entered the office an average of 16 times a day; after treatment it decreased to twice a day. Hallam (1974) successfully eliminated persistent requests to allay obsessive fears in a 15-year-old by placing her on a 24-hour extinction schedule.

Carr, Newsom, and Binkoff (1980) demonstrated the use of extinction with behavior maintained by negative reinforcement. Initial observations by the teacher suggested that the aggressive behavior of a retarded child was maintained by the termination of adult demands; when the child became aggressive, adults stopped giving him instructions. In the experimental situation, it was shown that when demand termination was stopped (he was given instructions regardless of whether he was aggressive), the aggressive behavior decreased.

Wolf and colleagues (1965) extinguished vomiting in a 9-year-old retarded girl by not allowing her access to what was considered to be the reinforcer maintaining the vomiting—namely, being allowed to return to her dormitory when she soiled her clothing from vomiting, which was quite frequently. The teacher in charge of the developmental class the child was attending was instructed to continue class as usual when the child vomited and not to allow her to return to the dormitory until class was over. The rate of vomiting decreased to zero over a period of 30 class days.

There are few recent studies that clearly demonstrate the use of extinction in applied settings. The procedure is so well established that most journals will not utilize space for one more replication of efficacy; when mentioned, extinction is embedded in complex treatment programs and cannot be evaluated independently.

In the classroom, the most common reinforcer to be withheld during extinction is teacher attention. The degree to which disruptive or undesired pupil behaviors are actually maintained by their attention surprises many teachers. Teachers often assume that their reprimands, or their commands to behave more appropriately, are punishing, when in fact they are often reinforcing. To investigate this, Madsen, Becker, and Thomas (1968) studied the effect of "sit down" commands on out-of-seat behavior. They discovered that the more the teacher told out-of-seat students to sit down, the higher the rate of out-of-seat behavior became. Conversely, ignoring such behavior resulted in its decrease. Madsen and colleagues demonstrated that ignoring inappropriate behavior while showing approval for desired behavior was an effective method of controlling classroom behavior. Hall and colleagues (1971) taught teachers to ignore talking out and disputing, and this, in combination with reinforcement of desired classroom behaviors, proved effective in decreasing the target behaviors.

Appropriate Target Behaviors for Extinction

Not all undesired behaviors should be treated by the use of extinction. Behaviors appropriate for treatment through extinction are ones that

1. Do not interfere with the work or well-being of other students.
2. Appear to be maintained mostly through teacher attention (or the attention of a person or persons in the environment who are amenable to cooperating with the teacher in an extinction program) or through some other reinforcer whose delivery can be controlled.
3. Are not destructive to the physical environment or to other children or adults in the area.

Using Extinction

After a teacher has determined that a given undesired behavior or behaviors might be successfully decreased or eliminated by the use of extinction, the teacher should perform the following steps before actually implementing extinction.

1. The teacher should write down the exact behavior or behaviors to be decreased. These should be specific behaviors, not classes of behaviors (such as "acting out") and not inferred factors (such as "negative attitude"). If acting out is a problem, exactly which behaviors this general description includes should be defined. If negative attitude is a problem, the behaviors which indicate a student's negative attitude should be described. Extinction procedures should then be applied to the specific behaviors, if they seem applicable.
2. The teacher should start with only the most serious one or two behaviors on the list. He can always go back to the remaining behaviors on the list if nec-

essary, but he will probably be more consistent in administering extinction if he concentrates on only one or two behaviors at a time. This will produce faster behavior changes in the pupil(s) and will reinforce the teacher more quickly for using extinction.

3. After each target behavior, the teacher should write down the reinforcer or reinforcers that he thinks are maintaining it. Most of these will be the attention of the teacher and/or peers.

4. If the teacher thinks that his attention is the reinforcer, he should decide on a behavior he can engage in while withholding his attention. This alternate behavior should be one that may be performed very quickly, not matter what other activity is being engaged in at the time. It should be as natural and low-key as possible under the circumstances. Typical alternative responses to attending to the undesired behavior might include slightly turning one's head away from the pupil(s) and looking back when the target behavior has stopped, briefly turning one's back to the students, or simply continuing with the task at hand without acknowledging the behavior in any way. This last alternative is probably the most difficult to learn to do, but it is often the most effective because the target behavior produces no visible effect on the teacher's behavior. For example, suppose a teacher was trying to get a pupil to stop interrupting other pupils during discussions. Each time the pupil interrupts, the teacher might simply maintain eye contact with the pupil who has been interrupted and, as soon as the interruption is finished, continue with the discussion as if the interruption had not occurred.

5. If it seems that the reinforcer for the target behavior is attention from other students, the teacher should explain to the other students why it is deemed desirable to decrease the target behavior, how it is felt their attention is helping to maintain it, and specifically what their response should be to the target behaviors. Once the extinction program has begun, the teacher should provide the peers with occasional feedback on the effect of their help and reinforce them for their willingness to help. A typical situation in which the help of peers must be engaged is when a pupil never or rarely completes assignments because of a constant exchange of banter with neighbors. If it seems that most of this off-task behavior is instigated by one pupil, peers could be taught to ignore this behavior except when it is appropriate (such as during recess, free-time periods, and so on).

6. The teacher should decide on a method for measuring the rate of the target behavior(s). Spending two or three days obtaining a measure of the behavior(s) before beginning the extinction program can help (see Chapter 7).

7. The teacher should begin the extinction program while continuing to measure the target behavior(s). This measurement should be as simple as possible. A cumbersome method either is not maintained or is inaccurate.

8. At the end of each day or instructional period in which the teacher uses the extinction program, he should add up all measures for the day and graph the results for that day.

9. If the extinction program is working, the teacher should see a steady decrease in the target behavior until its rate is consistently very low or it no longer occurs. This decrease should start within a few days of implementing the program, but it is extremely difficult to give specific time guidelines, as they will vary with a number of factors, including the length of time the target behavior had been previously reinforced, the schedule on which it had been reinforced, and the consistency of withholding the reinforcer(s) once the program has begun. If the

expected decrease does not occur or if the behavior does not decrease to a low enough rate, the teacher should implement another behavior-change program, either along with the program of extinction or in its place.

Advantages

Extinction has advantages over some of the other response-weakening procedures. It does not involve the use of aversive stimuli (as in removing a reinforcer or presenting a negative reinforcer), the effects are long-lasting, it is uncomplicated in that it requires no special equipment, and it is easy to implement.

Disadvantages

Paradoxically, the fact that the teacher must do nothing at all to carry out this procedure proves to be both one of its greatest strengths and greatest weaknesses. The weakness lies in the difficulty a teacher may have in doing "nothing" in response to a behavior to which she has previously attended. This disadvantage may be somewhat overcome by thinking of and carrying out an alternate behavior, as described previously, or by attending to the desired behavior in another child. The latter not only provides the teacher with something to do while trying to ignore the undesired behavior, but also provides an accurate model for the misbehaving child. Although extinction can be used effectively without additional behavior-change programs, a combination has been found to be more natural to most persons and more effective (Blessinger, 1974).

Another weakness in the extinction procedure is that when a teacher first begins to ignore a behavior which has been regularly attended to in the past, the behavior sometimes temporarily increases in frequency and/or intensity. Many teachers, finding it difficult to remain consistent in the face of this increase, return to attending to the undesired behavior. This has an unwanted effect; that is, it selectively reinforces more intense forms of the undesired behavior, provides intermittent reinforcement, and thus makes the problem worse. If nonattention (extinction) is to be used to weaken behavior, the teacher must be prepared to tolerate a temporary increase in intensity of the problem behavior without providing reinforcement.

Extinction alone usually has a gradual rather than a sudden effect in decelerating behavior. If behavior must be decreased quickly, it may be necessary to use extinction in combination with other behavior-change procedures. Behaviors in this category include aggression where there is danger to life or property and behavior that seriously hinders the learning of others.

It is often difficult to know ahead of time exactly what reinforcer is maintaining a certain behavior, and it often is not a reinforcer over which the teacher has complete control. For example, thumb sucking is often not dependent upon, nor reinforced by, teacher attention. It would be difficult to use extinction in such a situation to stop a child from thumb sucking.

Finally, extinction may have an undesired effect on the behavior of other pupils who are present when it is implemented; they may observe that a certain child is "getting away with murder" and the teacher is doing nothing at all about it! On rare occasions this may lead some children to begin modeling the undesired behavior that has been put on extinction. If this happens, the teacher should try to ignore the undesired behavior of all of the pupils involved, if possible. It may, however, be necessary to resort to some other method of decreasing the behavior.

A Special Problem

Sometimes a behavior that has been extinguished reappears briefly without having been reinforced since it was extinguished, a phenomenon known as *spontaneous recovery*. It is important for teachers to be aware of this possibility and treat it exactly as they did initially—that is, that they make sure the reinforcer is consistently withheld. It will then again decrease or disappear completely.

EXAMPLE

Mr. Sperry and Ms. Williams work together in a team-teaching situation in first grade. One of their objectives is to teach the children to raise their hands when they have a question or wish to show their work to the teacher, instead of leaving their work areas and following one of the teachers around the room until the teacher has time to attend to the child. They first make sure that the children understand the proper way to ask questions by explaining the procedure to the children and then asking several of them to model the behavior for the rest of the class. Once they are sure that the instructions are understood, they implement an extinction procedure for children who leave their work areas to ask questions or share with the teachers. When a child approaches one of them, the teacher simply continues what he or she is doing, ignoring the child's requests. If the child becomes too loud or insistent, the teacher may walk away a short distance or turn away slightly until the child stops. When the child returns to the work area and raises her hand, the teacher attending to that area reinforces that behavior by attending to the child (that is, by calling on her).

In the example just cited, the behavior treated by extinction was leaving the work area to ask questions or share with the teacher. This is not to imply that all teachers will consider this behavior undesirable. It happened that these teachers considered this behavior an impediment to learning to work independently, and they felt that much time was wasted when students left their work to wait in line for the teacher to attend to them. In this example, extinction was an appropriate technique for weakening the target behaviors.

Exercise

For the following list, circle each item for which extinction probably would *not* be a good choice as a response-weakening procedure. For each circled item, indicate *why* extinction might be a bad choice.

1. Johnny cries regularly in kindergarten. The other children ignore it, but the teacher usually asks him what the problem is and cuddles him.
2. Patsy frequently (twice a week on the average) loses her temper and hits other children with objects or stabs them with pens or pencils.
3. Mr. Wimpy has an entire unruly class. He is particularly bothered by Melinda, who, in spite of being "a pretty little girl" (his comment), uses a certain four-letter word excessively.
4. Whenever Mrs. Barkland looks at him, Streater sticks out his tongue.
5. At a later date, Mrs. Barkland has Streater on extinction for "filthy" language, sticking out his tongue, and asking unnecessary questions. Streater also makes spelling errors.
6. Ms. Desmond has had Molly's yelling on extinction for 9 weeks with no change.
7. Katrina has rarely been whining since the extinction program was started. Although there have been no school, class, or home changes, she starts whining again.

Feedback

2. The behavior is dangerous and must be stopped quickly.
3. Mr. Wimpy probably does not provide the major reinforcers, not can he control them.
5. Streater already has a lot of behaviors on extinction. It is doubtful that making spelling errors is a positively reinforced behavior; it is probably a skill deficit.
6. When a program is clearly not working, try something else.

3. USING RESPONSE-COST

In a response-cost procedure, points, tokens, privileges, or other reinforcers already given to an individual are removed contingent upon instances of a specific behavior or behaviors (Bellack and Hersen, 1977; Pazulinec, Meyerose, & Sajwaj, 1983). Although it is possible to use response cost without a token economy or a point system, it may be difficult to do it consistently and equitably. Some teachers remove privileges for specific rule infractions; this is about the best that can be done without a quantitative system. Many argue that removing privileges is usually not actually response-cost, as privileges the child already has are not removed; future privileges are prohibited.

As mentioned in Chapter 2, response-cost is really a form of punishment in which positive reinforcers are removed after a behavior. It is the only response-weakening procedure in which reinforcers already possessed by an individual are actually removed after an undesired behavior has been performed.

Response-cost has been used to decrease a wide range of problem behaviors. Siegel, Lenske, and Broen (1969) fined normal-speaking college students a penny each time they interjected or repeated meaningless sounds, words, or syllables; the result was a substantial decrease in disfluent speech. Winkler (1970) implemented fines for aggressive behavior in a token economy used with hospitalized chronic psychiatric patients, with the result of markedly decreasing noise and violent attacks on other patients and staff. In two studies involving predelinquent adolescents, Alexander, Corbett, and Smigel (1976) demonstrated that response-cost procedures can be used effectively with groups (see Chapter 10). Target behaviors included decreasing absenteeism and violations of curfew. Bornstein, Hamilton, and Quevillon (1977) used response-cost (in combination with other approaches) to decrease a 9-year-old boy's getting out of his seat inappropriately. Rosen and Rosen (1983) used response-costs as a major component of a classroom program to stop a boy from taking others' belongings (see box which follows).

Appropriate Target Behaviors for Response-Cost

Response-cost may be used to decrease or eliminate any behaviors (1) that have been difficult to decrease or eliminate through the reinforcement of competing behaviors and (2) that are not excessively damaging to other pupils or materials in the environment (see the section on time-out). It can be used where extinction is not a possibility, as the maintaining reinforcers are unknown or cannot be prevented from occurring after the undesired behavior. Response-cost is typically used to decrease behavior problems, but it has occasionally been used as a penalty for messy or grossly inaccurate work when it has been observed that the pupil has the skills to do better work. However, response-cost should never be used to punish errors unless they are errors only in the sense of being careless or sloppy. (Instead, the number of points or other reinforcers a pupil may earn during academic activities should depend upon the number of correct responses made during the activity.)

Using Response-Cost

The response-cost procedure usually works best if these steps (or an approximation) are followed in implementing it:

1. The teacher makes a list of the behaviors she feels are disruptive to the progress of the pupils and cannot be decreased efficiently through the use of extinction or the reinforcement of competing behaviors.
2. The teacher holds a discussion with the individuals involved and discusses each behavior on the list, explaining why she feels it is disruptive. These explanations should be short and clear, with an emphasis on decreasing behaviors that interfere with teaching and learning.
3. The teacher solicits pupils' opinions of the list and asks whether there are additional behaviors that they think should be included on the list.
4. The teacher should go over the list with the pupils after their suggestions have been added. She can delete any behaviors that either occur with such low frequency that they are not problems in the class (even though they might be if their rate increased) or do not interfere with teaching and learning. Inappro-

ELIMINATING STEALING

Steve, a 7-year-old male of borderline to average intelligence, was enrolled in a special-education class due to behavior problems. Each student in the class could earn tokens for being on task and for academic work. Tokens could be exchanged for breaks, extra reading, trinkets, and candy.

Steve frequently had things belonging to others in his possession. All of Steve's articles were marked with green circles. During treatment, each possession of unmarked items resulted in a 5-point fine and a reprimand.

"Stealing was reduced to .32 items per day from an average baseline rate of 6.0 stolen items per day. The token system was systematically eliminated and stealing averaged .09 per day during 31 days of follow-up."

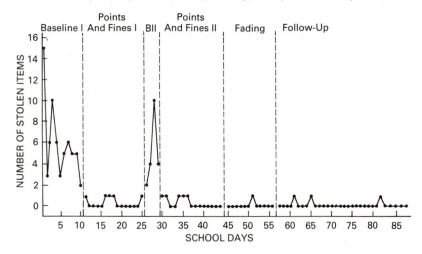

From H. S. Rosen and L. A. Rosen, "Eliminating Stealing: Use of Stimulus Control with an Elementary Student," *Behavior Modification, 7,* 56–63. Copyright © 1983. Reprinted by permission of Sage Publications, Inc.

priate dress or grooming might be an example. The objective is to come up with a list of a few seriously disruptive behaviors and begin working on eliminating them. If the list is too long, or concentrates on less serious behavior problems, or on behaviors that do not interfere with teaching and learning, the effectiveness of response-cost will be diluted. Remember, once the teacher has gotten rid of the most disruptive behaviors, she can always make up a new list with her pupils in order to "polish off" the few remaining behavior problems that might exist in the class.

5. After the list has been finalized, the amount of the fines is established with the students. Younger pupils (elementary-school age) often tend to set the fines unreasonably high, so the teacher should give some guidance in setting fines which are neither too stiff nor too lenient. The total fines the "worst" student might earn in a day should not exceed about half that student's daily earnings.

6. The teacher then makes a chart listing the behaviors to be fined and their amounts. The chart should be posted where it is visible to the class.
7. The teacher should go over the chart with the pupils, explaining that fines may be changed if it is discovered that they are too high or too low, but that the changes will be made on the chart and the class will be informed of the changes before they are implemented.
8. The teacher should role-play how fines will be administered, asking several children to model one of the undesired behaviors so that she may demonstrate how the fine will be delivered.

With very young or incompetent children, the teacher may have to make more decisions without student input. With unruly students, the teacher might start by soliciting input as described; if it is not forthcoming, the teacher should implement the program without student input.

Teachers usually find that response-cost is administered much more smoothly and without conflict if a set procedure is used consistently when the fine is made. The procedure might be something like the following:

1. The teacher states the reason for the fine and the amount in a neutral, matter-of-fact manner: "Tammy, I'm fining you 3 points for crowding in the lunch line."
2. The teacher "collects" the fine either by recording it in the records for the token economy or, if tokens or points carried by students are used, by collecting the fine from the student. For obvious reasons, fewer problems will be encountered if the fine is simply subtracted from the records rather than collected from the pupil.
3. No further mention is made of the misdemeanor. There is no nagging, no lecturing.
4. At the time the fine is made, it is not debatable. If the pupil objects, argues, pouts, talks back, and so on, the teacher may either quickly implement another fine (if pouting, arguing, or talking back are on the posted list) or simply ignore these emotional outbursts.
5. If pupils disagree with a certain behavior's being subject to fine, this must be discussed at some later time with the teacher and the whole class. It cannot be discussed at the time at which the fine is made.
6. The teacher should not implement a fine that is not on the posted list. If a behavior occurs and the teacher feels it should be on the list, one warning should be made to the offending pupil or pupils. "Bill and John, tripping people on the way to their seats is unacceptable. If it occurs again I will add it to the list for fining." Once a warning is made, it should not be made again. The next time the behavior occurs, it should be added to the list, along with the amount of the fine.

After the necessary preparations have been made to implement response-cost, it should be used consistently. Records for response-cost can be kept very simply. The teacher can keep a log of fines which includes the date, student's name, amount, and specific behavior fined. This log will allow the teacher to assess whether applying a response-cost to certain behaviors is producing the desired results. If it is not, several things might account for the ineffectiveness. First, pupils might be earning so many tokens (or privileges, money, candy, and so on) that the loss of some does not function as a punisher. Second, the size of the fines may not be large enough. Third, the back-up reinforcer exchangeable for points or tokens may not be potent. Finally, some students may not earn enough, with or without fines, to obtain back-ups.

Advantages

A major benefit of a systematic response-cost procedure is that it is usually quite effective in quickly reducing unwanted behavior, especially if used as part of a powerful token reinforcement system (Alexander et al., 1976). It is usually easier and less disrupting to "fine" a pupil than it is to place her in time-out. It produces more immediate effects than extinction used alone, unless the behavior is maintained only by social attention from the teacher or peers. If carried out accurately, response-cost rarely produces the extreme emotional behavior often seen as a side effect of punishment (presentation of an aversive stimuli, such as scolding or spanking), although it may produce some (Oliver et al., 1974; Sloane et al., 1977). Another advantage is that when response-cost is properly used, one must specify ahead of time the behaviors that will be fined. This is useful in reducing the ambiguity that may exist when teachers provide consequences for pupil behavior.

Disadvantages

One problem that often arises with the use of response-cost is misuse of the procedure. The fining may be conducted in a capricious manner if contingencies are not well planned and set. Teachers may fine too heavily or too much at one time. Also, if the initial introduction of the fining procedure is not carefully explained and rehearsed with pupils, an undue amount of time may be spent in arguing over fines and in trying to collect them. The solution to these problems is to carefully follow the steps on page 95. If a problem arises, it should be dealt with immediately and as many revisions as necessary should be made to get the desired results.

Special Problems

Determining the size of the fine.   A single fine should not significantly deplete the total number of tokens or points. It should, however, be large enough so that one or two fines have at least some desirable effect on the student's behavior. If one fine removes half of a student's points or tokens, it is probably too large. If a student is being fined many times, on the other hand, the size of the fine is probably inadequate. It is usually a good idea to make one fairly substantial increase in the fine rather than add several amounts at different times in the hope of finding an exactly correct amount because pupils may become "desensitized" to small increments in the fine.

A fine may be levied on a pupil who has no tokens to pay. The solution to this is to record the fine, allow the pupil to continue to earn tokens, and either collect the fine or subtract it when the pupil has enough tokens to pay it. If this occurs, it is important not to "give" the pupil unearned tokens in order to speed up the payment of the fine. However, some adjustment may be needed if a student or students are chronically "in the hole" and never have points or tokens to spend. This will defeat the purpose of the system, as such students never obtain reinforcement.

Teachers can become too dependent on response-cost. The third, and most serious, problem with the use of response-cost is that, because it produces results and is easy to use, teachers run the risk of becoming too dependent on fining (or other negative approaches). Data suggest that fining, time-out, and other negative procedures work best in a system that is otherwise overwhelmingly positive. If the negative is accentuated, pupils will tend to withdraw or rebel, and neither of these reactions will support the growth of functional social and academic behaviors.

EXAMPLE

The teacher and pupils in one fifth-grade class have decided that the 30-minute "special time" in the afternoons is generally working out very well. During the last 30 minutes of each day, the pupils trade in their points for "funny money," with which they can buy activities of their choice. The teacher has encouraged students to bring hobby materials, games, and books from home so that they will have something enjoyable and interesting to do during this time.

There are problems with the system, however. When the teacher gives a 5-minute clean-up warning, some pupils fail to heed this warning and leave a mess behind when the last bell rings. The teacher does not want to force pupils to stay after school to clean up because that punishes him as much as the pupils. The other problem is that some pupils use the "special time" to tease and mildly harass other pupils while ignoring their own activities. The teacher and pupils decide to implement a fine (response-cost) for these behaviors. When the teacher gives the 5-minute cleanup warning, he looks at the clock and after 30 seconds assesses a fine of 1 "dollar" on each pupil who has not begun to clean up. After another 30 seconds, each pupil who has not begun to clean up is fined 2 dollars. The same rule generally applies to harassing other students. The teacher says, "1 dollar for bothering John." If the harassment does not stop immediately after the first fine, the pupil is fined 2 dollars. If a student does not have enough "funny money" to pay the fine, the teacher makes a note of this in a record book and collects the fine the following day, immediately preceding the "special time" period. Pupils who do not have enough "funny money" to buy activities during "special time" spend the period in their seats not doing anything.

Exercise

In the list which follows, circle each item for which response-cost would probably *not* be a good choice as a response-weakening procedure. For each circled item, indicate *why* response-cost might be a bad choice or indicate other problems.

1. In an ordinary kindergarten, teachers are considering using response-cost for nondangerous tantrums in two children.
2. In a token economy class, Hugo always makes division errors because he does not know his multiplication tables. This is because he was always "goofing off" when multiplication was taught.
3. Mischa frequently steals tokens from other children.
4. Selena often tears up other children's papers during token period.
5. Tommy is fined so often that he usually owes the equivalent of a whole week's tokens.
6. Samantha complained bitterly when she was fined for a behavior not on the list.
7. The students all got upset when Mr. Jenkins suddenly started fining them for all sorts of behaviors.
8. Mrs. Gomez took 5 tokens from Marty's cup when he engaged in behavior 7 on the list (spitting).

Feedback

1. It is difficult to use response-cost without tokens or points.
2. Response-cost will not teach a new behavior.
5. The fines are too large, Tommy is unable or unmotivated to earn enough, or he is being fined for too many behaviors.
6. Do not fine for behaviors not on the list; give a warning and add to the list if necessary.

4. USING TIME-OUT FROM POSITIVE REINFORCEMENT

Time-out from positive reinforcement is one of the most effective response-weakening consequences. (Brantner & Doherty, 1983). In its most basic form, time-out excludes a pupil for a period of time from the opportunity to receive any reinforcement, including peer attention, teacher attention, activities, tokens, points, and so on. Denial of any reinforcement for a set time is, of course, contingent upon some specified behavior. Thus, time-out from positive reinforcement is like extinction in two ways:

1. Reinforcers are not delivered following the targeted behavior.
2. Reinforcers already in the pupils' possession are not taken away.

A time-out from positive reinforcement is a more extensive and involved operation than simple extinction, however. In extinction, the specific consequence that has been reinforcing an undesired behavior must be identified and then no longer delivered, while consequences for all other behavior of the individual are not changed. When time-out is used, reinforcement is withheld from all the individual's behaviors for a specified brief period of time. Time-out is usually quite effective, but it is also more difficult to carry out.

Time-out is usually carried out in the classroom by removing the pupil to some location in which no reinforcement can be received. Removal or isolation of the pupil is not necessary to program a time-out, however, nor does isolation or removal define time-out. For example, in a one-to-one tutoring situation, the teacher is usually the source of all significant reinforcers. Thus, the teacher can program a time-out by merely turning away and ignoring the pupil. In a regular classroom, there are usually many sources of reinforcement, such as other pupils, materials, or objects in the classroom. Thus, the only way to prevent all reinforcers from being available may be to isolate the pupil.

Appropriate Target Behaviors Without Isolation

As previously stated, time-out need not involve removal of the pupil from the setting in which the undesired behavior occurs. This is particularly true when the behavior is not harmful or dangerous to others in the environment or is not self-destructive. Porterfield, Herbert-Jackson, and Risley (1976) implemented time-out with a group of one- and two-year-old children by simply removing them to the sidelines of the play area and asking them to sit and watch the other children play appropriately for a brief period of time. Time-out has also been implemented during language-training sessions for an individual child by looking away from the child each time an undesired behavior occurred during the session. The trainer would not look back until the child was seated quietly and ready to work (Risley and Wolf, 1967). McReynolds (1969) used a similar procedure during language training to decrease "jargon," or unintelligible vocalizations.

Behaviors for which one might appropriately implement time-out in the immediate setting include such actions as getting out of a seat without permission, talking out, talking back, or disrupting others in the classroom by talking, laughing, or joking. These behaviors (and others falling into the same general category) can also be treated by response-cost; the advantage in using response-cost is that it can be administered more quickly than time-out from positive reinforcement. However, if the pupil has no reinforcers that may be "fined," time-out can be used because it involves implementation of a period of time during which no further reinforcers can be received, not the removal of any reinforcers.

Using Time-Out Without Isolation

Time-out without isolation may be used spontaneously as part of the minute-by-minute interaction between teacher and pupil, or it may be used in a more formal program. The teacher must withhold all reinforcement without removing the pupil from the classroom. Possibly the simplest way to program time-out without isolation is to ignore a pupil (or pupils) for a brief period of time. This works when the teacher is the only major source of reinforcement. This may be preceded by a short explanatory remark, such as "I'll be back to correct your work and give you points after you have worked quietly at your desk for 2 minutes," or "you can earn points again after you have been working at your desk for five minutes." During this brief period of time, no reinforcement is forthcoming. Reinstatement of the opportunity to earn reinforcement can be made dependent on the occurrence of a desired behavior, a contingency which goes beyond the time-out.

Physically turning away from a pupil and not turning back for a specified length of time can be an effective type of time-out. This technique is probably most appropriate for very young children or for severely retarded pupils who obtain nearly all reinforcers from the teacher. Another way of programming a time-out is to use a timer. When a student has acted in an undesirable way, he may not earn any kind of reinforcement for any behavior until the timer goes off. This may be used effectively with an individual, a small group, or even an entire class, if the teacher is the major reinforcement source.

There may be some confusion at this point between time-out without isolation and extinction. The difference is that in extinction, one specific behavior has previously been reinforced and is now no longer reinforced. In time-out, no behavior is reinforced for a specified brief period of time following the occurrence of an undesired behavior. If used successfully, time-out will usually decrease or eliminate the undesired behavior more quickly than simple extinction. It is important to remember that neither extinction nor time-out without isolation is appropriate if the undesired behavior damages other people or things in the environment. In these instances, it may be necessary to use procedures that remove the pupil from the environment.

Appropriate Target Behaviors With Isolation

Time-out involving isolation of an individual is a relatively involved procedure (Brantner & Doherty, 1983); it is also very powerful. For these two reasons, it is well to use it sparingly and only for chronically and seriously disruptive behaviors, such as tantrums (Nordquist, 1971), hitting, and other types of physical aggression against others; self-destructive behaviors; or grossly inappropriate behaviors, such as spitting, constantly using profane and insulting language, exposing the genitals in public, and so on.

Bostow and Bailey (1969) used time-out to decrease disruptive and aggressive behaviors in retarded patients in a state hospital. LeBlanc and colleagues (1974) used two types of time-out with an aggressive preschooler. The first type involved removing the child to a "time-out" chair when he committed an aggressive act. If the child did not stay on the chair until given permission to leave, he was then placed alone in an empty room where he was kept for 3 minutes after his last tantrum or yell. Three categories of aggressive behavior were decreased subsequent to implementing these time-outs.

Time-out from positive reinforcement through the use of isolation is not appropriate for decreasing behaviors whose main reinforcer is attention from one or two people. In these instances it usually suffices to teach these people to withhold their attention for the undesired behavior(s)—that is, to use extinction.

Using Time-Out With Isolation

How does a teacher "isolate" a student? The very word sounds ominous, conjuring up images of locking children overnight in pitch-dark closets with little air and no heat, only to draw them forth trembling and pale the next day, traumatized for life.

Possibly the best way to dispel this image is to think of time-out using isolation as a way of boring a pupil. Fear should play no part in effectively using isolation in time-out. One simply removes a screaming, crying, violent, and/or grossly inappropriate pupil to an area where he will not be seen (and preferably not heard) by anyone except the person administering the time-out, and where in addition, there is nothing to do, see, or use. In this setting no behavior of the pupil can be reinforced.

In employing isolation as a way of programming time-out, the teacher should use a set procedure. The following is recommended:

1. The teacher should not consider using isolation until other procedures have been tried. Often even the most serious behavior problems decrease and are eventually eliminated with a combination of praise and points for incompatible behavior and some mild form of response weakening. These other procedures should be given a fair chance before considering time-out with isolation.

2. Once a teacher is relatively sure that she will have to use isolation, she should write up a brief description of the exact time-out procedure to be used, the objectives of using it, and the rationale for its effectiveness. The description should include the behavior to be weakened and the procedure to be used to weaken it. Several copies of this written description should be made.

3. The teacher should meet with the administrator or director of the program or school to explain the situation, including details of the presenting problem and procedures that have been tried but have failed. The teacher should give a copy of the time-out procedure to the administrator, review it with her, and ask permission to implement it for this specific problem. If permission is not granted, the procedure should not be implemented. Instead the teacher should work with other response-weakening procedures in combination with response-strengthening procedures. If permission is granted, the next step should follow.

4. The teacher should prepare an isolation area—ideally a small room, at least 4 square meters in size, well-lit, completely empty, with an observation window

and a locking door. No toys, furniture, electric outlets, or electric lights or objects of any sort should be within reach of the child in the time-out room. The room should contain no windows that can be opened or broken. It should be available at all times and relatively near the instructional setting.

5. A fool-proof procedure must be outlined to guarantee that the pupil will not be left in the time-out room in an emergency or through oversight. The best procedure involves installation of a lock which opens automatically at the end of the preset period or immediately if there is a power failure or an alarm. The door should be monitored at all times.

6. The teacher should establish a beginning point by taking baseline data on the target behavior (see Chapter 6) on the day she decides she would like to use time-out isolation.

7. The teacher should arrange a meeting with the parents of the pupil and the administrator. At this meeting, she can explain the problem behavior, the steps that have been tried unsuccessfully, and what time-out using isolation is. The parents should be given a copy of the written description of the procedure. The procedure should be explained, and they should be shown the time-out area. Their concerns and questions should be solicited, and they should be given thorough answers. Their written permission to use time-out with isolation with their child should be obtained. (A form for this should be prepared in advance and approved by the administrator.) If the parents do not give their written permission, the procedure should not be implemented.

8. The teacher should write a description of the target behavior(s), limiting the list of behaviors to be "timed-out" to one or two.

9. She should then explain to the pupil that these behaviors are not acceptable. This explanation should be short, concise and not involve a long discussion about the problem behavior(s).

10. The next time the behavior occurs, the teacher should state the problem briefly (for example, "Spitting is not allowed.") This statement should be made in as calm and low-key a manner as possible.

11. The teacher should then take the pupil by the hand, lead him to the time-out room, shut and lock the door, and record on a form kept on the outside of the door the pupil's name, the time he entered the booth, and the reason for the time-out. The written plan should have specified the amount of time the student must spend in the time-out booth before being allowed to leave (3 to 5 minutes is typical), and the conditions under which the pupil will be allowed to leave. Typically, a pupil must have maintained a quiet period for a required minimal time, but this is not essential. For example, if a pupil was quiet in the booth for 2 minutes and then banged loudly on the door, the timing might have begun again until quiet was maintained for the required 2-minute time, or perhaps for just the final 30 seconds. It is not necessary to explain this to the pupil; he will learn it quickly from experience.

12. When the time period has passed, the total time spent in isolation should be recorded on the form. The teacher should then open the door. The teacher may either escort the pupil or let him return when he is ready. If the time-out booth is outside of the classroom, the person who is administering the time-out must accompany the pupil back to the room.

13. When the pupil returns to class, the teacher should reinforce an appropriate behavior as soon as it is legitimately possible. The teacher shouldn't lecture or joke about the problem behavior; it should be ignored completely except for administration of time-out.

14. At the end of the day, the teacher should graph the number of times the pupil was put in time-out, the length of each time-out, and the total time in time-out. If, after a week, there has not been a decrease in the number of times and the amount of time spent in isolation, the teacher should try to determine why. The teacher should also ask an independent observer to visit the classroom long enough to observe one of two instances of the administration of time-out. The independent observer should attempt to determine whether or not the teacher is administering time-out in an absolutely consistent manner—that is, that it is administered every time the target behavior occurs and only when the target behavior occurs.

The teacher should also make sure that the time-out is really a time-out from *positive* reinforcement. One of the most common reasons for the failure of time-out is that the isolation is more reinforcing than the environment from which the pupil has been removed. After the teacher has taken a careful look at factors that may be affecting the success of the time-out procedure, she may make any revisions necessary and try the procedure again for a week. If at the end of this period it has not begun to have an obvious effect in decreasing the rate of the target behavior, the teacher might want to use another procedure. In any case, if results have not been obtained in 2 weeks, the teacher should discontinue the procedure; the continued use of time-out with isolation in the absence of data to support its benefit is definitely unethical.

Advantages

A major advantage of the systematic use of time-out from positive reinforcement is its effectiveness in decelerating targeted behaviors. It is not necessary to know or control the reinforcer maintaining the undesired behavior. Time-out can be used in a class where points and tokens are not part of the environment. Research has shown that time-out is successful in reducing a wide range of undesired behaviors. Although this procedure does require more preparation, time, and effort than the use of extinction, it can be relatively easy to carry out. After long and unsuccessful attempts to decrease a serious behavior problem, the additional preparation and time to implement time-out are usually worthwhile.

Disadvantages

Since time-out is such a powerful procedure for eliminating undesired behavior, many problems can occur, particularly with time-out involving isolation. A common problem arises not from the fact that it doesn't work, but that it works too well. Time-out may be so effective in reducing a problem that it may be used to excess. It may be implemented, for example, before other techniques for reducing undesired behavior have been systematically tried. It may be used to decrease less serious types of undesired behavior, such as getting out of a seat, talking out, not answering quickly enough, and so on. When used in this manner, time-out is not contingent upon any response other than that response which the teacher doesn't like at a particular time. Most (if not all) of these disadvantages can be eliminated by strictly adhering to the suggested procedures for selecting appropriate target behaviors and implementing the use of time-out with, or without, isolation.

Another problem that teachers should be sensitive to is "holding a grudge." Some teachers have a tendency to require a pupil to be "extra" good or to perform outstanding work after returning from time-out. This additional "punishment" can have undesired effects. When a pupil returns from time-out, she should be treated exactly like the other pupils; reinforcement should be no easier or more difficult to earn than it is for other pupils.

Several pragmatic problems are involved in the implementation of time-out, especially when it involves isolation. The most obvious is finding an appropriate room. Some teachers have successfully solved this problem by using a special time-out "booth." Others have used areas separated by a screen that provides a visual barrier between the pupil in time-out and the rest of the class. If this sort of time-out is used with the most serious behavior problems, a pupil placed in an area that isn't physically confining may leave, or at least attempt to leave, with the result that the pupil receives attention from the class and the teacher. If the barrier is not heavy, the pupil may kick it, knock it down, or damage it. Shouts are easily heard by the class and may cause others to laugh or comment. This, of course, only reinforces the noise coming from behind the time-out barrier.

Finding a suitable time-out room tends to be difficult unless the school or program has had one specially built. Improvisations include the use of large closets, storage rooms, and even bathrooms. If these rooms are well-lit, contain no articles with which the pupil can be entertained or harmed, and are easily accessible to the classroom, they may be used. The decision to use a room for time-out should be made by the administrator and the teacher and should be shown to the parents as part of the procedure for getting their permission to use time-out.

Another problem that may arise in implementing time-out with isolation is that the teacher may have to leave the room to accompany the pupil to the time out area. Some staff member must remain by the booth for the entire time the pupil is inside. This means that the teacher's classroom could be left unsupervised for a relatively long period of time. This is illegal in most states. It also means that other pupils are robbed of instructional time while the teacher is away from the room. Therefore, some arrangement must be made for supervision of the class whenever a time-out occurs. This may be done by teaching an aide to administer the time-out (or leaving the aide to supervise the class, if this is permissible) or by enlisting the help of a school psychologist, the vice-principal, or any ancillary staff who may be notified on the spur of the moment that their assistance is needed. It should be noted here that in most cases the time-out will be effective relatively quickly and this type of arrangement need therefore be only temporary.

A problem that must be given serious consideration in the use of time-out involving isolation is the teacher's ability to enforce removal to isolation. If the pupil is full-grown, aggressive, and becomes violent when asked to leave the room, a decision must be made as to how much physical involvement the teacher can and should engage in to get the pupil into isolation. For example, if the pupil is being put into time-out for violent behavior against himself or others in the room, it could be necessary to have on call two husky, imposing staff members to "assist" the pupil into time-out. The best rule to follow in removing the pupil from the classroom to the time-out room is to refrain from touching the pupil any more than is absolutely necessary; if possible, do not touch the pupil at all. Simply ask the pupil to follow you to the time-out room. If he complies, good. If not, try a light hand on the pupil's upper arm. Do not struggle physically with the pupil. If a physical struggle seems imminent, request assistance. The pupil should be removed from the classroom to the time-out room as quickly, quietly, and with as little attention as possible.

When Time-Out Doesn't Work

Any sort of punishment is more effective if administered immediately after the occurrence of the target behavior (Azrin and Holz, 1966). If time-out is not working and if it is discovered that the time-out has not been occurring immediately after the target behavior, this should be one of the first things that is corrected.

Even more than with some other response-weakening techniques, time-out from positive reinforcement works best when there is a high rate of positive reinforcement in the classroom. If there is not, isolation could conceivably be preferable to the classroom and would not, therefore, function as a response-weakening procedure. Solnick and colleagues (1977) found that time-out failed to reduce the spitting and self-injurious behavior of a 16-year-old retarded boy until the environment from which he was removed was "enriched." In the same study, an increase in tantrums occurred in a 6-year-old autistic girl following the implementation of time-out. It was discovered that time-out provided her with an opportunity to engage in self-stimulatory behavior which was evidently more reinforcing than anything occurring in the environment from which she was removed. This clarifies the technical status of time-out. Time-out from positive reinforcement has a response-weakening effect on the target behavior by denying the student the positive consequences available under normal conditions, not because the procedure itself is intrinsically punishing. Thus, the use of the procedure in an effective, ethical, and technically correct manner depends upon the teacher's skills in developing a positive and rewarding classroom.

Another situation in which the effectiveness of time-out in reducing unwanted behavior is minimized occurs when the pupil has no alternative positive response that can be engaged in for reinforcement. This may be due to the fact that the required tasks are too complex, or it may be that there are not enough activities available with which to fill the time. In either of these situations, time-out will work more slowly than when there are numerous reinforcing alternatives available.

Time-Out Without Isolation

Julie was a second-grader who had a long history of whining and crying in school. Julie's first-grade teacher had felt that Julie was "immature," and each time Julie began to cry, the teacher had allowed her to sit at her desk or on her lap, or to engage in some other comforting activity.

Julie's second-grade teacher was determined to help Julie "mature." She began by quickly jotting down each incident that preceded Julie's crying. She didn't tell Julie or the rest of the class she was doing this. At the end of a week, she categorized the incidents on her list, and to her surprise nearly all of them fit into two categories. Most of the incidents occurred when Julie was required either to perform some task independently or to work with a small group of her classmates without teacher direction.

The teacher began observing Julie more closely throughout the day. She noticed that Julie did very well during most teacher-directed activities. Under these circumstances, she performed tasks well and interacted with the other pupils. The teacher also noticed that Julie was almost completely isolated during recess. The teacher concluded from the data she had recorded and from what she had observed informally that (1) her attention was important and motivating to Julie, and (2) Julie had few skills in independently interacting with peers.

The teacher began to teach Julie some independent study skills, and she also began to work specifically on getting Julie involved in social interaction during recess and at other times during the day. She concurrently began a time-out program for Julie's crying. The first time Julie began crying, the teacher said, "Julie, I know you are upset now. Would you please sit at your desk and put your head down until you feel better? When your tears dry up, you may come back and join the group." The teacher completely ignored Julie until she had stopped crying. Not until then did the teacher ask Julie to join the activity she had left, and after she had been engaged in the activity for a few minutes, the teacher quietly reinforced her by touching her on the back and praising something she was doing well. For subsequent crying episodes, the teacher merely instructed Julie to sit at her desk with her head down.

This use of time-out is particularly interesting because the teacher's attention was the main reinforcer withheld. This particular teacher did not run her class on a token economy, and the main reinforcers were activities and teacher attention. Teacher attention was the main reinforcer for Julie at the beginning of the year, so withholding attention was successful in eliminating the target behavior. As the year went on, Julie became more at ease with her peers because she was provided with many opportunities for getting to know them (and with few for avoiding them). She because less dependent upon the teacher, although the teacher's attention continued to be a strong reinforcer throughout the year.

It is instructive to contrast this time-out from positive reinforcement procedure with the use of extinction in the same situation. If extinction had been used, crying would have been ignored, but other appropriate behavior would have been reinforced at all times, even right after crying. This difference illustrates why time-out is often viewed as a more "severe" procedure.

Time-Out with Isolation

Barney was a fourth-grader who frequently disrupted the class by shouting obscene words. Although the behavior was not dangerous, time-out with isolation was considered because this shouting tended to send the class into an uproar. In addition, it was felt that the reactions of the class members, as well as attention from the teacher, were important reinforcers for this behavior. Because the reactions of other students are difficult to prevent, the use of time-out with isolation seemed easier to program than extinction, and the teacher believed it probably would be more effective.

Before starting the use of time-out in isolation, several other techniques were tried to decrease Barney's use of obscenities. None of them had any apparent effect. The teacher wrote a complete description of the time-out program and then obtained permission from the administrator and Barney's parents to use time-out. Before implementing the procedure, she explained to Barney that if he used foul language in class anymore, he would be separated from the other students and not allowed to take part in classroom activities for a while. When Barney asked the teacher what she meant, in a matter-of-fact manner she named unacceptable words he used. She explained to him that his use of these words disturbed the class.

A sheet of paper with columns marked "date," "start time," "end time," and "precipitating behavior" was taped on the door of the time-out booth. The required amount of quiet time, "3 minutes," was also recorded at the top of the sheet.

The first time Barney said one of his words, the teacher took him by the hand to the booth, saying, "You can't stay in class if you use that language." After Barney had been in the time-out booth for 1 minute, his yelling and kicking subsided, and he was quiet for 2 more minutes. He then began yelling again. When he had been quiet for 3 consecutive minutes (and in the booth for 6 minutes) the teacher opened the door and said, "When you're ready, you may come back to your group." Barney then returned to class.

The second time the teacher placed Barney in time-out, she again told him why he was being removed from the class. This time-out lasted for a little over 4 minutes. On subsequent occasions the teacher did not state the reason for the time-out.

While in time-out, Barney could not engage in any classroom activities. No materials were available for him in the booth. If he did not finish some work due to spending time in the time-out area, he did not receive credit for that work, and he was not allowed to make it up. Being in time-out was treated as an unexcused absence.

By the end of the second week, Barney was going to time-out zero times to two times a day, usually staying in the booth for the minimum 3 minutes. By the end of the third week, Barney had gone for four consecutive days without being in time-out. Periodically during the next month he had an occasional relapse and the teacher placed him in time-out.

Exercises

Critique each of the following descriptions, naming any procedural errors mentioned or any outstanding positive points. You may want to suggest improvements for some.

1. Each time Martha engaged in the target behavior she was placed in the time-out booth, as in the approved program description. Her teacher warned her she would have to stay in the booth longer each time she cried, yelled, or had tantrums.

2. Carlos became extremely violent in class Tuesday, although he had not been violent before. His teacher placed him in the closet for 10 minutes each time he was violent.

3. Marcos was put in time-out each time he could not sound out a word.

4. Each time Corinne kicked another student, she was asked to put her head on her desk for 5 minutes.

5. When Eddy used to say a "dirty" word, Mr. Folsom would reprimand him. Mr. Folsom decides to use time-out, so now he ignores these words.

6. Nancy occasionally set off firecrackers in class. After writing out the procedure in detail and clearing it with the principal and the parents, Ms. Joya started a time-out with isolation procedure.

7. Eli frequently dropped books on the floor while Ms. Nadine was talking to the class. The other students ignored him, but Ms. Nadine would usually yell at him. Then she wrote up a time-out plan, got it approved, and implemented it.

8. Because his aide was absent, Mr. Carter left Smitty in the time-out booth in the hall while he returned to the room and supervised the class.

9. Each time Big Bob was taken to the time-out room, he managed to break furniture, hurt himself or one of the three aides, or throw something through a window.

10. Mr. Beasley finally got Jim to stop fighting in class by using a well-designed and approved time-out program. He then used time-out for yelling, out-of-seat behavior, swearing, off-task behavior, noncompliance, not handing in work, throwing things, and whining.

11. Mr. Hunter was always very strict, yelled quite a bit, and used a lot of punishment, ridicule, and reprimands. He started a time-out program which included 10 minutes' isolation in the storage room for Kelley's pen-

cil-breaking. The number of pencils Kelley broke in a week tripled with the program.

Feedback

1. The teacher should not have commented on crying, yelling, or tantrums. This reinforces these behaviors.
2. Preliminary procedures were not followed.
3. Time-out should not be used for skill deficits.
4. Dangerous or disturbing behavior suggests isolation.
5. Sounds like extinction rather than time-out!
6. She might add checking for firecrackers before putting Nancy in the time-out booth.
7. Why not try extinction first?
8. Do Not leave an unsupervised child locked in time-out.
9. Try something else. Look up *contingency contracting* in the index.
10. Give a small boy a hammer and he will discover that everything needs pounding.
11. The classroom was so negative that the procedure was not a time-out from *positive reinforcement*. It sounds more like a time-out from punishment.

5. USING PUNISHMENT

Punishment was defined in Chapter 2 as the delivery of a negative reinforcer (aversive stimulus) following some specific behavior, resulting in a decrease in response rate. Although the authors do not condone or support the extensive use of punishment, it is felt that the legal and ethical ramifications of its use, as well as effective ways of using this response-weakening procedure, should be discussed thoroughly. There are two reasons for this. First, only if people fully understand the nature of punishment—including not only its use but also its effect on behavior—can it be used responsibly and stopped when it is used irresponsibly and/or unnecessarily (Van Houten, 1983). Second, there are certain instances in which the use of some types of punishment is indicated.

As dramatic as the definition of punishment sounds, punishment is a much-used procedure in childrearing, teaching, and other situations. Punishment often plays an overwhelming role in behavioral control. It sometimes seems that the only time a parent or teacher (or boss, or supervisor, ad infinitum) pays any attention to behavior is when punishing it. Although punishment can be used successfully, humanely, and justifiably, its indiscriminate and inappropriate use can and should be decreased.

For the purposes of this chapter, the use of punishment will initially be discussed in two separate categories: physical (or corporal) punishment and verbal reprimands.

Appropriate Target Behaviors for Physical Punishment

Physical punishment is the application of physical stimuli after behavior, resulting in a decrease in its future rate. A wide range of negative reinforcers have been used in physical punishment (Carr & Lovaas, 1983; Bailey, 1983).

Behavior that is so self-destructive and dangerous to the well-being of the individual that it must be eliminated as soon as possible is one type of behavior that often warrants the use of physical punishment (Newsom, Favell, & Rincover, 1983). This category of behavior might include the self-mutilation sometimes seen in severely retarded or psychotic individuals, a young child's running into the street without looking for traffic, or violent physical attacks against another person. All of these behaviors can often be decreased or eliminated through other procedures; however, the time involved before other procedures become effective might be prohibitive if severe damage to the individual or to other people is likely in the interim. When used properly, physical punishment can be an extremely effective means of quickly eliminating undesired behavior.

Lovaas and Simmons (1969) used electric-shock punishment to decrease the self-injurious behavior of a severely retarded 8-year-old boy. It was found that administration of shock contingent upon the boy's hitting himself quickly decreased this behavior. A concurrent decrease was also seen in the behaviors of whining and trying to avoid the adult in attendance. Young and Wincze (1974) tried to decrease self-injurious behavior in a retarded female adult through reinforcement of compatible and incompatible alternative behaviors. This met with little success. Upon the introduction of response-contingent shock, they were able to suppress the self-injurious behavior. In a study by Lang and Malamed (1969), persistent life-threatening vomiting (elicited by operant muscle movements) was successfully treated in a 9-month-old child through the use of brief shock initiated when vomiting occurred and continued until vomiting terminated. By the sixth session, vomiting had stopped; it recurred three sessions later, and the shock was again administered. Five months after treatment, the child's physician reported that the child was eating well, had stopped vomiting, and had gained weight.

In these cases, the use of physical punishment resulted in the elimination of seriously self-destructive behaviors. In all cases, the punishment was carried out under controlled circumstances in which data were kept on the effect of the punishment and the method of administering the punishment was closely monitored.

Using Physical Punishment

There should never be a need to use physical punishment with a regular classroom population. If there are severe behavior problems that cannot be treated by other response-weakening techniques in conjunction with positive reinforcement, the classroom structure and the teaching procedures should be carefully examined.

In special-education classrooms or institutions, there is a recommendation to use physical punishment, it should be administered under the direction of a licensed psychologist or psychiatrist with special training in behavioral techniques, and only in a well-monitored and controlled setting. Data should always be collected before, during, and after treatment to verify how the punishment is used and whether it is working. Administrators' and parents' or guardians' permission, along with other legal and ethical protections (see subobjective 7), should be obtained before using any method of physical punishment.

Appropriate Target Behaviors for Verbal Reprimands

Verbal reprimands range from severe, humiliating attacks on a person to milder and more common forms of correcting an incorrect response. The use of verbal reprimands is often abused. They may be given at such a high rate that they become a part of a background hum to which no one pays any attention. They may become so abusive, loud, and aversive that the person giving them is avoided as much as possible. They may produce the opposite of the desired effect by reinforcing the behavior they are intended to decrease. Nagging and other similar consequences may provide the attention a pupil cannot get in any other way and may thereby increase the undesired behavior. As "punishment," for example, a teacher may bring a pupil to the front of the room or otherwise direct attention to him. This attention from both the teacher and the pupil's classmates might reinforce those patterns the teacher is trying to eliminate. The study on "sit down commands" (Madsen, Becker, & Thomas, 1968), in which children "stood up" the more they were told to "sit down" illustrates these problems, as does a study by Burleigh and Marholin (1977) in which verbal prompts were shown to increase the deviant target behavior; in this case the verbal prompt served as a reinforcer for the undesired behavior. In addition, time spent on useless reprimands can often be spent more productively.

If viewed as a form of providing feedback, verbal reprimands may be used appropriately in response to any undesired behavior. Despite the potential for abuse, a low rate of verbal reprimands can play a useful role in classroom management. The effectiveness of verbal reprimands seems to depend upon their being delivered in an environment typified by an otherwise high rate of positive reinforcement. It is not clear why this is true, but it may be that due to contrast with the positive reinforcement, mild verbal reprimands become functionally aversive. In addition, in certain situations, reprimands may function as warnings which increase the likelihood of further occurrences of the undesired behaviors being punished (Wolf, Risley, & Mees, 1964).

Jones and Miller (1974) taught teachers in a school for educationally handicapped children to use a mild form of social punishment or reprimand called "negative attention" in conjunction with reinforcement of appropriate behaviors. In this study, training emphasized the following: (1) correct identification of potentially disruptive behavior, (2) development of a repertoire of brief verbalizations and gestures signifying that the child was out of order, (3) physical proximity to and orientation toward the disruptive student, (4) quick teacher response following disruptive student behavior so that negative attention often interrupted disruptiveness before it could elicit peer attention or approval, (5) facial expression and tone of voice consistent with disapproval, (6) immediate attention to and reinforcement of some other student who was behaving appropriately following the giving of negative attention, and finally, (7) reinforcement (and prompting, if necessary) of appropriate participation of the offending child as soon as possible following negative attention. This training produced a decrease in the frequency of disruptive student behavior.

O'Leary and coworkers (1970) showed that the loudness of reprimands had an effect on disruptive behavior. Contrary to what many teachers and parents may practice, this study showed that "soft reprimands" decreased disruptive behavior. During soft reprimands, the teacher spoke so that only the child being reprimanded could hear. Children participating in the study showed a decrease in disruptive behavior when soft reprimands were used.

Doleys and colleagues (1976) compared the use of social punishment with time-out and positive practice and found that social punishment produced lower levels of noncompliance than the other two procedures.

Using Verbal Reprimands

In order to use verbal reprimands as effectively as possible, the following steps should be used.

1. Before giving a reprimand, the teacher should state the pupil's name and wait until he stops what he is doing and establishes eye contact. Reprimands are often given in a half-hearted way to a half-hearted listener. Not only are they usually ineffective when so delivered, but they also teach people not to listen when a reprimand is given.

2. The reprimand should be stated in a neutral tone of voice. The teacher's facial expression should be neutral.

3. The reprimand should be brief. It should communicate one message clearly: what the undesired behavior is.

4. When describing the undesired behavior, the teacher shouldn't explain why it is undesirable. A simple statement, such as "John, smacking kids in my class is unacceptable. Don't do it again," is enough.

5. The teacher shouldn't threaten. He should make the reprimand once. If the necessary preparations have been made and the behavior doesn't stop, a consequence, such as a response-cost or a time-out, should be administered. If no preparations have been made, it is best not to reprimand. If this occurs, however, pupils behaving correctly can be praised and preparations made for future

misbehavior. The next time the behavior occurs, the teacher then provides that consequence. Administering the reprimand without a threat, but sometimes following through with a consequence, will teach pupils to listen and follow a request the first time with or without threats. Nothing is gained by threatening or warning, except more time to misbehave.

6. Once the teacher has stated the reprimand, he should watch for a desired behavior from the offender that he can praise or somehow attend to positively.

7. Reprimands should be kept to a minimum. Otherwise, they will establish a generally negative and aversive atmosphere in the class and they will cease to be effective. It is when they are used sparingly in a highly positive environment that they are most effective.

Advantages

As already stated, physical punishment, when sufficiently powerful, usually works very quickly. For certain dangerous or damaging behavior, this immediate effect of powerful punishment may justify its use. Verbal reprimands, when used at a very low rate and in conjunction with a highly positive environment, also usually work quickly for children in regular-education classes (Van Houten & Doleys, 1983).

Correctly used, verbal reprimands also provide pupils with an appropriate model of what a reprimand should be. Too often, correcting or scolding is done as an attempt to make the "offender" feel guilty, immature, dirty, and "bad." Reprimands can and should be delivered in such a way that they provide feedback about an unacceptable behavior in a particular situation. We all occasionally engage in such behaviors, and we all occasionally criticize such behaviors. Pupils must be taught to discriminate acceptable from unacceptable behavior in different situations, and verbal reprimands can help them do that.

Disadvantages

One of the problems with powerful punishment procedures is that, when used correctly, there is an almost immediate reduction of the objectionable behavior. Such immediate effects reinforce the teacher and thus greatly increase the probability that the teacher will continue to use aversive consequences to the exclusion of positive consequences. If this vicious cycle continues, evidence suggests that the desired effects of the aversive consequences will be lost as the children become "hardened veterans" of a punitive, hated classroom environment.

A second major problem in the use of punishment techniques is that they are often not applied contingently. Teachers (and parents) sometimes punish children, not contingent upon the child's behavior, but contingent upon how the adult feels at that particular moment. Punishment that is not consistently contingent on specific undesirable student behaviors will have unpredictable results. Students may become afraid to respond at all unless some aspect of the teacher's behavior is clearly discriminative for reinforcement, not punishment.

A third problem, closely related to the second, is produced by the tendency of many teachers and parents to have someone else (principal or father) carry out the punishment. This often results in a long delay between the act and the consequence. While such a long delay might not diminish the effectiveness of a punishment on older children, it probably would lessen its impact on younger children (primary age) and might punish other behavior that is closer in time to the punishment than the target behavior.

A fourth problem arises because a stimulus that can weaken a behavior that it follows can also strengthen those behaviors that avoid or terminate the stimulus (see Chapter 2). Children may thus learn a range of "avoidance" behaviors which circumvent, terminate, or reduce the punishment, and which it is not desirable for them to learn. Thus, when punishment is used, crying, lying, cheating, staying home, and other behaviors tend to become more frequent, because of all these attenuate or avoid the punishment. It is difficult for a teacher to prevent this from happening, and it is a common phenomenon in classes where punishment is used a great deal.

A fifth problem relates to the long-range effectiveness of punishment. Some research suggests that the effects of punishment can be temporary. All of the reasons for this are not clear, but one factor appears to be that the use of punishment does not remove the preexisting reinforcement for the behavior. The teacher may punish Johnny for yelling funny remarks, but the other children still laugh. Thus, when the person who carries out the punishment is not present, the behavior may reappear in strength. Permanent suppression of a behavior also appears to relate to the intensity of the punishing stimulus (Azrin and Holz, 1966). In most school settings, punishment probably is not of an intensity to totally suppress a behavior.

A sixth problem, related to the fourth, is the possibility that the teacher who uses punishment may himself acquire punishing characteristics. If this occurs, the pupil will tend to avoid the teacher, with the result that his ability to learn from that teacher will be seriously impaired. The avoidance behaviors can take an even more dramatic turn: The child can learn to physically fight with or verbally abuse the teacher if such actions cause the teacher to punish the child less. The child may also develop a high level of absenteeism. Such negative patterns of interaction are frequent when punishment is used.

A final problem, widely recognized if not completely understood, involves the development of emotional behavior when punishment is used. Some data strongly suggest that when punishment is used, aggressive behavior or general suppression of responding may develop (Oliver, West, & Sloane, 1974; Sloane, Young, & Marcusen, 1977). Most teachers do not feel that it is desirable to teach children to be aggressive or withdrawn. This seems particularly likely to occur if the contingent relation to a specific behavior is not clear—that is, when the relationship between behavior and punishment is capricious, inconsistent, or unclear due to overwide use of punishment.

EXAMPLE

Ms. Johnson taught reading to her first grade in small groups of four or five children each. During the time she spent with each group, she provided skills instruction and practice for the children, and she expected each pupil to participate in the practice. For the most part, she received cooperation and participation from the children. She was very positive, joked with the children mildly throughout the lesson, and patted and shook the hands of those who performed particularly well. She concentrated on reinforcing desired behavior and ignoring undesired behavior.

After the first 2 weeks of school, the children were all performing quite well, with a few exceptions. Ms. Johnson decided to reprimand some of the occurrences of undesired behavior. She did this by making direct statements, such as "Sally, do not play with Susan's hair during reading." This usually produced the desired results, but when it didn't, Ms. Johnson told the child involved that she could earn the privilege of rejoining in the reading group by not emitting the undesired behavior for 3 minutes. During the 3-minute period, the child was ignored for all behavior (time-out). When the child began participating again, she was again attended to by the teacher. In this classroom, reprimands were cues that future occurrences of the reprimanded behavior would be punished.

Exercises

Indicate whether each of the following is true or false. If an item is false, state why.

1. Punishment is rarely used in every-day life.
2. Fighting and leaving the room are behaviors for which physical punishment might be used in a regular fifth grade.
3. Electric shock might be used to eliminate self-destructive eye-gouging in a 9-year-old autistic boy.
4. In item C, the teacher should start a punishment program as soon as the behavior is observed.
5. Reprimands will be more effective when administered by a generally positive teacher than when administered by a very punishing teacher.
6. Reprimands may increase or decrease undesired behavior, depending upon various factors.
7. Reprimands should always explain why the reprimanded behavior is "bad" or undesirable.
8. Threats will make reprimands more effective.
9. Effective punishment is a positive reinforcer for the teacher behavior of using punishment.
10. Because teachers are human, it is good for children to learn that people's

tolerance varies and to get punished for behavior on one day they may "get away with" on another.

11. Kids who are punished will learn discipline and will not learn behaviors like lying, cheating, or being "manipulative."

12. As we know from studying emotional disorders, punishment permanently suppresses the punished behavior in all situations.

13. Children who receive a lot of punishment, particularly inconsistent punishment, are usually docile and nonaggressive.

Feedback

Feedback is provided for false items only.

1. Punishment seems to be widely used in schools and work situations, and in the course of child-rearing.

2. Punishment should not be necessary in a regular classroom; check other aspects of the classroom situation and other response-weakening procedures.

4. Because the behavior is dangerous, physical restraint should be employed to stop it at once. However, a program using physical punishment should not be started without various approvals and ethical and legal safeguards.

7. Reprimands should be brief and should not include explanations of this sort.

8. If all reprimands include threats, they will have no effect. If only reprimands followed by consequences include threats, students will learn to ignore those without threats.

10. Punishment used like this has unpredictable and potentially undesirable effects.

11. Using a lot of punishment is one of the most effective ways to teach children to lie, cheat, and be manipulative.

12. Most of the time the effects of school-type punishment used alone are temporary and situation-specific.

13. Research suggests that punishment, particularly with unclear contingencies, is one cause of aggressive behavior.

6. USING OVERCORRECTION

Developed by Foxx and Azrin (1972), overcorrection has two basic variants: restitutional overcorrection and positive-practice overcorrection. (For a recent review see Foxx & Bechtel, 1983.) *Restitutional overcorrection* requires that the subject restore the environment to a better-than-original state. Thus, a student who throws his book, notebook, and pencil on the floor when asked to begin working might be required not only to pick up the objects he threw, but also to pick up papers on the floor, straighten the desks, and tidy up the room. With this type of overcorrection, the subject experiences some realistic consequences of his behavior.

Positive-practice overcorrection is a reeducation procedure in which the subject is provided with a task or tasks to practice for a set amount of time contingent on the emission of the target behavior. These tasks are related to the undesired target behavior in that they teach the subject a desired competing behavior. For example, a child who erased a rule the teacher had written on the board might have to rewrite the rule 100 times.

Appropriate Target Behaviors for Overcorrection

Overcorrection has been used to decrease the occurrence of a wide range of problem behaviors, including incontinence (Azrin & Foxx, 1971), self-stimulatory behavior (Foxx & Azrin, 1973; Wells, Forehand, & Gren, 1977), stealing (Azrin & Wesolowski, 1974), wandering, (Rusch et al., 1976), stereotyped behavior (Barrett & Shapiro, 1980; Shapiro, Barrett, & Ollendick, 1980), not sharing (Barton & Osborne, 1978), self-injurious behavior (Conley & Wolery, 1980; Gibbs & Luyben, 1985), and aggressive and disruptive behaviors (Foxx & Azrin, 1972; Shapiro, 1979).

Overcorrection may be administered to some students without the necessity of physical prompting. In such cases, overcorrection may be used more or less spontaneously. An example of this was suggested by Martin (1978) for remediation of certain academic errors, such as reversals during reading or writing. In other cases, it may be necessary to gently prompt the desired behaviors; in this situation a teacher should be certain that a procedure that is less restrictive than overcorrection will not work as well or better.

In both restitutional overcorrection and positive-practice overcorrection, if the student refuses to comply with the requests of the person implementing the procedure, he is physically guided through the overcorrection procedure until the task is completed. Much skill is required in deciding to use overcorrection, and in implementing it, to avoid the likelihood of a physical confrontation.

Using Overcorrection Without Physical Prompting

If the student complies readily with the requests, the following rules should be used to implement overcorrection:

1. The procedure should be implemented as soon as possible following the target behavior.
2. The main characteristics of overcorrection—that the student should experience realistic consequences of his behavior or practice of a desired competing behavior—should be kept in mind.
3. During the time overcorrection is administered, reinforcement should be withheld except as it is used in the procedure.

OVERCORRECTION

An excellent example of the use of positive-practice overcorrection is a study conducted by Azrin and Powers (1975). This study was conducted with six boys ranging in age from seven to eleven. The target behaviors were speaking out and/or getting out of one's seat without permission. The positive practice centered around the rationale that speaking out and getting out of one's seat are not disruptive behaviors per se, but that permission should be asked and granted before the behavior is emitted. Four procedures were compared in treatment of these disruptive behaviors: (1) warnings, reminders, and reinforcement; (2) loss of recess (a type of response-cost); (3) delayed positive practice; and (4) immediate positive practice. Both delayed and immediate positive practice consisted of the following steps:

1. The teacher asked the pupil to repeat the correct procedure (getting permission) for talking in class or leaving one's seat.
2. The student repeated the procedure.
3. The student then role-played the correct procedure by raising his hand and waiting for the teacher to call on him by name.
4. The student asked for permission.
5. The student was given feedback as to the correctness of his practice and was then required to practice again.

If the practice was "delayed," it was conducted during recess. An average of five to ten practices were performed in a five-minute period. During the "immediate" practice procedure, the teacher asked the student to repeat the correct procedure for the disruptive behavior, practice the correct procedure once, and then finish the practice session during the next recess.

The results of this study showed the positive-practice procedures to be more effective than either the warnings or the loss of recess. Delayed positive practice was almost as effective as immediate positive practice.

Azrin and Powers contend that in many classrooms, delayed positive practice may be more easily implemented than other response-weakening procedures.

Using Overcorrection When Physical Prompting is Necessary

Physically coercing a person to perform a task is an extreme procedure. A teacher who finds physical force necessary should not use overcorrection. Highly skilled persons with special training usually do not have to use actual physical force. For instance, if the overcorrection procedure requires a child to raise his hand ten times, and the child does not comply with a verbal instruction, the teacher should place a hand under the child's arm and gently raise it. If the child resists the movement, the teacher should stop for a moment and then try again. This should be repeated as many times as necessary until the child raises his hand. The response is then repeated for the required number of times.

The use of overcorrection with physical prompting in a regular classroom should be kept to an absolute minimum and should be used with a great deal of caution and only as a last resort, either instead of time-out from positive reinforcement in isolation or instead of physical punishment. This procedure is probably most appropriately used with fairly severe and persistent behavior disorders in a mildly to severely retarded or disturbed population. Data on its effectiveness with older, more competent children are sparse. If the procedure is to be used, the following steps for implementation are recommended.

1. First, other procedures or combinations of procedures that are less restrictive should be tried, and data on their effectiveness should be collected.
2. If the behavior persists, the teacher should write a brief description of the overcorrection procedure, the problem behavior, and the specific overcorrection tasks that she will request the pupil perform. A description of the type of physical prompts that will be used and the additional personnel (if any) who will be asked to assist should be specified. Several copies of this description should be made.
3. The teacher and her administrator should meet to review the description. The administrator should approve the procedure. If permission is not granted, the procedure should not be implemented. The teacher should work with other response-weakening procedures in combination with response-strengthening procedures. If permission is granted, the next step can be taken.
4. A meeting with the pupil's parents should be arranged. The problem should be explained, they should be given a copy of the written description of the proposed program, and any questions or doubts they may have should be answered. The teacher should request their written permission to implement the program. (A form for this should be prepared in advance and approved by the administrator.) If permission is not granted, the procedure should not be implemented. If it is, the next step can be taken.
5. As soon as the teacher receives permission to use overcorrection, she should start to collect baseline data on the frequency of the problem behavior (see Chapter 6). Data collection may start even earlier.
6. The teacher should review the written description of the program with any other personnel who will be involved in implementing it. She might role-play physical prompting, demonstrating the appropriate amount of strength.
7. The teacher should briefly tell the pupil (if he is able to comprehend) that the target behavior is unacceptable.
8. The overcorrection procedure should be implemented the next time the behavior occurs, and it should be repeated every time the behavior occurs until treatment is formally terminated.
9. The teacher should continue to keep data on the frequency of occurrence of the behavior, making sure she has a record of the date the overcorrection procedure was implemented.
10. At the end of the first week, data should be reviewed to see whether the rate of the behavior has begun to decrease. If parts of the procedure are weak, the

program can be revised. The program should be continued for another week. Using a graph similar to those described in Chapter 6, the teacher may want to graph the number of times overcorrection is implemented each day.

11.   If the results are not clearly positive at the end of 2 weeks, the procedure should be discontinued.

It should be noted that the proper use of overcorrection, especially when the pupil must be prompted to go through the restitution or positive-practice procedure, requires much skill and patience. If a student will not go through the restitution or positive-practice procedure when instructed, although physical prompting can be used, force still should not be used. Gentle prompting, not force, is used on all trials, resistance is ignored (and counterforce not used), and the procedure is then repeated. As physical prompts become unnecessary, they are discontinued. This very delicate procedure must be subtly carried out if it is not to become a "power struggle"; it is best used by those who are specifically trained.

Advantages

Overcorrection has some advantages over the use of other powerful response-weakening procedures (Foxx, 1977; Foxx & Azrin, 1973). It is usually less cumbersome, less expensive, and may be less controversial to implement than time-out in isolation. It is usually preferable to the use of physical punishment and should always be tried before physical punishment is implemented. It is carried out in the environment in which it occurs, which means that it is quickly implemented. No special equipment is required for its implementation, other than the occasional need for additional personnel.

Disadvantages

Overcorrection is one of the newer response-weakening procedures; the data indicating the degree of its effectiveness in a wide range of situations are therefore limited. Much research is needed on this procedure, particularly in the area of its potential side effects (Rollings, Baumeister, & Baumeister, 1977; Epstein et al., 1974; Foxx & Bechtel, 1983).

It should also be noted that implementing a procedure such as this in the environment in which it occurs can backfire. For example, there are people for whom the entire procedure might well serve as a positive reinforcer, strengthening rather than weakening the behavior. The intensity of attention provided during the administration of overcorrection, including the physical prompts, is certainly a strong reinforcer for many. The entire procedure must be administered in a completely nonemotional manner. This will be difficult for many teachers; for some it will be impossible. The target behavior may elicit anger in the teacher, resulting in excessively applied strength while physically prompting, responding inappropriately to pupil baiting, and so on. No procedure that requires the possibility of physical contact is easy to implement calmly and nonemotionally, and overcorrection is no exception.

EXAMPLES

Sally was a 4-year-old child in a special-education class for educable mentally retarded (EMR) children. Instead of eating, Sally often spent the lunch period throwing her food at other children, pouring her milk onto the floor, and generally making a mess and a nuisance of herself. A number of plans had been tried to eliminate the behavior, and none of them had worked. The staff and the parents objected to the use of time-out in isolation, but they agreed to try an overcorrection procedure using restitution.

The first step in the procedure was to request that Sally clean up the food she had thrown, along with any other food lying on the table or floor. Her parents were uncertain about this task because they felt that she was "too little" to be held responsible; however, they decided that it should be tried. At first Sally refused to pick up any of the food. She was physically prompted to do so. The teacher took her by the arm, guided her hand to the food, closed her hand over it, brought it to the garbage pail, and opened Sally's hand so that the food was dropped in. In the beginning, Sally often resisted the physical guidance given. When this occurred, the staff member working with Sally merely stopped the guidance until the resistance ended, and then gently continued again. Force was not used; much patience was necessary.

In addition to picking up the food lying on the table and the floor, Sally was required to pick up another tray of food, take it to the table, sit down, and eat one bite from one food on the tray. She then returned the tray to the serving counter, set it down, picked it up, and returned to the table. This was done five times. When she refused to perform a certain task, she was physically prompted.

The first few times the procedure was implemented, it took approximately 35 minutes to complete, thus preventing the teacher from taking her class back to their room to begin the next activity. The teacher requested, and was given, temporary assistance from an aide, who took the children to their room and initiated the next activity. When the teacher and Sally entered the room, Sally was taken to her seat, the teacher replaced the aide, and Sally was provided with positive reinforcement as soon as possible for an appropriate behavior.

The teacher recorded the occurrence of, and the time taken to administer, each overcorrection. By the end of the first week the rate of Sally's food throwing had greatly decreased, and at the end of 3 weeks it had stopped completely. The teacher repeated the overcorrection each time the behavior recurred. By the end of the year Sally had gone for 4 months without throwing food in the cafeteria.

In a second example of overcorrection, positive practice rather than restitution was used. James would frequently slam his book on his desk with a resounding "bang" that would startle the entire class. This effect appeared to be the reinforcer for this behavior. It was difficult to implement an extinction procedure in which the entire class would ignore the sudden noise because it usually happened at unexpected moments. As no formal reinforcement system was in effect and as the behavior occurred several times a day, a response-cost procedure was impractical. Physical considerations and the teacher's inclinations suggested that a time-out procedure (which would probably require isolation) was also impractical. Reprimands were ineffective, and physical punishment seemed unwarranted, so overcorrection was used after the necessary preparatory steps had been taken.

Each time James slammed his book on the desk, the teacher required him to raise it and place it gently on the desk ten times. In addition, fifty further delayed positive practices, supervised by the student teacher, were given during recess. A minor amount of physical guidance (prompting) was initially necessary, but James quickly learned that the procedure would continue until he had met the requirement and cooperated. Records kept by the teacher and student teacher indicated that slamming objects on the desk was no longer a problem within 1 week, and the procedure was discontinued.

Exercises

Indicate whether each of the following is true or false. If an item is false, state why.

1. Mendel had to touch his toes 500 times after pulling his hair out; this is an example of restitutional overcorrection.
2. The teacher had Arlene write her name correctly 200 times after she had written it illegibly; this is an example of positive-practice overcorrection.
3. Overcorrection should never require physical prompting.
4. Overcorrection with physical prompting may, on occasion, be appropriate for a regular classroom if properly used.
5. Because overcorrection with physical prompting is nonrestrictive, it can be instituted without formal permissions or procedures.
6. Overcorrection is usually easier to use, less restrictive, less expensive, and more socially desirable than time-out in isolation.
7. The main disadvantages of overcorrection include possible use of physical force, side effects, reinforcement of undesirable behavior by attention in some cases, and overemotional reactions by the teacher.
8. Overcorrection is known to have permanent response-weakening effects.

Feedback

Feedback is provided for false items only.

1. This is an example of positive-practice overcorrection.
3. Gentle physical prompting that does not become a forceful confrontation is used in overcorrection.
5. There are many less restrictive procedures to try first; formal permission and formal procedures should be used.
8. Overcorrection is a relatively new procedure, so its long-range effects are not known.

7. ETHICAL AND LEGAL CONSIDERATIONS

The use of response-weakening procedures can raise many legal and ethical issues, regardless of the theoretical framework from which the procedures are derived. It is impossible to review all of these issues here, let alone the relevant legislative background and the new cases and executive actions that may change applications. (Interested readers are referred to Martin (1975, 1977), Griffith (1983), and to the quarterly *Law and Behavior.*) This section will briefly cover several particularly relevant topics. (It should be understood that there is no intent in this section to render legal advice or services, which should be sought from an expert in that field or from one's local school district. Cases cited may currently be pending appeal or may later be appealed.)

The use of response-weakening procedures, by the nature of both the procedures themselves and the social and behavioral context in which they are used, is particularly liable to intentional or inadvertent violation of the legal rights of others. Awareness of the dimensions of potential legal or ethical misuse obviously reduces the probability of inadvertent violations. It is often extremely difficult to separate the responsibilities and liabilities of the individual teacher from those of the school, school district, or other administrator or administrative unit, and no attempt to do so will be made in this section.

A Right or a Privilege?

Some response-weakening procedures directly involve removing something from a pupil (as in response-cost) or preventing a child from access to something (as in time-out from positive reinforcement). Several court cases have affirmed that institutions cannot deprive individuals of things that are constitutional rights rather than privileges. These have included such items as access to water or to the bathroom, exercise, education, grooming, social interaction, and other activities routinely available to all students (*Wyatt* v *Stickney; Morales* v. *Turman*).

In *Goss* v. *Lopez,* high school students suspected of being involved in a lunchroom disruption were summarily suspended from school. The court held that this action was a deprivation of constitutional liberties without due process because it deprived the students of freedom of association and affected the way they were viewed by teachers and other students. It should be noted that the court did not rule that suspension itself was illegal, but rather that suspension without due process was illegal. As will become clear, issues such as due process and the right to treatment in the least restrictive environment (as well as the general right to treatment or to education) are general considerations that interact with more specific ones in a number of ways. For instance, the legality of a procedure may be affected under due process by the degree to which it can be shown that it is the least restrictive alternative, that the treatment will produce an individualized and beneficial result for the particular student, and that this result is a reasonable goal for the school to maintain (Martin, 1975, Ch. 5).

The Right to an Education

In recent times, the right to an education has usually been considered a basic constitutional right, and this right is incorporated in many state constitutions and in legislation. Despite this, many schools have suspended or excluded children from school on the basis of their behavior, frequently with the implicit assumption that this is part of a response-weakening procedure.

In *Mills v. Board of Education of District of Columbia*, students labeled retarded, hyperactive, behaviorally disordered, emotionally disturbed, or otherwise handicapped were suspended, transferred, or otherwise excluded from school programs on a temporary or permanent basis. The court held that all school age children are entitled to public education, and that assignment to other than regular classrooms could be made only if the alternative was more suited to their educational needs, if due process was followed, and if these procedures were documented. The Education for All Handicapped Children Act of 1975, as implemented by Public Law 94–142 (as well as several court cases), requires free education for all handicapped children. The definitions of *handicapped* in P.L. 94–142 are comprehensive enough to include all children a teacher is likely to consider atypical or problematic.

Although this law has numerous implications, misuse of response-weakening procedures, such as extensive time-out or response-cost, which systematically deprive a child of educational opportunities, could be considered violations of P.L. 94–142 in a number of ways, one being that the effect of such procedures may deprive a child of an education. Other implications will be considered in later sections. Furthermore, as most teachers are aware, this law requires individualized educational goals which benefit the student, not merely the teacher or the institution (Martin, 1975, Ch. 2). Undue time on response-weakening procedures that benefit the teacher or the school, but not the student, could be construed as depriving the student of educational opportunities (see also *Morales v. Turman*).

Least Restrictive Alternatives

P.L. 94–142 has established the requirement that children be educated in the least restrictive environment suited to their needs. Martin (1975, Ch. 4) indicates that, based on various legal precedents, the particular procedure selected may have to balance restrictiveness against effectiveness even within a single setting. As procedures were discussed throughout this chapter, suggestions concerning use of the least restrictive approach were mentioned, beginning with the assumption that response-weakening procedures should be used only when alternative approaches have failed.

Many have interpreted the Supreme Court decision that corporal punishment in the schools is not unconstitutional as meaning that teachers are free to use this type of punishment. Teachers who act on this assumption are quite possibly leaving themselves open to serious legal as well as ethical challenges. At a minimum, the use of corporal punishment would seem to require the following: data on the failure of all other less restrictive alternatives, informed consent, due process proceedings, documentation of need, documentation that the behavior to be weakened is not a constitutional right and seriously impedes education, followed by data monitoring the effectiveness of the corporal punishment or documentation of its cessation within a limited time. It is difficult to imagine many situations in a public school in which the necessity for corporal punishment could be documented in a manner that would meet legal and ethical requirements.

Due Process and Informed Consent

The requirements for due process before placing a student in any alternative program and for certain restrictive or experimental procedures are complex, and school authorities should be consulted in these matters. Steps have been recommended for certain procedures on the assumption that permission from school authorities will include a number of other due process steps not described here. The right to due process is embodied in the constitution and has been interpreted and reaffirmed in court cases (for example, *Stroud* v. *Swope*) as well as in P.L. 94–142.

Privacy and Records

Federal law now ensures the privacy rights of parents and children (amendment to P.L. 93–380, regulations published in the Federal Register, June 17, 1976, and included in P.L. 94–142, Section 504), including the right of access to all records, the rights of parents to amend records, and the right to restrict others' access to records. These rights mean that teachers must be aware of challenges that they are "stigmatizing" a child. Martin comments: "The cumulative file should no longer be a garbage pail into which any subjective and unverified comment about attitudes, home environment, and so forth can be dumped" (1975, p. 122).

Response-weakening procedures are used when a teacher feels that something is "wrong" with a child or his behavior. Documenting the need for some procedures requires that records be kept. The value of objective records of actual behavior, rather than subjective evaluations, cannot be overemphasized. Such objective records are much less likely to be open to criticism than are opinions, ratings, or anecdotes. In many situations, data must be kept to determine the effectiveness of a procedure. Teachers should be aware that parents have the right of access to such records, as well as the right to have such records protected from access by other persons who lack a right and need to see them. In addition, disclosure of such records to unauthorized persons is protected against, and such records should be destroyed when they are no longer needed.

Issues Related to Time-Out

Time-out has been a particular concern in several litigated cases (*Morales* v. *Turman; Wyatt* v. *Stickney; New York State Association for Retarded*

Children v. Rockefeller; New York State Association for Retarded Children v. Carey; Horacek v. Exon). In general, courts have suggested that time-out durations exceeding 1 hour without a "break" may violate constitutional protection from cruel and unusual punishment or other civil rights of children. It has been further suggested that such time-outs require various due process procedures, including both a warning of intent to discipline which specifies the target behavior and a hearing which allows the individual in question time to prepare a defense. However, the courts have suggested that short time-outs, with a duration measured in minutes, may not warrant such due process protection. The duration of time-outs suggested in this chapter, which have been found to be effective with school children (1 to 5 minutes), probably fall within this limit. The time-out must also be contingent upon a behavior that warrants it and take place in an environment that protects the child from harm. A time-out procedure that does not meet these requirements, as well as others suggested in the section on using time-out, may well violate legal restrictions.

Medication

Although use of medication as a response-weakening procedure is not a topic covered in this book, the use of medication is common in some schools. Various drugs are used to alter the behavior of children judged "hyperactive," "anxious,""attention deficited," or fitting some other label.

Aside from the traditional requirements for legal and ethical prescription and administration of medication (which are sometimes ignored), court cases have suggested other restrictions (*Morales v. Turman; Wyatt v. Stickney; New York Association for Retarded Children v. Rockefeller*). These cases indicate that medication cannot be used as a substitute for a program or if it hampers a program (if, for example, it renders a child too sedated or sleepy to respond). When there is a legally mandated plan to individualize children's educational programs, medication used to control undesirable behavior cannot hamper or invalidate the observation and assessment necessary to preclude the possibility of unwarranted diagnoses or prescriptions. In addition, medication cannot cause irreversible damage. This latter requirement raises some serious issues, because data on the long-term effects on children of chronic administration of the drugs used to control hyperactivity or to tranquilize children are currently incomplete.

Legal Issues and Behavior Analysis

The consideration of legal and ethical issues brings this discussion of the uses of response-weakening procedures full circle. Although these concerns apply to all aspects of school programs, behavioral strategies, especially response-weakening procedures, have been the focus of several legal cases and ethical debates. In general, decisions have reflected the following principle: Ethical and technically correct use of behavioral response-weakening techniques that meet requirements for informed consent, due process, and so forth, is sound educational practice; abuse of these procedures, as with abuse of any approach, is often not only illegal and unethical but also counterproductive in the classroom. Concern for children, technical skill, and awareness of ethical standards and legal guidelines are prerequisites for the successful use of behavioral approaches in a school setting.

EXAMPLES

Ms. Mila used reading group as a reinforcer; students had to earn points for appropriate behavior in order to participate. The school decided this could violate a student's right to an education, so an after-school activity was substituted.

Because of Carter's many obnoxious and dangerous behaviors, he spent several hours a day in time-out. His parents, in a hearing, claimed that he was being deprived of an education because he was often removed from the educational setting. Changes were made that included briefer time-outs, tolerance of minor behaviors, extinction for a behavior maintained by teacher attention, and home-based response-cost for several others.

Teresa was put in the time-out room for 10 minutes each time she wandered around the classroom. It was decided that a variety of techniques, such as reinforcing incompatible behavior (seatwork), had to be tried first, so a change was made.

Marlon, a noncompliant and disruptive 16-year-old, was just as disruptive after positive procedures, extinction, response-cost, overcorrection, and time-out at his desk as he had been before. A program using a brief time-out in isolation was also ineffective. A formal due process hearing attended by his parents and their advocate was held before a program involving a 20-minute time-out was attempted.

Marlon's parents requested and obtained the right to periodically monitor the records of how often and how long Marlon was in time-out, and of whether or not this changed his disruptive behavior. They checked weekly, at a time convenient to both them and the school. These records, along with other records of the due process hearing, were not available to a potential employee, although Marlon and his parents did agree to this individual's seeing some school records.

In another school, students were placed in time-out for having a "bad attitude" and for "misbehavior." As it was difficult to document these highly subjective behaviors, this school eventually became involved in a costly law suit, and the professional and ethical reputation of some of the staff suffered.

In the same school, Sammy's parents sued when, because of his "noncompliance," Sammy was placed in a special program for severely conduct-disordered students. It was shown that, on the advice of the school, Sammy had been placed on tranquilizing drugs which caused sedation; when he did not respond in school he was judged noncompliant. A hearing ruled that Sammy had to be reevaluated under nonsedated conditions.

In another school, behavioral procedures were carefully used. The emphasis was on using positive reinforcement to develop appropriate behavior in order to avoid undesirable behavior. For the few children who did not respond to this, carefully planned and implemented response-weakening procedures were carried out. The least restrictive appropriate approach was always tried first. Due process, informed consent, careful documentation, good technology, and common sense were used. The program was very successful, and students, parents, teachers, and administrators were happy with the school.

Exercises

Each of the following descriptions fails to take into account one or more legal or ethical considerations. Name the failure in each.

1. The first time he threw a book, he was put in time-out for an hour.
2. In order to go to the reading class, it was necessary to earn points by following the rules.
3. Fighting resulted in a loss of bathroom privileges for an hour.
4. John waved his hands wildly to be called on each time a question was asked. His new teacher immediately moved his hands down by his sides 500 times after each incidence of this behavior.
5. The principal showed Ms. Edwards Tom Jenson's record to prove to her that the boy was not so unusual.
6. A time-out program was started for Kate (a fourth grader) without her knowledge or that of her parents.
7. The principal would not show Kate's parents her file because it contained the "private opinions" of her teachers.
8. Because Richard spent a great deal of time wandering around the class, the principal persuaded his parents to get him a prescription for Ritalin.

Feedback

1. Due process procedures were not used; less restrictive procedures were not tried first.
2. The students are being denied the right to an education.
3. This is a right, not a privilege.
4. Try a less restrictive approach, such as extinction, first.
5. The right to privacy was violated.
6. Informed consent was not obtained.
7. Parents have a right to see records.
8. Medication is being substituted for a program without first attempting the program.

FAST TRACK

REVIEW

Positive procedures, which strengthen desirable behavior and thus compete with undesirable behavior, should be emphasized. The instructional setting should be analyzed, and weaknesses corrected, before response-weakening procedures are attempted.

Response-weakening procedures do not teach new behavior; they merely weaken existing behavior. Such procedures should be used only when there is a documented need, records are kept, due process and informed consent are followed when necessary, and other safeguards are in place.

Extinction is a response-weakening procedure in which reinforcement does not follow an undesirable behavior. It requires that the teacher be able to identify and control the relevant reinforcer(s). Extinction is an appropriate procedure for behaviors that are neither dangerous nor seriously disruptive, as it does not work quickly, nor does it remove the child from the class. It is easily implemented, although many teachers may find doing "nothing" difficult when confronted by inappropriate behavior. Extinction is gradual, and there may be a brief increase in the behavior when extinction starts.

Response-cost involves the actual removal of a reinforcer following a targeted behavior. It is thus easiest to use within the context of a token or point system. It can be used for a wide range of behaviors that are not dangerous in the short run, as its effects are not immediate, but they occur more quickly than do the effects of extinction.

Time-out from positive reinforcement involves removing the possibility of reinforcement for any behavior for a brief period following the target behavior. In situations in which nearly all reinforcers are teacher-delivered, this can be done without isolation. Isolation is usually necessary, however, as peers, activities, and materials may be potential sources for reinforcers. Time-out, especially with isolation, is one of the more complex, restrictive, and powerful response-weakening procedures. As such, due process is very important in implementing a time-out program. Physical, procedural, and technical requirements demand careful planning and skill.

Punishment involves weakening behavior by presenting negative reinforcers after the target behavior. When a verbal negative reinforcer is delivered after inappropriate behavior, the punishment is usually called a *reprimand*. The form and context in which reprimands are delivered is a major determinant of effectiveness. *Physical*, or *corporal*, punishment is usually used only with severe problems such as dangerous, destructive, or life-threatening behavior. It should not be used in the typical classroom. All punishment procedures other than minor verbal reprimands require careful planning and adherence to due process procedures. Physical punishment is rapidly effective and powerful. When used sparingly and clearly, reprimands work well with typical children in highly positive classrooms. The many disadvantages associated with physical punishment should be reviewed when its use is considered, as should all necessary procedures.

In *positive-practice overcorrection* the student is provided with a positive task or tasks to perform or practice for a set amount of time following a targeted behavior.

The tasks practiced usually are similar to, but incompatible with, the targeted behavior. In *restitutional overcorrection,* following the targeted undesired behavior, the subject is required to restore the environment to a better-than-original state. In both, guided physical prompting may be used if necessary, but force should be avoided. Overcorrection can be used with a wide range of target behaviors. The invasiveness of the procedure depends to a great extent upon the individual circumstance. Procedural safeguards should be observed.

The use of response-weakening procedures raises a number of ethical and legal considerations. School and district authorities should be consulted, although teachers should be aware that authorities cannot legally or ethically provide a teacher with permission to do what is illegal or unethical. Procedures should not remove, nor prevent children from obtaining, anything considered a right rather than a privilege; this includes not removing the right to an education through procedures such as extended exclusion from the teaching situation. Children have a right to the most appropriate education and educational procedures in the least restrictive setting or with the least restrictive appropriate procedures. Restrictive procedures require various due process safeguards, which include, but are not limited to, informed consent, documentation, and permissions.

Students and their guardians have the right to examine records. They also have the right to be assured that the privacy of these records is secured from examination by individuals who lack the legal right and need to see them.

The use of time-out with isolation has raised several legal and ethical questions. Courts have suggested that time-outs exceeding an hour may be considered "cruel and unusual" punishment with certain students under certain conditions. Careful attention to legal process and ethical concerns is absolutely necessary when time-out with isolation is used, particularly with extended time-out periods.

Although the use of medication as a response-weakening procedure is not an applied behavior analysis technique, it is often used in situations in which such procedures are also used, or might be used. Medication cannot be used in a way which denies a student's rights, such as when it is used in lieu of providing an educational program, or when its side effects preclude accurate assessment of a student's needs and capabilities.

"Behavior analysis" procedures have been mentioned in many legal cases. Questionable procedures are always associated with incorrect use or abuse. Abusive procedures are usually counterproductive; perhaps their worst effect is that they reduce the chance that beneficial procedures will be used.

CUMULATIVE EXERCISES

1. List five factors related to the instructional setting to assess before initiating response-weakening procedures.
2. Would you use extinction to stop a child from running out into the street if you were *sure* that parent attention was the reinforcer? Why?
3. Would extinction be a reasonable procedure to stop fingernail biting? Why?
4. List factors that would suggest the use of response-cost as a response-weakening procedure.

5. What might you suggest to a teacher using time-out when a child stutters?
6. List at least five things to consider before starting a response-weakening program using time-out in isolation.
7. Would you agree that no type of punishment should be used in the regular classrooms?
8. Would you agree that physical punishment should not be used in special-education settings?
9. What effects does punishment have when it is not clearly contingent upon specific behaviors?
10. What might you do differently before using social reprimands compared with physical punishment?
11. What might be an appropriate response-weakening procedure for a child who occasionally takes things out of the storage closet one at a time and puts them on the floor?
12. Describe an overcorrection procedure you might use for a child who washes his hands with cold water and no soap, and then comes down to dinner.
13. To teach an overactive child who frequently got out of her seat during work period to remain in her seat, the following positive-practice procedure was used. Each time she got up during work period, she had to stand up and then sit down and cross her hands on her desk twenty times. What should have been done before the procedure was started?
14. After all appropriate preliminary procedures had been satisfied, a time-out period in isolation was started to decrease Tim's *severe* biting of other children. The time-out room was in the hall. Tim was accompanied there and returned by an aide, who stayed there for the duration of the time-out. In the first week he averaged 3 hours a day in time-out; in the third week this had decreased to 2 hours. Comments?
15. Kim's parents do not speak English. What additional requirement will be necessary before starting a time-out program?
16. Students who assist in the administrative office have been reading other students' files. What right does this violate?
17. One of the aides does not allow disruptive students to go to lunch. Comment?
18. If you have reason to believe that both extinction and response-cost will work to weaken a nondangerous inappropriate behavior, which would you try first? Why?
19. What is the best way to weaken undesirable classroom behavior?

Feedback

1. The following factors should be assessed before initiating response-weakening procedures:

a. Are classroom activities effective, motivating, well-sequenced, and organized according to objectives?
b. Can the teacher work with individuals, with groups, and with the entire class?
c. Are students grouped according to skill and learning rate?
d. Are they regrouped as needed?
e. Do the community and professionals consider the subjects being taught to be important?
f. Are easy activities alternated with difficult ones?
g. Is the classroom easy to monitor?
h. Are activities well paced with comfortable transitions?
i. Is contingent social reinforcement used?

2. This dangerous behavior calls for a rapidly effective procedure. Extinction by preventing parent attention, would be slow.

3. No, because the likely reinforcer (feel and taste) can't be prevented.

4. The following conditions suggest the use of response-cost:
a. Tokens or points are already in use.
b. Less restrictive procedures have already been tried.
c. The behavior is not dangerous if not stopped at once.

5. Use something else. This procedure is not for a problem that involves mainly skills and new teaching.

6. Consider the following:
a. Is the classroom environment positive?
b. Is the problem behavior carefully described in writing?
c. Is the problem behavior dangerous or seriously disruptive?
d. Have less restrictive procedures been tried, with resulting data on their ineffectiveness?
e. Has the time-out procedure been described in writing?
f. Has administrative approval been obtained?
g. Has an adequate time-out area been prepared?
h. Have arrangements been made to ensure that the child cannot accidentally be left in time-out and can be released in an emergency?
i. Have baseline data on the target behavior been collected?
j. Has parental approval been obtained?
k. Has the program been explained to the child?

7. Physical punishment is unnecessary in regular classrooms; reprimands, if used correctly, may be useful.

8. Dangerous behavior may warrant using physical punishment in special-education classes, particularly for very impaired children.

9. It appears that punishment, when not clearly contingent upon specific behaviors, may increase aggressive behavior, have other vague effects, and may weaken desired behaviors without weakening undesired behaviors.

10. With mild reprimands, no special precautions of a formal nature may be necessary. With physical punishment, all technical, ethical, and legal safeguards must be observed.

11. Restitutional overcorrection would be appropriate; the child could straighten out the entire closet.

12. The following positive practice could be used: Walk upstairs, wash hands with warm water and soap, turn off water, replace soap and towels, come back downstairs; repeat five times.

13. The following should have been assessed or carried out before initiating the procedure:
    a. Is the classroom environment positive?
    b. Is the problem behavior carefully described in writing?
    c. Have less restrictive procedures been tried, with resulting data on their ineffectiveness?
    d. Has the procedure been described in writing?
    e. Has administrative approval been obtained?
    f. Have baseline data on the target behavior been collected?
    g. Has parental approval been obtained?
    h. Has the program been explained to the child?

14. The amount of time being spent in time-out suggests that the program may be depriving Tim of his right to an education. The small decrease in average number of hours spent in time-out suggests that the program is not being well implemented.

15. A translator should be obtained to ensure informed consent.

16. This violates the right to privacy of records.

17. Lunch is a right, not a privilege, and cannot be withheld under usual circumstances.

18. Extinction should be tried first. It is less restrictive because it does not involve actually taking anything away from the child.

19. Use positive procedures to make desirable behavior so strong that there is no time for undesirable behavior.

FIVE

Measuring Behavior

OBJECTIVES

After completing this chapter, you will be able to define several measurement and assessment methods that are used with applied behavior analysis procedures. To do this, you will learn to:

1. Discriminate between traditional and behavioral approaches to assessment.
2. Label various criteria for judging assessment procedures.
3. Pinpoint target behaviors.
4. Identify several behavioral assessment procedures.
5. Identify several behavioral observation techniques.
6. Graph data in three different formats.
7. Use several single-subject designs.
8. Describe methods for implementing an effective information feedback system for students.

Measurement is important in virtually all aspects of life—cooking an omelette, checking the oil in the engine of a car, balancing a checkbook, or taking the temperature of a sick child. In all of these cases, measurement is used to discern the current status of something and to make a decision about what to do next. It is difficult to make a meaningful decision without some type of measurement. If we do make a decision without measurement, we risk leaving the outcome to chance and guesswork. Most decisions are too important for such a haphazard approach, particularly educational decisions.

Teachers need valid, reliable, and useful measurement techniques to gather data for basic decisions about students' academic progress and behavior. Sound behavior modification programs depend on accurate and meaningful measurements of initial behavior, progress, and end behavior. Teachers cannot know whether students have met behavioral goals if they have no way to measure the criteria.

Unfortunately, some of the measurement tools that teachers have had to rely on have not been helpful in clarifying student academic performance or measuring behavior in a meaningful way. Many measurement techniques proposed for teachers are time consuming, difficult to implement in the classroom setting, and, most important, not helpful in making decisions in the classroom.

Advances in applied behavior analysis and behavioral assessment have been particularly helpful in enabling teachers to measure student progress objectively. Behavioral assessment techniques are being used in such varied areas as the continuous assessment of children's academic performance, precision teaching techniques, classroom behavior comparisons, social skills training, new computer applications for decision making, and Individual Education Plans (IEP) for special-needs children. Since behavioral techniques are objective measures with few theoretical assumptions, they stand legal tests in education very well. This chapter will cover the difference between traditional and behavioral assessment, how to judge measurement techniques, how to define behaviors, behavioral interviewing, behavior checklists, observation techniques, single-subject designs, and the effects of performance feedback on students. Many teachers will find these measurement techniques helpful both in improving their own instructional and behavioral management procedures, and in enabling them to read and understand the scientific literature of applied behavior analysis.

PURPOSES OF ASSESSMENT AND EVALUATION

Assessment

Many teachers feel that assessment and measurement are psychological techniques that are primarily the business of psychologists and researchers. However, we all make assessments in everyday situations. **Assessment** is merely information gathering that leads to some type of decision (Cole, 1978; Cronbach, 1970; Lidz, 1981). It is important to note that this definition has two components: information gathering and decision making. *Information gathering* can involve observing classroom behavior, structured testing, interviewing, or simply grading a paper. Information is often gathered in a nonsystematic manner; frequently used approaches are rumors about a difficult child from another teacher, informal observations, anecdotal reports from other children in the classroom, and some testing approaches, such as projective tests (ink blots, stories, sentence completion, and drawings) (Gelfand, Jenson, & Drew, 1982). Gathering information in a structured, systematic way reduces errors in the information that is collected and makes it more useful.

The second component of assessment is *decision making.* From the information they gather, teachers make all sorts of decisions about students. Such decisions can include what type or level of group a child might be placed in for academics, or they can involve a curriculum or instructional change if a child is having difficulty with a particular subject. Assessment information can also lead to decisions about classroom behaviors. A teacher may need to know whether a child's behavior warrants special help. For example, an excessively shy or withdrawn child might be observed on the playground or in the lunchroom to determine whether he needs social skills training or encouragement to interact with other children. In more severe cases, a teacher's initial assessment of a child may start the process for a referral for more intensive special services.

Information gathering *without* a decision is a costly, inappropriate process. The child is exposed to a needless information-gathering procedure and possible labeling, and money and time are wasted. Decisions are needed even if the conclusion is that no program change is necessary. The decision component directly relates to the "utility" of an assessment procedure, which will be discussed later in this chapter.

Evaluation

Assessment involves information gathering and decision making for a single child; **evaluation** is this process applied to an entire program. For example, a teacher may want to determine whether or not a particular set of instructional materials produces greater gains than others. In such a case, it is not enough merely to know whether individual students are making progress. The teacher wants to know *why* they are making progress. Is it due to the program itself, or to changes unrelated to the program or academic materials, such as parental encouragement? Applied behavior analysis programs in education are particularly well suited for this type of evaluation process. Both assessment and program evaluation are important to teachers who want to improve their programs and provide an optimal educational experience for children. Most of the material covered in this chapter can be applied to both individual-student assessment and program evaluation.

THE DIFFERENCE BETWEEN BEHAVIORAL
AND TRADITIONAL ASSESSMENT

Applied behavior analysis programs are a particular type of assessment called **behavioral assessment,** which differs from traditional educational and psychological assessment in a number of ways. First, behavioral assessment is concerned with directly gathering a sample of information about specific behaviors. The behaviors defined from this sample are the starting point of many behavioral programs, so the data collected are of primary importance. Traditional approaches are more concerned with "underlying causes" of a problem behavior. The sample of information gathered is of secondary importance and is considered only a reflection or symptom of an underlying problem which cannot be directly measured. For instance, a behavioral assessment approach would indicate that the behavior of an aggressive child should be observed in the classroom and a *baseline* established to determine the frequency of the behavior. A program of direct classroom interventions would then be designed to reduce the aggression and replace it with more accepted behaviors. More traditional approaches would assume that the observed aggressive behavior is a symptom of an underlying emotional disturbance. Instead of direct classroom interventions for the aggressive behavior, a more indirect or nondirectional approach would be used to treat the assumed underlying cause. Such approaches can be costly in time and resources, and they can be extremely frustrating to teachers who want direct, effective methods.

Besides initial assessment and definition of target behaviors, behavioral assessment approaches emphasize definition of specific target behaviors and collection of continuous (prior, during, and after the intervention) assessment data to improve or change a program. Traditional approaches to assessment describe personality functioning instead of defining target behaviors, and they tend to collect assessment data on a before-and-after basis instead of continuously.

Assessment methods also differ between behavioral and traditional assessment. Behavioral methods emphasize such information-collection techniques as direct observation, behavioral checklists, and structured interviewing. Traditional approaches emphasize more indirect information-collection methods, such as projective testing (ink blots, unstructured drawings, sentence completion, and story telling), unstructured interviewing, self-reports, and anecdotal histories. A more detailed comparison of behavioral and traditional assessment is given in Table 5–1.

EXAMPLE

John has been assessed by his classroom teacher and the school psychologist for behavioral difficulties in the classroom. The teacher assessed John by administering a standardized achievement test and asking him questions about his home life. The psychologist used a variety of assessment measures that included a developmental history (John's mother answered the questions), a sentence-completion test in which John supplied answers to open-ended questions, and a draw-a-person test. The psychologist also administered an individualized intelligence test. When all of the information was gathered, the teacher and psychologist wrote a report that diagnosed John as emotionally disturbed with learning difficulties due to emotional traumatization. Because special placements were limited, however, they decided to wait and assess John again at the end of the year.

Exercise

How is this assessment different from a behavioral assessment of John's problems?

Feedback

This assessment differs from a behavioral assessment in the following ways:

1. The assessment procedures emphasized underlying difficulties instead of gathering a direct sample of some of John's in-class behaviors.
2. No baseline information was gathered.
3. John's behaviors were assumed to be a symptom of an underlying cause.
4. None of John's behaviors were pinpointed. Instead, the assessment addressed personality structures.
5. The assessment was not continuous. There will be a long gap between the current assessment and the next assessment.
6. No decisions were made about interventions that could be tried with John in the classroom.

JUDGING MEASUREMENT TECHNIQUES

Not all measurement techniques are created equal. Decisions about the value of an assessment technique are based on the answers to four basic questions: (1) Does the assessment lead to a decison? (2) Does the assessment technique have validity? (3) Does the assessment technique have reliability? (4) Does the assessment technique have utility?

All assessment and evaluation measurements are subject to error because they are only approximations of the phenomena they are supposed to be measuring; Even with the best assessment and evaluation procedures, only samples of information are gathered. For example, classroom observations are carried out for only limited amounts of time. The child's behavior is not observed for the entire school year. Similarly, structured academic achievement tests sample only specific subject areas, such as reading or mathemat-

TABLE 5-1 Differences Between Behavioral and Traditional Approaches to Assessment

	Behavioral	Traditional
I. Assumptions		
1. Conception of personality	Personality constructs mainly employed to summarize specific behavior patterns, if at all	Personality as a reflection of enduring underlying states or traits
2. Causes of behavior	Maintaining conditions sought in current environment	Intrapsychic or within the individual
II. Implications		
1. Role of behavior	Important as a sample of person's repertoire in specific situation	Behavior assumes importance only insofar as it indexes underlying causes
2. Role of history	Relatively unimportant, except, for example, to provide a retrospective baseline	Crucial in that persent conditions seen as a product of the past
3. Consistency of behavior	Behavior thought to be specific to the situation	Behavior expected to be consistent across time and settings
III. Uses of data	To describe target behaviors and maintaining conditions	To describe personality functioning and etiology
	To select the appropriate treatment	To diagnose or classify
	To evaluate and revise treatment	To make prognosis; to predict
IV. Other characteristics		
1. Level of inferences	Low	Medium to high
2. Comparisons	More emphasis on intra-individual or idiographic	More emphasis on inter-individual or nomothetic
3. Methods of assessment	More emphasis on direct methods (e.g., observations of behavior in natural environment)	More emphasis on indirect methods (e.g., interviews and self-report)
4. Timing of assessment	More ongoing; prior, during, and after treatment	Pre- and perhaps post-treatment, or strictly to diagnose
5. Scope of assessment	Specific measures and of more variables (e.g., of target behaviors in various situations, of side effects, context, strengths as well as deficiences)	More global measures (e.g., of cure, or improvement) but only of the individual

Reprinted with permission from D. P. Hartmann, B. L. Roper, and D. C. Bradford (1979). Some relationships between behavioral and traditional assessment. *Journal of Behavioral Assessment, 1,* 3–21. (New York: Plenum).

ics. Children do not read all of the available material nor complete all of the possible math problems for a specific grade level. Because the information gathered is only a sample, it is susceptible to error. No assessment or evaluation approach is error free, and the very act of gathering a sample of information can produce error. Two basic types of error are associated with information gathering: **random error** (the error occurs intermittently) and **systematic error** (the error occurs every time the measure is used) (Althauser and Herberlein, 1970; Carmines and Zeller, 1979; Nunnally, 1978).

Validity

A measurement technique must have validity. A **valid** measure is one which actually measures what one wants to measure. Measurement techniques can lack validity for several reasons. They may be inappropriate for the competency level or age of the students. For instance, the arithmetic section of a general achievement test for sixth graders is not likely to be valid for measuring the beginning math of a first grader. It does not measure progress or status at the first-grade level, and it is therefore said to lack validity for this purpose. If we used the test with first graders, it would **systematically** be in error every time it was used with this population.

The validity of other measurement techniques may depend on the purposes of the measurement or the context in which it is carried out. For example, the number of pages a child reads in a set amount of time may be valid if the teacher is interested in amount of reading, but it may lack validity if the teacher is interested in reading comprehension. The number of times a child asks a teacher for help may or may not be a valid measure of the effect of a program designed to teach independent seat work. It may depend on whether the questions asked are in reference to some new subject matter, how the teacher has presented it, or the method of teaching used.

Some measures simply do not, or cannot, measure what they are supposed to measure. Educational or psychological theory frequently suggests that a measure is valid when it may in fact lack validity. According to some clinical theory, for instance, potential aggressive behavior may be measured and predicted by the number of aggressive images that a child reports in looking at an ambiguous stimulus such as an ink blot (a projective test). If the teacher's interest is in the child's aggressive behavior then interpretations from ink blots may not provide a valid measure of such behavior (as reviewed by Gittelman-Klein, 1980). The developers of an ink-blot test may purport that their test measures or predicts aggression, but research may not support such an assertion. In this case, the test would be said to lack validity.

Validity describes how well a technique measures what it purports to measure. A valid measure for one student population or one type of situation may not be valid for another population or situation. If an assessment technique is used invalidly, then the measure will produce a systematic error each time it is used.

Reliability

Reliable measurements produce consistent results over a period of time regardless of the person doing the measurement, and the same results can be predicted for each use of the measurement. Reliability is a measure of the consistency of the information gathered by various assessment techniques (Gelfand and Hartmann, 1984). Inconsistent results which cannot be replicated are a result of nonreliable assessment methods and **random error.**

The most important reliability measure for applied behavior analysis involves the similarity or consistency of results between two observers using an observation system. For example, a teacher and an aide may observe a child in a classroom setting using a coded observation system. If the definitions for the observation codes are vague and can be intrepreted in a number of ways, the teacher will probably get different results than the aide even though the teacher and the aide observed the same child at the same time. They will get inconsistent or different results each time they use this vague system due to their individual interpretations of the observation codes. They are literally looking for different behaviors. This type of reliability is called **interrater reliability.** It is generally measured as the percentage of agreements between the two observers, divided by the sum of their agreements and disagreements; it can be calculated by using a simple formula, given in the EXAMPLE.

The repeated use of a reliable assessment technique over time yields consistent results. If a teacher administers an achievement test to a child and then readministers the same test 2 weeks later, the difference in the test results can be used to judge the reliability of the test. Since the child has probably not learned enough significant academic information in 2 weeks to account for a difference in scores, any difference is the result of random measurement error. If the difference is large, then the reliability of the test would be suspect. If the difference is small, then test would have good reliability. This type of reliability is called **test-retest reliability.**

Obviously, if a measure is not reliable, it cannot be valid. A measure that gives different results every time it is used cannot measure what it is supposed to measure. An unreliable measure automatically lacks validity.

Utility

It is important for teachers to gauge the **utility** of any measurement or assessment technique that is recommended for use in the classroom. Even if an assessment technique has superb validity and reliability, it must be feasible for use in the classroom and offer good data so that decisions can be made. It is easy to become excited about a new assessment technique only to realize that there are large hidden costs in time and money. If a measure requires far too much time or costs too much money, then it is not practical for routine classroom use: It lacks utility. In addition, if a measure does not readily yield data that can be used to make decisions in the classroom, it lacks utility. For example, if an assessment system requires that a great deal of time be spent collecting, scoring, and compiling the data for use, the results will probably sit in a file drawer while more pressing classroom needs are attended to.

For an assessment procedure to have utility, it must be economical and the results must be useful for a teacher. They must give information concerning a child's progress, suggest a course of action, or indicate a program's effectiveness.

EXAMPLE

Two raters are using an interval-observation system of 25 intervals and recording data on the "talk outs" of a child in a classroom. The number of agreements (A) and the number of disagreements (D) between intervals must be determined. In the following sample line, an X in an interval indicates that a behavior occurred and an O indicates that no behavior occurred for that interval.

A A D D A A A A A A A D D D A A A A A A A D A A A
lxlxlolxlolxlolxlolxlxlxlxlololxlolxlxlolxlolxlolxl   Rater #1
lxlxlxlololxlolxlolxlxlololxlolxlolxlxlolxlxlxlolxl   Rater #2

Exercise

Calculate the interrater reliability.

Feedback

If the raters agree on 20 of the intervals, but disagree on 5 of them, the data can be put into a reliability formula:

$$\text{Reliability} = \frac{A}{A + D} \times 100$$

or

$$R = \frac{20}{20 + 5} \times 100 + = 80\%$$

An 80 percent reliability between two observers is considered reasonably good consistency for a classroom behavior analysis project.

SELECTING AND DEFINING BEHAVIORS

Most teachers know of a number of difficult behaviors that they would like to see reduced in their classrooms. In general they include such problem behaviors as noncompliance, defiance of the teacher, not attending to academic work, and not completing assignments. Teachers should emphasize appropriate behaviors to replace the problem behaviors, such as attending to academic tasks, improved cooperation with teacher requests, and improved social skills with peers. For each problem behavior selected for a behavior analysis program, a positive replacement behavior should also be selected.

Behaviors can be broadly classed into three basic categories (Gelfand and Hartmann, 1984). Behavior **excesses** are problem behaviors that occur too much and that teachers would like to reduce (talking out in class, noncompliance, aggression). Behavior **deficits** are appropriate behaviors that teachers would like to increase (politeness, amount of academic work, positive social interactions with peers). Behaviors that are **inappropriately controlled by environmental stimuli** are behaviors that are generally considered appropriate but that are occurring at inappropriate times or under inappropriate conditions. (Examples are a shy child who learns to start conversations and then begins to talk out in class during teacher lectures, or a child who learns undressing skills at home and then proceeds to disrobe in the grocery store.)

Once a behavior has been selected by a teacher, parent, or student to be included in a behavior analysis program, it must be objectively defined before it can be assessed. All behavioral assessment techniques, including direct observation, behavior checklists, and structured interviewing, require objectively defined, or **pinpointed,** behaviors—behaviors that are "pinned down" so that they can be observed and measured in a reliable way. The behavior must be defined so that it includes the following components: (1) a descriptive name, (2) a specific definition, (3) a description of parts of the behavior, (4) typical examples of the behavior, and (5) examples of borderline, questionable, or difficult conditions (Gelfand and Hartmann, 1984; Hawkins, 1982). It is important that the defined behavior accurately reflect what the child actually does (validity) and that two people can agree on when the behavior is occurring by using the definition (reliability). An example of a behavioral definition for *noncompliance* is given in the next EXAMPLE.

After a behavior is defined, a behavioral objective that can be included in a behavior change program must be defined. In a sense, behavioral objectives are goals to be reached by a behavioral program. (A more detailed explanation is given in Chapter 10 on task analysis.) Behavioral objectives have three basic parts: (1) the behavioral definition, or pinpoint; (2) the situations in which the behavior occurs or is to occur, which can involve settings, times, people, or materials; and (3) the criteria of determining when the objective has been accomplished (Mager, 1962; Sulzer-Azaroff & Mayer, 1977). Behavioral objectives are a "road map" to a program. They tell a teacher specifically where a student started, how much has been accomplished, and when the student will be finished. However, a teacher should ask a number of questions concerning behavioral objectives before they are implemented.

EXAMPLE

John is not doing what the teacher wants him to do in the classroom. He does not follow through with requests from the teacher.

Exercises

Write a behavioral definition and objective for compliance.

Feedback

Definition: Compliance is the appropriate initiation and completion of a behavior that is made in response to a teacher's request. The behavior must start within 5 seconds of the teacher's request.

Behavioral Objective: John's (people) compliance (as defined as a pinpointed behavior) to the teacher's (people) requests will improve in the classroom (setting) from 40 percent to 80 percent (criteria) within 2 weeks (time).

TYPES OF BEHAVIORAL ASSESSMENT TECHNIQUES

Teachers use a number of behavioral assessment techniques, usually without being aware of doing so. These techniques include interviewing others for information, using checklists to assess a child, observing children in the classroom, and collecting academic performance information. The basic difference between using these techniques informally and using them for an applied behavior analysis program is *consistency*. When these techniques are used informally, the validity and reliability of the information is often compromised.

Behavioral Interviewing

Interviewing is possibly the most frequently used assessment technique. It simply involves asking someone for information about a subject. The difference between informal interviewing and behavioral interviewing is that the latter approach is structured to help define target behaviors, to determine under what condition the behaviors occur, to get a sense of how often the behaviors occur (the rate), and to discover what has been tried in the past to change the behaviors. Behavioral interviewing has several advantages: (1) it uses a verbal format that helps establish a relationship with the person giving the information; (2) it allows flexibility in that interesting or new information can be pursued; and (3) it can be used with both adults and children to get both sides of the information. An example of a behavioral interview with the parent of a student is given in Table 5–2.

Behavior checklists. The use of behavior checklists is becoming more widespread in educational settings because of their ease of use and general utility for teachers. They are used to identify behavior disorders (Achenbach, 1978; Achenbach & Edelbrock, 1978; Quay & Peterson, 1975; Walker, 1976), hyperactivity (Conners, 1969), and infantile autism (Krug, Arick, & Almond, 1980). Checklists are lists of specifically defined behaviors which are completed by persons familiar with the child. For example, a checklist that helps

---

TABLE 5–2   Initial Caretaker Interview

These are the basic questions to ask caretakers concerning the child's problem behavior:

1. *Specific Description.* Can you tell me what (child's name)'s problem seems to be?
   (If caretaker responds in generalities such as, "He is always grouchy," or that the child is rebellious, uncooperative, overly shy, then ask him to describe the behavior more explicitly.)
   What, exactly, does (he or she) do when (he or she) is acting this way?
   What kinds of things will (he or she) say?

2. *Last Incident.* Could you tell me just what happened the last time you saw (the child) acting like this?
   What did you do?

3. *Rate.* How often does this behavior occur?
   About how many times a day (or hour or week) does it occur?

4. *Changes in Rate.* Would you say this behavior is starting to happen more often, less often, or staying about the same?

5. *Setting.* In what situations does it occur?
   At home?
   At school?
   In public places or when (the child) is alone?
   (If in public places) Who is usually with him? How do they respond?
   At what times of day does this happen?
   What else is (the child) likely to be doing at the time?

6. *Antecedents.* What usually has happened right before (he or she) does this?
   Does anything in particular seem to start this behavior?

7. *Consequent Events.* What usually happens right afterward?

8. *Modification Attempts.* What things have you tried to stop (him or her) from behaving this way?
   How long did you try that?
   How well did it work?
   Have you ever tried anything else?

Reprinted with permission from D. M. Gelfand and D. P. Hartmann (1984). *Child behavior: Analysis and Therapy.* New York: Pergamon Press.

assess classroom behavior problems might include an item like "Is overactive, restless, and/or continually shifting body positions" (Walker, 1976).

Checklists are behavioral in the sense that the person filling out the checklist is gathering a sample of behavior, either from memory or by observation. The specific items in a checklist can be used as starting points for applied behavior analysis programs. The basic drawbacks to checklists are that many of the items can be vaguely defined and that the person filling out the checklist will generally do it from memory rather than by direct observation. Both of these factors can affect the reliability of checklists and limit their use. Even with these problems, however, checklists are popular and can be used effectively in conjunction with other behavioral assessment methods.

Permanent products. This term means that the behavior being measured has left a permanent environmental effect that can be easily observed and measured. The most common forms of permanent products in a classroom are the outcomes of behavior such as the worksheets or tests the children have completed. A teacher does not have to see a child complete each problem or spell each word; he has only to review the results of the child's efforts. The effects are durable, tangible, and easily measured. Other types of permanent-product results found in the home and school can include a clean room, a written paragraph, and books checked out at the library.

Permanent products are ideal for incorporation into the behavioral objectives of a program. Since they are durable, a teacher can wait until he has time to count or measure to determine whether a criterion has been met. Although there are advantages to permanent products, there are also distinct disadvantages, particularly if the child is not periodically observed to make sure he is engaging in the target behavior. In the classroom, for example, a child may receive inappropriate help from a peer with spelling words. At home, an older (or younger) sibling may help clean up the room. It is wise to randomly observe a child unannounced when using permanent-product approaches.

Observation systems. Of all the behavioral assessment approaches, direct observation of behavior gives the most accurate recording of ongoing behaviors. Permanent-product recording involves measuring an outcome of behavior; observation measures behavior that is actually occurring. Behavioral observation has been used to measure behavior in classrooms (O'Leary, Romanczyk, Kass, Dietz, & Santagrossi, 1971), in the home (Patterson, 1982), and on the playground (Walker et al., 1978). But behavioral observation involves more than simply defining a behavior and going into the classroom to observe. It requires a system.

The systems used to collect observational data require some type of code, which is a set of clearly defined behaviors. Such behaviors for a classroom system might include out-of-seat behaviors, off-task behaviors, talking-out behaviors, and disruptions. Figure 5–1 lists a set of behavioral codes that were designed for behavioral observation.

Some dimensions of behavior are particularly important for behavioral observation and can determine which observation system will be used. For instance, the *discreteness* of the behavior is important; that is, the behavior should have a clear onset and ending. Discreteness is important when accurate counts of behaviors are needed. The *length* of the behavior is another important aspect. Some behaviors occur too quickly for some recording systems. The *rate* at which the behavior occurs is also important in the selection of a system. If the behavior occurs at a high rate, it may happen so quickly and frequently that the observer misses behaviors and becomes confused. If the rate is too low, waiting for the behavior to occur will waste the observer's time.

Five basic systems can be used to collect observational data in the classroom. As with other assessment approaches, teachers must decide what is feasible in their classrooms within the confines of limited resources and time.

1. Frequency (tally or event) method. This is the method many novices use when first recording data. It is the easiest to conceptualize in that the teacher merely counts the number of times the behavior occurs in a given block of time. An example of the frequency method could involve counting the number of off-task behaviors in a class period. Another example might be counting the number of times a child raises his hand during a 30-minute period (see Figure 5–2a).

Frequency recording has some severe limitations if the behaviors are not discrete. It is difficult to count a behavior, such as a conversation, if you are not sure when it is stopping or starting. Do you count the number of words, sentences, or pauses? Similarly, if the rate of behavior is too high or extremely low, a frequency system may be inadequate. It is easy to lose count if behaviors are occurring so rapidly that it is difficult to separate one behavior from the next. Similarly, the frequency system is generally restricted to recording one behavior at a time and behaviors of the same general time duration. When the observer tries to observe more than one behavior or the length of time varies for each behavior, it is very easy to become confused. To reduce confusion, simple recording instruments are often used to record frequencies. These include golf counters, knitting counters, beads on a string, or masking tape worn on the wrist with an ink mark for each behavior.

2. Interval recording method. This method is probably one of the most useful for educational applications because it can be used with a number of nondiscrete behaviors at the same time. To use this method the teacher breaks the observation period into short intervals (usually from 5 seconds to 1 minute, depending on how frequently the behavior occurs) and records whether or not the behavior occurs during each interval (see Figure 5–2b). What is recorded is the presence or absence of a behavior during each interval—for

FIGURE 5-1   Behavior Recording Sheet from the Classroom Observation System

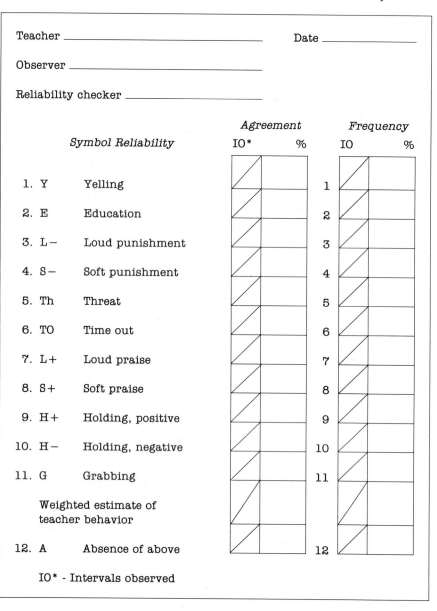

Reprinted with permission from D. K. O'Leary, R. G. Romanczyk, R. E. Kass, A. Dietz, & D. Santogrossi (1971). *Procedures for Classroom Observation of Teachers and Children.* Unpublished manuscript. State University of New York at Stony Brook.

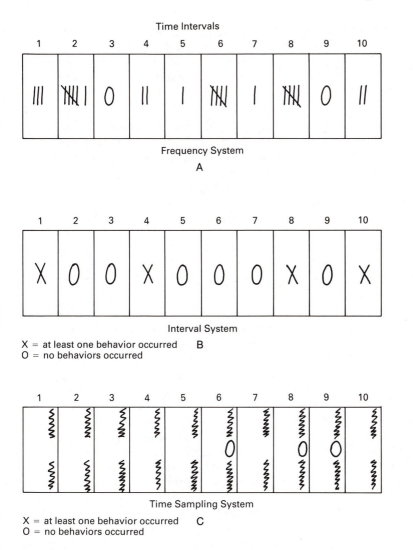

Time Intervals

Frequency System

A

Interval System

X = at least one behavior occurred   B
O = no behaviors occurred

Time Sampling System

X = at least one behavior occurred   C
O = no behaviors occurred

FIGURE 5-2

example, "paying attention or not paying attention." Thus, whether a be-havior occurs once or several times during an interval, it is checked just once to indicate that it occurred during the interval.

With interval recording, only one occurrence of the behavior is recorded if it occurs in the interval. All others are disregarded. This makes it easy to record a number of nondiscrete behaviors of varying time length. Simple signaling devices, such as an egg timer or a "beep" on a cassette audio tape (used with headphones), have been used to signal teachers that an interval is starting and they should be observing for the occurrence of a behavior.

It is important to note that since interval recording is measuring only one instance of a behavior across each interval, it generally underestimates the true frequency of the behavior. However, this underestimate is considered tolerable because only relative rates before an intervention and after an intervention are made.

3. Duration method.   The duration method of recording measures the length of a behavior. To use this method, the teacher runs a stopwatch continuously while the behavior is occurring during a specified length of time. An example of the use of this method would be recording the amount of time a student spends talking in class. While the student talks, the watch is running. When the student stops talking, the watch is stopped. What is recorded is the amount of time during which a specific target behavior occurred.

The duration method gives both a frequency count of a behavior and a duration count. As with the frequency method, the behaviors have to be discrete and not too frequent. However, the lengths of time for the individual behaviors can vary greatly.

4. Instantaneous time-sampling method.   This method is actually a variation of the interval recording method, although it requires less work. As with the interval recording, intervals of a certain length are set up. Instead of noting the occurrence or nonoccurrence of the behavior in question throughout the interval, however, the observer merely looks at the student for an instant at the end of the interval and scores the behavior as occurring only if the person is engaging in it at that moment (see Figure 5–2c). Such a measure gives a relative estimate of the behavior and can be used to determine whether some behavior is becoming more or less frequent as a function of some changes in procedures. The instantaneous time-sampling method has been shown to lack precision and should be used when only a rough measure of large behavior change is desired (Repp, Deitz, Boles, Deitz, & Repp, 1976; Repp, Roberts, Slack, Repp, & Berkler, 1976).

A good use for the instantaneous time-sampling method is with behavioral assessment of a group. For instance, if the observer is interested in changes in the degree to which children attend to their seat work, he chooses an interval—4 minutes, for example. At the end of each four minute interval, the observer quickly scans the group, counts the number of children doing seat work, and then starts to count another observation interval. If the group size changes, he will also have to record this. At the end, the teacher computes the percent working during each interval (Risley & Cataldo, 1973).

5. Self-monitoring method.   This behavioral observation is very different from the other four for two reasons. First, the child observes herself instead of being observed by the teacher or classroom aide. In a sense, the child is collecting data on herself. Self-monitoring is a "process involving self-observations and the systematic recording of observations" (Haynes, 1978).

Second, the self-monitoring observation system may be more of a behavior change procedure than a data collection system. This behavior change is a result of the reactivity of having the child collect the data. **Reactivity** means the changing of the natural occurrence of a behavior simply by the process of observing the behavior (Nelson, 1977). Having a child watch for a particular behavior in himself and then recording the behavior will temporarily change the frequency of the behavior. This procedure has been used successfully to improve academic work (Broden, Hall, & Mitts, 1971—see EXAMPLE), to reduce irritating throat clearing in the classroom (Jenson, Paoletti, & Pettersen, 1984), to reduce hair pulling (Horne, 1977), to improve study skills (Broden et al., 1971; Richards, 1975), and to reduce talking out in class (Broden et al., 1971). Self-monitoring is particularly useful with problem habits or behaviors that a student is unaware of but wants to change.

Self-monitoring generally involves having the child collect data with a frequency method. One researcher (Kunzelman, 1970) used cartoons called "countoons" to help children keep track of the behaviors they were self-monitoring. The use of recording instruments seems to increase the reactivity of the self-recording and improve the effects. The behavior change effects of self-monitoring are only temporary, however, and a back-up behavior management program is generally needed to consolidate the changes permanently. In addition, students who are motivated to change but have difficulty getting started are the ones who are most likely to benefit from the procedure. Even though additional reinforcements are necessary, self-monitoring can be an effective method to start behavior change, particularly for difficult or chronic problem behaviors.

EXAMPLE

In this study (Broden et al., 1971), an eighth-grade student, Stu, had trouble remaining quiet in his math class. The teacher referred him to the experimenters to find some means to "shut Stu up." The "talk outs" were defined as "any verbalization that occurred during class and that had not been recognized by the teacher." Since not all of Stu's talk outs were audible to an observer in the classroom who was taking data, both audible talk outs and Stu's lips moving were counted as talk outs. After a baseline was collected for 9 days, a self-monitoring phase was started. During this phase, Stu was given a piece of paper with a rectangle marked on it and told to record a mark every time he talked out.

The design used in this study was a series of alternating baselines and treatment phases (reversal design). During the baselines, Stu's talk outs averaged approximately 1.5 per minute. During the treatment phase using self-monitoring, talk outs dropped to approximately 0.4 per minute. Over the course of the experiment, however, the positive effects of the self-monitoring slowly decreased. This decrease shows that self-monitoring has only temporary effects. To make it last, another intervention, such as a behavioral contract reinforcing no talk outs, should also have been used.

Exercises

1. What type of observation system was used in this example?
2. How was the target behavior defined?
3. Was the behavior change permanent?
4. What other procedure could have been used to make the behavior change permanent?

Feedback

1. A self-monitoring system that utilized a frequency recording of talk outs was used.
2. The target behavior was defined as "any verbalization that occurred during class and that had not been recognized by the teacher."
3. No, the behavior change was not permanent.
4. A behavioral contract could have been used to make the change permanent.

ESSENTIALS OF GRAPHING DATA

Once the data have been collected using an observation system, they have to be graphed to be useful. It is confusing to look at data on a raw data sheet and try to make a decision. Some easy, systematic way to display the data is needed, and graphs are the quickest and most effective.

Conventional graphs consist of a vertical line and a horizontal line, called axes. The vertical axis is also known as the **ordinate,** or **y axis,** and is generally used to display frequencies (number of talk outs, for example), percentages (percent of correct words spelled), means (the average number of times out of seat), or durations (amount of time spent attending to a task). The horizontal axis, also known as the **abscissa,** or **x axis,** is used to display time units such as minutes, hours, days, weeks, or sessions.

The general rule for graphing is that time is placed on the abscissa and behavior is placed on the ordinate. The y axis and x axis intersect at zero (the corner of the graph), where the graph plotting is started. For example, if you were to graph the number of assignments completed each day by a student, you would start with Day 1 and the number of assignments completed for that day. The next data point to be connected would be Day 2 and the number of assignments for this day (see the EXAMPLE). Problems occur with conventional graphs when the intervals for the abscissa or ordinate are changed inconsistently—plotting for a day and then for a week on the abscissa, for example. When the values are changed inconsistently, meaningful comparisons cannot be made.

A variation of the conventional graph is used by some teachers to show continuing change in a behavior. This graph is called a **cumulative graph** because the data from a new session is added to the total data of all the previous sessions, resulting in an upward "negatively accelerated" curve. The essential difference between a conventional graph and a cumulative graph is that on a conventional graph, each data point does not take into account any of the previous sessions, while the cumulative graph keeps a running total of all the previous sessions. The cumulative graph's curve also offers a way to judge the rate of response or improvement. For example, a flat line (no slope) indicates no change, a steep slope indicates a rapid change, and a gradual slope indicates a slow change.

Cumulative graphs are most useful when a teacher wants to determine the total behavior change since the start of a new procedure. It gives the whole picture of behavior change. Conventional graphs are more convenient for representing daily performance changes. Both forms of graphing are acceptable in most classrooms, but they each have some drawbacks. **Precision teaching,** a new way of representing data, offers some new and innovative approaches to charting and graphing.

Precision teaching is a technique that has been particularly advanced by Dr. Ogden Lindsley (a former student of B. F. Skinner) and an avid group of practitioners. The term *precision teaching* can be misleading, however. It is not actually a new method of teaching; rather, it is an alternative way of graphing data and making educational decisions. The precision teaching approach uses a "semilogarithmic" 6-cycle graph paper which can give a more accurate picture of performance changes than conventional arithmetic graphs. For example, if a teacher plots the improved performance of student 1 and the student moves from reading 1 page per day to 2 pages per day, then the percentage increase that would be plotted on a conventional graph would be 50 percent. However, if student 2 is reading an average of 10 pages per day, that student would have to improve her reading rate by 20 pages to get a 50 percent increase. If we are only comparing percentage improvement as plotted on a conventional graph, then student 1 appears to have improved as much as student 2. This is called the "gee whiz" effect, and it can be misleading.

Precision teaching uses a 6-cycle, semi-log graph (see Figure 5–3) which helps correct for this misleading effect. **Logs** are mathematical expressions which represent numbers as ratios of other numbers. Conventional arith-

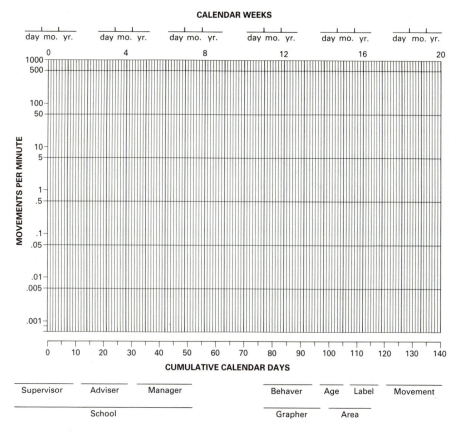

FIGURE 5-3   A 6-cycle precision teaching graph.

metic graphs represent behavior as an equal interval increase or decrease, which can lead to gee whiz–type problems. Precision teaching graphs represent behaviors as a function of logs; this helps to smooth out performance because increases or decreases are plotted as ratios instead of as equal intervals. In our example of improved reading skills, the improvement from 1 to 2 pages would be plotted with a much smaller interval than from 10 to 20 pages. The graph has 6 cycles so that a behavior can be represented from as few responses as 0.001 per minute to as high as 1,000 per minute. It is called *semilogarithmic* because, although the responses are plotted as a function of logs, the time on the x axis is still plotted in conventional equal intervals. (For a more detailed description of precision teaching and its uses, see O. R. White and N. G. Haring [1980]. *Exceptional Teaching,* 2d ed. Columbus, Ohio: Charles E. Merrill.)

EXAMPLE

1. (See Figure 5–4.)
2. (See Figure 5–5.)

Exercises

1. How are simple and cumulative graphs similar?
2. How are they different?
3. How do they differ from a precision teaching graph?

Feedback

1. Simple and cumulative graphs are similar in that they record frequencies and percentages on the y axis and time on the x axis.
2. They are different in that with a simple graph, data from previous times (sessions, days, weeks, and so on) are not added together. With a cumulative graph, however, they are added together and form a running total. In addition, a simple graph can decrease or dip down, but a cumulative graph never dips; it only becomes flat.
3. Simple and cumulative graphs represent data in equal intervals on the graph, which can cause "gee whiz" problems. Precision teaching graphs use a semilogarithmic representation of data to avoid this problem.

FIGURE 5–4   A standard graph of assignments completed.

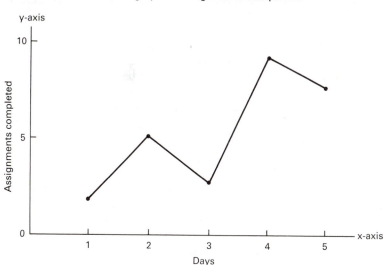

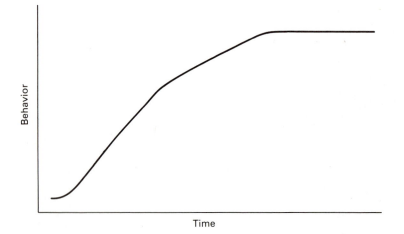

Time

FIGURE 5-5   A cumulative graph.

SINGLE-SUBJECT DESIGNS

It is a short step from learning how to collect data and graph it to developing single-subject research designs. A research design is a method of organizing interventions so that the results can be accurately measured against a control. **Single-subject designs** can involve only one subject or child at a time. The same subject provides data for the baseline, or control, and for the results of the intervention. Single-subject designs are easier for teachers to implement than group designs, which require numerous students and a separate control group against which the results of the intervention are measured.

Teachers may wonder what an understanding of a sophisticated research design can contribute to their classrooms. First, teachers can use these designs to make basic decisions about which techniques are effective and which are not. Second, teachers need to understand basic single-subject design so they can understand educational research. Many research reports use both group and single-subject designs. If a teacher is interested in applied behavior analysis, a knowledge of single-subject designs is required. This section will discuss three of the most frequently used single-subject designs.

Baselines

Defined generally, a **baseline** is "the strength or level (e.g., rate, duration, latency) of a behavior before an experimental variable or procedure is introduced" (Sulzer-Azaroff & Mayer, 1977). Measuring the behavior before the intervention provides a **control,** or standard against which the same behavior after the intervention can be compared in order to judge its effectiveness.

A teacher might want to collect baseline data on the number of times a child is out of his seat, the number of completed assignments turned in, or the number of social interactions during recess. In each case, the teacher would collect *repeated* samples over hours, days, or sessions before an intervention was tried. Generally, the minimum number of repeated samples of a behavior before intervention is 3 (3 hours, 3 days, or 3 sessions), and each sample represents 1 data point graphed on the abscissa and ordinate (see Figure 5–7) (Hersen and Barlow, 1976). The behavior is plotted on the ordinate and the time variable on the abscissa; the data point is plotted at the point at which they meet. An example of a 3-point baseline for out-of-seat behavior with a sample collected each day is shown in Figure 5–6.

Simple baselines are problematic when the data are very variable and unstable—that is, when the data points randomly rise and fall from session to session. A varying baseline does not provide a standard against which to compare treatment to determine whether it was effective. A practical rule for determining whether a baseline is stable is that the total (minimum) number of data points should equal the number of data points already collected plus 1 additional data point for "each 10 percent of variability in the data already collected" (Gelfand & Hartmann, 1984). Variability in the data already collected is defined as the difference between the largest and smallest data point, divided by the largest data point. For example, if the largest data point to date equalled 100, and the smallest equalled 90, the difference would be 10. Divided by 100, this would give 1/10. As one additional day is suggested for each 10 percent variability, this would suggest 1 more day of baseline. The general formula is as follows:

$$\text{Number of additional days} = 10 \, \frac{(\text{largest} - \text{smallest})}{\text{largest}}$$

FIGURE 5-6   A 3-point baseline.

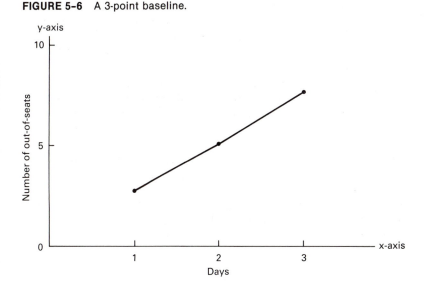

In another example, if after 3 days of baseline the number of homework problems solved varied from 6 to 20, the number of additional days of data collection would be as follows:

$$\text{Number of additional days} = 10 \, \frac{(20 - 6)}{20} = 7$$

The *directionality* of a baseline is also important in determining the effectiveness of an intervention. The ideal baseline is flat (no trends) with little variability (less than 10 percent of the mean). If the baselines are ascending, descending, or curved, it may be difficult to decide whether the change in direction (trend) is due to an intervention or to some external variable that is affecting the baseline.

AB Design

The **AB design** (also known as the *case design* or *quasi-experimental design*) is one of the most useful designs for teachers. All of the more advanced single-subject designs are expansions or variations of the AB design. AB stands for the two phases of the design, with A being the baseline phase and B being the intervention phase. The data are graphed in the two phases, A and B, with a broken line between the phases. The difference between the A and B phases, as measured by an increase or decrease in the amount, rate, percentage, duration, or trend (direction) of the data points, determines the effectiveness of the intervention.

Figure 5–7 is an example of an AB design used with an aggressive 4-year-old in a nursery school setting. The baseline sample was collected on the percentage of time that the boy exhibited aggressive behaviors (hitting, kicking, pulling on others, or destroying property). After 3 days of baseline data had been collected, an intervention was implemented which included placing the child in a chair in the corner for each aggressive response. As Figure 5–7 shows, aggressive behaviors dropped quickly during the intervention phase, suggesting that the intervention was effective.

The cautious phrase "suggesting that the intervention was effective" is used in this example instead of a stronger statement because AB designs have a drawback for strict research studies that might be published. The drawback is that we cannot be sure that some unknown variable did not occur at the same time as the chair-in-the-corner intervention was implemented. The fact that this unknown variable, and not the intervention, might actually be responsible for the behavior change affects the validity of the design. The casual observer might say that such an event was unlikely; however, if the research is to be published, all doubt should be removed. To ensure the reliability of data, other single-subject designs have been developed. For educational and clinical use, however, the AB design is practical and easy for teachers to use.

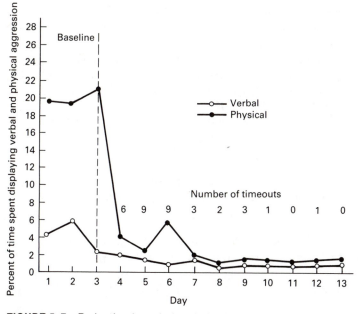

FIGURE 5-7 Reduction in verbal and physical aggression from baseline A to treatment B.

Reprinted with permission from P. Firestone (1976). The effects and side effects of timeout on an aggressive nursery school child. *Journal of Behavior Therapy and Experimental Psychiatry, 7,* 79–81.

Reversal Designs

A **reversal design** is an extension of an AB design that removes the threat to the validity of the design. A reversal design generally includes four phases—ABAB; it is actually two AB designs spliced together. First, data are collected for the baseline phase before any intervention. Second, the intervention is implemented during the experimental phase B. Third, there is a return to the baseline condition, which is generally called a *reversal.* Fourth, the intervention is reimplemented for a final experimental phase. The reversal phase corrects for the problem of the validity of the design. However, the reversal also brings up an ethical question.

Reversal designs are not always appropriate for classroom use because the teacher is required to temporarily stop using a procedure that may be working. This could be unethical in many applied situations—if the procedure appeared to be beneficial to a student, for instance (Gelfand & Hartmann, 1984). A teacher would have difficulty reversing a procedure for a child who had started to do his academic work for the first time in his school career because of a new intervention. A second type of problem can occur when the new behavior change is so rewarding for children that they will not return to baseline when the reversal is implemented. When this happens, it is impossible to demonstrate that the intervention was responsible for the behavior change, although it may be a positive development for the child. Other common problems associated with reversal designs include starting out in the intervention phase (BABA) instead of the baseline phase, or having two intervention phases or slightly different phases next to each other with no separation by a baseline (AB[1]B[2]A).

Figure 5–8 is a graph of an experiment in which a reversal design is used. The four conditions of the design (baseline, experimental I, reversal, and experimental II) are described next.

Baseline.   Observations made on the behavior prior to a direct manipulation of that behavior indicated that the rate of correct responses averaged 10 percent of the total response in each session. This lasted 5 days.

Experimental I.   During this first experimental, or manipulation, phase, the rate of correct responses increased to between 40 percent and 70 percent as a result of some procedure. During the last 4 sessions, the percent of correct responses was consistently above 60 percent. The condition lasted 7 days.

FIGURE 5-8   A graph of a reversal design study.

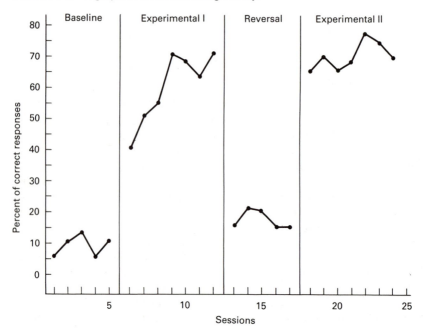

Reprinted with permission from P. Firestone, The effects and side effects of timeout on an aggressive nursery school child, *Journal of Behavior Therapy and Experimental Psychiatry, 7* (1976), 79–81, Pergamen Press, Ltd.

Reversal. A return to baseline conditions (that is, the withdrawal of the experimental I procedure) for 5 days produced a drop in the percent of correct responses to between 15 percent and 25 percent, which is well below the rate observed during experimental I.

Experimental II. The rate of correct responses increased immediately to between 65 percent and 80 percent of the total responses when the experimental procedures were reinstituted.

Because the percent of correct responses was substantially higher in each experimental period than in either baseline or reversal conditions, it would be safe to assume that the new teaching procedure was more effective than that which had been used previously.

Multiple-Baseline Designs

When reversal designs are not appropriate because of ethical concerns, a multiple-baseline design may be needed. A **multiple-baseline design** can be viewed as a series of simultaneous AB designs (discussed previously) in which the baseline A varies. The multiple-baseline design does not include a reversal phase, and the varying baselines control for the problem of an unknown variable, rather than the intervention, causing the behavior change. For example, in Figure 5–9, the panels for Jim, Jon, and Will look like an AB design, except that the intervention occurs at different times (day 8 for Jim, day 12 for Jon, and day 16 for Will). Since the interventions occur at different times, and since the behavior of increased math performance improves with each intervention, it is safe to say that the intervention caused the improvement. It would be extremely unlikely that an unknown variable occurred at exactly the same time the intervention was implemented for all three children.

The multiple-baseline design just described is *across subjects* because the same target behavior is tracked with three children (subjects). A similar multiple-baseline design can be used with only one subject but with three target behaviors. This type of multiple-baseline design is called *across behaviors*. Figure 5–10 is an example of the third type of multiple-baseline design, *across settings*, since in this case the same type of behavior, lateness, is tracked across the same subjects, fourth graders, but in different settings.

This example treats a fourth-grade class of students as a single subject in a multiple-baseline design across settings. Arriving late to a class in a fourth-grade group may occur in three settings: the first period of the day, the first period after lunch, and the second period of the day. A baseline is taken on the behavior of lateness in each of the three situations. A treatment is applied, which in this case consisted of posting names on the board for early birds. The treatment was applied starting on the twelfth day for the first-period class, starting on the fifteenth day for the after-lunch class, and starting on the eighteenth day for the second-period class. The results are present in Figure 5–11.

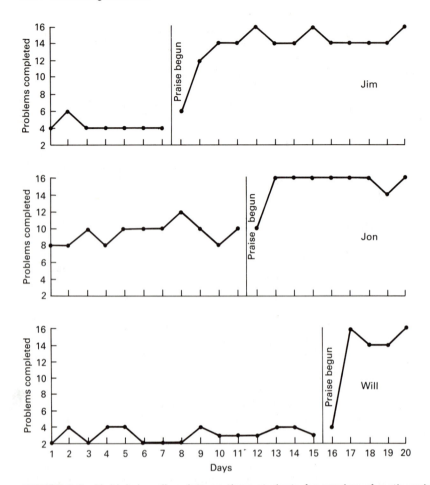

FIGURE 5-9 Multiple-baseline data on three students for number of math problems done correctly in study period under baseline conditions and under treatment conditions where teacher gave students verbal praise for work done.

The data may be interpreted as follows. On the first period of the day, lateness during the baseline period was fairly stable at about six students per day and dropped to zero or one per day after treatment was begun on the twelfth day. For the after-lunch and second-period classes, baseline lateness was also stable but higher (about ten per day), and it again dropped dramatically after treatment was begun. It appears from the data in the multiple-baseline design that the technique of posting "early birds" was effective for this group of fourth graders. Public posting of names had a positive effect on the children, increasing their punctuality.

There are some problems associated with multiple-baseline designs that can limit their use in classrooms. First, it can be relatively difficult for a

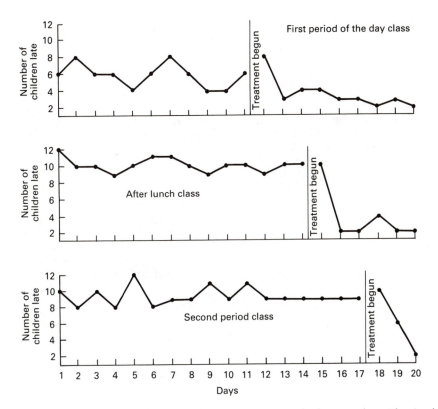

FIGURE 5-10 Multiple baseline data on fourth-graders for lateness in getting to class in three different classes under baseline conditions and under treatment conditions.

teacher to keep track of three or four baselines until they reach stability. Second, there may be a practical and ethical problem of having some children in a treatment group and some children still in a baseline phase. Third, multiple-baseline designs assume the independence of the target behaviors being tracked. This means that if an intervention is started for one target behavior, a behavior that is still in a baseline phase should not change. This assumption is generally safe. However, some behaviors in the baseline phase will also change when a related behavior undergoes an intervention procedure. This is called response generalization, and it is not always possible to forecast which behaviors are not independent.

All of the designs have applications in educational settings, and each design can be used to document change. AB designs can be easily implemented in classroom settings with teachers who have limited time. The other designs, such as reversal and multiple-baseline designs, are more limited in their everyday use, but are excellent for research purposes. However, teachers should be familiar with all of the basic single-subject designs so they can read the literature and make judgments about the quality of educational research.

EXAMPLE

AB designs are very useful to teachers in the classroom. This design might be considered a building block design for the other two single-subject designs (multiple-baseline and reversal designs) described in this section.

Exercise

1. How are AB designs used as building blocks in reversal designs?
2. How are AB designs used as building blocks in multiple-baseline designs?

Feedback

1. A reversal design could be viewed as a string of two repeating AB designs—for example, AB,AB.
2. A multiple-baseline design could be viewed as a series of AB designs used with different subjects or behaviors, or in different settings. However, the baseline in each A would have to be of increasing length—for example, a multiple-baseline design across subjects:

    Subject 1 AB (baseline 3 data points)
    Subject 2 AB (baseline 5 data points)
    Subject 3 AB (baseline 7 data points)

PERFORMANCE FEEDBACK SYSTEMS IN THE CLASSROOM

Measurement and assessment are important for a teacher's decision making. But one of the most important functions of measurement and assessment—performance feedback to the students—is often overlooked in classrooms. Some children are always in the dark about their behavioral and academic performance. They know little of their actual standing until "report card" time, by which time inappropriate patterns may be well established.

Performance feedback combines a measurement system and a feedback system that is immediate and precise. This feedback should be used during two basic phases in the learning process for both academics and new behaviors (Van Houten, 1979). The first phase is **acquisition,** in which a child is first learning or "acquiring" a new skill. The second phase is **practice,** in which the child has learned a skill but now needs to practice it until mastery is obtained. Van Houten (1984) has devised a set of rules that teachers can use to give performance feedback to children for both the acquisition and practice phases. However, one of the most powerful performance feedback systems for students is public posting of performance gains.

Publicly posting the results of performance so that children can immediately see their results is one of the most important ways to enhance a measurement system's effectiveness for changing both academic and behavioral difficulties (Figure 5–11). It has been used to improve reading skills,

FIGURE 5-11 More complex chart showing students' performance during five class days, their highest day, and highest week.

NAME	Day 1	Day 2	Day 3	Day 4	Day 5	Highest day	Highest week
KEN	1	0	1	1	0	1	2
PAUL	1	0	2	1	1	2	4
LAX	3	2	3	3	3	3	15
SANDRA	1	0	1	1	1	1	5
LEE	3	2	3	3	4	3	13
MARK	2	2	2	1	2	2	7
ROSE	5	8	4	7	8	8	33
ELLEN	3	2	3	3	3	3	12
MIKE	1	0	1	2	1	2	5
ANN	1	1	0	2	2	2	4
CLASS	21	17	20	20	24	24	100

Reprinted with permission from R. Van Houten (1984). Setting up performance feedback systems in the classroom. In *Focus on Behavior Analysis in Education*, W. L. Heward, T. E. Herson, D. S. Hill, and J. Trap-Porter (eds). Columbus, Ohio: Chas. E. Merrill.

mathematics and science performance, copying from the board, and follow-ing instructions (as reviewed by Van Houten, 1984). Feedback is given to students using a large data chart with letters and numbers at least 3 centimeters high so that they can be seen from anywhere in the classroom. Confidentiality can be maintained by using a coding system to identify the students.

Charts should be based on daily performance. The chart in Figure 5–12 represents all the days of the week. This particular chart records the number of reading assignments completed each day, with the student's highest previous day's performance and the highest previous week's average performance. In addition, the average class performance is also recorded at the bottom of the chart. The teacher records the data on the chart each day. Some teachers prefer to change the chart data when the students are out of the room—before class or during recess, for example.

The effect of public posting can be dramatic, with the most marked effect for the children who perform most poorly. Figure 5–12 shows the performance data of two classes—one twelfth-grade and one night-school class. This is a multiple-baseline design study, with the classes functioning as subjects. Each class was divided into the top-half-performing students and the

FIGURE 5-12   Mean test scores for top half and bottom half of twelfth grade and night school students during baseline; public posting by coded numbers; and public posting by names.

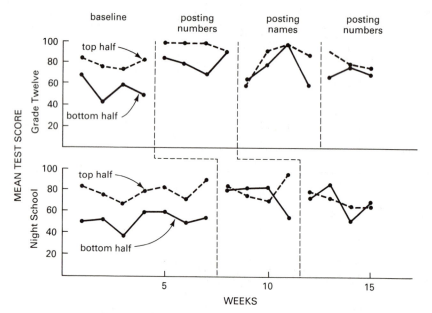

Reprinted with permission from R. Van Houten (1984). Setting up performance feedback systems in the classroom. In *Focus on Behavior Analysis in Education,* W. L. Heward, T. E. Herson, D. S. Hill, and J. Trap-Porter (eds). Columbus, Ohio: Chas. E. Merrill.

bottom-half-performing students. For some weeks, the data were plotted by number to ensure confidentiality, and for other weeks they were posted by the students' names. The results showed that, overall, the public-posting procedure improved academic performance, particularly for the lowest-performing students. However, posting by confidential number or by name made no difference in the actual academic performance.

FAST TRACK

REVIEW

Measurement is central to teaching based on applied behavior analysis and is frequently called *behavioral assessment.* This measurement, or assessment, involves structured information gathering that leads to decisions about the effectiveness of a teaching program or behavioral intervention. The basic difference between behavioral assessment and more traditional assessment approaches is that behavioral assessment emphasizes the measurement of behavior as the important object of a teaching or behavior change program, while traditional approaches assume that problem behaviors are just the symptoms of an underlying cause that cannot easily be measured directly.

Decisions about the value of an assessment technique are based on the answers to four basic questions: (1) Does the assessment lead to a decision? (2) Does the assessment technique have validity? (3) Does the assessment technique have reliability? and (4) Does the assessment technique have utility? *Validity* judges whether the technique actually measures what it purports to measure. *Reliability* judges the consistency of the assessment measure over time or from observer to observer. And *utility* is a judgment about a technique's practical use and worth.

Most behavioral assessment approaches involve defining and pinpointing valid "target behaviors" that can be measured and observed in reliable ways. These approaches include behavioral interviewing, checklists, observation, permanent product measurement, and self-monitoring. The behavioral observation systems are frequency counting, interval sampling, duration of behavior, and time sampling.

Once a behavior has been pinpointed, data on it must be collected with a behavioral assessment technique. *Designs* ensure that data is collected in systematic ways so that meaningful comparisons can be made. Most behavioral designs start with a *baseline,* which is simply data collected on a behavior before an intervention or program to change the behavior is started. Baselines serve as a standard of comparison to judge the effectiveness of an applied behavior analysis program. Several formal designs that use baselines include the AB case study design, the multiple-baseline design, and the reversal designs. Teachers can use the simple single-subject designs, such as the AB case study design, in their classrooms. But they should also understand the more complex designs so they can read the research literature and keep up with new findings and techniques.

Behavioral assessment data can also be used with the students themselves through performance feedback systems that allow students to judge their own progress on an ongoing basis. Performance feedback involves some type of graphing system or chart that represents a child's progress. This system can be enhanced by using immediate feedback, public posting, and student scoring. Allowing students to assist with scoring and maintaining a performance feedback system will also reduce the amount of time and effort that the teacher has to invest in a data collection system.

CUMULATIVE EXERCISE

A student has been exhibiting a number of problematic behaviors, including talking out in class, bothering others, and not doing in-seat academic work. Define each of these behaviors in objectively measurable terms and write a behavioral objective for each one. Describe a data collection system that could be used with each behavior. Draw a graph that uses an AB single-case design for each behavior.

Feedback

1. Make sure that each behavior is described so that it can be observed or measured accurately. For example,
   a. A "talk out" is defined as making any verbalization or gesture during class time without the teacher's permission.
   b. "Bothering others" is touching another child, making faces, taking others' property, or talking with another child without permission.
   c. "Not doing academic work" is failing to complete all assigned academic tasks at the 70-percent-correct level during designated work times.
2. A behavioral objective should contain three basic components: (1) behavioral definition, or pinpoint, (2) the situations in which the behavior occurs or is to occur, and (3) the criteria of determining when the objective has been accomplished.
3. Make sure the data collection system can adequately gather data for all three behaviors and that it can accurately handle nondiscrete behaviors; an interval observation system is an example.
4. Draw the behaviors on a graph, making sure that the baselines have at least three data points and that the data are stable.

SIX

Token Economics

OBJECTIVES

After completing this chapter, you will be able to describe how to set up and use token economies effectively. To do this you will learn to:

1. Decide when a token economy is appropriate and useful.
2. Specify the steps in setting up a token economy.
3. State several ways to make the token economy more effective.
4. Identify and solve common problems with token economies.
5. Specify steps for fading out the token economy.

Most societies use some medium of exchange as an intermediary step between work performed and acquisition of desired items. Our society, for example, commonly reimburses its workers with money, which they then exchange for such items as food, clothing, entertainment, and other necessary goods or services. Few adults would work unless they received some type of token reinforcement (money, paycheck, or credit) that could be exchanged for "reinforcers"—food, housing, services. Since a token economy is the way the "real world" works, its use in the classroom can be seen as a legitimate method of reinforcing students for their "work." Clearly, regular classrooms are not self-contained societies. However, a number of similarities exist that make an exchange system possible. For example, children are generally willing to do academic work and behave appropriately in exchange for a number of goods and services. However, children receive these classroom reinforcers as a matter of daily routine without having to earn them. A formal exchange system, or **token economy**, simply establishes the contingencies for earning classroom reinforcers, thereby improving performance. It may not be necessary for all classrooms, but it can make many of them far more efficient.

How the Token Economy Works

Tokens, such as money, are not intrinsically reinforcing. Tokens become generalized reinforcers because they can be exchanged for a wide range of specific reinforcers. One of the reinforcers that a job provides for adults is money. Because of money's exchange value, it becomes a reinforcer. Similarly, in a classroom, tokens become generalized reinforcers because, after a child earns enough of them for completing specific social or academic activities, they are exchanged for reinforcing items or activities called **backup reinforcers.**

An effective token economy system should establish a continuous process of *positive* interaction between teacher and student which results in a cycle of earning and spending. Students are reinforced for appropriate behavior and work with some sort of token, along with social reinforcement. Then, at designated times during the day or week, depending on the age of the children, the tokens are used to purchase privileges, activities, or materials. After exchanging the tokens for reinforcers, the children return to work and a chance to earn more tokens, which will be used to buy reinforcers at a later time. In classrooms where a token system is operating properly, there is a clear connection between working hard, behaving appropriately, and receiving classroom reinforcers. The basic token reinforcement system requires three primary parts:

1. the *tokens* to be dispensed
2. the *rules* for earning the tokens
3. the *backup reinforcers* to be earned

This system sounds simple. However, token economies are one of the most intricate behavior management systems for a regular-education teacher to implement. They have the potential to become overly complex, and they can easily be abused. A teacher should understand when a system is needed, how to set up a token economy, how to run it effectively and solve common problems, and how to phase out a token economy when the students no longer need its powerful reinforcing qualities.

Are Token Economies a Form of Bribery?

The question of bribery and the use of systematic reinforcement and token economies has been addressed by a number of researchers (Blechman, 1986; O'Leary, Poulos, & Devine, 1972; Vargas, 1977; Walker & Buckley, 1974). The conclusions are similar. Many adults feel that children are "paid off" for something that they should do naturally or because it is the proper thing to do. We have already mentioned, however, that few adults, including teachers, would work unless they received some type of token reinforcement that could be exchanged for backup reinforcers. It is illogical to think that a child should work at difficult academic tasks or behave appropriately in a classroom and receive nothing. We all work for something, and we do not feel it is bribery.

A closer examination of the word *bribery* shows that this word has two meanings (Walker & Buckley, 1974).

1. Bribery is an incentive for someone to do some illegal, immoral, or illicit.
2. Bribery is offering a child an incentive at the time *he is not performing* to get him to perform.

First, token reinforcement is not bribery because schoolwork and appropriate classroom behavior are not illegal, immoral, or illicit. Second, to promise a child an incentive when he is not working is an inappropriate use of a token system. If it is used in this way, the child will learn that waiting and not performing will lead to the promise of bigger rewards. Good token economy applications clearly specify the rules for earning tokens and obtaining privileges *before* the procedures are started. Children are not threatened or cajoled into working.

WHEN TO USE A TOKEN ECONOMY

How Token Systems Have Been Used in the Past

Token systems in general society are as old as money itself. Their systematic application with special populations is much more recent, however. It is interesting to note that with nonhandicapped populations, the use of money or token systems has been viewed as necessary for motivation for thousands of years. In the case of children and handicapped populations, however, we have simply expected them to work "because they ought to."

Token systems have been used with a variety of populations in a variety of settings, and their effectiveness and limitations have been extensively reviewed (Ayllon & Azrin, 1968; Kazdin & Bootzin, 1972; Kazdin, 1977; Kazdin, 1982; O'Leary & Drabman, 1971). For example, token systems have been used to reduce apathy in psychiatric patients (Schaefer & Martin, 1966); to improve social skills in delinquent females by teaching them to accept criticism without reacting negatively (Timbers et al., 1973); to reduce stuttering (Andrews & Ingham, 1972); and to teach self-care skills to the mentally retarded (Horner & Keilitz, 1975; Spradlin & Girardeau, 1966).

In schools, token systems have been used extensively in both special-education and regular-education classes. Disruptive classroom behaviors that have been reduced by token economies include talking out without permission, not complying with instructions, disturbing others, and reducing aggression (Kazdin, 1977; O'Leary, 1978). Token economies have also been used to increase appropriate classroom behaviors, particularly academic work; examples include improving accuracy, completing assigned work, attending and working independently, creative writing, and improving the amount and accuracy of homework assignments returned (Hendersen, Jenson, & Erken, 1985; Kazdin, 1977; Malyn & Jenson, 1986; Walker & Buckly, 1974).

Possibly the largest single application of token economies in the classroom occurred in the behavior analysis follow-through project (see Chapter 1) (Bushell, 1978). This program served over 7,000 disadvantaged children from kindergarten through third grade in 300 classrooms in 15 cities. A teacher-run token economy system served as the motivational backbone of this giant educational project. The point should be made that token economies are not experimental or new techniques. They have been used extensively, and one of the most frequent uses has been in the classroom.

Deciding to Use a Token Economy

Token economies are usually most beneficial when used (1) to make classroom management easier with a disruptive class, (2) to get better results from children who are making little academic progress, or (3) to improve the motivation of children who are disinterested in their classroom work. Several groups of children benefit especially from the token economy approach. Children who are incompetent in several skill areas (academic, social, and behavioral), such as slow learners, mentally retarded children, or behaviorally disordered children, generally improve with token economies. These children appear to need the concreteness of a token economy, with its immediate and direct reinforcement. Children whose school or social histories make social reinforcement from a teacher relatively ineffective may work better under a token system. Classrooms that are out of control with extremely disruptive, unmotivated, and noncompliant children may warrant a token system.

By and large, however, a token system should not be instituted until it has been shown that other behavior management procedures have not worked. There are several reasons for this. For the majority of regular-education students, the existence of classroom problems suggests some failure in current teaching procedures that can be improved by an effective system of increased social reinforcement or better teaching practices, such as improved design of teaching tasks, systematic instructional planning, better scheduling, or improved presentation and pacing. Adding a powerful token system may prevent the teacher from correcting basic teaching deficiencies. Also, student gains under a token system used in place of sound teaching techniques are unlikely to be as great as they would be if other teaching problems were corrected first. In addition, the use of a token system, even when successful, can create future problems. If the system is not handled carefully, students' problems are likely either to recur when the token system is discontinued or to continue to occur in other settings (Kazdin, 1982). These problems can be averted, but it is preferable to try other approaches first and avoid the problem completely.

Before starting a token economy system in the classroom, a teacher should ask the following questions:

1. Have other behavior management and effective teaching procedures been tried and their failure documented?
2. Are there children in the classroom whose learning difficulties are due to other disruptive children who could be managed by a token system?
3. Are there children who need the concreteness of a token system? Or will the token system be overly controlling for the majority of the children in the classroom?
4. Are there children who do not value social reinforcement from a teacher and therefore need a token system? Or is there a problem with the teacher's social reinforcement approach to the children? (that is, is the teacher not very verbal or warm, or does he not provide the class with a high rate of reinforcement?)
5. Are the behaviors to be controlled and managed by a token system important ones for the child's long-term growth and success? Or are the behaviors to be controlled basically for the convenience of the teaching staff? (that is, is the goal to teach children to be quiet and docile and to endure classroom boredom without protest?)
6. Is the teaching staff organized, trained, and precise enough to manage a token system?
7. Are the time, resources, and energy that will be required by a token economy worth the effort? Or will the management of the system (the dispensing, exchanging, counting, and recording of tokens and providing of new reinforcers) take too much valuable teaching time?
8. Should the token economy be used with the entire class? Or can a modified token system be used with only a few children as a temporary approach?

EXAMPLE

Ms. Jones is having difficulty getting her new class to behave and produce acceptable academic work. She particularly wants the children to be quiet so she can organize the classroom better and accomplish more. A school psychologist has observed in the classroom and has suggested that a token economy be started for the entire class. Although resources are scarce, he feels they can run a token economy effectively and improve the classroom.

Exercises

Using the questions previously listed, decide whether Ms. Jones needs a token economy for her class.

Feedback

1. She has not tried other less complex behavior management techniques in her classroom.
2. An analysis has not been made of which children in the class are difficult and what the possible causes of the disruption are.
3. It has not been determined whether the whole class needs a token economy or whether just a few children need it.
4. Being quiet so that Ms. Jones can become more organized is not an important behavior for the children. They may be bored or reacting to Ms. Jones's disorganization.
5. No provision has been made to train Ms. Jones or her staff in the use of a token economy.
6. The classroom has limited resources. There may not be enough time, money, or backup reinforcers to run the program.

SETTING UP A CLASSROOM TOKEN ECONOMY

It is essential that a token economy be well planned, with a careful analysis specifying the behaviors to be changed, backup reinforcers, the cost of the reinforcers, the types of tokens to be used, and the procedure for dispensing the tokens (Ayllon & McKittrick, 1982). Unless these decisions are made *before* the token system is started, failure is likely.

Specifying Behaviors

Before setting up a token economy system, the behaviors to be increased or decreased by the system must be precisely defined. Without precise behavioral definitions, the classroom staff is apt to carry out different programs for different sets of behaviors. The effectiveness of a token economy depends on consistently applying token reinforcers for a well-defined set of behaviors.

Token economy systems are effective at both increasing and decreasing sets of classroom behaviors. The behaviors that teachers generally want to increase are academic performance, social interaction skills, and appropriate classroom behaviors such as paying attention or doing what the teacher asks. Teachers generally want to diminish nonworking behaviors, such as day-dreaming or failing to complete academic assignments, and disruptive behaviors, such as talking out, noncompliance, or bothering other children. A good token economy builds more behaviors than it tries to reduce. Token economies should be primarily positive and should improve students' skill levels instead of simply reducing inappropriate behaviors.

The process of defining token economy behaviors should include the following steps:

1. The behaviors should be specifically defined so that a teacher has an objective criterion to determine whether the behavior has occurred. The behaviors should be observable, leave a permanent product (such as completed academic assignments), and be measurable.
2. The behaviors should be defined so that the children can understand the definitions. In too many instances, the definitions are written in adult terms.
3. There should be more appropriate behaviors to be increased than inappropriate behaviors to be decreased. The token economy system should be primarily positive and skill building.
4. There should be no more than ten behaviors defined for a classroom token economy. If the number exceeds ten, it becomes too difficult to track and reinforce the behaviors.
5. The specific amounts or criteria should be defined for some token economy behaviors—for example, 90 percent correct on an academic assignment or 10 minutes attending to an academic task.
6. The behaviors should be publicly posted in the classroom so that children can read and understand what is expected of them. If the behaviors change, then the changes should be discussed by the class.

Here is a sample list of simple token economy behaviors to be posted in a classroom:

How to Earn Tokens During Seat Work

1. Complete your seat work with 80 percent correct (increase).
2. Do not touch your neighbors or their things (decrease).
3. Stay in your seat during work periods (increase).
4. Raise your hand before talking (increase).

Backup Reinforcer Selection

Tokens maintain and acquire their reinforcing value because they can be exchanged for items, activities, or privileges, called *backup reinforcers,* which are intrinsically reinforcing. The most effective token economies use a wide variety of backup reinforcers that are periodically changed and updated. This helps ensure that there is always something reinforcing available for each child. (Chapter 3 discusses the selection of reinforcers; these procedures should be used in developing a variety of backup reinforcers.)

It is important to involve the students in the selection of the backup reinforcers. They can compile lists of reinforcers and rank what they want to earn. It is also a good idea to allow them to sample some of the reinforcers prior to making up a list; they can have a day, for example, when they sample some of the edible reinforcers and play some of the games.

Most effective token economies provide a wide range of reinforcers of varying types and "prices." Ideally, some small items that most children can earn within a day should be included along with larger reinforcers that may be earned only infrequently and after the child has saved for them. The backup reinforcers should also include a variety of types, such as material reinforcers (small toys), edible reinforcers (small candies, fruit), and activity reinforcers (free time, games with a friend, drinks of water from the principal's water cooler). The material and edible reinforcers can be kept in a "classroom store" along with a menu of reinforcers and their costs. Teachers should realize that the costs for reinforcers can easily get out of hand. Creativity in selecting low-cost but highly attractive reinforcers is important. For example, "junk" from the classroom staff's garages or attics can be used. Some items are surprisingly valued by children; one teacher sold the overabundance of zucchini from her garden in a token economy.

Backup Reinforcer Cost

The number of tokens required to earn backup reinforcers must also be determined. There is no hard-and-fast rule to follow in determining the price to charge for backup reinforcers. Some small reinforcers should be priced so that the typical child can earn some each day. Larger activities, privileges, or goods should require larger numbers of tokens, so a child can earn them only by saving his tokens or points over a period of time. This may require a "classroom bank" and some minor record keeping for the teacher. The "bank" can be a large-sized list of the students' names, covered by a plastic sheet that can be written on with a washable marker and then erased as the total of token points change for each child (see Figure 6–1). Publicly posting the bank amounts provides feedback to the students about how well they are doing with the token economy and fosters competition to earn more points for appropriate behavior.

Pricing of the backup reinforcers is important. If they cost too little, children will be able to earn many reinforcers in a short period of time and motivation will be reduced. If the backups are too expensive compared to the number of tokens a child can earn, then reinforcement will be insufficient to maintain behavior. When first deciding on the cost of an item in the classroom store, the actual cost of the item should be equated with a number

Reinforcer Classroom store	Point cost
1. 10 minutes extra free time	100
2. Snack	150
3. Teacher's helper	75
4. First in line	50
5. Choice of games	50
6. Work with a friend	150
7. Mystery grab bag	75
8. Small toy	300
9. Recess monitor	20
10. Wear a hat in class	30

Classroom Bank—Points Saved 200 Points Possible Each Day

Name	Mon	Tue	Wed	Thur	Fri	Total for Week
Charlie	150	90	20	150	75	**485**
Marty	200	100	75	200	150	**725**
Sue	150	75	25	200	0	**450**

FIGURE 6-1   Classroom Store and Bank

of classroom tokens. For example, the exchange rate can be set at 5 tokens for each cent that an item actually costs (that is, a small toy that costs 25 cents would equal 125 tokens). Time for an activity or privilege reinforcer should be computed on an hourly basis. The exchange rate might be 10 tokens for 5 minutes of a game or free time. These rates are established on the basis of how many tokens a student earns on the average each day. For example, the costs just listed would be reasonable for students who earn on the average of 50 tokens a day. This is only a starting point, however, and the actual classroom demand for individual backup reinforcers should set their price in tokens. A teacher should not be afraid to change the token economy prices.

Choosing the Tokens

A variety of tokens can be used with children. There are physical items such as poker chips, marbles, beans, play money, buttons, beads, or washers. Physical items are better for use with younger children because they like to have "things" they can collect or earn. The teacher must be careful, however, that the tokens are not swallowed or stuck up an ear or nose. One teacher had a student who put a small token economy bean up her nose. Fortunately, the student sneezed just as the teacher closed the student's unblocked nostril and the bean came flying out. Small containers (baby food jars, boxes, or bags) can be used for storing the tokens. If children play with tokens while they should be working, they should lose the tokens.

Written points, stamps, or marks made by the teacher on a paper card are easily dispensed tokens. These marks are generally made on a small card that is divided into a number of squares. If a child earns a point for an appropriate behavior, the teacher marks the number of points on the card and initials it (see Figure 6-2). To prevent children from marking their own cards,

FIGURE 6-2   A classroom point card with points assigned around the edge of the card.

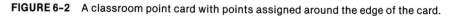

Home −6	+5	+5	+10	−5	+10				

Blue

Name _____ Date _____

Chart moves

Homework . . . . (yes)   no
Reading . . . . (yes)   no
Math . . . . (yes)   no
Spelling . . . . (yes)   no
Comprehension . . . . yes   (no)
Language . . . . (yes)   no

yes   no

Left edge (top to bottom): +10, +10, +10, +10, +10, −5

Right edge (top to bottom): +10, +10, +5, +5, +5, +5, −5

Lunch −7	+10	+10	+10					Recess −16

Warm fuzzie tries	Contracts	Warnings	Missed points		
		NPA	NPA −5	OS	
+ 10	1. _____		NFD	TO	
	2. _____	NFD	NFD −5		
Recess: +45		TO	Hands −5	Theft	
Lunch: +30			PA	TOS	

a specially colored pen that only the teacher is allowed to have can be used for marking. The cards can be gathered at the end of the day and used as a data source. The marks that a child has earned or lost can be used to assess her progress in the program.

Dispensing Tokens

Once behaviors are specified, tokens decided upon, and backup reinforcers selected, the teacher must decide on some system for delivering tokens. The type of dispensing system will depend on (1) the number of children to whom tokens must be given, (2) the age of the children, (3) the length of the day over which the tokens must be dispensed, and (4) the behaviors that are to be reinforced with tokens.

Most young children like physical tokens that can be collected and saved in a container. The teacher can circulate around the class and put tokens into the children's containers for appropriate behaviors. It is preferable for the teacher to place the tokens into the container, rather than giving them directly to the child. Handing the tokens to the child can be distracting or may encourage the child to play with the tokens. A child who wants to be involved in the token-dispensing process can hold the container while the teacher places the token into it.

The disadvantage of physical tokens is that they must be carried by the teacher, which can be a chore if the teacher must carry them throughout the school day. In addition, they may be stolen if they are left around the classroom. In most circumstances, it is best to dispense the tokens to small work groups—to reading groups or during table work, for example. The teacher can simply bring the token container to a small work group instead of carrying it for the entire day. Marks on paper are the easiest way to dispense token points because the teacher has to carry only a pen. When appropriate behavior occurs, the teacher takes a token economy card, marks it with the appropriate number of points, and initials the number. Counting the tokens that each child has earned at the end of the session gives them feedback about their performance in that particular group.

Tokens should be dispensed quickly and unobtrusively, unless the teacher is attempting to provide a model for other children to observe. The teacher should "slip" tokens quickly into a child's token container or mark a point on a card on the child's desk. The teacher should quietly socially reinforce the child when the token is dispensed and then move on to the next child.

Speed in delivery of tokens is important for at least three reasons: (1) The behavior that is reinforced is most likely to be the one that occurs immediately before the token delivery, so the teacher will want to reinforce the target behavior before anything else can happen. (2) Too much time spent delivering tokens will reduce the amount of time the teacher can spend instructing and reinforcing. (3) The children will be less distracted from their tasks when reinforcement is delivered quickly.

Speed of token delivery is not a reason to neglect to pair the token with a social reinforcement such as a smile, a comment on the good work, or a touch on the shoulder. Dispensing tokens without this social reinforcement is mechanical. However, socially reinforcing students without taking them off task is an art that must be practiced. When the teacher's social response is paired with the token, the teacher's comments are enhanced by the tokens and the token system's motivational properties are improved by the teacher's social response.

Delivering Intermittent Token Reinforcement

Ideally, when a target behavior is first being learned or acquired, reinforcement should be delivered after each occurrence of the behavior. This continuous reinforcement is the most effective strategy for quickly accelerating a new behavior. Once a behavior has been acquired, however, continuous reinforcement is very ineffective for maintaining it. The schedule of reinforcement must gradually shift from continuous to intermittent. If the shift occurs too abruptly, the student is likely to refuse to work. With a younger child, for example, a shift may occur from a token for each correct response (continuous reinforcement) to a token for every other response (fixed ratio 2), then randomly on average for every 3 responses (variable ratio 3), and finally, randomly on average for every 5 responses (variable ratio 5).

There are several methods for programming intermittent token reinforcement that are practical and maintain a clear relationship between appropriate behavior and token reinforcement. One method is to write each student's name on an index card and turn the cards over at periodic intervals (1 to 5 minutes). If the student whose name is on the card is working, he is reinforced. The card is then randomly replaced in the deck. Another variation of intermittent reinforcement delivery is to set an egg timer at random intervals. When the bell rings, the teacher scans the class and gives points to the students who are behaving appropriately. After the bell has rung, the teacher randomly resets it at an interval unknown to the students. Alternatively, reinforcement beeps can be randomly placed on a cassette tape and played in class. An intermittent reinforcement approach using a "secret agent" invisible-ink pen and "chartmoves" is described in the EXAMPLE.

Rules and Implementation

The rules for earning tokens and the specific behaviors for which tokens can be earned should be posted in the classroom. The rules and behaviors should be printed in large letters and displayed prominently. The rules and behaviors should be explained to the students in a "training session," during which the students role play appropriate behaviors and receive tokens that are then exchanged for backup reinforcers. A series of examples and nonexamples of the behaviors and rules for earning tokens can be used. This training session can also be used to determine whether all members of the classroom staff can correctly implement the program.

EXAMPLE

The use of "chartmoves" and the "special agent" pen is a unique token economy system for improving homework compliance (Malyn & Jenson, 1986). With this token system, a student draws a picture of a favorite object, such as a rocket (see Figure 6–3). The rocket is then made into a dot-to-dot chart with approximately 150 small dots.

A secret agent pen is used to put invisible-ink reinforcement dots (approximately 30 to 50) randomly on some of the regular dots. A secret agent pen, which can be purchased at most novelty shops, is filled with invisible ink on one end; on the other end is an ink that will make the invisible ink visible when it is touched. When a student brings a completed homework assignment to class, the teacher allows him to take a "chartmove," which involves connecting two of the dots in the picture and touching the last connected dot with the special agent pen. If this dot has been treated with invisible ink, it will show up, and the child is permitted to choose a backup reinforcer.

Exercises

1. What determines the intermittent schedule of reinforcement in this example?
2. What are the tokens?
3. What are the specific behaviors?

Feedback

1. The intermittent schedule of reinforcement is based on the random invisible dots.
2. Tokens are the chartmoves.
3. The specific behavior in this example is completion of homework assignments.

MAXIMIZING THE EFFECTIVENESS OF A TOKEN ECONOMY

Once the token economy has been designed and begun, there are a number of simple procedures that can enhance its effectiveness as a reinforcement system (Kazdin, 1982). The following steps can be used to improve the effectiveness of a classroom token economy:

1. Vary the magnitude of reinforcement. This simple procedure involves assigning differing values to the backup reinforcers. Those reinforcers that are not greatly valued should cost less than highly valued reinforcers. This range in value improves children's responsiveness to a token economy, particularly if there are special items for which to work.

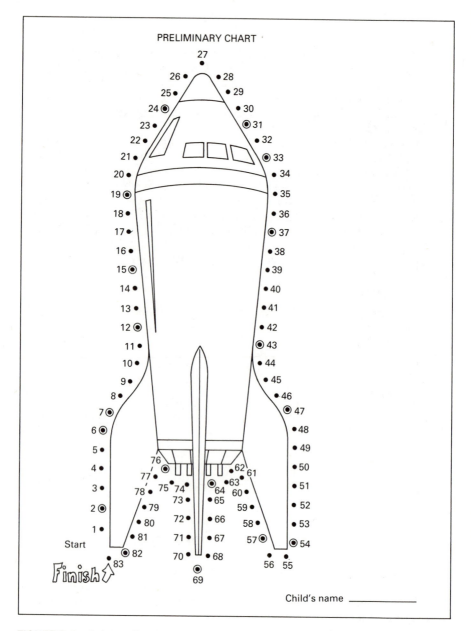

PRELIMINARY CHART

FIGURE 6-3   A dot-to-dot chart with reinforcer and nonreinforcer dots exposed.

   2. Allow reinforcer sampling.   With reinforcer sampling, a student is allowed to sample some of the backup reinforcers noncontingently—without having to pay. For example, a student might be allowed to eat a few of the edible reinforcers from the store or engage in a special activity for a few minutes. This procedure enhances children's motivation to earn the tokens to purchase more of the backup reinforcers that have been sampled.

3. Permit peers to share the backup reinforcers.   Allowing peers to share the earned backup reinforcers helps to improve children's motivation to earn reinforcers. The child whose reinforcers are shared is encouraged by other children in the classroom to perform and earn tokens. This procedure is a form of group contingency.

4. Use a peer management system.   Using peers in the classroom to help dispense tokens, administer backup reinforcers, and withdraw tokens can improve children's motivation to earn tokens. A peer management system involves the entire class in the token economy. In fact, the privilege to help operate the classroom token economy can be a backup reinforcer that children have to buy.

5. Pair tokens with a social response.   It is important to pair the dispensing of a token with a positive comment from a teacher or a peer. This social pairing amplifies the value of the tokens and at the same time enhances the value of positive comments from the teacher. Dispensing a token unaccompanied by positive feedback is clearly inappropriate.

6. Combine a token system with a classroom level system.   A level system is a multistep management system in which each step signifies a number of target behaviors that a child must master. After the child has mastered the behavior on one step, she progresses to the next step, which generally comprises more complex or challenging target behaviors. Figure 6–4 shows a simple three-step system in which a child must master the behaviors listed under each step. A token economy can be used with a level system so that (1) a child earns tokens for the specific behaviors listed under each step, (2) when a child earns enough tokens, she can spend them to go on to the next step, and (3) the backup reinforcers are more valued on each of the higher steps. The combination of a level system and token economy system should be viewed by the teacher as a formalized shaping system which helps students through the program by enabling them to successfully master simple classroom behaviors (first step), then intermediate behaviors (second step), and finally complex behaviors (third step). When a child has effectively mastered all of the steps in a level system, he can be faded off the level system and the token economy.

7. Combine a token economy with a group contingency.   Combining a token reinforcement system with a group contingency is one of the most powerful behavior management techniques that a teacher can implement with the least investment of teacher time (see Chapter 7). With a token–group contingency, the entire group's performance determines whether each individual in that group will earn a token. For example, the teacher sets a

```
┌─────────────────────────────────────────────────────────────┐
│                                    Level 3                    │
│                                    Use polite language        │
│                                    Contribute                 │
│                                    Help others                │
│                                                               │
│                       Level 2                                 │
│                       Follow directions                       │
│                       Pay attention                           │
│                       Do all assignments                      │
│                                                               │
│        Level 1                                                │
│        Stay in seat                                           │
│        Hands to self                                          │
│        Work independently                                     │
│        No talk outs                                           │
└─────────────────────────────────────────────────────────────┘
```

FIGURE 6-4   Example of a Classroom Level System.

kitchen timer and when it goes off, he scans the classroom. If one child is off task, then the whole class misses their tokens. An even more effective approach is to split the classroom into teams or rows, which are treated as groups. When the teacher gets the signal (a random beep or ring) to scan the classroom, he scans each team or row to see whether every child is working. If so, each child on the team or row receives a token reinforcer; if not, no one on the team or row receives a reinforcer. Research has shown that using teams improves the performance of a classroom over that obtained when the whole classroom is treated as a group in a group contingency (Harris & Sherman, 1973). It appears that the use of teams fosters competition. A program developed by Erken and Hendersen (1976), the *Practice Skills Mastery Program*, combines all of the elements of classroom token–group contingency with preprogrammed random beeps on cassette tapes.

The effectiveness of a combined token–group contingency approach has been well established in the research literature (Barrish, Saunders, & Wolf, 1969; Greenwood, Hops, Delquadri, & Guild, 1974; Hendersen, Erken, & Jenson, in press). However, a number of precautions should be taken to ensure (1) that all the children in a group can meet the requirement for reinforcement and (2) that there is not a "spoiler" in the group who enjoys ruining the chances of reinforcement for other children. A full description of how to set up a group contingency and the precautions to be observed are provided in Chapter 7.

8. Combine response-cost and tokens.   To this point, we have talked about a token reinforcement system only as a paying reinforcement system. But token economies can also be used in combination with mild punishment systems in which earned points are lost for inappropriate behaviors. This punishment system, response-cost, involves taking a predetermined number of token economy points away for previously defined inappropriate behavior. It is similar to being fined for a traffic violation. The most important aspect of response cost procedures is that the behaviors to be punished must have been previously defined. The rule should be "no surprises." The number of token points to be taken away should also be predetermined so that the child is not overly punished when the teacher is angry. The actual number of points to be lost should depend on the severity of the inappropriate behavior. For example, if a child in the classroom earns approximately ten points per hour, then the most severe behaviors, such as aggression or swearing, should cost ten points. Lesser inappropriate behaviors, such as being off task or talking with a neighbor, might cost three tokens.

When points are subtracted for inappropriate behaviors, the child should be informed of the behavior, and the points should be subtracted in an unemotional way. A child who is angry may, if given the opportunity, try to persuade the teacher not to take away the points. When this happens, the procedure's effectiveness is reduced and the entire class can be disrupted. Do not interact with the child verbally or physically about the point loss. If a child will not give up the actual tokens or the point card so that a subtraction can be made, then points can be taken from the child's token bank. Indicate to the child that an additional "five points" will be taken away for not following the direction to hand over the point card or tokens, and take them later from the classroom bank.

Unfortunately, response-cost systems can turn a positive token economy into a negative token economy when a child goes "into the hole" by owing more tokens than he has earned. If a child has a deficit (below zero points) in the bank and has to earn more points just to get back to being even, his motivation will be destroyed. If a child has lost all of the banked token points, switch to another technique, such as time-out, to provide a consequence for negative behavior, instead of letting a child go into point debt.

EXAMPLE

Ms. Jones's classroom token economy does not seem as effective as it once was. The children have lost interest in the backup reinforcers, and the target behaviors no longer appear to be controlled by the tokens. In fact, there is now a small group of disruptive children who seem intent on disturbing the rest of the class. Nothing seems to work, and Ms. Jones has started to take tokens away in a response-cost program.

Exercises

1. List five ideas for revitalizing Ms. Jones's classroom token economy.

Feedback

1. She should change and vary the magnitude of the backup reinforcers and allow a free reinforcement sampling day.
2. She could use a peer management system to help manage the token system, and allow the better-behaved children to assist as a privilege.
3. She should make sure that she is socially positive in dispensing the tokens.
4. She should make sure that her response-cost program is not too severe.
5. She could use a group contingency program in conjunction with the token economy to help handle the small group of disruptive children.

TROUBLESHOOTING A TOKEN ECONOMY

As with any behavior management procedure used in the classroom, problems can occur with a token economy. However, the complexity of token systems makes them vulnerable to special problems. In addition, token economies require a significant amount of effort to design and implement. Teachers cannot become so invested in a token economy that they resist changing the system if problems do occur. Some of these problems follow.

Duplication and Theft of Tokens

As with any valued medium of exchange, counterfeiting and theft will occur with tokens or points if the system is not closely monitored. Standardized tokens, such as poker chips, printed play money, or beans, are generally difficult to duplicate but easy to steal. Most duplication occurs when points are written on a token economy card. It is a relatively simple task for a child to write his own points on the card and claim they were given by the teacher.

A number of methods can be used to stop point duplications. The teacher can initial a card each time points are given; it is more difficult for children to copy a teacher's initials. Or, the teacher can carry a specially colored pen to assign points and not permit the students to have a similarly colored pen. Alternatively, points can be assigned with a unique rubber stamp.

If point duplication or theft of tokens occurs, an appropriate response-cost consequence should be instituted. A consequence for theft of tokens might require that a child pay double the amount of the tokens back. For duplication of points, a child might have the card taken away for half a day and not be allowed to earn points for this period.

Inflation, Depression, and Hoarding

Inflation and depression in a token economy are signs that the rules for earning tokens and the cost of backup reinforcers are inaccurately set. *Inflation* means that the cost of buying a backup reinforcer slowly increases, particularly the costs of the more valued backup reinforcers. For example, students may continue to buy out a valued small toy or candy item as soon as it is replaced. After the children buy out the valued reinforcers, they complain or simply save their tokens until more expensive reinforcers are put in the store. As a reaction, the teacher raises the price of the valued reinforcer. Token inflation suggests that the contingencies for earning tokens are too lenient and that children have too many tokens to buy reinforcers. The teacher should reexamine and adjust the contingencies for earning the tokens instead of raising prices in the classroom store (as happens in our society).

Token *depression* is the opposite of token inflation. With depression, the contingencies are too high and the children earn so few tokens that many of the backup reinforcers cannot be purchased. The danger of token depression is that it can eliminate students' motivation to behave and work. The teacher should make sure the number of tokens earned is reasonable and that some of the students are capable of buying the most prized backup reinforcers by saving. To improve a depression situation, the teacher can design token bonuses for work on specific projects, such as 100 percent of homework handed in by the end of the week. These special *token behavioral contracts*, which allow students to earn a relatively large number of tokens for a specific task, help reduce token depression.

Some children *hoard* tokens for no apparent reason. In most situations, saving is a valued behavior; if too many tokens are saved, however, it can disrupt a token economy. Children with large hoards of tokens may feel that they do not have to work, or they may buy all of the prized backup reinforcers in one day. Procedures to reduce hoarding include placing expiration dates on the tokens or having a classroom store sale or auction.

The auction option is a particularly enjoyable one. The rules for an auction are that (1) all savings are dropped to zero the day after the auction, (2) students bid against each other for backup reinforcers, and (3) students cannot lend each other points for the auction. The classroom staff can bring in "junk" from their attics and basements and sell these prized pieces to the highest bidder at the end of the day. It is interesting to note what children buy at auctions. One teacher watched an old ski being sold for 5,000 points after hard bidding between children. A schizophrenic girl bought the ski for the points that she had hoarded for almost two weeks and walked home with it on a fine spring day.

The Unresponsive Child

Some children just do not seem to be affected by a token economy. They indicate that they do not want to participate, and they reject an opportunity to earn tokens or points. Several steps can be taken to encourage a child to participate in a token economy. First, allow the child to hold back for a week or so and watch other children participate. The child's nonparticipation should be ignored because a great deal of teacher attention for nonparticipation may be reinforcing for the child. Simply let the child not earn tokens and thus be unable to buy reinforcers from the store when other children buy them. Second, after a week or two, the child should be primed. *Priming* means that the child should be allowed to have a free day when she is given a number of tokens noncontingently so she can sample the backup reinforcers. The day after priming, the teacher should make it easy for the child to earn a few tokens and then slowly increase the requirement for earning tokens. Third, if ignoring and priming do not work, a group contingency (see Chapter 7) may be needed. In that situation, if the child agrees to earn some tokens and participate, then the whole class will earn bonus points that could be used for a party at the end of the day.

Legal Problems and Token Economies

Legal difficulties that arise from the use of token economies generally involve two basic issues: (1) being required to participate and (2) being stripped of basic necessities (Myers & Jenson, 1985). The right to participate in a token economy should be given by the child's parent after the system has been explained to them. The teacher should be careful to describe the advantages of the system, the rules for earning points, what a child can purchase, and what privileges can be taken away. If a parent gives the teacher permission for a child to participate and the child refuses, then the previously listed procedures for an unresponsive child should be used. If a parent refuses to give permission for a child to participate, then the system should either be modified to meet the parent's objections or not be used.

The second area of difficulty comes from withholding basic privileges and rights until they are earned in a token economy (Greenberg & Meaghers, 1977; Martin, 1975; *Clone* v. *Richardson*, 1974; Schwitzgebel & Schwitzgebel, 1980; Wexler, 1973; *Wyatt* v. *Stickney*, 1974). Basic necessities, such as access to lunch, water, the bathroom, or the use of their own clothes, should not be withheld from children through a token system. However, these activities may be regulated so they are not abused. For example, having a child eat lunch in the classroom or giving a reasonable number of drinks of water and trips to the bathroom instead of free access are activities that all teachers control. It would be inappropriate, however, to have children earn their lunches, access to water, or the opportunity to go to the bathroom. In addition to basic rights, children should not lose so many points that they are not able to earn basic classroom privileges and the social company of other children for extended periods of time.

EXAMPLE

Tony is an unresponsive child who does not care much about the token system or about doing well in the classroom. In fact, he makes a show of not caring.

Exercises

1. What can the teacher do to motivate Tony to participate in the token system?
2. What safeguards should the teacher take in order not to violate Tony's rights as a student?

Feedback

1. The following steps should be used to motivate Tony:
   a. He should be allowed to hold back for a week or so and watch others participate.
   b. His show of nonparticipation should be ignored.
   c. After a week or so, he should be primed—given tokens noncontingently so he can earn reinforcers.
   d. If he still does not participate, a group contingency should be considered.
2. In order not to violate Tony's rights, the teacher should take care in allowing him access to lunch, water, the bathroom, and use of his own clothes. If a response-cost system has been used with Tony, care should be taken so that he does not "go into the hole" and be unable to buy basic classroom privileges or the social company of other children for an extended period of time.

GETTING OFF OF A TOKEN ECONOMY

Token economies are artificial and should be faded out as soon as a student is capable of maintaining target behaviors through natural classroom reinforcement. Teachers should be particularly concerned with overcontrolling a classroom by keeping all of the students on a token economy when it is no longer needed. A student should be given the opportunity to get off the token system by maintaining a standard of appropriate classroom behavior and academic performance. We have already discussed the use of a classroom level system to help shape classroom behavior and eventually fade a token system. Two other procedures that can be used to fade a token system include the following:

1. "Earning Off" a Token System

This system requires a child to earn his way off a token system by earning a minimum number of regular tokens that he can spend for the backup reinforcers in the classroom store. In addition, each day the child earns the minimum number of points, he is also given special "earn-off" bonus points that can be spent only for getting off the token system. When a child has earned enough special points, he is off the token system. For example, a child might have the minimum number set at 100 regular tokens a day. Each day the child earns 100 or more regular points, she is given 20 earn-off bonus tokens that are recorded and saved. When the child has 1,000 earn-off tokens, she is off the token system. This system ensures that a child must have at least 50 days (20 earn-off tokens ÷ 1,000 cost to be off token system = 50 days) on which her behavior was good enough to earn the minimum number of 100 points. It is important that the child be allowed to spend regularly earned points for backup reinforcers and not have to save them to earn his way off the token system. Only the special earn-off points can be used to get off the token system.

Having a child earn off a token system has only one major problem: Many children do not want to get off the token system because it is simply too reinforcing. This problem can be managed in two ways. First, incentive to get off the system can be provided by giving a special bonus or prize to each child who "graduates" from the token economy. Second, children who are off the system should be given noncontingent access (as long as they reasonably maintain their behavior) to some of the backup reinforcers that children on the token system have to purchase and also to special privileges that children on the token system are not allowed to buy.

Having a student earn himself off a token system is an effective procedure for weaning students from a highly structured token economy. There is also evidence that the earning-off procedure actually increases the effectiveness of a token economy (Kazdin & Mascitelli, 1980).

2. Self-Monitoring and Fading a Token System

Having a child rate her own behavior on a token economy card and match it to the perceptions of a teacher is a powerful technique to fade a child from a token economy system. With this technique, a child rates her own behavior for the behaviors listed on a token economy card. The teacher also rates the child, and at the end of the day a comparison is made between the child's and the teacher's ratings. If there is a close match, then the child gets the points. If there is not a close match, the child loses the points.

This procedure has been particularly useful in generalizing a child from one setting to another. The researchers in one study (Rhode, Morgan, & Young, 1983) used a random matching procedure to generalize behaviorally disordered children on a token economy system from a resource room to a regular classroom using random (unpredictable) matches. The children monitored their own behavior in the regular classroom and marked their points for following the classroom rules and doing the academic assignments. Without their knowledge, the regular classroom teacher also monitored the children's behavior while they were in the classroom. Surprise matches were made back in the resource room, where the children's recorded points were matched to the regular-classroom teacher's recorded points. If there was a 90 percent correspondence between the teacher's and the child's recording, the children got the points; if not, the children lost the points.

The random matchings between the teachers and the children had a number of advantages. First, it maintained control of the children's behavior in a regular-education setting with little effort from the teacher. In the study by Rhode and colleagues, the matches were faded to only once a week, with the children behaving appropriately in the classroom at least 80 percent of the time. Next, this procedure was used to fade the children off the token economy. Gradually, the children were told only to record their behavior and that they would no longer get token points that could be exchanged for backup reinforcers. Then the students were told to privately evaluate their behavior and work without the use of a card or points. With this last condition, the appropriate behaviors continued in the regular classroom without the need for the token economy.

EXAMPLE

Ms. Jones has a difficult student who has responded very well to the classroom token economy. In fact, the child has responded *too* well and refuses to be faded off the system.

Exercise

1. What systematic steps can be taken to get the child off the token economy yet maintain behavioral and academic gains in the classroom?

Feedback

1. a) The teacher could increase the price of backup reinforcers and slowly reduce the number of points this child earns.
   b) The teacher could implement a classroom level system under which the child is systematically shaped off the token economy.
   c) The teacher could have the child earn herself off the token system, with a bonus when she is off. The bonus could include having the child (1) get free access to the reinforcers as long as she maintained her behavior and (2) she could become a teacher helper to assist in running the token economy.
   d) The teacher could use a random matching of the teacher's rating of the child's performance program and slowly fade out the random matches. This approach could also be combined with a bonus when the child is off the token system.

FAST TRACK

REVIEW

A *token economy* is a behavior management system which uses some medium of exchange to reinforce specific target behaviors. The basic token reinforcement system requires at least three basic parts: (1) tokens to be dispensed, (2) rules for earning tokens, and (3) backup reinforcers. Token economies are particularly useful for managing disruptive classrooms, for getting better results from children who are making poor academic progress, and for motivating children who are disinterested in their classroom work. However, token systems should not be used to overcontrol a classroom or increase sitting, docile, or quiet behavior in a boring or unstimulating classroom.

The basic steps to setting up a token economy require that behaviors are specified, backup reinforcers selected, reinforcer costs established, tokens selected, and procedures for dispensing tokens chosen. The behaviors to be specified must be precisely defined, observable, and measurable. Selection of backup reinforcers should involve the students, and they should be allowed to have a day to sample the reinforcers. The costs of the reinforcers should be established so that they are not too expensive but cost enough to motivate the children. For younger children, tokens can be physical items such as poker chips, buttons, or beads. For older children, paper cards are preferable. Tokens should be dispensed quickly and unobtrusively, but with a pairing of a social reinforcer from the teaching staff. Intermittent schedules of reinforcement work best for maintaining classroom behaviors.

The effectiveness of token economies can be maximized by varying the magnitude of the backup reinforcers, allowing reinforcer sampling, permitting peers to share the backup reinforcers, using a peer management system, pairing tokens with social responses from the teacher, combining the token system with a classroom level system, or combining the token system with a group contingency. A response-cost procedure can also be added to a token economy, but children should not be allowed to go into debt or be overly punished. Troubles develop with token economies when tokens are duplicated or stolen, inflation occurs, a token depression occurs, or children hoard the tokens. Children who are unresponsive to the token system can be particularly difficult and can be handled by allowing them to observe the token system and not participate for a week or so, giving them some tokens and letting them sample the backup reinforcers, or developing a group contingency for them. A teacher must be careful, however, in withholding basic classroom privileges and making a child earn them on a token system. For example, items such as access to lunch, water, the use of a bathroom, or the use of a child's own clothes should not be used as backup reinforcers in a token economy.

Fading a child off a token economy can be a problem, particularly if the child prefers the system. A classroom level system can be used to fade a child from a token system. Or, children can earn their way off the system with a bonus when they are off the token economy. Children can also be faded off a token system by using random matches of the teacher's rating of their behavioral and academic performance with their ratings. This is an excellent method to combine fading with a generalization of the effects of a token economy.

CUMULATIVE EXERCISE

You have a classroom of thirty regular-education sixth-grade students who have a history of being disruptive and poorly academically motivated. Other behavior management programs have failed in the past, and a token economy is needed. Design the steps for implementing a token system.

Feedback

Your design should include the following features:

1. Selection and specification of target behaviors that are observable and measurable.
2. Selection of backup reinforcers that the children help select. A day of reinforcement sampling is a good way to get started, and the magnitude of the reinforcers should be varied. The costs of the reinforcers must also be determined.
3. Selection of the tokens—probably paper point cards for this age level.
4. Design of a system of rules for earning and dispensing tokens. These rules should be posted in the classroom and a meeting held to explain the rules.
5. Design of a classroom bank.
6. A classroom level system that interfaces with the token economy.
7. A plan to deal with the difficulties of inflation, depression, hoarding, and the unresponsive child.
8. A plan to fade children off the token system.

SEVEN

Contingency Contracting and Behavioral Self-Management

OBJECTIVE

After completing this chapter, you will be able to use contingency contracts to help students improve their academic performance and social behavior and teach them to manage their own behavior. To do this, you will learn to

1. Develop, implement, and evaluate a contingency contract with elementary or secondary students.
2. Define behavioral self-management and develop student-written contracts to help students acquire self-management skills.

WHAT IS CONTINGENCY CONTRACTING?

Previous chapters have outlined some general aspects of behavior analysis that may be applied in the classroom to improve students' academic progress and social behavior. The basic principles include specification of desired target behaviors; identification and application of positively reinforcing consequences; the use of shaping, instructions, or prompting; and a program for consistently and systematically applying these procedures. One such program is the use of contingency contracting.

A **contingency contract,** as used in education, is a written document in which a teacher and student agree that when a student satisfactorily completes a stated amount of an objectively defined academic or social behavior, he will be able to engage in a stated amount of some privilege, preferred activity, or other reinforcer. Figure 7–1 is a sample contract between a student and a teacher. Using task cards, the teacher specified the work to be

FIGURE 7-1 A sample contract. Konio was a 14-year-old junior high school student. Each day at the start of class, his history teacher handed out "task cards" to each class member. (A task card is a minicontract specifying the requirements and reinforcers for a specific task or assignment. It usually interprets the daily requirement to meet some more general and more encompassing contingency contract.) On Tuesday morning, Konio received this task card.

Daily Contract

Date   Tuesday, November 10

Read   Unit 8 (pages 123–126 of history text).

Complete   the dittoed Unit 8 progress check.

If passed   (8 or more correct), take 5 minutes free time in back of room, then get new task card.

If failed   (7 or less correct), see teacher for remedial unit.

_____
Teacher

_____
Student

---

completed and the reinforcer (5 minutes of free time) that the student could earn.

When is Contracting Useful?

Contracts, of course, are not only used in education, but continually influence adult activities. There are marriage contracts, rental contracts, contracts to buy and sell a home, contracts to make time payments, to work, and to buy a car. Contracts encourage accountability by specifying in writing the expectations for all involved parties. Familiarizing students with contracts while they are in school is good preparation for the future.

The use of contingency contracts in education has been diverse. Contracts have assisted in improving the reading, spelling, math, and handwriting performance of elementary students. Disruptive and aggressive behaviors have been eliminated and positive social behavior increased. High school students have been motivated to complete homework assignments via contracts. Contracts have been used in elementary and secondary schools, special-education programs, correctional institutions, and at home. Counselors use contracts to improve school attendance. Psychologists and behavior therapists contract with adults to decrease smoking, to assist weight loss, to improve social skills, and to resolve marital conflict.

For teachers, contracts provide an excellent procedure for meeting the needs of individual students who may be struggling academically, off task or disruptive in class, or unmotivated. Contracts may be part of a class-wide program to individualize curricula.

An example of the use of contingency contracting with an extremely hostile group of junior high school– and high school–age students who were uninterested in academics has been reported by Cannon and colleagues (1971). In a program for institutionalized male juvenile delinquents, contingency contracting was used to increase academic performance in programmed reading. The class average increased from two pages completed per day before contracting to six pages per day during contracting. The contracts used points exchangeable in a dormitory store for various goods as reinforcers. Using money as a reinforcer, J. Moffat (1972) obtained similar results with college students for increases in time spent studying; S. Moffat (1972) had corresponding success with college students using daily activities as reinforcers. White-Blackburn, Semb, and Semb (1977) found that contracts for on-task behavior (time spent at work) reduced disruption and increased assignment completion with disruptive sixth graders; improvements were noted in all areas, including grades. Regular class activities and privileges were used as reinforcers. While contracts were in effect, the problem students compared favorably with the top-performing students chosen as models.

Contracts may also aid in the transition from teacher management systems to student self-management. By teaching students to develop their own contracts, teachers can help students learn to use such procedures as self-recording, self-evaluation, and self-reinforcement to manage their own academic and social behavior.

CONTINGENCY CONTRACTS

When used to greatest advantage, the contracting procedure is closely attuned to the student's knowledge, special abilities, and personal characteristics. The teacher and the individual student together make decisions and set standards—what behavior needs to be changed, how much work must be completed, the criteria for accuracy, what the reinforcement is to be—based on information about that particular student. Students who are involved in the development of the contract can negotiate changes with the teacher if they feel that the contract is inappropriate. Similarly, the teacher has an opportunity to describe to the student in advance the work that will be required, the standards, the reinforcement, and the rationale for the work and the specific contingencies. This advance notification of what is required, combined with the opportunity to negotiate changes, appears to increase students' cooperation.

The contracting procedure seems to students to be an "adult" procedure because, unlike some traditional classroom approaches that may make older students feel that they are being treated as "children," it is a two-way process. Contracting is particularly beneficial whenever it is necessary to motivate students, particularly if the students tend to be uncooperative, rebellious, or antagonistic (Lovitt, 1973; Lovitt & Curtiss, 1969; Fixsen, Phillips, & Wolf, 1973). Students who require special assistance because of academic or social deficits often need individualized programs; contracts are one way to provide individualization.

Developing a Contract

The development of a contingency contract involves four basic procedures: specifying target behaviors, establishing performance criteria, identifying appropriate reinforcers, and writing the contract.

Specify behavior. The first step in contracting is to identify the behaviors that will be included in the contract. This sounds simple: "Bill will be a good student," "Mary will complete her work," "Sally will be nicer to other students." One of the positive aspects of contracting is that it involves the student in setting goals for himself. However, Sally may not perceive "being nicer" in the same way her teacher does. To Sally, it might "be nicer" not to bloody Billy's nose but rather to hit him over the head with a ruler. It's doubtful that the teacher would agree to such a contract. Before a contract can be written, the student and the teacher must agree on what both will do and not do. As in all behavioral management procedures, the behaviors must be defined specifically; ambiguity leads to a misunderstood and unsuccessful contract.

The specified behavior must be one that the child can perform. Under duress or even with the best of intentions, Mary might agree in a written contract to complete her work. Chances are, however, that if she hasn't done it in the past, it may be too big a step for her to complete successfully. It would be more effective to specify a behavior that approximates the final desired behavior. Rather than contract to "do all her work," it might be preferable to have Mary initially contract to do ten problems in one class, then half a page, then a page, then a class assignment, then class homework assignments. As she succeeds with each small step, she learns that she can be accountable for her own behavior and that she can set realistic goals for herself.

Contract behaviors should be specified as positive behaviors to be performed rather than as negative behaviors to be avoided. Since support from others is critical in behavior change, it is helpful to contract to increase behaviors that are likely to be noticed by others and be reinforced. If, for instance, we state that Johnny won't scream at other students, it is unlikely that anyone will say "It is nice that you're not screaming." If we stated behaviors that Johnny should perform, we might state that Johnny "will ask in a quiet voice to play with another student." This is a more positive approach, and the student may acquire an appropriate social behavior that will be acceptable to his teacher and peers after the contract is completed.

The behavior to be performed by the student must be precisely and adequately specified in language that is clear to the student. Table 7–1 lists six examples of behaviors or tasks that might be improved by developing a teacher–student contract. Table 7–1 also provides brief analyses of the precision and clarity of the target behaviors, including a discussion of the limitations. As you can see from the examples and the analysis, some behavioral statements lack the clarity necessary to avoid ambiguity in the contract.

In connection with defining the target behaviors, the teacher should select the appropriate method to collect data (see Chapter 5, Measuring Behavior). The teacher should then collect baseline data to verify the need to intervene with the contract.

Specify the criteria. It is not enough to identify the behavior to be contracted for without specifying how much behavior and what level of behavior will be required for obtaining reinforcement. Example a in Table 7–1 specified that a student should read Unit 8 and take the progress check. However, it does not define the level at which he must pass the progress check to earn the reinforcer. If the progress check consists of ten objective questions, and the student fails all of them, is the student eligible for reinforcement? An acceptable wording might be "Read Unit 8 and take the progress check, answering 80 percent of the questions correctly." Similarly, example b in Table 7–1 must specify the criterion. If "stay in your seat" were adequately defined, it might read "Stay in your seat during your history lesson with less than 3 minutes out of seat."

Identify appropriate reinforcers and amounts. Contracting should create situations in which positive rewards are clearly given for successes, and penalties are clearly spelled out for lack of a desired behavior. In contingency contracting, activities, privileges, and home-based reinforcers are often extremely practical to use, as is time in a reinforcement area. Tokens (points)

TABLE 7-1   Examples of Target Behaviors and Analyses

Target Behaviors	Analyses and Limitations
1. Read Unit 8 and take the dittoed progress check.	1. The adequacy of this specification will depend on the progress check. If the questions have definite correct and incorrect answers listed on a score sheet, this is adequate; that is, the description is adequate if there will be no question as to whether an answer is correct or incorrect. However, if the questions are items such as "discuss the role of such-and-such," this specification probably will not be adequate.
2. Stay in your seat during history lesson.	2. How is "staying in your seat" defined? Is turning around in it but remaining with the buttocks in contact staying in your seat? Is standing on your chair also remaining in your seat? Until this is specified, this contract will not be adequate.
3. Complete Chapter 10 in your text.	3. How does one tell if Chapter 10 is "completed" and at what level? This is definitely not sufficient.
4. Read and fill in ten frames of programmed math.	4. Will any fill-in be satisfactory? Suppose the student wrote "the teacher is an idiot" in each frame. Would this be sufficient? This item is not specific enough.
5. Behave appropriately for 15 minutes without a single exception.	5. Item 5 may be the best example of how a behavior requirement should not be defined. It is a global statement, not a direction.
6. Do not speak more than three times between 2:00 P.M. and 2:30 P.M. unless you have first raised your hand and been given permission to speak by the teacher. Any vocal or verbal noise or word counts as speaking. Any time you stop making noise for over 5 seconds, the next time you make noise will be counted as speaking again.	6. Example 6 is wordy and trivial, but satisfactory.

may often be given for completion of specific contract requirements, accumulated, and later exchanged for a reinforcer.

Rewards for desired behavior need not be big, expensive, or time-consuming. The most effective rewards are those that occur frequently and can be administered immediately; examples are 15 minutes to read a comic, 10 minutes of listening to the radio or a favorite record, or an opportunity to take a note to the principal.

The initial success of a contract may depend on a student's wanting to earn the contracted reward; it is important that he be allowed to choose a reward appealing to him, whether or not it is appealing to the teacher. Designing a bulletin board at the end of the week might appeal to the teacher, but it might not be as interesting to a student as choosing and playing for the class a popular rock record for a few minutes during math period.

Involving the student's family in rewarding successful contract completion can be helpful. At a back-to-school night or a parent–teacher conference, parents might fill out cards stating two or three things that they are willing to do for or with their child, such as a trip to the local ice cream store, popcorn with a video movie, or a bike picnic. These should not be treats that the child is likely to get in any case. The child may earn these cards for

FIGURE 7-2 Contract for a ninth-grade girl, for improving work at school and receiving reinforcers at home.

I, *Jane Smith*, agree to
1. Be on time for my math class.
2. Bring my book, pencil, and note paper.
3. Work quietly during study time and complete my in-class assignment.

Ms. Benson agrees to give me the following points:

1. On time	5 points
2. Bring materials	5 points
3. Complete assignment	10 points
Total possible	20 points

My parents agree to exchange the points I earn as follows:

10 points	30 minutes of television
20 points	1 hour of television
30 points	2 hours at a friend's house
80 points	have a friend stay overnight

_____   _____   _____
Student   Teacher   Parent

_____   _____
Start   End date

---

successfully fulfilling the contract. Unless the parents fulfill their part of the agreement as soon as possible after the child brings home the card, this system will lose its effectiveness. The parents' responsibility could be written into the contract so that they are made accountable just as the student is accountable. Figure 7–2 is an example of a school contract with home reinforcement.

Penalties are implicit in most contracts. If the student does not perform the contracted behavior, the student does not receive the stated reward. For difficult students, the target behavior may be established more quickly if an additional penalty for contract failure is clearly stated, such as forfeiting a recess and doing work instead, paying a fifty-point fine for each aggressive incident, working in a room alone during a class activity, or not watching television at home for one night. The penalty should be severe enough to make the student want to avoid it, but not so severe as to make the contracting process undesirable should the child occasionally fail to fulfill the contract requirements. Penalties may also be specified for teachers or parents failing to complete their part of the contract. Such a penalty might require the adult to double the student's reinforcer.

Establish a written contract by negotiation.   A contract should be a written agreement. In the beginning of contracting, the teacher will probably specify fairly easy contract tasks to which the student will agree. The teacher should get *explicit, voluntary, informed agreement* from the student before finalizing and signing a contract. Specify the length of time that the contract will be in effect and the evaluation procedure.

Include evaluation criteria and procedures in the contract. Simple graphs or charts which the student might keep herself can be effective in motivating student performance and in evaluating the success of the contract. If the child is not meeting the terms of the contract, it is time to analyze the contract for potential problems and rewrite it until success is achieved.

The conditions under which the behavior and reward should take place should be discussed, agreed upon, and specified in the contract. If a reward is an activity that should take place for only 10 minutes, the contract should state the time limits. If a behavior should take place only at certain times or on certain days, those conditions should be specified. For instance, appropriate social interactions might be monitored only "during lunch hour while eating in the school cafeteria."

Contracts traditionally specify those behaviors expected of the student, whereas teacher responsibilities are only implied. It is helpful to specify in writing what the teacher's responsibilities in the contract are and what the consequences of his behavior will be. Many contracts fail because the teacher does not administer the contract consistently.

The form of the written contract is also important. For younger children, contracts must be simple and enticing. Figure 7–3 illustrates a contract used with a second-grade boy to motivate work completion. As students mature, contracts become more "adult-like," with fewer frills and more details.

CONTRACT

I, Billy Jones, agree to work in my handwriting workbook during writing period (2:00 PM to 2:20 PM, Monday, Wednesday, and Friday). I agree to complete at least 3 pages, with 80% of the work correct. Ms. Brown agrees to give me 10 minutes of extra recess if I earn 15 points. Extra points can be saved; when I earn 50 extra points, the whole class gets a treat. Each time I disturb another student, I will lose 5 points. This contract will be reviewed in 4 weeks.

_____	_____
Student	Teacher
_____	_____
Principal	Date

FIGURE 7-3   Example of a simple contingency contract for a second-grade boy.

Figure 7-4 is a sample contract that specifies the contingent relationship between a ninth-grade girl's completing her school work and receiving special privileges at home.

Implementing the Contract

After the contract has been developed and the content agreed upon, all parties sign the contract, thus officially implementing it. It is important that the student achieve success and be reinforced right from the beginning. Therefore, the initial steps in the contract should be relatively easy for the student to master. Shape improvement gradually, if necessary, but make sure the student is successful.

A series of contracts may be required in order to produce any real change in student academic performance and skills. Planning the strategy to be used in this sequence is as important as planning the technical requirements of an individual contract.

The day-to-day operation of the contract is straightforward. Data are collected on the student's performance and evaluated by comparing the data with the contract criterion. If the student has completed his part of the contract, the teacher, parent, or other responsible person provides reinforcement immediately, or as soon as possible, according to the contractual agreement. If the student did not fulfill his part, the teacher provides brief corrective feedback, as needed, and encourages the student to try harder.

I, *Mona Lott,* agree not to complain about how hard my math assignments are and not to disturb other students by asking them to help me with my work. Instead, I agree to work quietly, complete my math assignment before I go to recess, and raise my hand to ask the teacher for help. Points will be earned as listed below:

1. 5 points for every 5-minute period of quiet work.
2. 10 points for completing my work on time.
3. 20 points if my math assignment is at least 90% correct.
4. 2 points for raising my hand and waiting quietly for Mr. Johnson to call on me (not more than 3 times per period).

I may also lose 10 points each time I disturb another student. I may use my points to buy home reward cards. If my parents fail to provide me with the rewarding activity I select within 3 days of earning it, I will get 2 rewards.

Student   Parent   Teacher

Date

Reward Cards

50 points Ice cream	200 points Go shopping with Mom	300 points Video movie and popcorn

FIGURE 7-4   School performance contract with home reinforcement cards.

A note of caution: The student should never fail to meet criteria on several consecutive days. Repeated failures indicate a flaw in the contracting program and adjustments should be made or the contract should be rewritten.

As the student's behavior improves, contract responsibilities should gradually be shifted to the student. Unneeded contract procedures should be faded out. The amount of reinforcement given should be diminished, and natural consequences should be used as much as possible. When the contract is no longer necessary, discontinue it and replace it with self-management procedures.

Evaluating the Contract

Aspects of evaluation have already been mentioned as part of the discussion of contract development and implementation. Evaluation occurs in two ways: (1) *daily*—evaluating student performance in relation to the criteria, and (2) *periodically*—evaluating the effectiveness of the contracting program.

The daily evaluation has already been described. The periodic evaluation involves the examination of student performance over time—several days and weeks. The first, and perhaps easiest, evaluation question is "Has the goal of the contract been accomplished?" If the student has reached the goal for the objective, the contract ends and, if necessary, a new one is written for another objective. If the student has not reached the goal, we ask "Is the student making progress toward the goal?" If the answer is yes, continue with the contract. A negative answer requires the teacher to examine the program for problems. Modifications are made as necessary.

Problems with Contracting

If a contract is not producing behavior change, check the following list:

1. Did the student have a say in the contract?
2. Were behaviors specified clearly?
3. Was the contract written so that not too many behaviors were required for the reward?
4. Was the contracted behavior something the child could unquestionably perform?
5. Were data collected on the specific behaviors included in the contract?
6. Was the contracted behavior one that would gain recognition and praise from other people in the student's environment?
7. Were the stated reinforcers frequent and immediate?
8. Was an effective communication and follow-up channel established if other people were involved in the contract?
9. Was an evaluation system established to ascertain contract effectiveness on a regular basis?
10. Were teacher violations of the contract occurring?

A common problem is the use of rewards that are not really reinforcing. You can usually determine that it is a reinforcer problem if students are not excited about earning and selecting the available reinforcers. If this is the case, don't scrap the whole contract; find new, more powerful reinforcers (see Chapter 3 on identifying effective reinforcers).

Another problem that can arise with contracting has to do with its obviousness and explicitness. Students may learn, under certain conditions, to perform only those desirable behaviors for which a contract exists. As a general rule, this tends to occur when the teacher gives little other reinforcement for behavior. A teacher who never praises, gives privileges, or otherwise encourages good work or appropriate behavior may teach students that only behaviors specified in contracts are reinforced; students will behave accordingly. The solution to this is to maintain a classroom that is generally reinforcing and to use contracts only for problems or to reverse specific deficits.

One way to minimize the problems that may develop when contracting is discontinued is to use rather long-term contracts in the final weeks. Another way is to proceed to self-contracting and let the students provide their own reinforcement. For example, a student can be encouraged to write a contract for himself which specifies that when he completes a task, he will go bowling after school. Many of the procedures mentioned in Chapter 6 for fading token reinforcement are also applicable.

Specific Contracting Rules

Homme and colleagues (1970) have formulated ten rules as a practical guide to developing, implementing, and evaluating contingency contracting.

1. *Immediacy.* The reinforcement provided in the contract should be immediate, especially when the procedure is first being used. The importance of immediate reinforcement was discussed in Chapter 2.
2. *Small approximations.* Single contracts should require small approximations (tasks) leading to the desired goal behaviors. Early contracts should require *extremely* small approximations. It is important that beginning contracts require small amounts (rather than large "chunks") of behavior that can be performed easily. Large academic units, chapters, or assignments might best be broken into several small contracts or task cards.
3. *Frequent reinforcers.* This rule follows from the first two. Contracts should be written so the student receives frequent, small reinforcers rather than infrequent, large reinforcers. Casella (1971) showed that even college students will increase their study time if reinforced with frequent visits to an activity area.
4. *Accomplishment, not obedience.* If the teacher wants students to learn skills that will serve them in school and afterwards, his contracts should reinforce accomplishment, not obedience. A contract that specifies that the student will "do what he is told within 20 seconds eight out of the next ten times" does not reinforce an accomplishment. The teacher should anticipate what the student will be required to do and contract for these actual performances. Thus, a contract might specify that a student will get his materials out on time, start on time, and so on, rather than "do what he is told."
5. *Reinforcement follows behavior.* This seems obvious, but many teachers do just the opposite. For example, if a student requests to speak to another student, he should be told, "Finish your spelling and then you can talk to Bart," rather than "You can talk to Bart if you will go right back to your spelling when you are through." Contracts should follow similar form: "When you complete your math assignment, you may have 5 minutes of free time."
6. *Fair.* A contract should be fair in that the amount of reinforcement provided should be appropriate for the amount of performance required. If it is too small, the student's behavior will extinguish; if it is too large, the student will not reach his objective.
7. *Clear.* There should be no ambiguity as to what behavior is required, how much

and what quality is required, what the reinforcer is, how much of it will be earned, and how it will be judged.

8. *Honest.* An honest contract is one which is carried out as it is written. The teacher should not contract with students if she cannot fulfill their contractual agreements.

9. *Positive.* Contract for desirable behavior rather than for the absence of undesirable behavior. A contract requiring that the student stay in her seat and complete a certain amount of work is preferable to one which specifies that she will not wander around and bother other students. The goal is to teach the child something, not merely to extinguish or suppress behavior.

10. *Systematic.* To be effective, contracts must be used in a systematic and ongoing manner. Sporadically using one or two contracts during a troublesome week is unlikely to have much effect; a planned series of contracts over a term based upon considerations of shaping and progressions may have a substantial effect.

Contracts for Specific Purposes

Figures 7–5 through 7–9 are sample contracts illustrating the use of contracts with schoolwork, homework, study skills, and social behavior.

Task cards and contracts.   Some teachers like to write a more general, "large" contract for an entire academic unit or behavioral goal and then break this contract into a series of "small" contracts, called *task cards.* They feel that giving the student a greater overview of what is to be accomplished allows the student to budget time realistically and motivates the student by letting him see what he will accomplish in terms of skills. In this case, the large contract might tend to be somewhat less specific and might violate some of the requirements for adequate contracts previously discussed.

The task cards meet the requirements for adequate contracts and avoid these weaknesses, however. For instance, a teacher and student might write a large contract specifying that the student will complete an entire text by the end of the term, hand in two papers, and do six in-book exercises (Figure 7–5). The big contract might state that classroom privileges will be given for completing individual assignments that help to meet this large goal; it might also state how the grade will be determined. For example, it might say that each exercise and the papers will be graded from 0 to 100 percent, that each paper will count as 20 percent of the final grade, and that each exercise will count as 10 percent of the final grade. A task card would then be written for each assignment (Figure 7–6). The result of all the task cards would be in agreement with the overall contract and meet its requirements. The task cards would also specify the daily or weekly in-class reinforcers, in addition to the final grade.

Contracting for schoolwork.   As has been illustrated by Figures 7–5 and 7–6, most uses of contingency contracting will have to do with academic work done in school. Three strategies are available to guide the teacher in determining how a sequence of contracts or task cards should be formulated:

Social Studies Class Contract

I, ————————————————, understand that my assignments for my fourth-quarter social studies class include the following:

1. Read Chapters 25 through 30 in the text.
2. Complete the exercises at the end of each of the six chapters.
3. Write two papers—one on the executive branch of government and one on the legislative branch.

When I complete each individual task card, I may engage in the reinforcing activity listed on the card. I understand the following grading criteria will be used to determine my class grade.

Grade		% of Assignments Complete	% of Accuracy
A	=	100%	90% to 100%
B	=	100%	80% to 89%
C	=	100%	70% to 79%
D	=	80% to 90%	60% to 69%
F	=	Less than 80%	Less than 60%

———————————— ———————————— ————————————
Student   Teacher   Date

FIGURE 7-5 Contract specifying the assignments and contingencies for a fourth-quarter social studies class. The contract is used with task cards (see Figure 7-6).

1. For a student who does little work, each contract might require a slightly greater amount of work than the last one.
2. For a slow student who does work regularly, each contract might require that a set amount of work be done in a shorter amount of time than the last contract required.
3. For a sloppy or inaccurate student, each contract might require a slightly higher degree of accuracy, neat work, a higher grade, or fewer errors than the previous one.

Contracting for homework. Teachers can contract with students for homework as well as for schoolwork. Some have suggested that home-based (parent-controlled) reinforcement is especially appropriate when contracting for homework.

1. For a student who does very little homework, each contract can require a slightly larger amount to be done than the last contract did.

....

Name __Willie Maket__ Date __March 20__ Assignment No. __25__

Amount of Task __Read Chapter 25 and complete the chapter exercises__

Reinforcing Activity __10 minutes of in-class free time__

Due Date __March 28th__

....

Name __Willie Maket__ Date __March 25th__ Assignment No. __First term paper__

Amount of Task __Complete an outline of the first term paper__

Reinforcing Activity __25 points toward class video party__

Due Date __April 3__

....

Name _____ Date _____ Assignment No. _____

Amount of Task _____

Reinforcing Activity _____

Due Date _____

....

FIGURE 7-6 Sample task cards used in connection with a contract written for an entire fourth-quarter social studies class.

2. For a student who does not get her homework in on time, each contract can specify a deadline, and the deadlines can be made shorter and shorter in successive contracts until they are the same as the deadlines given students who perform well; or, progressively more severe penalties can be assessed for late work.

3. For a student who puts things off until the last minute and then does a sloppy rush job, task cards can break down the work into smaller amounts with a due date for each portion of the project or assignment (Figure 7–7). Task cards could be used to specify the work in detail and list each reinforcer.

Science Project Contract

I, _____, agree to complete each step of my science project by the following due dates:

Task	Due Date
1. Select a project.	Oct. 10
2. Find the necessary resource materials.	Oct. 14
3. Outline the project.	Oct. 17
4. Collect the needed equipment.	Oct. 20
5. Develop the project.	Oct. 27
6. Try it out.	Oct. 28
7. Make the necessary modifications.	Oct. 30
8. Prepare the project for class presentations.	Nov. 5
9. Present project in class.	Nov. 10–14 (day to be assigned)
10. Outline paper.	Nov. 19
11. Write rough draft of paper.	Nov. 24
12. Rewrite paper.	Nov. 26
13. Final paper due.	Dec. 3

I will turn in each task card when the task is completed and pick up the next card. The task cards will list the reinforcing activity that I will earn if the task is completed on time.

_____   _____   _____
Student   Teacher   Date

FIGURE 7-7 Contract designed to help a student who procrastinates when working on assignments. The teacher assists the student by contracting for task completion leading to punctual assignment completion.

4. For sloppy or inaccurate work, each contract can require a slightly more accurate paper, a lower error rate, or a higher grade than previous contracts.

Contracting for study skills.   Teachers can also contract for study skills.

1. For the procrastinator, contracts can be written for starting classwork within a certain amount of time. Each contract can require a faster start.
2. For the student who schedules his homework poorly, contracts can be written to start homework at a set time and place each day (Figure 7-8). Successive contracts can have stricter requirements.
3. For the student who "forgets" books, materials, or supplies, contracts can be written to require that these be in the correct place at the correct time. In each successive contract more items can be included.

I, _____, agree to do the following:

1. Study the subject _____ in _____ and no other place.
2. Start studying the subject at _____ and terminate studying the subject at _____.
3. Report honestly the amount of studying accomplished each day.
4. Study the subject on the days assigned.
   Mon.   Tue.   Wed.   Thurs.   Fri.   Sat.   Sun.
5. Engage in one of the following rewards only when the contracted studying is completed:

   a. _____

   b. _____

   c. _____

   d. _____

   e. _____

6. I will receive _____ points for every assignment handed in to my teacher with _____ percent correct.

_____
Student

_____
Parent

_____
Teacher

FIGURE 7-8   Contract for improving study at home.

Contracting for social skills and appropriate classroom behavior.   A sequence of contracts for social skills requires expert use of shaping procedures and of correct progressions. Following are some general strategies:

1. Each contract can require a slightly better approximation than the previous one. For instance, one contract might require a student who is a "loner" to

I, <u>Wally Wanderer</u>, agree to use the social skills listed below, during the morning and afternoon recess. I will receive 5 points each time I do one of the following:

1.	Invite another student to play with me	5 points
2.	Accept an invitation to play with others	5 points
3.	Compliment three other students	5 points
	Total	15 points
		possible per recess

When I earn 200 points, the whole class will get 20 minutes of extra recess.

_____   _____   _____
Student   Teacher   Date

FIGURE 7–9   Contract designed to help a socially withdrawn child interact with other students. The contract is designed to encourage the student to use skills taught during a social skills class.

score another student's quiz, while the next contract might also require him to go over the scoring with the other student.

2. Each successive contract can require a slightly higher or lower frequency of some behavior. For instance, if a student talks out excessively at inappropriate times, each contract might require a slightly smaller number of such behaviors than the last. (Note: A "negative" contract is not ideal in terms of rule number 9 of contingency contracting.)

3. Each new contract can require either that some desired social behavior (see Chapter 9) occur in more situations than the last one did or that an undesired behavior occur in fewer situations. For instance, one contract might require a student to help another student in some way during reading; a second might require that he do this at least once during both reading and math.

Figure 7–9 is an example of a contract designed to improve social behavior.

EXAMPLE

Mr. Brown, an eighth-grade social studies teacher, is concerned about one of his students, Phil. Mr. Brown believes that Phil is a bright and capable student but that he is not reaching his full potential. Phil does well on most of his tests but rarely completes all of his assignments. Mr. Brown gives the students some time to work on their social studies assignment in class but expects some of it to be done at home.

Mr. Brown decides to analyze the problem. For one week Mr. Brown gives the students a daily assignment to read and answer questions from their social studies text. He allows 20 minutes of the class period to work on the assignment and then asks the students to complete it at home. He checks Phil's work each day to see how much of the assignment he has completed, and he compares what Phil has completed with other students in the class. He learns that Phil is completing almost no work in class, while other students are completing about 20 to 30 percent of the assigned questions. He also questions Phil to see whether he has done any reading during class time and finds that he has done very little. Phil spends most of his time doodling or looking out the window, and completes only about 40 percent of the questions at home. From this analysis, Mr. Brown determines that Phil has a problem both in doing his work at school and in completing it at home.

Mr. Brown has a parent–teacher conference with Phil's parents. He explains his concerns and suggests that he, Phil, and Phil's parents enter into a joint contract to try to improve Phil's study behavior both at school and at home. The parents agree and the three of them specify the following target behaviors: Phil will work quietly in class when he is given independent study time. He will attempt to read the assignment in class and answer at least three questions before the end of the class period. Phil will take the rest of his work home, where he will complete the remaining questions at his desk from 7:00 to 8:00 each night. He will then have his parents check the work and initial that he has completed it.

Next, Mr. Brown discusses with Phil's parents the concept of positive reinforcement. He suggests that they identify rewards they can give to Phil at home and suggests that these rewards be activities rather than tangible reinforcers. Phil's father says that he feels he should be spending more time with his son. He agrees to set up activities that he can do with Phil each evening for about 30 minutes if Phil completes his assignment. Mr. Brown compliments Phil's father on the suggestion; he asks him to write down some of the activities that father and son might do together and to ask Phil for some suggestions. Mr. Brown agrees that he will write up the contract.

The next day, Mr. Brown invites Phil to come in after school to meet with his parents and Mr. Brown. Mr. Brown delineates his concerns and shows Phil the contract he has written. He explains what the behaviors are that he and Phil's parents would like to see Phil improve on. Phil agrees that he needs to improve his study habits and assignment completion, and he likes the idea of earning activities he can do with his father. Phil also asks about what happens if he earns the reinforcer but his father doesn't come through with the activity. They agree to write in a penalty clause for the parents, stating that if Phil's father fails to provide an earned activity on a weeknight, Phil gets a special half-day activity with his father on the weekend. All parties agree and sign the contract. They also agree to meet again in a month to evaluate the contract and its effectiveness.

Exercise

1. Write a sample contract for a student who needs to work quietly, remain in her seat, stop talking to other students, and complete her assignments.

Feedback

1. The contract should include the following: clearly specified target behaviors, a performance criterion for each behavior, reinforcers, contingencies for earning reinforcers, the teacher's responsibilities, a method of collecting data, and a statement of how often reinforcers can be earned and how long the contract will be in effect. The contract should be organized and written so that it is easy to read and understand, and it should have a place for dates and signatures.

BEHAVIORAL SELF-MANAGEMENT

Previous chapters described the use of the principles of reinforcement to motivate student academic performance and modify social behavior. Research has demonstrated that these behavior modification procedures effectively alter both the academic and social behavior of school-aged children in classrooms (Rosenbaum & Drabman, 1979). Although these procedures are effective, external agents are required in order to arrange and administer the programs.

Teachers, aides, peers, and parents can spend a great deal of time conducting behavior change programs. With all of the demands placed on educators today, it is highly desirable to have students be able to control their own behavior rather than requiring assistance from external agents for that control. O'Leary and Dubey (1979) have suggested five reasons for teaching self-control or self-management procedures to children in public school settings:

> First, acting independently is valued and typically expected by our culture. Second, the child's teacher and/or parent may not always be capable of successfully implementing external controls. Third, when a child controls his/her own behavior well, adults can spend more time teaching the child other important skills. Fourth, the self-controlling child is able to learn and behave effectively when adult supervision is not available. Fifth and finally, teaching children to control their own behavior may lead to more durable behavioral changes than relying solely on external means of influence. (p. 449)

Self-management programs have been successfully used at all grade levels in public school settings. Glynn, Thomas, and Shee (1973) used a behavioral self-management procedure to maintain the on-task behavior of students in a second-grade elementary classroom. The on-task behavior had initially been established with externally administered reinforcement procedures. Brigham and colleagues (1985) used a self-management program to improve the disruptive behavior of students in a middle school. "Repeat offenders" in violating school rules and disrupting classes were invited to participate in a self-management class. Students attended the class, learned the procedures, and then implemented them to improve their classroom and school behavior.

Gottman and McFall (1972), using a self-management procedure with potential high school drop-outs, significantly increased their participation in their school program. Rhode, Morgan, and Young (1983) used self-evaluation procedures to help elementary-aged, behaviorally handicapped students generalize their improved classroom behavior from a resource room to their regular elementary classrooms. These research studies are a few of many that have demonstrated that self-management procedures can be effectively used by teachers in public school settings. The procedures are effective with elementary, junior high school, and high school students, as well as with special education and nonhandicapped students.

The term **self-management** refers to any of several procedures or combinations of procedures designed to help an individual change and/or maintain his own behavior. The self-management procedures discussed in this chapter include identifying target behaviors and establishing goals, self-recording, self-evaluating, self-reinforcing, and self-instructing. The use of contracts to provide transition from teacher management to self-management programs will also be discussed.

Behavioral self-management.   Self-control, or behavioral self-management, as it is often called by behavior analysts, is not an issue of a lack of, or an abundance of, willpower. Rather, it requires only the application of the principles of behavior discussed in previous chapters in this book. **Self-management** is the arranging of environmental events so that they modify an individual's subsequent behavior. The same basic principles used in externally managed programs are applicable.

First, the problem is identified and a specific target behavior is defined. Next, baseline data are collected on the target behavior. An intervention procedure—which will probably include rearranging behavioral antecedents (events occuring prior to the problem behavior), behavioral consequences (events following the target behavior), or a combination of antecedent and consequent changes—is programmed so as to assist in the modification of the behavior. The self-management program is implemented, further data collected, and the program modified as necessary to produce the desired results. After the results have been achieved, the program components can be gradually faded out, or they can be maintained indefinitely based on the individual's needs. Self-management programs are distinguished from externally controlled behavior change programs in that the individual establishes and conducts his own program, or at least is the primary person involved in implementing the program.

Identifying Target Behaviors, Establishing Goals, and Evaluating Performance

For a self-management program to be effective, the individual involved must have identified a specific behavior that she would like to modify. A teacher who observes that a student is disruptive or misbehaving may state,

"Jane lacks self-control." However, Jane may be in complete control, behaving exactly as she wants to behave. The problem is not a lack of self-control or self-management; rather, it is a disagreement between the teacher and the student as to how the student should behave in the classroom. On the other hand, if Jane expresses a willingness to change her behavior and to be more compliant with classroom rules but needs assistance in accomplishing this, then a self-management program may be effective. The individual implementing a self-management program must have a personal goal to change the specific behavior for which the program is designed.

Defining the problem behavior, specifying when and where the behavior should and should not occur, and listing the typical consequences of the problem behavior will provide information that will help the individual establish the self-management program. For a younger student, the teacher may have to be involved in collecting this information and establishing the parameters of a program which the student will then implement. More capable students may gather this information with only minimal help from the teacher.

Setting a goal or a standard for each target behavior is also important. In a study by Smith and colleagues (1986), high school students were taught to set daily and weekly academic goals and evaluate their accomplishments. In the first phase of training, students were taught to (1) identify and list all of the tasks in an academic assignment, (2) sequence the tasks in the order they would complete them, and (3) divide the tasks by the number of days they had to complete the assignment. These steps were initially written to assist the student in formulating a daily goal (see Figure 7–10). The teacher allowed the students 20 minutes in class each day. At the end of the study time, students evaluated whether or not the goal had been achieved. The students received points (exchangeable for backup reinforcers and used in grading) for setting appropriate goals and achieving them. If the student did not accomplish the goal, a new goal was set for the next day.

Part of a self-management program is self-evaluation. The individual cannot determine whether reinforcing or punishing consequences should be self-administered if he does not first evaluate whether or not the behavior has met the criterion or standard established. An effective evaluation always includes comparing one's performance to a preestablished standard. Agreeing that 20 pages should be read each evening as part of a student's homework, establishing that no aggressive acts will occur on the playground, or stating that the student will not disrupt the class more than once per hour are all examples of goals or behavioral standards that may be established. The standards, whatever they are, may be established by the student or teacher, or in a conversation between the two. Once the behavioral standard is established and understood by the student, the student can proceed to record and evaluate her own behavior.

After the students demonstrated the goal-setting skills and were achieving the goals consistently, phase 2 was initiated. Students were asked to "think" through the assignment (that is, identify the tasks, sequence them, and divide them into days, but not write out each part) and write daily goals.

Point Card

Name _____ Date _____

GOAL SETTING

                                                    Points

Label: 0   1

Sequence: 0   1
1.

2.

3.

Divide: 0   1

                                                    Points

Today's goal: (2) _____

Did I meet my goal?   (3) _____

Total number of goal setting points   = _____
Total number of points for meeting goal = _____
Total number of points earned   = _____

FIGURE 7-10 Point card for setting and accomplishing daily goals.

Points were still given but were used only for grading purposes. The students' academic and on-task behavior improved.

Self-recording. The purpose of measurement or data collection in education or any behavior change program should be to provide a basis for making decisions about the effectiveness or ineffectiveness of the programs. Data provide the basis for deciding whether to continue a program in its present form, modify it in some way, or discontinue it. Direct and frequent measurement of our own behavior assists us in evaluating our progress toward behavioral goals.

Behavioral self-observation and self-recording involve teaching individuals to monitor their behavior and record the occurrence of each instance of specific behaviors. Self-recording involves monitoring and recording information about behavior but minimizes the requirement of making a judgment about the behavior. Self-recorded data provides the student and the teacher with information used to determine the effectiveness of the program and reinforcers or the need for program modification.

Self-monitoring and self-recording are important steps in the development of any self-management program. Self-recording can also function as a behavior change technique. Several suthors have found self-recording alone to be effective in producing behavior change (see O'Leary & Dubey, 1979; and Rosenbaum & Drabman, 1979, for reviews). When self-recording is used in connection with self-evaluation (comparing one's own behavior with the established standard and making an evaluative judgment), the combined procedure is more effective than either alone. Self-recording and self-evaluation are further enhanced by adding a self-reinforcement procedure. Self-recording is also effective as a procedure to maintain behavior change established with some externally controlled behavior management program.

Self-evaluation. As previously stated, self-evaluation is used in connection with self-monitoring and self-recording. Self-evaluation is the process of comparing one's own behavior to a preestablished behavioral standard. Self-evaluation is a prerequisite skill for determining whether positive or negative consequences should be self-administered. Self-evaluation, along with self-recording and self-reinforcement, has been demonstrated to be an effective technique in public school settings (Bolstad & Johnson, 1972; Drabman, Spitalnik, & O'Leary, 1973; Rhode, Morgan, & Young, 1983; Robertson et al., 1979).

Rhode, Morgan, and Young (1983) provide an example of how teachers can assist students in learning to evaluate their own behavior. In that study, the teacher first used an external reinforcement system to establish instructional control in a resource-room setting. The teacher explained to the students that they could earn points based on ratings of how well they followed the classroom rules and completed their academic assignments. Students were told that ratings they received for work and behavior were to be converted to a corresponding number of points (for example, a rating of "5" would convert to 5 points). The zero-to-five rating scale was used according to the criteria presented in Figure 7–11.

After the teacher had established a high rate of appropriate classroom behavior through the use of the point system, a self-evaluation procedure was introduced. The teacher asked students to rate their own academic work and behavior by awarding themselves rating for each behavior on the zero-to-five point scale during their resource-room sessions. An example of a student–teacher rating card is illustrated in Figure 7–11.

Teacher _____ Date _____

Student _____ Period _____

	Subject _____				
	Academic Work		Student Behavior		Points
Monday	3	4			4
Tuesday	4	4			5
Wednesday	3	3	3	3	8
Thursday	2	4	1	3	0
Friday	2	4	3	3	4

Teacher   Student   Teacher   Student

Please rate each student, for each period, on a scale of 1 to 5 according to the guidelines below.

Criteria for Ratings

Teachers will rate the behavior of each student for each session according to the following criteria:

Student Behavior	*Academic Work*
5 = *excellent*—Followed all classroom rules for the entire interval.	5 = Work 90 to 100% complete and judged to be correct and neat.
4 = *very good*—Minor infraction of rules (e.g., talked out or was out of seat once), but followed rules during the rest of the interval; worked for almost the entire interval.	4 = Work at least 80% complete and judged to be correct and neat.
3 = *average*—Did not follow all of the rules for the entire interval, but there were no serious offenses. Followed rules approximately 80% of the time. (Inappropriate behavior may have in-	3 = Work at least 70% complete and judged to be correct.

FIGURE 7-11 Self-evaluation rating form.

volved talking out or being out of seat.)	
2 = *below average*—Broke one or more rules to the extent that the behavior was not acceptable (involved in a higher-level misbehavior that disturbed others), but followed the rules part of the time.	2 = Work at least 60% complete and judged to be correct.
1 = *poor*—Broke one or more rules for almost the entire period, or engaged in a higher degree of inappropriate behavior most of the time.	1 = Work at least 50% complete and judged to be correct.
0 = *totally unacceptable*—Broke one or more rules for the entire interval. Did not work at all or all work incorrect.	0 = Work less than 50% complete and judged to be correct.

The teacher independently rated students' work and behavior by awarding points in a similar fashion. The student would then match her self-evaluation with the teacher's evaluation of her work and behavior at the end of each time period. If a student was within one point of the teacher's rating (either higher or lower), she kept the number of points she had given herself. If the two ratings were exactly the same, the student earned a bonus point. If there was more than 1 point difference (higher or lower) between the teacher and the student rating, no points were earned for that interval (see Figure 7–11). After the students had used the self-evaluation–matching procedure for several days and their appropriate classroom behavior was being maintained at a high level, the teacher gradually faded out the matching procedure. After the teacher–student matching procedure had been completely eliminated and students were evaluating their own behavior, they were asked to use the same procedure in the regular elementary classrooms.

In order to help the students establish the use of the self-evaluation procedure in the regular classroom, they initially matched their ratings with the rating of the teacher. The points earned in the matching and/or self-evaluation procedure were exchanged for back-up reinforcers in the resource room. The matching procedure and the points were quickly faded out and students continued to self-evaluate their own behavior. After a period of time of successful use of the self-evaluation procedure in both the resource room and the regular classroom, the use of the rating card was eliminated.

The research indicated that the procedure was effective in changing the students' behavior in both the special-education and the regular-education classrooms. The procedure also maintained appropriate classroom behavior after all self-evaluation procedures and the use of the self-evaluation card were discontinued.

Self-reinforcement.　People have used self-reinforcement procedures to help improve their own behavior for years, most frequently in the form of "If I complete this task, I may then engage in this reinforcement." For example, an individual may say, "When I get the house cleaned, I will take a break and have a cup of tea," or a student may say, "After I have read 10 pages of my homework assignment, I will watch a television program." If the principles of reinforcement already discussed in this book are followed, self-reinforcement can be effective in modifying behavior (O'Leary & Dubey, 1979). That is, the administration of the self-reinforcer must follow contingently upon successful completion of the target behavior (this is where self-evaluation is a necessary part of the self-reinforcement procedure), and reinforcement should be immediate and appropriate to the amount of work or effort expended to complete the target behavior. The self-reinforcement procedure is ineffective if the student "short-circuits" the contingent relationship and self-rewards noncompletion of the behavior (Martin & Pear, 1983).

Self-instruction.　Self-instruction is a procedure whereby one uses statements to prompt or cue a specific behavior. O'Leary and Dubey (1979) mention that children often use self-instructions, such as "*i* before *e*, except after *c*" and "stop, look, and listen," to facilitate the correct performance of the subsequent response" (p. 450).

Self-instructional procedures have been used to help students increase their ability to demonstrate a variety of academic skills (Burgio, Whitman, & Johnson, 1980; Douglas et al., 1976; Robin, Armel, & O'Leary, 1985). Self-instructions have also been used to train hyperactive children to increase their attending and on-task behavior (Barkley, Copeland, & Sivage, 1980; Meichenbaum & Goodman, 1971; Peters & Davies, 1981). Burron and Bucher (1978) used self-instruction to assist children in decreasing rule-breaking and increasing rule-following behavior. Teaching students verbal statements that they can use as prompts or self-instructions to assist them in performing certain behaviors or resist performing inappropriate behaviors is an effective technique that teachers can use with students.

Contracting as a Transition Strategy to Self-Management

One way to facilitate the use of self-management skills, particularly with academic performance, is to use contingency contracts. As mentioned earlier, contingency contracts can bridge the gap between teacher-managed programs and student self-management. Behavior management programs can be individualized through the use of contracts, which can gradually shift from being teacher-developed to being student-written, so that students learn to specify behaviors and reinforcers, determine the amounts of work and reinforcement, establish the contingent relationship, identify the roles of the involved parties, specify the timeliness, and outline the evaluation procedure.

The following procedure details how the transition from teacher-managed programs can take place and how students can learn, through the use of contracts, to manage their own academic performance. When the student writes a contract, it is presented to the teacher, who may disagree with it. After they negotiate their differences, they both sign. This usually saves the teacher a lot of time and allows the student to develop a self-management skill she can use in other classes or in work situations.

Before students can write their own contracts, two things must happen. First, they must know what tasks and assignments need to be completed in the next 3 to 4 weeks. Given this list, students can break their chores into a series of small tasks, budget their time, and then plan a sequence of contracts to accomplish these tasks.

Second, the teacher must train students to write satisfactory contracts, which usually requires that they have some experience with teacher-written contracts. A six-step process can systematically move students from teacher-written to student-written contracts.

1. *Teacher-written contracts.* The teacher should write the contracts for at least two weeks. For students who are having trouble with the contracts, this period should be longer.

2. *Teacher suggestion of reinforcement.* The teacher writes the part of the contract specifying the behavior but leaves the reinforcement part blank. The teacher suggests a reinforcer and amount and then asks the student to write down what she feels is appropriate. If the student specification is about the same as the teacher's, they can agree on it. If what the student writes substantially disagrees with the teacher's specification, they can negotiate until a fair amount of reinforcement is agreed upon. When the student specifies an amount that is in agreement with the teacher suggestion for 4 to 5 days, she can go on to the next step.

3. *Student specification of reinforcement.* The teacher asks the student to write in the type and amount of reinforcer. If it seems appropriate, the teacher accepts it and praises the student. If it seems unfair, they negotiate. When the student-specified reinforcement seems appropriate for 4 to 5 days in a row, she can go on to the next step.

4. *Student specification of reinforcement and negotiation of amount of work to be accomplished.* The student is responsible for specifying the reinforcement in writing and verbally suggesting the amount of work to be accomplished. The teacher accepts the suggested amount of work or negotiates a different amount.

5. *Student specification of reinforcement and amount of work to be accomplished.* The student is responsible for specifying both the amount of reinforcement and the amount of work in writing. The teacher still checks the written contract and determines whether the amount of work and the amount of reinforcement appear to be reasonable; the teacher then accepts the proposed amounts or negotiates. The teacher adds other contract details as needed, including dates, times, and penalties.

6. *Student-written contract.* In this step, the student writes the entire contract, including details. If the teacher approves, he signs it. Otherwise, negotiations are required. If the contract written by the student is way out of line, the teacher and student return to an earlier step.

EXAMPLE

Ms. Waterton, a fifth-grade teacher, is concerned about Butch's aggressive behavior on the playground. Butch is a good student, but during recess, when no
one invites him to play, Butch gets angry, pushes and shoves the other kids,
grabs their playthings, and runs away. Ms. Waterton decides that it's time to
teach him some social skills (see Chapter 9 on teaching social skills) and set up
a contingency contract to improve his behavior.

Ms. Waterton meets with Butch after school and teaches him how to
politely ask others if he can join their game and how to invite others to play
with him. They role play and practice the behavior until Butch is proficient at
it. The teacher then explains how Butch can compliment other students, which
will make them feel good about him. After their social skills instruction, Ms.
Waterton explains that she wants to set up a contract to encourage Butch to
stop fighting and to use the social skills about which they have been talking.

The contract specifies that each time Butch asks if he can play with
someone else or invites them to play with him, he can earn 5 points (up to
three times per recess, or a total of 15 points); each time he praises or compliments other students, he will earn 2 points (up to 10 points per recess); and
each time he gets in a fight, pushes or shoves other students, or takes their
playthings, he will lose 10 points. The contract specifies that if Butch earns 75
points in a week, the entire class will receive extra recess, free time, or a party
on Friday afternoon. Ms. Waterton tells Butch that she's going to explain
Butch's new contract to the class and ask the students to help and encourage
him. She believes that this approach will help increase Butch's social standing
in the class and encourage the other students to cooperate. Butch agrees to the
contract and they sign it.

Three weeks later, Ms. Waterton calls Butch in after school to tell him
that he has been doing a great job. She is proud of the fact that he has earned
a group reward on each of the last three Fridays. Butch says that he thinks the
program is great, that he's having fun with the other students, and that he feels,
for the first time, that he's making friends. Ms. Waterton suggests that they
write a new contract for the next 2 weeks to encourage the same behaviors but
require Butch to earn 150 points over 2 weeks before the class can earn a group
reward. (She is doing this to fade reinforcement.) Butch agrees, but he asks
whether, since it takes 2 weeks to earn a reward, the class can have a party for
an hour instead of 30 minutes. Ms. Waterton agrees and they sign a new contract.

Exercise

1. List and explain five self-management procedures.
2. Write a contract that involves one or more of the five self-management
   procedures just discussed.

Feedback

1. The following is a list of five self-management procedures.
   a. Identification of target behaviors and setting of goals—The individ-

ual identifies his own target behaviors and the criterion of acceptable performance in observable terms.

b. Self-recording—The individual collects data on the occurrence or nonoccurrence of his own behavior.

c. Self-evaluation—Using the self-recorded data, the individual determines whether he has met the performance criterion.

d. Self-reinforcement—if the self-evaluation indicates that the performance criterion has been met, then the individual praises himself and/or engages in reinforcing activities.

e. Self-instruction—The individual prompts himself to perform the correct behavior at the right time and place.

2. The contract should include the following: clearly specified target behaviors, performance criterion for each behavior, reinforcers, contingency for earning reinforcers, responsibilities of the teachers, method of collecting data, how often reinforcers can be earned, and how long the contract will be in effect. The contract should be organized and written so that it is easy to read and understand and has a place for dates and signatures. The contract must also include one of the following: student goal setting, self-recording, self-evaluation, self-reinforcement, or self-instruction. (See sample contract below.)

The following is an example of an acceptable response:

I, Patty, agree to bring my pencil or pen, notebook, and English book to fifth-period English every day. I also agree to write down all assignments and their due dates. I will self-record my performance and have Ms. Brewer initial it each day. I will be responsible for turning in the self-recording card to Ms. Brewer each Friday.

Ms. Brewer will give me up to 30 points each week. I may earn these points as follows:

1 point each for having paper, pencil, and book in class
1 point for writing down the daily assignments
1 point for writing down the due dates
(5 points possible per day plus 5 extra points for turning in the card on Friday)

The bonus points will be used to improve my class grade. I will also reinforce myself with a stop at the ice cream parlor on Friday afternoon if I earn all 30 points.

We will review the contract in 1 month.

_____   _____   _____
Patty   Ms. Brewer   Date

FAST TRACK

REVIEW

Many students, especially those who have not done well in school, feel that they don't really have a "handle" on what is expected of them. They may feel that someone has changed the rules in the middle of the game or that in some way they just don't measure up. Judicious use of *contingency contracts* can help students effectively cope with these feelings and the problems they cause. Contracts can help teacher and student alike better focus on goals and methods of reaching those goals.

Teachers should comply with the basic contracting procedures: specify the behavior in measurable and observable terms; specify the criteria for reinforcement; identify appropriate reinforcers and amounts of reinforcement; and establish a written contract, including evaluation procedures, with the student. The following contracting rules, specified by Homme and colleagues (1970), are also an excellent guide for the teacher when developing a contract: reinforce immediately; reinforce small approximations of the target behavior; reinforce the behavior frequently; reinforce accomplishment; follow the desired behavior with the reinforcer; make sure that the contract is fair; make sure the contract is clear and free of ambiguity; have an honest contract in which all parties fulfill their commitments; contract for positive, desirable behaviors rather than undesirable behaviors; and use contracts in a systematic fashion.

Problems arise in contingency contracting when the contract is unclear, when the student or teacher has violated the stipulations, and when there is little positive reinforcement in the classroom apart from the contract. Problems with discontinuing contracts can be handled by moving the students to self-management contracts.

Contingency contracts are an excellent transition from teacher-managed programs to student self-management. Several self-management procedures can be effectively used with students in public school situations. These include: identifying target behaviors and establishing goals, self-recording one's own behavior, self-evaluating one's behavior against some preestablished criterion, learning self-instructions to prompt or cue certain positive behaviors, and using self-reinforcement contingently for emitting the desirable behaviors. Since our society values the attribute of self-control, or behavioral self-management, teachers can provide an important service to students by systematically teaching them to use self-management procedures to control their own behavior. Teaching self-management also reduces behavior management demands on the teacher's time, thereby allowing more time for instructional activities.

CUMULATIVE EXERCISE

1. Ellen does her written work very well, but she never volunteers answers during oral review periods. She also exhibits other withdrawn, shy behaviors. Write a contract for Ellen. Her teacher uses a token reinforce-

ment system. Immediate reinforcers are points, which are marked on a grid on Ellen's desk.

Feedback

1. Following is a sample of the kind of contract to which Ellen and her teacher might have agreed. Yours will probably be different in several respects, but it should be similar in a number of ways. The contract should include the following
   a. the behavior
   b. the criteria
   c. the reinforcers and amounts
   d. plans to negotiate the contract

   It should also
   a. provide immediate reinforcement
   b. use small approximations
   c. provide frequent reinforcers
   d. reward accomplishments, not obedience
   e. allow reinforcement to follow behavior, not vice versa
   f. be fair—that is, provide reasonable reinforcement for the amount of behavior required
   g. be clear and unambiguous
   h. be honest—that is, a contract that can and will be carried out
   i. be positive rather than negative
   j. be part of a systematic plan

Contract

Each time Ellen raises her hand to volunteer an answer during social studies review, she will receive 1 point. The teacher will call on Ellen at least four times each period. Each time the teacher calls on Ellen, if Ellen gives a verbal answer that is loud enough to be heard by the teacher and speaks in a complete sentence, she will receive an additional 5 points. Ellen's hand must be fully raised for her to be called on.

Behavior: Raising hand and giving answer.
Criteria: Hand fully raised, voice loud enough to be heard clearly by teacher, and use of complete sentences.
Reinforcers: 1 point for raising hand when not called on; 1 point if called on and 5 additional points for a good verbal response. Points will be exchanged for reinforcers on the class menu.

Negotiate: The contract was originally written by the teacher and did not specify that the teacher would call on Ellen any number of times. Ellen requested the addition of being called on four times.

_____   _____
Date   Teacher's Signature

                         _____
                         Student's Signature

EIGHT

Group Contingencies

OBJECTIVES

After completing this chapter, you will be able to use group contingencies and peer control to improve academic and social behavior. To do this, you will learn to:

1. Identify the advantages of different types of group contingencies, with appropriate targets and situations.
2. Set up group contingencies.
3. Identify and correct problems with group contingencies.
4. Use less formal peer-control procedures.

What is a Group Contingency?

In simple terms, a **group contingency** is a rule that specifies exactly how a consequence, positive or negative, is applied to a group. The behavior of one individual or of many can determine how a consequence will be applied. For example, Schmidt and Ulrich (1969) used access to a preferred activity time (the consequence) as a reward if the noise level of a fourth-grade class (the group) was held below a certain level (the rule or criterion). When the noise level was held down, the whole class received additional activity time. When the noise level increased beyond a certain level, however, the whole class missed the activity time. In this example, the group as a whole, not just one individual, determined the consequence. If the group was too loud, the preferred consequence was lost for the whole group.

Why Use Group Contingencies?

Group contingencies allow efficient use of teacher time and effort. The teacher's time and attention are essential but limited resources in today's large regular-education classrooms. Teachers can be trapped into spending a lot of time attending to a few problem children and neglecting other children who need help. This teacher attention is often negative and punishing because the teacher feels frustrated by the lack of the resources needed to manage classroom behavior and teach effectively. These problems significantly affect teacher morale; the main reasons that new teachers leave education after the first year are basic discipline problems and a feeling of having lost control of the classroom.

As you have already seen, many discipline problems can be solved by using behavioral analysis procedures in well-planned, systematic programs. Unfortunately, in a crowded classroom it is not always possible to set up and properly administer a separate behavior management program for every problem student. Effective systems for managing the behavior of a large number of students are necessary to overcome the limitations on teacher time and attention.

It is also necessary to recognize that although the teacher does have a large degree of control over classroom behavior, the students themselves also have a considerable measure of control over peers and over the teacher (Solomon & Wahler, 1973). Peer influence, which is profound, increases as children get older, and the most troublesome children are the most negatively influenced by their peers. If a child receives peer attention for misbehavior or lack of academic work, then the teacher's attention for positive behavior and achievement may be diminished.

Group contingencies provide an economical behavior change technique that maximizes a teacher's effectiveness because they require less time investment than individual behavioral programs. They capitalize on peer influence and use it to reinforce appropriate behaviors in difficult children.

The use of group contingencies in the classroom also teaches students an attitude toward groups that is fundamental for the well-being of society as a whole—that is, the concept of working for the good of the group even when it is against one's personal inclinations. In effect, group contingencies are what make societies function. Our language is filled with references to group contingencies. Such common sayings as "We're all in this together," "We're all depending on you," and "He's not a team player" reflect the natural application of a group contingency. It could be said that the environment is a natural group contingency for today and tomorrow. If a few individuals foul the environment by dumping toxic waste, then a larger group suffers the health and economic consequences. The environmental or ecological movement is an attempt to make this contingency obvious, to set up a situation in which noncompliance with the group will have definite short-term, as well as long-term, consequences. This example may seem broad; however, the same forces apply in the minisociety of a school classroom. If a few individuals misbehave in a classroom and are reinforced by peers, the effectiveness of the learning environment can be significantly reduced for the whole group. A group contingency program sets up explicit consequences for compliance or noncompliance for the benefit of the group as a whole.

Is a Group Contingency Fair?

When a group contingency is started in a classroom, students and their parents frequently ask, "Why should the whole group suffer because one or two students engaged in inappropriate behavior?" The answer is that they should not suffer consequences that are dependent on another student's behavior *if* they have no influence over that student. This is rarely the case, however.

Several studies (Buehler, Patterson, & Furiness, 1966; Solomon & Wahler, 1973) have shown that peers play an important role in controlling other students' behavior. Attention for a misbehavior, a comment, or a smile from a peer can help maintain a misbehavior. Even a negative reaction from a peer who is teased can positively reinforce the acting-out child to continue teasing. If a child continually misbehaves in the classroom, it is safe to assume that either the teacher is reinforcing the behavior by reacting and attending to it, or other students are reinforcing the behavior with their attention and reactions, or both. In many classroom situations, it is impossible to tell exactly which students are rewarding the inappropriate behavior. Many of the student-initiated reinforcers that reward a misbehavior are so subtle that treating the classroom as a whole is not only fair, but possibly the only way to manage a difficult classroom problem.

A different side of the fairness question involves the individual's taking responsibility for members of the peer group. Parents and teachers usually want students to learn to be responsible for themselves and their friends. They expect children to be actively involved in helping friends who are in trouble. Unfortunately, all too often in our society we see instances when this lesson was not learned. Many adults just "don't want to get involved." High crime rates, documented public apathy when a crime is openly being committed (Fatane & Varley, 1970), and the failure of people to help their neighbors are all too pervasive. Correctly applied group contingencies can teach students about being appropriately responsible for a peer's behavior. They learn to discriminate when their attention or social reinforcement is getting another child into trouble. The question about group contingencies might therefore be better posed as, "Is it fair *not* to teach responsibility and cooperation through group contingencies in the schools?"

The rest of this chapter will introduce the use of group contingencies as a positive technique to manage problem behaviors in large regular-education classrooms. In addition, it will review the use of peers as tutors, graders, and classroom managers.

ADVANTAGES, TYPES, AND TARGETS FOR USE OF GROUP CONTINGENCIES

When Are Group Contingencies Useful?

Teachers who are considering using a group contingency program should carefully consider whether or not the classroom problems warrant this solution. Since this technique makes demands on both the teacher and the students, it should not be used for minor problems. Teachers who feel that the classroom is out of control despite their best efforts or that they are spread too thin to properly administer individual behavior programs should seriously consider a well-designed group contingency program.

The following questions can be useful in helping a teacher decide whether a group contingency is needed:

Do peer attention and recognition generally appear to be important rewards for both appropriate and inappropriate students?

Is there a group of children having the same behavioral difficulties, and do these students appear to be reinforced by each other for the inappropriate behaviors?

Have other individual techniques failed, such as the use of behavioral contracting, a simple token economy, or tangible reinforcers?

Is there a need to improve student cooperation?

Group contingencies seem most appropriate when there is reason to believe that peer reinforcement is either maintaining a misbehavior or could be used to change the misbehavior. If a student misbehaves and then looks for or waits for a reaction from his peers, it is probable that peer reinforcement is important. Being the class clown, defying the teacher for the benefit of other students, or engaging in obnoxious habits such as making funny noises are all problems that are commonly reinforced by peers. These behaviors are **attention-based**—that is, if the attention is removed, the problems stop.

When several students in a class engage in misbehavior and peer attention is suspected of maintaining this misbehavior, it is often impossible for the teacher to monitor all the students individually to determine who is engaging in the behavior or providing reinforcement for the others. A group contingency program can turn inappropriate peer attention around so that it is used to reward appropriate behavior. For example, if accuracy on arithmetic problems is a desired behavior and several students are encouraged to be sloppy or not turn in assignments by the reinforcement of other students, then the teacher might consider a group contingency to turn peer reinforcement of poor class work into peer encouragement of accuracy. As an added bonus, the time the teacher spends grading incorrect papers and trying to instruct unmotivated students can be saved if there is a group incentive to do well on academic assignments.

Teachers who are considering group contingencies need to consider their effectiveness compared with available alternatives. Which is most effective: an individual program for each difficult student or a classroom group contingency? Some research data (Hamblin, Hathaway, & Wordarski, 1971; Shapiro, Albright, & Ager, 1986; Taylor & Sulzer, 1971) seem to indicate that there is little difference in the treatment effectiveness between carefully planned individual and group contingencies. Other evidence (Gresham & Gresham, 1982) indicates that group contingencies are more effective than individual contingencies and tend to foster peer tutoring (Sulzer-Azaroff & Mayer, 1986; Van Houten & Van Houten, 1977). However, Walker and Hops (1973) have found that when individual and group contingencies were combined in a classroom, the behavioral effects were more potent than using either technique alone.

If the answer to most of the questions asked before is yes, then a group contingency should be considered. But what type of group contingency?

Types of Group Contingencies

Litow and Pumroy (1975) have described three basic types of group contingencies that can be used with children. The first provides a group consequence (positive or negative) that is dependent on the performance of a single individual—for example, giving an extra snack to the whole class if the least-motivated student completes 80 percent of his daily assignments. This system is called an **individual-all group contingency**. As the name implies, only one *individual* must perform in a certain way for *all* of the group to receive some consequence. This type of contingency has been used to improve the behavior of hyperactive children (Patterson, 1965), to decrease off-task behavior (Coleman, 1970), and to accelerate academic performance (Evans & Oswalt, 1968).

There are several variations to the individual-all group contingency. First, a teacher can randomly select the individual each day so that each student has an equal probability of being the individual to meet the criterion. Second, the teacher can select an individual and keep the name secret until the student's performance is evaluated to see whether it met the criterion.

This procedure has the advantage of motivating all of the students, because they are not sure whether they have been selected, yet allowing the teacher to evaluate only one student. For instance, the teacher might select a student randomly and keep the name secret, with the rule that the selected student could not talk out or be out of seat more than once without permission. If the rule is met, the class receives a free-time period at the end of the day. If the criterion is not met, the class has an extra academic assignment to complete at the end of the day. The teacher has to keep track of only the randomly selected student's behavior, instead of that of the whole class. However, the class does not know who the selected student is and behaves as if the whole class has been selected to meet the rule. When using random selection of an individual, it is important to ensure that the selected students are not teased or threatened if they do not meet the criterion.

In the second type of group contingency, each member of the group must individually earn a reinforcer based on individual performance. The same performance is required for each group member, and the consequences are the same for each. For example, an extra snack can be given to each group member who correctly finishes 80 percent of the math assignment. Those students who do not correctly finish 80 percent do not get the extra snack. This type of contingency has been called an **independent group contingency** (Gresham & Gresham, 1982; Litow & Pumroy, 1975) because each child is independently meeting a criterion. This is actually an individual contingency that is the same for each group member. Variations of this system have been successfully used to increase academic performance (Hopkins, Schutte, & Garton, 1971) and to reduce disruptive behaviors (Hall et al., 1971). However, the independent group contingency seems to be less effective than a true interdependent group contingency, for which children have to cooperate to meet the criterion.

The third, and possibly most frequently used, group contingency program is one in which the criterion is the same for all group members and the consequences are applied to the group as a whole depending on the group performance. With this **all group–all group contingency,** the individual members of the group are truly dependent on each other for meeting the criterion and receiving or avoiding the consequences. An example of this type of group contingency is making an extra snack available to the entire class if the entire class completes 80 percent of the assigned problems. If the criterion is not achieved, none of the group members gets a snack.

There are several ways to calculate how the group criterion is met. The first method is to require that all members of the group perform at the criterion level. If one student falls below the criterion, no one in the group receives reinforcement. This is a severe standard and requires careful analysis of student capabilities. A lower standard for the group is usually used at first, and the standard is gradually increased in a series of approximations.

The second way to calculate the performance standard is to average the score of the lowest and the highest performances. This method has the advantage of motivating students to perform at their peak, especially when a bonus is given for superior performance. It has the disadvantage of the potential for a few low-performing students to drag down the class's average.

One useful variant of the all group–all group contingency system is to divide the group into competing teams. Barrish, Saunders, and Wolf's (1969) early application of the "good behavior game" is an excellent example. A fourth-grade class that included several troublesome children was divided into two teams. The math period for this class was selected as the time during which to implement the group contingency because much out-of-seat behavior and talking occurred during this period. A game was developed in which each team member received marks on the chalkboard each time one of its members talked, got out of his seat, or moved his desk without the teacher's permission. *Both* teams were winners if they had five or fewer marks on the board. If one team had more than five marks and the other team had less, the team with the fewer marks was the winner. Therefore, both teams could win if the criterion was met, both teams could lose if the criterion was not met, or one team could win and the other could lose.

The consequences for the winning team(s) were victory tags to wear, stars next to their names on a winner's chart, 30 minutes of free time that day, and the privilege of lining up first for lunch. The losing team worked on assignments as usual during the other team's free time and stayed after school if their assignments were not complete. Other researchers (Medland & Stachnick, 1972) have found the good behavior game to be extremely effective, with 97 to 99 percent reductions in talking-out, disruptive, and out-of-seat behavior.

The team variant of the all group–all group contingency fosters competition, which can dramatically improve classroom performance. However, it is important to design this system so that both teams can win if they meet the criterion.

Desirable side effects. Group contingencies have several desirable side effects for the classroom. Shared responsibility and cooperation between students are increased by group contingencies (Sloggett, 1971). Spontaneous peer tutoring is also increased by this method, with group reinforcement increasing general learning rates (Hamblin et al., 1971). Group contingencies also enhance the effects of reinforcement for appropriate behavior and achievement. Social reinforcement from a teacher may have far less effect than the same type of social reinforcement from valued peers, particularly for older children. Interestingly, the children themselves as well as the teachers appear to prefer group contingencies to no group contingencies. Barrish and co-workers (1969) found that most of the students who participated in the Good Behavior Game appreciated the game, offering such comments as, "I like the game because I can read better when it is quiet," "I like it cause it was fun," "You give us free time," or "I like the morning game because it helps keep people quiet so we can work." If a group contingency is well designed, most students will like it. There will be some students who do not, however; generally these will be the students who need the procedure the most (Barrish et al., 1969). These children, who may try to sabotage a group contingency, may have to be taken out of the program and have an individual program designed for them.

EXAMPLE

**Reducing Disruptive Bus-Riding Behavior
Through a Group Contingency**

Riding the bus can cause serious problems for children, especially when the behavior of a few students gets out of control. Approximately 200 deaths and 7,200 injuries occur on school buses each year, and disruptive student behavior contributes to these accidents. Greene, Baily, and Barber (1981) conducted a study using an all group–all group contingency to decrease the disruptive behavior of sixth-through eighth-grade students. The bus ride took about 25 minutes, typically with a full capacity of 44 students, 2 in each seat. The *target behaviors* that were monitored by an observer on the bus included being out of seat, roughhousing, and coercive comments from the bus driver. The *criterion* was unusual in that it was measured by a "noise guard"—an instrument that was sensitive to sound. The noise guard would register excessive noise on the bus, counting each time the noise went above a threshold and giving the students *feedback* through a panel of lights at the front of the bus. The *consequences* included music played on a cassette tape the day following a low-noise bus ride. In addition, raffles were held for hamburgers the day after the noise criterion was met and for movies after 5 consecutive days of low noise. The raffled rewards were later slowly phased out. One *rule* stated that if a student consistently lost the reward for the rest of the students, she would be reported to the school principal.

The results of this experiment showed that when loud noise was targeted with a group contingency, (1) the loud noise decreased, (2) out-of-seat behavior decreased, (3) roughhousing decreased, and (4) coercive comments from the bus driver decreased. Instead of trying to track all the out-of-seat behavior and roughhousing, these authors chose a by-product of these behaviors—noise. They also found an easy and automatic way to record the noise through the noise guard instrument, which was easy to operate, gave accurate counts, and gave the students feedback through lights.

Exercises

In the following list, mark the situations for which a group contingency probably would not be appropriate.

1. Much encouragement from one student is causing the class to be out of control. The principal is asking Mr. Smith to get his class under control.
2. The class is lagging behind in academic performance, but the teacher has not completed an academic assessment of all of the children.
3. Charley Tough keeps causing problems in the classroom and seems to delight in getting other children into trouble.

Feedback

1. In this situation, it would probably be acceptable to try a group contingency after some individual behavior management programs have been tried and have failed, and if the principal is in agreement with trying a group contingency.
2. The teacher should understand each student's academic abilities to ensure that a group contingency criterion is not placed too high for some students.
3. It seems that Charley Tough likes to get other students in trouble and would probably enjoy the negative attention he would receive for causing a group contingency to fail. The teacher should first try to design an individual program for Charley before trying a group contingency.

DESIGNING AND IMPLEMENTING A GROUP CONTINGENCY

All behavioral programs must be well planned and well written; this is especially important with a group contingency program, however, because it affects not one student, but several. The first step is to define the target behaviors and set the criteria.

Three general types of target behaviors are appropriate for group contingencies. Response excesses are the first type, including such behaviors as talking out, being out of seat, and noncompliance. The goal is to reduce the frequency of these behaviors. The second type of target behavior is response deficits, such as poor academic work or the lack of appropriate social skills. The idea is to increase the frequency of the target behavior; examples include increasing the rate of correctly spelled words or the number of appropriate social contacts at recess. The third type of target behavior is that which is not inappropriate per se but which occurs in the wrong place or at the wrong time. An example is doing art projects during a reading period. The teacher generally wants to reduce the occurrence of such behaviors in the inappropriate settings without reducing them in the appropriate settings.

The target behavior should be well defined in an objective, measurable way (see Chapter 5). The response should be overt and observable, and there should be no guesswork about whether or not it is occurring. Conflicts can run high if children perceive that a teacher is unfairly judging their behavior. The general cause of such perceptions is a poorly defined target behavior. "Bad habits," "poor attitude," or "sullen behavior" are examples of poor choices of target behavior. They are difficult to measure, and it is difficult to get two observers to agree that the behaviors are occurring. Good target behaviors might be noncompliance with a teacher's request, incorrect answers to arithmetic problems, or being out of one's seat without permission. For example, *noncompliance* might be defined as not responding within 5 seconds to the teacher's first request.

When choosing target behaviors involving academic competence, it is important to remember that group contingencies can be used only if all of the students are capable of the required behavior. Accurate assessment of each student's academic level and capabilities is necessary before planning target behaviors and criteria that require a specific level of competence.

Once the target behaviors have been clearly defined, baseline data should be collected to determine at what level the behaviors are occurring. The frequency of occurrence and the number of individuals engaging in the behaviors can be counted and tracked for a period of time. The criterion for the group contingency can then be defined. A 10 to 15 percent increase in a deficit behavior, or a 10 to 15 percent decrease in excessive behavior or behavior inappropriate to the situation, is a reasonable starting point. The criterion can gradually be changed as the behaviors improve. Both baseline and data collection systems are discussed in Chapter 5.

The third step is to determine a feedback system that lets the group know how well they are doing in meeting the criterion. A feedback system allows students to gauge their progress. It also facilitates cooperation among group members and competition between teams. The good behavior game mentioned in the last section used chalk marks on the board as the feedback system; other methods are marbles in a mason jar on the teacher's desk, beads on a large abacus, or happy or sad faces on a bulletin board. Feedback is an important part of a motivation system for a group contingency.

The nature of the consequences to be used in a group contingency are also important. The major consequences for use with group contingencies should always be positive, although a well-balanced combination of positive and negative consequences can be extremely effective. A poorly designed group contingency is one that uses only negative consequences and leaves out the positive consequences (Walker & Buckley, 1974). A negatively oriented system is likely to fail, leaving the students with hostile feelings. A good behavioral consequence has an effect on all of the group members—either positive for all of them or negative for all of them. The consequences should also occur fairly frequently—at least once a day when the program is starting.

Examples of positive group consequences are being permitted to immediately leave one's seat when the bell rings for a class or period change, early release from school, extra recess time, the chance to use coin-operated vending machines, and free reading or art time. Reasonable negative consequences could include having to wait 30 seconds after the bell rings before being allowed to leave, having to work on extra academic assignments during free time, or the loss of a privilege such as the extra recess. Poor consequences generally make students wait too long before they are reinforced or are too severe and deny basic rights. Examples of poor consequences are waiting for a week for a class party for younger children, not being able to eat lunch, or being detained after school without the teacher's informing parents or arranging transportation.

It is important to have a variety of reinforcers that the children help select as consequences for a group contingency (see Chapter 3). Once a list of possible reinforcers is developed, choices for each day can be made by using spinners (Jenson et al., 1982) and grab bags (Jenson & Sloane, 1979). First, they allow a more valued reinforcer to be considered for completing a group contingency. Second, this more valued reinforcer need not be given each time a group contingency is completed to have an effect on behavior. Third, an element of chance is introduced, which enhances most reinforcers.

To make a spinner, a circle is divided into unequal areas and an arrow is attached so it can be spun (see Figure 8–1). The divided areas on the circle correspond to the various reinforcers. The easiest or least costly reinforcers are on the larger areas. The more costly or more valued reinforcers are on the narrow area, which reduces the possibility of the arrow's landing on them. When the criterion is met for the group contingency, a child is selected to spin the arrow for the group. The area on which the arrow lands determines the reinforcer for that day. It is important to have the child spin only *after* the group has performed for that day.

A grab bag is similar to the spinner. The reinforcers are written on slips of paper and placed in an opaque container. The more costly reinforcer appears on only one slip of paper, while the less costly reinforcers may appear on five or six slips in the container. When the group meets the criterion, a child is selected to dip into the container without looking and select a slip of paper that determines the reinforcer.

When the group contingency has been planned and discussed with the students and the classroom aides, the details should be written down in outline form. The details and rules of a group contingency are easily forgotten, and an outline helps remind both the teacher and the students. It is also

FIGURE 8-1

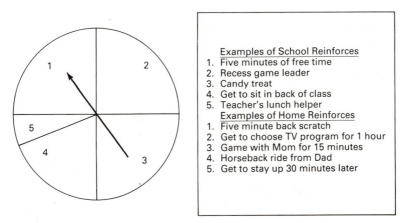

Examples of School Reinforces
1. Five minutes of free time
2. Recess game leader
3. Candy treat
4. Get to sit in back of class
5. Teacher's lunch helper
Examples of Home Reinforces
1. Five minute back scratch
2. Get to choose TV program for 1 hour
3. Game with Mom for 15 minutes
4. Horseback ride from Dad
5. Get to stay up 30 minutes later

Reprinted with permission from W. R. Jenson, M. Neville, H. N. Sloane, & D. P. Morgan (1982). Spinners and chartmoves: A contingency management system for school and home. *Child and Family Behavior Therapy, 4,* 81–85 (New York: The Haworth Press, Inc.).

important for training aides or classroom volunteers, who may not understand all the components of the group contingency and will tend to change it, particularly when the teacher is not present. The group contingency outline should be posted in the classroom so that all classroom personnel and students have access to it.

EXAMPLE

The following outline is designed to help plan a group contingency program for a classroom. In this example, the program is designed to reduce talk outs and increase reading behavior.

Target behaviors

1. Reduce student talk outs, which are defined as any verbal remarks, notes, or gestures made to other students without the teacher's permission.
2. Increase reading behavior, which is defined as the number of pages read with the correct comprehension answers made in the programmed reader (fill-in-the-blank type).

Type of group contingency

Individual-All

Feedback systems

1. For each talk out, the teacher will make a mark on the board
2. For reading behavior, the teacher will graph the number of pages read per day with fewer than four errors on the written comprehension answers in the workbook. Graphs are kept on the students' desks.

Composition of group

All students in the fourth grade class (no teams).

Positive consequences

If the criteria are met for *both* talk outs and reading material, the consequences for the group will be decided by spinning the spinner. The consequences to be given at the end of the day include one of the following:

1. an extra snack
2. 30 minutes of story reading by the teacher in a high-interest adventure book
3. a popcorn party
4. 30 minutes of art projects
5. 30 minutes of extra recess
6. an unknown surprise

Negative consequences

If the criteria are not met, the students will work on their reading for an extra 30-minute period with no snacks for the next day.

Criteria

1. Less than eight talk outs for the day for the entire class.
2. At least three pages read in the programmed reader, with fewer than four errors on the reading comprehension written assignment.
3. Both the talk-out and the reading criteria must be met for reinforcement.

Procedure

The teacher will select three students at random, and their work will be checked to see whether they meet the criteria for their ability levels.

Rules

1. No student can be made fun of or threatened by another student. If this happens, it will count as a talk out for the whole group.
2. If one or two students consistently fail to meet the criteria and lose the consequences for the whole group, these students will be treated as a group by themselves.
3. Only one spin can be taken to determine the consequence. If students complain, they lose the reward.

Program implementors

The teacher, the teacher's aide, and the principal.

Cautions

1. The students' parents and the school principal must be informed that the group contingency is in effect and give their permission.
2. If a small number of students continually miss the criterion, their skill level in reading should be reassessed. If the teacher feels the failures are deliberate, the children should be counted as a group by themselves.

In this outline, the target behaviors are well defined and observable. The contingency type is an individual-all group, so that a random sample of individuals must meet the criteria for the entire group to obtain the positive consequence. The positive consequence involves only 30 minutes of extra time or a snack. However, the teacher should periodically change the rewards on the spinner with input from the students as to what they would like.

Exercises

1. How could this example be changed to an all group–all group contingency?

2. If it is changed to an all group–all group contingency, what precautions should be taken?
3. What should be done if the students have problems earning the positive reinforcement and the program becomes primarily negative?

Feedback

1. To make it an all group–all group contingency, the performance of the entire class would be averaged. Or, the highest and lowest performance in the group could be averaged.
2. The major precaution with an all group–all group contingency is to make sure that one student does not continuously ruin the average for the whole group.
3. The criterion and the way it is calculated (one individual missing the criterion, group average, or high and low average) should be reassessed and changed.

IDENTIFYING AND CORRECTING PROBLEMS

Group contingencies are very effective, but there are cases in which group contingencies do not work, or do not work well. Fortunately, the majority of failures are caused by a few common factors.

A common problem with group contingencies that fail is that their consequences are not well planned or effective. Some teachers make the mistake of assuming that they know exactly what will reinforce a group. If a group contingency does not appear to be working, the teacher should evaluate the consequences that are being used. It is important to ask again what the children want, and then watch them. The students' behavior is the best indicator of what is reinforcing. What do they rush to do? Is it a game or a special activity? What do they ask for more of? A treat or a snack? (See Chapter 3 on selecting reinforcers.)

A second source of program error is the inconsistent application of consequences. This can generally be traced to a few factors. The first is poorly defined target behaviors that cause confusion. If it is difficult to tell exactly when a target behavior is occurring, the consequences for that behavior will be inconsistent. Is there confusion among students and teacher about the exact count of the target behaviors? It does little good to have a contingency system outlined and a performance criterion established if the count of the target behavior is impossible to determine accurately.

Poorly informed or poorly motivated staff assistants is another factor that will surely lead to program failure. If the assistants who administer the program are uninformed about, or do not care about, the program goals or procedures, the program is bound to fail. It is a good idea to explain the benefits of the program to assistants and invite them to help design the program so they are invested in its success. In addition, the classroom assistants and the teacher should read the group contingency outline and take a simple competency test on the specifics of the program. Cooperation and demonstrated knowledge by the staff should be ensured before starting the group contingency.

The presence in the class of a particular child who cannot perform the required target behavior is another factor that can lead to the failure of a group contingency. An 80 percent accuracy criterion for arithmetic is impossible if one or more children do not have basic arithmetic skills. Group contingencies work to motivate students who have already mastered or almost mastered a skill.

Group contingencies are also useful when children need to reach the next level of skill development by trying harder or doing more work. For example, a class may need to practice a skill like multiplication facts to a higher level of accuracy, with new multiplication facts added slowly. To set criterion levels too high or with too big an increment leads to frustration and failure for all the children.

The fact that students in a class may have different skill levels can be accommodated in the criteria if the academic diagnoses and prescriptions were correct. In the sample group contingency presented earlier, one criterion required all students to read at least three pages per day with fewer than four errors on the written comprehension assignment. However, each child was reading individually prescribed materials at his own level. Accurately placing students at appropriate levels allows all students who work to meet the criterion. Inadequate diagnosis or prescription would seriously undercut this program and result in repeated failure for the improperly diagnosed students.

When a negative consequence is applied to the group or a positive consequence is withdrawn, some children may say that it is "unfair" if they have met the criterion but the group has not. They will usually express this unfairness to the teacher and possibly to their parents. The teacher should inform the children that they share the responsibility for the behavior of their classmates and should encourage them to help their peers behave or complete assignments. It should be explicitly stated that no aggression or threats toward classmates will be tolerated. If the student persists in complaining, the teacher should ignore the behavior.

If the group frequently fails to meet the criteria, the teacher should seriously assess whether criteria are inadequately set or whether some children are being rewarded by having the group fail. There will occasionally be a student in a group for whom getting the whole group to fail seems to be reinforcing. This problem confronted Barrish, Saunders, and Wolf (1969) in some of their original research on the "good behavior game." One student "emphatically announced that he was no longer going to play the game" and refused to participate. If he had been kept in the group, his nonparticipation would have penalized the other students who were trying. The teacher therefore dropped this student from the group and treated him as if he were a group by himself (independent contingency). When he would not participate and misbehaved, he was given penalty marks, which effectively changed his behavior. A similar approach of an independent contingency was used by Crouch, Gresham, and Wright (1985) to handle children who were reinforcement "spoilers" for students participating in a group contingency to reduce off-task and disruptive classroom behaviors.

EXAMPLE

Ms. Jones has implemented a group contingency in her classroom. Everything appeared to go well for approximately a week. She had selected reinforcers that she thought would be effective, and defined misbehavior and not doing academic work as the target behaviors. She discussed the program with her classroom aide and volunteers and felt good about their acceptance of the program.

Exercise

1. Analyze the foregoing example, steps from the preceding section, and the outline on how to set up a group contingency from the previous EXERCISE, and describe what Ms. Jones did wrong.

Feedback

1. She selected the reinforcers without including the children's input.
2. Her target behaviors are poorly defined and easily misunderstood.
3. She did not assess the students' ability prior to implementing the program.
4. She did not set explicit behavioral standards for the children to meet.
5. She did not list a set of classroom rules that regulated how children were to behave with a group contingency.
6. She only discussed the group contingency with her classroom staff; she did not train them in its application.
7. She did not discuss the group contingency with the students' parents or the school principal.

LESS FORMAL USE OF PEERS IN THE CLASSROOM

Group contingencies are useful in a classroom because they help control inappropriate peer attention and turn it to useful purposes. Peers can also be used to help a teacher with the everyday tasks that are needed to run a classroom effectively. They can be used as successful student tutors, as reinforcing agents, as classroom managers, and as graders (Kalfus, 1984). It is important to emphasize that when peers are used, they must not be exploited.

Peers should get something for their help, whether it is recognition, extra attention from the teacher, or some type of contracted reward.

Peers as Tutors for Academic Behaviors

Peers have been used to successfully tutor other students in spelling, reading, and arithmetic. There is some evidence that peers can sometimes be as effective as, or more effective than, a teacher in the instruction of certain subjects through modeling, practice, and feedback (Greenwood et al., 1984; Jenkins et al., 1974). These studies found that when peer instruction was used in addition to teacher instruction, students responded more often, weekly scores were higher, and the students who benefited most were the lowest-performing students.

Most of the tutoring research has compared the effects of trained and untrained tutors to that of independent study by students. The research has shown that unstructured or untrained tutors are superior to independent student study (Harris et al., 1972; Harris & Sherman, 1973). Untrained tutors are simply assigned to tutor another student in a subject. The effectiveness of trained peer tutors is well documented (Dineen, Clark, & Risely, 1977; Johnson & Baily, 1974; Parsons & Heward, 1979). To increase tutor effectiveness, the teacher should spend a short time assessing the peer's knowledge of the academic area and training him in basic teaching techniques such as reinforcement, modeling, data collection, ignoring, and giving positive feedback.

Setting up a peer tutoring program is easy for most teachers. Specific curriculum areas such as math facts, spelling words, and reading are areas in which peers can give students extra practice. Teachers should select students who are fluent in the topic area, but they should *not* select only the best students to be peer tutors, leaving the rest of the students feeling less skilled or inferior. If possible, all students should be given the opportunity to both tutor and be tutored. Almost all students have an area of competence in which they can help others. For example, a student who may be a good speller but a poor mathematician can tutor in spelling and receive tutoring in arithmetic. Teachers can pick some less academically advanced students to be tutors for the less rigorous subjects such as sports, art, or crafts. Research has shown that tutoring improves the academic skills of the tutor as well as of the tutored (see EXAMPLE 1).

The classroom area selected for tutoring should be quiet and secluded from other peers, but easily monitored by the teacher; a desk carrel or a classroom corner with dividers makes a good place for peer tutoring. A data collection system is also necessary so that teachers can assess students' progress. Public posting or self-recording are effective techniques to combine with peer tutoring.

It is important to teach the tutors basic reinforcer skills and to stress that their feedback should be positive. The following steps are suggested for a tutor training program:

1. The peer tutor observes three or four tutoring sessions conducted by the teacher or an experienced peer tutor.
2. The peer tutor becomes familiar with the tutoring materials before beginning the tutoring sessions.
3. The peer tutor conducts sessions with the teacher acting as a student. The teacher gives the tutor feedback, with modeling for difficult steps and reinforcement for correct teaching methods.
4. The teacher and the tutor then alternate roles.
5. The teacher conducts an actual tutoring session, but the peer tutor rewards the students.
6. The peer tutor conducts a session with the teacher observing.
7. The teacher randomly observes and receives a "consumer evaluation" from the student being tutored about the peer tutor's method and positive approaches.

Peers as Classroom Graders

Grading papers can be one of the more time-consuming and less challenging aspects of teaching. Peer grading can be incorporated into a peer tutoring program to take some of the load off the teacher. Careful procedures can be designed to enable students to grade their own papers with acceptable accuracy and honesty (Farnum & Brigham, 1978; Hundert & Bucher, 1978).

Peer grading techniques require choosing a curriculum area in which little judgment is needed to decide if an answer is correct. Subjects such as arithmetic, spelling, and programmed (fill-in-the-blank) material for reading are good areas. Subjects that require subjective or qualitative judgments, such as handwriting or English composition, are poor areas for peer grading.

Confidentiality is extremely important in grading papers, and steps must be taken to preserve it. If a peer is helping a teacher with grading, the confidential nature of the task should be emphasized to the student or the names on the papers should be removed or coded so the peer grader doesn't know whose paper she is marking.

A separate area of the classroom should be designated as the grading station, and the teacher should monitor this area. The peer graders can use special colored pens for marking the papers to reduce the chance of cheating by other children. The peer grader should grade a set of papers using an answer sheet and the special pens. When she is finished, the teacher should randomly regrade approximately 10 to 20 percent of them with the peer grader present to explain any problems.

An effective alternative grading approach is to have children grade their own papers with special pens at a grading station, and then have peer tutors explain the missed problems.

Peers as Classroom Managers

Peers can also be used to help teach and maintain nonacademic behaviors in the classroom. With training, a group of socially valued peers can be taught to manage disruptive behaviors, teach social skills, and monitor classroom behavior or management systems. These tasks can be done as part of a group contingency program or by themselves. For example, Solomon and Wahler (1973) taught a group of sixth graders, through observation and discussion, to use social reinforcement for appropriate behaviors, extinction for inappropriate behaviors, and differential reinforcement (a combination of social reinforcement and ignoring) to change the behavior of classroom peers. Similarly, Hendersen, Jenson, and Bingell (1982) used instruction on the use of simple extinction and reinforcement with peers to change the disruptive behavior of several classmates (see EXAMPLE 2).

It is important to train socially valued and motivated peers as classroom managers. Rehearsal, modeling, and video taping sessions are excellent techniques for teaching the necessary skills. Feedback booster sessions with discussions of actual classroom incidents are necessary so that the peer managers can assess their performance.

Peers can also be used in classroom situations to help children with social deficits. Generally, a peer is assigned to a child having difficulty with social skills and both of them undergo the social skills training with a particular program. The advantage of peer training is that they can be used as models both during the training process and to help the trainee generalize the newly learned skills to other situations (Butler & Lahey, 1979; Lancioni, 1982).

Peers can also help as monitors or managers of behavior management systems (Greenwood, Sloane, & Baskin, 1974; Phillips et al., 1973). For instance, peers can be used to help dispense reinforcers that have been earned on individual student contracts, they can serve as data keepers for other students' progress through a program, or they can help run a classroom token economy. Greenwood and colleagues (1974) effectively used peers to run a token economy by having them monitor earned points, subtract points for inappropriate behaviors, and praise students for appropriate behaviors. The effectiveness of peer tutoring programs is enhanced by having the class elect peer managers and making this function a classroom privilege contingent upon being fair and positive (Phillips et al., 1973).

EXAMPLE 1: PEER TUTORING AMONG ELEMENTARY STUDENTS

This study by Dineen, Clark, and Risely (1977) investigated the education benefits that tutors gain from instructing other children. The three children (ages 9 to 10 years) who were tutored were from an open-environment classroom and had an average 2-year reading deficiency. Spelling behavior was targeted for tutoring.

The teachers spent 20 to 30 minutes training the tutors. During the training session, the teacher modeled the appropriate behaviors and then assumed the role of the student while the peer tutor acted as the tutor. The teachers verbally rewarded such tutor behaviors as spelling a word slowly or verbally correcting an error tactfully. The peer and the teacher then alternately switched roles of tutor and student until all of the basic skills were mastered.

The peer tutoring session in which spelling was taught lasted for approximately 20 minutes. Two boxes of index cards were on the table. The peer tutor held 15 spelling-word cards so that the student could not see them. The tutor said the word on the card and waited for the student to write the word and then spell it aloud. If he did so correctly, the tutor circled the word on the student's paper in red, praised him, and dropped the index card into the "plus" box. If the student's written or oral spelling was incorrect, the peer tutor drew a line through the word on the paper and described the error. The peer tutor then slowly spelled the word while the student wrote it. The student then spelled the word aloud and wrote it again. If both versions were correct, the tutor circled the word and placed it in the "minus" box. If the student misspelled the word again, the process was repeated until he spelled the word correctly.

After the 15 cards had been presented, the student was given a blank piece of paper, and the words in the minus box were again presented. Cards from the minus box were used in successive rounds until they were all placed in the plus box. After the session, the student was given a spelling test on the 15 words, which had been previously recorded on a tapeplayer, the test was graded, and the tutor and student were told the number of words spelled correctly.

The results from the experiment showed an impressive 59 percent increase in correctly spelled words. The peer tutors also experienced a 47 percent increase in correctly spelling the tutored words. The peer tutors never wrote the words or took a test. The interaction between the peer tutor and the student seemed to help the tutor almost as much as the student.

EXAMPLE 2: MANAGEMENT OF THE BEHAVIOR OF EMOTIONALLY DISTURBED CHILDREN THROUGH SOCIAL REINFORCEMENT BY PEERS

Four male students in the fourth, fifth, and sixth grades were the subjects of this study. These four subjects had an extensive history of disruptive behaviors that included acting aggressively, talking out, being out of seat, destroying objects, throwing objects, and not complying with teacher requests. These behaviors were observed and baselines collected in the subjects' original classrooms and then in the peer treatment classroom.

Nine regular students were selected to make up a treatment classroom. The nine students were taught by the teacher through modeling and role playing to ignore inappropriate behaviors, to selectively reinforce with attention and social approval, and to integrate the subjects into both social and classroom work settings. The behaviorally disruptive students were then transferred into the treatment classroom. These students left 20 minutes early each day so that the regular peers could explore ways to improve their techniques.

The results were impressive. The rates of talk outs, out of seat behaviors, throwing objects, hitting, and noncompliance dropped from initially high rates in the original classroom to low or nonexistent rates in the peer treatment classroom. Attending to tasks increased and academic performance improved. Instead of being sent to special classes where they would be surrounded by other behaviorally disordered children, the four disruptive subjects were successfully treated by their peers and were then faded back into their regular-classroom settings (Henderson, Jenson, Bingell, 1982).

Exercise 1

Design a classroom program that uses peers in two or more ways to help a teacher.

Feedback 1

Your peer programs should include an academic component and a nonacademic component. The academic component should stress easy-to-teach skills that are easily graded, and it should have a data collection system to help measure student progress. The nonacademic program should use peers to help reinforce appropriate classroom behaviors and ignore inappropriate behaviors.

Exercise 2

In designing two peer programs for a classroom, think of a reinforcement system to reward the peers for their help.

Feedback 2

The reward system can include behavioral contracting for a special reinforcer, extra free time, and social attention from the teacher. Picking all motivated students, rather than just the best achievers, to be tutors can be extremely rewarding in itself.

FAST TRACK

REVIEW

Group contingencies are rules that specify consequences for specific behaviors and are applied to a group of students. Group contingencies are best used when (1) peer attention appears to be an important reward for behavior, (2) other behavioral techniques have failed, and (3) there is a need to improve student cooperation. There are various types of group contingencies. In the *individual-all* group contingency, the consequences for the group are determined by the behaviors of one individual. In the *independent* group contingency, the same consequences are in effect for the whole group, but individuals work independently to achieve the consequences. This is actually an individual contingency with the same consequence for every member of the group and no sanctions if the group fails to meet the criterion. In the *all group–all group* contingency, the behavior of the whole group determines the consequence for the group. A variant of this contingency, generally called the "good behavior game," consists of forming teams which compete for the consequences.

The basic components of any group contingency involve defining observable, measurable *target behaviors*, developing a *feedback system* so that students can continuously assess their progress, and determining *positive consequences* for meeting the criteria and *negative consequences* for not meeting the criteria. The group contingency should have a primarily positive emphasis. Criteria describing the exact conditions under which the target behaviors lead to positive or negative consequences must be carefully developed. General rules must ensure that students will not be threatened or teased if they do not meet the criterion for the group.

A group contingency can fail for several reasons. First, the staff may not be well trained or may not have been involved in designing the group contingency. Second, the consequences may be inconsistently applied because of poorly defined target behaviors. Third, there may be a child in the group who lacks the skills to perform the criterion behavior. Fourth, there may be a child in the group who is reinforced by having the group fail.

Students can be used in the classroom in a teacher-assistant role. Peers can tutor other students in basic academic subjects and mark objectively graded papers. Peers can also assist in nonacademic areas: They can reinforce appropriate behaviors and ignore inappropriate ones, help other students with social skills problems, and help the teacher with classroom behavior management systems such as token economies. Students used in these functions must not be exploited, but must be systematically rewarded for their help.

CUMULATIVE EXERCISE

Describe the steps for designing a group contingency and peer tutoring program for a classroom with the following characteristics:

Some children do not achieve academically; others are disruptive.

The teacher is unsure of the academic ability of some of the students.

The teacher has little time to grade or consistently monitor all of the children's disruptive behaviors.

The teacher has a limited budget for reinforcers.

Feedback

1. The teacher should consider a combination group contingency and peer tutoring program which will work to increase academic performance and reduce disruptive behavior.
2. The teacher must assess the academic abilities of all of the children to set a fair academic criterion.

3. Disruptive target behaviors should be defined in objectively observable and measurable ways so that they can be reduced.

4. Criteria should be set for increasing the academic behaviors and reducing the disruptive behaviors.

5. Consequences should be developed that are effective but not costly. Student input can be important for determining both the positive and negative consequences.

6. An all group–all group contingency with a random sampling of student performance should be considered since the teacher has limited time.

7. Use of the "good behavior game" should be considered.

8. Peer tutoring could be carried out within the teams to help improve academic performance and team performance.

NINE

Teaching Social Skills

OBJECTIVE

After completing this chapter, you will be able to teach the skills students need to become socially competent. To do this, you will learn to

1. Define the term *social skills,* list the characteristics of socially skilled persons, and identify curriculum programs for use in teaching these skills.
2. Assess students' social competence.
3. Specify and describe the procedures commonly used to teach social skills.

Social competence is a key element in a satisfying and successful life. Social skills include such behaviors as greeting another person, being polite and using good manners, complimenting others and providing encouragement, asking others to participate in an activity with you or accepting an invitation to join others in an activity, carrying on a conversation, and, at appropriate times, being assertive. These behaviors, performed and timed appropriately, enable individuals to make friends, be liked by others, and successfully interact in social and work situations.

Many individuals acquire the skills necessary to behave in a socially competent manner as part of their natural development. Others need specific instruction and practice to develop appropriate social behavior. Many teachers have become aware of the need to teach students to be socially, as well as academically, competent.

In recent years, educational and psychological researchers have discovered that many individuals with social skill deficits often have problems in many aspects of their lives, including school. Researchers have identified methods and procedures that are effective in teaching social skills to children and youth. This chapter presents the rationale for teaching social skills, discusses methods for assessing social competence, and presents the instructional procedures that are most effective in helping individuals become socially competent.

In a comprehensive review of social skills training with children, Ladd and Asher (1985) state that difficulty in getting along with others and relating to peers may interfere with progress in school. Researchers estimate that 6 to 11 percent of the students in third through sixth grades have no friends in their classes (Gronlund, 1959; Hymel & Asher, 1977). Asher and Renshaw (1981) stated that 5 to 15 percent of all elementary students have significant interpersonal problems. Ladd and Asher (1985) pointed out that "there is some evidence to suggest that children's early patterns of peer interaction and their acceptance in the peer group remain relatively stable over time" (see Asher & Hymel, 1981; Coie & Dodge, 1983; Van Alstnyne & Hattwick 1939; Waldrop & Halverson, 1975). This suggests that social incompetence in childhood may have a lifelong detrimental effect. Children who have difficulty in relating to peers are also more likely to drop out of high school (Barclay, 1966; Ullman, 1957), commit suicide (Stengel, 1971), be seen in mental health clinics (Rinn & Markle, 1979), seek psychiatric assistance as adults (Cowen et al., 1973), experience behavior or character disorders or become juvenile offenders (Roff, Sells, & Golden, 1972), have school maladjustment problems (Gronlund & Anderson, 1963), and/or become alcoholics (Robins, 1966). French and Tyne (1982) point out that these findings are correlational and that an actual causal relationship between poor peer relations and the aforementioned problems has not yet been established. However, the high correlations reported are cause for concern.

Lack of basic social skills is a serious problem. Consider the elementary student who spends the entire recess period wandering around the playground watching others play but never participating, or the high school student who eats lunch alone every day, or the junior high student who fails an assignment because she doesn't know how to ask for assistance. These students usually feel alone, left out, and rejected. If they can learn to start conversations, make requests, be assertive, invite others to play with them, or ask to join in, they may become part of the socialized world around them.

Of equal concern is the aggressive child who lacks appropriate social skills—the sixth grader who demands, "Let me play or I'll knock your teeth out," or the secondary student who swears at and threatens his teacher. Children who are aggressive, socially withdrawn, have low levels of peer acceptance, are unpopular, and have no close friends can usually benefit from social skills instruction.

For training students with social skills deficits, Young, West, and Smith (1984) recommend that groups include socially competent as well as socially deficient students. Socially competent students already have most targeted social skills, or acquire missing skills quickly. They can thus model appropriate behavior for the other students. Use of the social skill by the competent model also validates the social acceptance of the behavior and increases the probability that the other students will risk trying their newly learned social skill in nontraining settings. Another advantage of including socially competent students in the instructional group is that these socially competent students become more aware of the social skills being emitted by other, less competent students, and the more competent students may reinforce the less competent students for using appropriate skills. In other words, all students can benefit from social skills instruction.

SOCIAL SKILLS: WHAT ARE THEY, WHO HAS THEM, AND HOW ARE THEY TAUGHT?

What Are Social Skills?

Stated simply, **social skills** are those behaviors which allow an individual to successfully interact with others. Psychologists and educators have proposed many variants of this definition, five of which are included in Table 9–1.

Young and West (1984) examined the term *social skills* and the characteristics of socially skilled persons and pinpointed three fundamental aspects of the definition. First, the word *social* refers to interpersonal interaction—in other words, behavior that involves more than one person. Therefore, any time we talk about social skills, we must be talking about behavior that involves interpersonal interaction between two or more people. Thus, having a conversation with another person, making a polite request, or asking someone to play are all examples of a social interaction between two or more people and thus qualify as social skills. Personal hygiene behaviors such as showering, applying deodorant, and dressing in clean clothes may be important prerequisites for social skills, but since they are done in private

TABLE 9-1 Definitions of Social Skills

A repertoire of verbal and nonverbal behaviors by which children affect the responses of other individuals . . . in the interpersonal context . . . the extent to which (children) are successful in obtaining desirable outcomes and avoiding or escaping undesirable ones *without inflicting pain on others* is the extent to which they are considered socially skilled. (Rinn & Markle, 1979, p. 108)

Those responses which, within a given situation, prove effective or . . . maximize the probability of producing, maintaining, or enhancing positive effects for the interactor. (Foster & Ritchey, 1979, p. 626)

The ability to interact with others in a given social context in specific ways that are socially acceptable or valued and at the same time personally beneficial, or beneficial primarily to others. (Combs & Slaby, 1977, p. 161)

Those identifiable, learned behaviors that individuals use in interpersonal situations to obtain or maintain reinforcement from their environment. (Kelly, 1982, p. 3)

An individual's ability to interact successfully with others in his natural environments; at school, home, and work. (Hersen & Eisler, 1976, p. 362)

and are not part of interpersonal interactions with others, they do not qualify as social skills.

Second, *skills* are behaviors; they show action. A person is usually referred to as "skilled" if he possesses a talent, or has had enough training and practice to achieve the ability to perform a behavior well, not just in a mediocre way. The word *skill* does not refer to what one *doesn't* do. When asked what social skills they would like students to acquire, some teachers will respond by saying, "I would like them not to fight and not to tell lies." While not fighting and not lying are admirable characteristics, they cannot be considered social skills. A social skill must be a positive action. Not creating problems in class is not a social skill, but raising one's hand and politely asking the teacher for assistance or complimenting and praising other students for things they do well would be examples of social skills.

Third, a person who is socially skilled must be capable of displaying social skills at the appropriate time. For example, a socially skilled person knows when to be assertive and when to be compliant; he knows how to perform the social skill and when to perform it.

Another characteristic of social skills is that they are valued by society. People must think that behaving in a certain manner (the social skill) is important and worthwhile. In some cultures, praising and complimenting other people is considered a very positive behavior; in other cultures, however, complimenting a person is considered a negative act and may be insulting. Social competence is defined by the society and the cultural groups within the society. In gangs of delinquents, the gang member who can best insult a person in authority might be considered the most socially skilled member of the gang. In a classroom, however, a student who follows directions and is compliant with authority figures is usually considered socially skilled. It is important to assess the immediate environment in order to determine what social skills are considered important and acceptable by those within that environment.

A socially skilled person is not only capable of displaying social skill at the right time, but also performs those appropriate social behaviors repeatedly and consistently. We all may have flashes of brilliance, but skilled persons regularly perform well. Since a socially skilled person uses her social skills regularly, the social behavior appears to be a natural and comfortable part of her behavior.

In summary, then, social skills are interpersonal interactions between two or more persons; the skills involve action (they are not a description of what is *not* done); and the interactions are positive, and effective, and valued by society. Socially skilled persons successfully display these interpersonal behaviors at the appropriate times, in the appropriate situations, regularly, consistently, and in a natural manner.

Young and West (1984) have described five categories of social skills based on the goal of the interaction. Following are examples of social skills grouped by these five categories:

1. *Social skills can promote interaction.* Some social skills are designed to promote or develop social interactions. Some examples of these social skills include greeting others, inviting others to play, accepting an invitation to play with someone else, asking questions, sharing, offering assistance to others, praising or complimenting others, saying "thank you," making polite requests, asking for clarifications, expressing affection, offering information, expressing interest, and offering comfort.

2. *Social skills can help us deal with unpleasant circumstances.* The following social skills may help us deal with unpleasant circumstances: denying requests, handling name calling and teasing, giving negative feedback, resisting peer pressure, apologizing, making a complaint, and dealing with an accusation.

3. *Some social skills are designed to handle or resolve conflict.* Social skills that may help us resolve conflict include negotiating, compromising, and problem solving.

4. *Other social skills may help us maintain social interactions that have already begun.* Some examples of social skills that maintain interactions include conversing, asking questions, providing information, seeking clarification, listening, and taking turns.

5. *Assertive behaviors are often classified as social skills.* Assertiveness skills include expressing your feelings, reiterating requests, clarifying understandings, saying no, dealing with accusation, expressing concerns.

Curricular Programs for Teaching Social Skills

Several readily available curricular programs have been designed to teach social skills. Educators and support personnel can use these programs with relatively little training. Most of the programs were designed for small group instruction but can be used in larger class settings.

TABLE 9-2   Commercially Available Social Skills Training Materials

Program	Publisher
ACCEPTS—*A Curriculum for Children's Effective Peer and Teacher Skills,* H. M. Walker, S. McConnell, D. Holmes, B. Todis, J. Walker, & N. Golden.	Pro-Ed 5341 Industrial Oaks Blvd. Austin, Texas 78735
ASC—*Achieving Social Competence,* D. P. Morgan & K. R. Young	Dept. of Special Education Utah State University Logan, Utah 84322-6500
ASSET—*A Social Skills Program for Adolescents,* J. S. Hazel, J. B. Schumaker, J. H. Sherman, & J. Sheldon-Wildgen	Research Press Box 31779 Champaign, Illinois 61821
Getting Along with Others: Teaching Social Effectiveness to Children, N. F. Jackson, D. A. Jackson, & C. Monroe	Research Press
Skillstreaming the Adolescent, A. P. Goldstein, R. P. Sprafkin, N. J. Gershaw, & P. Klein	Research Press
Skillstreaming the Elementary School Child, E. McGinnis & A. P. Goldstein	Research Press

Table 9-2 lists some commercially available social skills programs, all of which have been proven effective. Each of the programs listed in Table 9-2 identifies social skills to be taught, has checklists and other assessment procedures, suggests teaching and management strategies, and includes support materials such as videotapes and program forms. The ASC and ACCEPTS programs have video training tapes to assist instructors in learning how to teach social skills. Instructors should initially follow the program closely; as they become more experienced, some modifications may be appropriate.

To illustrate the skills that are often included in a social skills curriculum, the skills taught in the *Achieving Social Competence* program (Morgan & Young, 1984) are listed in Table 9-3. A teacher could select any one of the listed skills or a combination of skills and, following the scripted lessons, teach the skills to a small group or an entire class.

EXAMPLE

Mr. Harwood, a fifth-grade teacher, was concerned that several students in his class were being impolite to one another and were often negative in their interactions. He was particularly concerned about five students who were constantly teasing others. He was also concerned about a student who was shy and withdrawn, and was the brunt of a lot of the name calling and teasing. In discussing this problem with the school psychologist, Mr. Harwood discovered that what he wanted was for his students to develop social skills and that there were social skills curriculum programs available for use by teachers. The school psychologist suggested that they use the *Achieving Social Competence* (ASC) curriculum to teach social skills to the class.

In reviewing the materials, Mr. Harwood decided that the *Being Positive and Making Friends* program was exactly what he was looking for. Teaching the students in his class to praise and encourage others, to invite others to play with them, to share and help, and to be polite were all skills that he wanted the students in his class to develop and use. The school psychologist offered to help Mr. Harwood learn more about how to assess the class to determine the skills they needed most and how to teach the skills. Mr. Harwood borrowed the program and retired to the faculty room to review the instructor's manual. (In the next two sections, Mr. Harwood will learn how to assess the social skills of the students in his class and how to help those who are socially deficient become socially competent.)

Exercise

1. Define the term *social skills*.
2. List five characteristics of a socially skilled person.

Feedback

1. Your definition should include the following points: (a) social interaction between two or more persons, (b) involves action, (c) the interaction is performed in a positive and/or effective manner, (d) at the appropriate time, and (e) the behavior is valued by society and considered appropriate.
2. A socially skilled person emits (a) the correct social behavior, (b) at the right time, (c) in the appropriate situation, (d) consistently, and (e) in a capable manner.

ASSESSING SOCIAL COMPETENCE

Like any good instructional program, teaching social skills requires procedures for assessing and evaluating the behavior that is being taught. It is important that teachers of social skills assess student behavior before, during, and after instruction. Although many methods have been developed to assess and evaluate social skills, the process is not always a simple one. Several characteristics of social skills make the assessment process more difficult than academic assessment.

First, social skills are almost always "opportunity-bound"; that is, social skills must occur in the right context or situation. For example, one does not compliment or praise another person when that person has made a mistake or a blunder. Praise should follow appropriate behavior, or at least an improvement in previous performance. Another example of opportunity-bound

TABLE 9-3   Social Skills Taught in the Achieving Social Competence Curriculum

Skills Taught

This program contains four instructional packages, each of which contains four or five separate lessons. The packages and accompanying lessons are as follows:

I. Basic Social Interaction Preskills
   1. Getting the person's attention/Establishing and maintaining eye contact
   2. Speaking with appropriate voice volume and tone
   3. Maintaining an appropriate distance
   4. Don't interrupt/Wait until other person pauses before speaking

II. Talking with Others: Teaching Conversation Skills to Children and Adolescents
   1. Keeping it going by providing additional information and answering questions
   2. Asking a question and making comments
   3. Changing the subject
   4. Providing positive feedback
   5. Starting and ending a conversation

III. Assertiveness Skills for Adolescents
   1. Asking for a clarification
   2. Making a clarification
   3. Making requests
   4. Denying requests
   5. Negotiating

IV. Being Positive and Making Friends
   1. Praising
   2. Encouragement
   3. Invitations to play
   4. Sharing and helping
   5. Being polite

behavior is engaging in a conversation. To have a conversation, one must have the opportunity to speak to others, and the opportunity to have a conversation during a school day is usually restricted to free time, recess, lunch period, or other nonacademic times. One can't just hand a student a piece of paper, as one would with math or reading assessment, and tell him to start displaying social skills. Students must perform those behaviors in an appropriate context.

A second consideration is that most social behaviors occur infrequently. The number of times that we perform certain social behaviors is usually limited, largely because social skills must occur at the appropriate time. In other words, while a student may read thousands of words at school each day or solve dozens of math problems, it is unlikely that a student will praise and compliment others fifty times, or ask someone to play with her thirty times. For some social behaviors, therefore, we would have to watch students for long periods of time in order to evaluate whether or not they are using the social skill.

Another consideration in the assessment of social skills is that many social skills are private in nature and are therefore difficult to observe and evaluate. For example, one might apologize quietly, speaking only to the person to whom the apology is directed. A young man who is appropriately asking a girl for a date is not likely to do so in front of the class. Praise and compliments are often given quietly, in small groups or individually. In spite of these restrictions, methods for assessing and evaluating social competence have been developed.

Screening Methods

Screening is the first type of assessment procedure. Initial screening is used to determine which students could benefit most from social skills training. Two assessment procedures are helpful for initial screening: (1) completing a social skills checklist and (2) collecting sociometric data.

Social skills checklists.   Most commercially available social skills curricula contain a social skills screening checklist, which simply lists the specific social skills and subskills that the socially competent child should be able to perform. Figure 9–1 is an illustration of the preskills and conversation skills listed in the ASC Social Skills Checklist. Someone who knows the child well, usually a teacher or parent, reads each item on the checklist and scores the individual's level of competence. Most checklists use a rating-scale format. In Figure 9–1, a rating of 3 indicates that the individual frequently uses the social skills, which suggests a high degree of social competence. A rating of 2 indicates that the person sometimes uses the social skill. A rating of 1 means that the rater believes the student never uses the skills, which suggests little or no competence in this area. The rater is also given an opportunity to check that he has not had an opportunity to see the student perform the skill and is therefore not able to rate that particular behavior.

FIGURE 9-1   Example of a social skills checklist.

Social Skills Checklist

Student's Name _____ Date _____

Rater _____

Directions: Please read each statement below and circle the rating which best describes the student's current level of performance on the skill. A number 1 indicates that the student never demonstrates the skill; a number 2 indicates that the student sometimes demonstrates the skill; and number 3 indicates that the student frequently demonstrates the skill. Circle a 0 if you have not had the opportunity to observe the student demonstrating the skill or are unsure about the student's current level of performance.

		Not Observed	Never	Sometimes	Frequently
I.	Preskills				
	1. Establishes/ maintains eye contact.	0	1	2	3
	2. Speaks with appropriate voice volume.	0	1	2	3
	3. Maintains appropriate distance when speaking with others.	0	1	2	3
	4. Does not interrupt conversations.	0	1	2	3
	5. Speaks in appropriate tone of voice.	0	1	2	3
II.	Conversation Skills				
	6. Begins conversations appropriately.	0	1	2	3
	7. Keeps conversations going (asks and answers questions).	0	1	2	3
	8. Provides positive feedback during conversations.	0	1	2	3
	9. Presents and/or responds to information.	0	1	2	3

Sociometric measures.   Checklists are typically filled out by parents or teachers who know a child well. **Sociometric techniques** are used to obtain information regarding a student's social status with his peers. In other words, they measure how well liked or disliked a child is by his peers. Asher and Hymel (1981) discuss the two major methods of sociometric assessment—nomination and rating scales—pointing out that the peer nomination method developed by Moreno (1934) is the most commonly used technique. Children are asked to nominate a certain number of classmates that they especially like and/or dislike. The procedure is helpful for identifying children who are experiencing high levels of peer rejection, which in turn suggests the need for social skills training.

The rating-scale technique (Asher & Hymel, 1981; Roistacher, 1974; Singleton & Asher, 1977) is implemented by asking students to rate each of their classmates according to a specific criterion. A common rating scale calls for circling a number from 1 (for someone they like to play or work with a lot) to 5 (for a student with whom they don't like to play or work). A variation of the technique is to use "faces ranging from a frown to a smile." These "accompany the scale to help communicate the meaning of each of the numbers" (Asher & Hymel, 1981, p. 129). Figure 9–2 illustrates a sociometric instrument using faces (Young, West, & Smith, 1984). The form was given to all students in the class; each student rated all other students. Those students with the highest number of "don't like" faces were further screened for social skills deficits.

Social skills checklists and sociometric measures are good screening instruments and do indicate which students are likely to benefit from social skills training. However, screening instruments only reflect the opinion of others who associate with the student. The best method of determining whether a student can perform a particular social skill and use that skill in the natural environment is by observation.

Observational Methods

Because of the aforementioned problems inherent in social skills assessment (that is, the fact that social skills are opportunity-bound, often occur at low frequencies, and are often performed on a one-to-one basis or in a private situation), it is difficult to collect observational data to verify their existence. There are, however, three procedures for conducting behavioral observations of students performing social skills: observation via role-play tests, contrived situations, and naturalistic observation.

Role-play tests.   A **role-play test** consists of creating a hypothetical situation which calls for the use of a particular social skill to solve a problem or to promote a positive social interaction between the student and another individual. During the role-play tests, the student has the opportunity to perform the social skill that she would display under similar conditions in the natural environment. Even though the role-play test is hypothetical, it should

Name _____

Directions:
  Put an X on the circle that shows how you feel about each of the
  people in your class.

Ann	Friend	All right	Don't like	Don't know
	☺	😐	☹	?

Bill	Friend	All right	Don't like	Don't know
	☺	😐	☹	?

Bob	Friend	All right	Don't like	Don't know
	☺	😐	☹	?

Carol	Friend	All right	Don't like	Don't know
	☺	😐	☹	?

Dick	Friend	All right	Don't like	Don't know
	☺	😐	☹	?

FIGURE 9-2   Sample sociometric rating scale.

represent a real-life situation and be structured to emulate natural conditions. Once meaningful situations have been identified, the appropriate responses for those situations must be determined. An evaluation procedure is then devised to rate students' responses during the role-play test. This can be accomplished by conducting a task analysis of the appropriate social behavior to successfully complete the role-play situation and then developing a score sheet for an observer to record whether each step of the task analysis was performed correctly.

Cartledge and Milburn (1980) have suggested guidelines for the successful use of role-play assessments:

1. *Practice situations.* Provide students with an opportunity to practice role playing before actual testing occurs. This will help students learn what is expected prior to the test.
2. *Standard script.* Preparing a written script for introducing the role-play situation helps to standardize the test from one administration to the next.

3. *Prompts.* A prompt is used to initiate the role play. After presenting the scripted scene, give the student a prompt to which he should respond by displaying the appropriate social skill.

4. *Use audio- or videotaping for evaluation.* Where possible, it is a good idea to make a video or audio tape recording of the student's response to the role-play situation. This provides a permanent product of the response and makes evaluating the correctness and the quality of the response easier.

An example of a role-play test item may help to clarify how these procedures are put into practice. If you were establishing a social skills unit to teach students how to greet a potential employer and ask for a job, you would first identify some potential work sites in the community where the students might apply for jobs. You might identify two or three fast-food restaurants, grocery stores that hire students to bag groceries or stock shelves, or other businesses in your community that typically hire young people. You could then create situations in which a student would have to greet the manager of one of these establishments. Next, you would analyze the steps involved in greeting the manager and asking for a job. Then, based on these steps, you would create standard scripts and a scoring sheet for rating the students' responses. Next, you would select a prompt to initiate the actual interaction and then organize all of these materials on a form in order to standardize the role-play assessment.

Although role-play tests can be helpful in assessing whether or not the student can perform the social skill appropriately, this assessment procedure does have limitations. A role-play test does not indicate whether a student can actually perform the social skill in the natural environment (generalization). Therefore, role-play tests should be supplemented by other instruments that give the instructor feedback on whether or not the student does use the social skill in real-life situations. Figure 9–3 is an example of a role-play test item for making requests at school.

Contrived situations.   Another procedure for observing students' social behavior is to establish a contrived situation in which social behaviors are likely to occur. For example, a teacher instructing students in how to share their possessions with one another might create a situation in which two or more students are placed at a table to do an art project. Each student would be given different types of materials to use. The instructor could then observe the situation and record how many times the students share their materials with each other.

This situation is different from role-play tests in that it is less structured and specific prompts are not given to the students. This contrived situation requires the instructor to define sharing behavior and devise an observation system (see Chapter 5). Contrived situations are usually limited to short time periods of 5 to 10 minutes. This procedure is very helpful for allowing instructors to observe students in situations in which they are likely to have the opportunity to use the skills that are being taught.

Social Skill: Making polite requests

Settings (where skill may be used): School, home, work, social activities

Role-Play Situation:
      You have been sick all week and haven't been able to finish a homework assignment. You need more time for your work and want to ask your teacher for a couple of extra days. You have just walked into class and your teacher sees you.

Prompt: Teacher says, "Hello (Name). I'm glad to see you're feeling better."
        (Note: If no response, say, "What would you say?")

Evaluation Checklist (Task Analysis):

		Yes	No
1.	Eye contact	___	___
2.	Pleasant face	___	___
3.	Appropriate tone of voice	___	___
4.	Appropriate voice volume	___	___
5.	Appropriate distance	___	___
6.	Got attention	___	___
7.	Didn't interrupt	___	___
8.	Provided rationale for request	___	___
9.	Made request in form of question	___	___
10.	Was polite (e.g., said please, thank you)	___	___

Percent of steps completed correctly: _____

FIGURE 9-3 Example of a role-play test item and evaluation checklist.

Naturalistic observations. Some social skills do lend themselves to naturalistic observations and, when it is possible, this is the most desirable method of collecting information about how well a student behaves socially. Some behaviors occur naturally during the course of the school day and are therefore relatively easy to observe; examples include inviting someone to play during recess, taking turns, praising or complimenting another student, or having a conversation. These behaviors might occur during recess, at lunch, or during free-time activities. To conduct an observation, the social skills being taught must be defined and an observation system developed. The instructor can then observe the students during appropriate situations and record each occurrence of the specific social skill. This type of observational system is helpful because it indicates that the student can and is performing the social skill in real-life situations. Two methods that are particularly helpful in recording social behavior in naturalistic settings are frequency recording (each occurrence is counted) and checklists detailing the steps of the social skill. Figure 9–4 is an example of an observational recording form.

Self-monitoring/self-evaluation.   Monitoring the progress of students' mastery of social skills is as important as monitoring any other subject. Because of the nature of social skills, the monitoring process is more difficult. Students' self-monitoring and recording of their own behavior is an excellent procedure for collecting progress data. As part of the social skills lessons, students are taught to become more aware of whether or not they are performing the desired social behavior and to record each occurrence of the behavior on a form. Students are usually assigned a specific number of social behaviors to practice as homework. The students return the self-monitoring card to the instructor and are reinforced for their performance.

The principle of shaping should be used when giving students homework assignments and teaching them to self-monitor. Students are initially given very easy assignments that require only one or two instances of the social behavior. It may even be necessary to prompt people in the student's environment that the student has been assigned to perform the social behavior so that they can be helpful when she attempts to use the skill. If there are concerns about the accuracy of the self-recording, others can be alerted to the assignments and asked to initial cards when they see the behavior being performed. Teachers, playground aides, parents, and peers have all been used successfully to assist in checking the accuracy of self-recorded data.

For some social skills, it is also helpful to teach the student to evaluate the quality of the social skills that they are practicing in addition to recording the occurrence of the social skill. This can be done by preparing a checklist for the student to indicate whether he completed each of the steps in the task analysis. The student may also be required to rate how well he did. Again, the principle of shaping can be used by reinforcing the student for gradually improving the quality of the use of the social skill and including all of the steps.

Jenne and colleagues (1986) taught conversation skills to three socially withdrawn high school students. The students acquired the skills and displayed them in a contrived setting but not in nontraining situations. The authors then developed a self-recording procedure and taught students to evaluate their own conversational behavior. The addition of the self-evaluation procedure resulted in improved conversational behavior in other settings. A four-month follow-up indicated that the students were considerably less withdrawn and engaged in conversations with other students at appropriate times.

SOCIAL SKILLS PROGRAM
Data Collection Form

Student's name: _____ Date: _____

The total time during which these observations were made: _____

Person filling out this form: _____

1. Following Directions (Give a minimum of ten directions per day)
   / = A direction   + = Direction followed

   Total number of directions given: _____
   Total number of directions followed: _____

2. Praising, Complimenting, or encouraging others

   Total day =

3. Negative talk

   Total/day =

4. Excuse me/I'm sorry

   Total/day =

5. Demands or impolite requests

   Total/day =

6. Making a polite request (please . . .)

   Total/day =

7. Thank you

   Total/day =

FIGURE 9-4 Sample data collection form for collecting frequency data on seven social skills.

EXAMPLE

Mr. Harwood reviewed the skills taught in the "Being Positive and Making Friends" part of the ASC program. With these skills in mind, he reflected upon the social competence of each of the students in his class and picked out six students whom he felt needed particular help. He then rated each of these six students' social behavior on the ASC social skills checklist. He found that all six had skill deficits in the areas of praising and complimenting, sharing and helping others, and being polite.

He decided to obtain more assessment information by observing these six students during their morning and noon recess periods. He observed the students and counted each time he saw and heard them compliment someone, offer to share or help, or use the words *please, thank you,* or *excuse me.* His observational data confirmed his suspicion that the students did not emit these social behaviors in their social interactions with others.

Mr. Harwood then decided to construct and administer role-play tests for each of those three skills to see whether they knew how to perform each skill appropriately. The students performed better on the role-play tests than they had during the recess periods. However, Mr. Harwood concluded from his assessment data that social skills instruction would be very appropriate for these students. In further consultation with the school psychologist, Mr. Harwood decided to divide the six target students into two groups of three and add three socially competent students to each of those two groups. Mr. Harwood and the school psychologist would then teach social skills to each of these two groups separately, for 30 minutes a day twice a week. Before they commenced the social skills lessons, the school psychologist suggested that Mr. Harwood learn more about how to teach social skills.

Exercise

1. List six methods of assessing social competence.
2. Explain the guidelines for conducting role-play tests.

Feedback

1. The methods commonly used to assess social competence include checklists, sociometric ratings, role-play tests, observations of contrived situations, naturalistic observations, and self-recording.
2. Guidelines for role-play tests include (a) provide an opportunity to practice before the test, (b) prepare a standard script, (c) prompt the initiation of the role play scene, and (d) evaluate (when possible, make a video or audio tape recording of the role-play interaction).

SPECIFYING AND DESCRIBING INSTRUCTIONAL PROCEDURES
FOR SOCIAL SKILLS

Social skills instruction may be conducted by regular-classroom teachers, special educators, school counselors, school psychologists or social workers, or administrators. Frequently, two or more individuals team teach social skills to students. The skills may be taught individually, in small groups, or to an entire class. Regardless of who teaches the skills or to what group size, the same basic direct instructional procedures should be used.

Several instructional procedures are common among the various social skills instructional programs: defining the social skill to be taught, conducting a task analysis of the steps involved, presenting a rationale for the importance of the social skill, modeling the social behavior (via either videotaped or live role-play scenes), using role play and practice activities, coaching and prompting, providing positive reinforcement, giving homework assignments, and teaching behavioral rehearsal strategies. Some instructional programs also present *nonexamples* of the social skill (a role-play scene in which the social behavior is emitted incorrectly) in order to help students discriminate between the appropriate and inappropriate use of the skill.

Defining the Social Skills to be Taught

In the introduction of the lesson, the students are told specifically what social skill they will learn in that particular lesson (for example, the teacher would say, "Today we are going to learn how to praise others"). The social behavior is then defined and an example given: "Praising is telling someone that you like them, something about them, or something they did or accomplished. For example, I might say, 'John, you sure played a great baseball game today.' " The brief definition and example should give the students a clear picture of what they are going to learn to do.

Presenting a Rationale

Next, the students are provided a rationale for the importance of learning this new social skill. The instructor might say, "Praising others is one way to make friends. When you compliment others, they are more likely to compliment you in return. They will like you better and you will like them." At this point in the lesson, the students should be able to explain the importance of learning the skill.

Explaining the Steps

Social skills often involve several behaviors performed in sequence. To teach the skill, the instructor must know each step in the sequence. Therefore, task analyses are conducted to identify the steps (see Chapter 10 for more information on task analysis). In some social skills programs, the steps are presented as rules. Each step or rule is explained and modeled by the teacher. As the lesson proceeds, the students are asked to recall each step in performing the skill.

EXAMPLE

Figure 9-5 is an example of a social skill definition, task-analyzed steps, and a rationale for the skill. Lesson 1 of *Being Positive and Making Friends* (Likins, Morgan, & Young, 1984) is on praising. The "overview" provides a rationale, the "goal" is the objective, and the "skills" are the task-analyzed steps that a socially skilled person might use to praise others.

FIGURE 9-5   Sample social skills lesson.

LESSON I: PRAISING

Overview

This lesson introduces the student to several rules for effective praising. It includes basic conversational components (preskills) as well as skills which facilitate positive peer interactions. Research indicates that praising has a reciprocal quality; that is, when a child praises or compliments another child, his chances of receiving reinforcement in return are increased. A child who appropriately praises or compliments other peers will likely be viewed more positively by peers and adults.

Goal

Student will exhibit the skills necessary to appropriately praise/compliment peers.

Skills

1. Student will exhibit the basic social interaction preskills.
2. Student will identify a praiseworthy act or object.
3. Student will state what it is that he likes.
4. Student will use appropriate tone when making praise statements.
5. Student will use physical gestures, when appropriate, to indicate approval.

Reprinted from Likins, Morgan, & Young (1984). *Being Positive and Making Friends.* Logan, Utah: Dept. of Special Education, Utah State University.

Modeling the Social Skill

Teacher instructions are not always sufficient for teaching a particular skill; it may be necessary to demonstrate some behaviors. This is often referred to as *modeling* a behavior. Most students imitate a model; in fact, much of what children and adults learn is acquired by imitating models (Bandura, 1969). Several factors can affect the degree to which learning occurs through modeling:

1. Selecting models with attributes similar to the students you are teaching, particularly models of the same sex, age, and race as the learner (Bandura, 1969; Goldstein, 1981)
2. Selecting "prestigious" models—those with high status, who are viewed as highly skilled by the learners (Bandura, 1969; Gelfand, 1962; Goldstein, 1981)
3. Reinforcing the model's behavior (Bandura, 1969; Mayer, Rohen, & Whitley, 1969)
4. Combining modeling with instructions (Zimmerman & Rosenthal, 1974)
5. Keeping the modeled behavior simple and clear (Bandura, 1969)

Modeling is used extensively in the process of teaching social skills, either with live models (usually the instructor) or via video or audio tapes. The method used is not particularly important, but the social skill being taught must be clearly demonstrated to the students.

Commercial programs often use videotape presentations to model examples and nonexamples of social skills (Morgan & Young, 1984). Students observe others using the social skill in a particular situation; the tape is then stopped and the scene is discussed and critiqued. If the scene was a nonexample, the students explain what was missing and how it could have been improved. If the scene was a positive example, then the students would point out the elements that made it so. Additional examples and nonexamples of that social skill in a variety of situations are then presented.

If videotapes are not available, the same process can be carried out by having the instructor(s) and/or students act out examples and nonexamples of the skills. Again, after each role play, the scene is discussed and critiqued by the students. This process helps students discriminate between appropriate and inappropriate use of the particular social behavior. It also facilitates students' mastery of the social skill steps.

Role Play and Practice

The role-play and practice portion of the lesson is a critical part of social skills training. Students must practice the skills if transfer of the behavior from the classroom to natural situations is to occur. During every social skills lesson, each student should have several opportunities to role play the skill being taught. The instructor may initially role play the social skill with the students playing subordinate roles. The roles gradually reverse, with the instructor playing subordinate roles and the students demonstrating the use of the skill.

When using role-play situations, the principal of shaping (the reinforcement of successive approximations toward the final desired behavior) is a very important part of the teaching process. Initial role-play activities should be brief and easy for the student to perform. The instructor may break the social skill down into its components and have the students participate in a role play using only a portion of the complete social skill. For example, the praising lesson might include the following steps: (1) getting the person's attention, (2) looking the person in the eye, (3) formulating the praise statement, (4) speaking in the appropriate tone of voice (showing interest and enthusiasm), (5) speaking in an appropriate voice volume, and (6) making the complimentary statement. The initial role play might include only the first two steps. The student would say, "Hi, John," and look John in the eye. Each subsequent role play might add an additional subskill until the student is role playing all of the steps.

The instructor should initially use guided practice by providing feedback and coaching to the students. Guided practice also uses corrective feedback. The instructor should not hesitate to correct the student's inappropriate use of the social skill. Corrective feedback should always be positive. Corrective feedback should be provided by complimenting the student on what she has done correctly, then pointing out the problem, modeling the correct way to perform the skill, having the student role play the situation again, and reinforcing improvement.

After the student can successfully perform the social skill in role-play situations, the instructor moves into student-initiated practice. During the role-play activities, the situations were developed by the teachers or came from a social skills curriculum program. Practice activities now shift from artificial situations to those that occur naturally in the student's environment. The students are asked to think of situations in which they might use this new social skill. The instructors ask the students to provide as much detailed information about this potential situation as possible: who might be involved in the situation, where it might take place, what might be said, what activity might be going on prior to the performance of the social skill. Using this information, the instructor creates a role-play situation similar to the natural situation described by the student. This type of practice promotes generalization.

Coaching and Prompting

Coaching involves the use of prompts, encouragement, and praise. Several types of prompts may be utilized: *gestural prompts*—such as gesturing for the student to lift his eyes and direct them toward the person to whom he is speaking; *verbal prompts*—cueing the student on the next step or reminding him of how to perform a particular step; and *physical prompts*—physically assisting the student through a step necessary to complete the skill. Words of encouragement are beneficial for students who are having difficulty completing the role-play activity. Praise for all improvements and accomplishments should be specific and immediate.

Reinforcement

Like other behaviors, social skills must be reinforced to be strengthened. Social skills that are not reinforced will eventually extinguish. Some social skills are reinforced naturally; a polite request is frequently granted, complimenting others is often reciprocated, an act of sharing will likely be returned. However, other reinforcers are usually needed during instruction. For many students, praise is sufficient to increase, then maintain, their attempts at using new social behaviors. Other students require more tangible reinforcers, such as point systems with backup reinforcers. (The guidelines discussed in Chapter 3 on positive reinforcement and Chapter 6 on token reinforcement can be applied to social skills training programs.)

Homework and Behavioral Rehearsal Strategies

Homework in a social skills training program is designed to facilitate the transfer of learning from the classroom to the student's natural environment. Each day, the teacher gives the students assignments to use the skill in an outside setting, to be completed before the next social skills lesson. For example, students might be asked to praise four other students during recess time, share their materials with students during their afternoon art project, make a request, negotiate a solution to a problem with their parents, or have a conversation with another student during lunch. Special assignment cards, such as the one illustrated in Figure 9-6, are often helpful in facilitating the completion of homework assignments. Before the lesson is completed, the student writes the homework assignment on the card. As the student completes the assignment, he checks off his accomplishments. The card is then returned to the instructor for praise and other reinforcement.

Some students have difficulty completing homework assignments, either because they are uncomfortable using the skill or because they forget. The first problem may be solved by one of two methods. First, the instructor may use the student-initiated practice procedure to identify some specific situations in which the student believes he can complete the homework assignment. The student then practices with the teacher and other classmates under simulated conditions. This procedure may help the student gain some confidence in using the social behavior in the natural environment.

Students may also be taught to use a behavioral rehearsal strategy. They specifically plan what they will say and do when using the social behavior, and they rehearse the behavior with others or in front of a mirror until they feel comfortable with it. The behavioral rehearsal strategy is particularly helpful for secondary-age students.

A second strategy for improving the completion of homework is to involve others in the assignment. Teachers, secretaries, school administrators,

---

SOCIAL SKILLS PRACTICE CARD

Name _____   Date _____

Things to remember:
  Use your new skill.
  Take this card with you and mark it when you use the social skill.

Social Skill: _____

	Where?	How many times?				
		1	2	3	4	5
1.	In class					
2.	On the playground					
3.	At lunch					
4.	At home					
5.	Other					

FIGURE 9-6 Example of a self-recording form.

---

parents, or the student's peers may be prepared to assist the student when he attempts to perform the social behavior. These people can be asked to reinforce the student, encourage improvement, and assist or prompt the student as necessary. The involvement of parents or siblings can help with the transfer of the skills from school to home. A study conducted by Young, West, and Smith (1984) demonstrated that a cooperative school–home social skills program can effectively enable students to perform the social skills in both environments. It is essential that the instructor follow up on homework assignments, discussing problems and reinforcing the students for successfully completing assignments and using the skills.

Teaching Interactions

Learning is not restricted to formal lessons. In addition to formal group instruction, informal individual instruction is important. In fact, most learning takes place informally, in our interactions with others. This is particularly true with social behavior.

We begin learning how to behave socially in infancy, and we continue to learn and modify our social behavior throughout our lives. Parents affect their children's social behavior in thousands of incidental teaching interactions or teaching moments—those brief moments when the situation establishes a learning environment.

A teaching moment for a social skill might occur at the dinner table. The preschool child might say, "Give me the butter"; the socially astute parent quickly capitalizes on the teaching moment and says, "Say, 'please pass me the butter.'" The child is then encouraged to ask for the butter again in a more socially acceptable manner, whereupon the correct behavior is reinforced by receiving the butter. Most children learn appropriate social behavior in this informal, incidental manner; however, some children have not had socially appropriate behavior modeled for them and/or they have not had their attempts at appropriate social behavior reinforced by significant others.

TABLE 9-4   Social Skill Teaching Interaction

---

1. **Positive approach to youth**—The teacher makes initial contact or opening statement in a nonpunitive manner. May be a greeting or descriptive praise, but should not include punishing statements.

2. **Description of inappropriate behavior**—The teacher describes inappropriate behavior in detail to youth.

3. **Description of appropriate behavior**—The teacher describes desired or appropriate and effective behavior to youth.

4. **Rationale for the appropriate behavior**—The teacher describes consequences, both good and bad, that could be received following appropriate and inappropriate behavior.

5. **Modeling of desired behavior**—The teacher demonstrates the appropriate (and may include the inappropriate) ways to perform the defined social skill.

6. **Request for youth to practice**—The teacher requests that the youth practice the desired behaviors in a role-play situation. The teacher develops the role-play scene to include other peers, adults, etc.

7. **Feedback during practice**—The teacher provides both positive and negative feedback on youth's performance by describing those behaviors that are good, adequate, or need improvement and by offering constructive suggestions for future performance.

8. **Requests for additional practice by youth**—The teacher requests that the youth attempt to role play situations again and suggests specific behavior changes and improvements to be included.

9. **Praise for accomplishments**—The teacher delivers praise to the youth for performance and participation.

10. **Homework practice assignment**—The teacher requests that the youth attempt the trained social skill in another setting, at another time, or with different people. Desired behaviors and rationales to be utilized by the youth are reemphasized. (p. 2)

Reprinted from Clark, Northrop, & Wood (1980). *Social Skills Development: Applications of Individual and Group Training,* unpublished manuscript, Las Vegas, NV: Children's Behavior Services, Mental Health Center. Adapted from E. L. Phillips, E. A. Phillips, D. L. Fixsen, & M. M. Wolf, *The Teaching-Family Handbook,* University of Kansas, 1974.

Therefore, teachers may need to informally teach social behaviors when the situation provides a learning opportunity.

Clark, Northrop, and Wood (1980) outlined a ten-step process referred to as "social skills teaching interactions." Instead of teaching formal social skills lessons, teachers, counselors, and other school personnel become observant of the social interactions in which children are engaged. When a child is observed behaving in a socially inappropriate manner, the teacher capitalizes on the learning opportunity and engages in a social skills teaching interaction. Teaching interactions involve the same skills that are used in a formal social skills lesson, but they are organized to be used in a teaching moment with one or two students. Table 9–4 presents and defines each of the ten steps in the teaching interaction.

TABLE 9-5   Key Steps for Achieving Generalized Use of Social Skills

1. Teach behaviors that will maximize success and minimize failure.

2. Make the training realistic. Use relevant examples and nonexamples. Role-play and rehearsal activities should reflect what actually happens in the students' "real life."

3. Make sure the students learn the skills in the direct instruction part of the program. Demonstrating mastery of the skills is more likely if there are plenty of supervised practice opportunities.

4. Extend practice by providing "real life" homework assignments. The use of homework assignments allows the students to practice outside the training situation.

5. The self-report following a homework assignment is critical. Reinforcing contingencies should be programmed into the homework assignment which provide positive consequences for: (a) the accuracy of the self-report, and (b) the achievement of homework assignment tasks. If the student "fails" his homework assignment or his self-report is inaccurate, the teacher should employ problem-solving/positive practice procedures prior to beginning the next lesson.

6. The natural environment will need to be reprogrammed to support performance of the targeted skills. Teachers, other school personnel, peers, and parents must be involved in reinforcing and prompting the newly learned social skills.

7. For more difficult cases, there is a need to "go the extra mile" to facilitate generalization. This involves the gradual transfer of stimulus control procedures. That is, the trainer may actually follow the student into a variety of nontreatment settings to prompt, coach, correct, and reinforce the targeted skills. The trainer would then "fade" and other individuals in the environment would take over this role.

8. Fade special reinforcement programs to eventually approximate the reinforcement schedules existing in real life.

9. Teach self-management skills which the student can use to help maintain improvements in social behavior.

10. Use periodic "booster shots" if the student's behavior deteriorates or if only as a preventative measure. The student would be recycled back to the appropriate lesson.

Reprinted from Morgan & Young (1984). *Teaching Social Skills: Assessment Procedures, Instructional Methods, and Behavior Techniques.* Logan, Utah: Dept. of Special Education, Utah State University.

Generalization of Newly Learned Social Skills

Social skills instruction is not complete until the social behavior *generalizes*. Generalization takes place when newly acquired social skills occur in settings other than the training setting. Many students who can master social skills in a classroom setting have difficulty using them at other times and in other places. Social skills are of little value unless they are emitted in the right situations. The lack of generalization is a problem reported by several authors (Berler, Gross, & Drabman, 1982; Gresham, 1981). The problem is that students often do not display the same level of the skill outside the training situation. The social skills successfully rehearsed and practiced in the classroom should ultimately transfer to other times, places, and situations. Morgan and Young (1984) outlined ten procedures that are helpful in achieving a generalized use of social skills; these procedures are presented in Table 9–5.

EXAMPLE

After learning the basics of how to teach social skills, Mr. Harwood started his instruction with Lesson 1 of "Being Positive and Making Friends." Lesson 1 was on how to praise other students. (Figure 9–5 is a page out of the ASC program that introduces the praising lesson by providing an overview, a goal statement, and the task-analyzed steps to be taught.) Mr. Harwood taught the praising skill by following the lesson manual. He presented the skills and the steps to be learned and a rationale for the importance of learning to praise and compliment others. He also provided the students with role-play experiences for practicing the skills. After each lesson, Mr. Harwood gave the students a homework assignment, which usually consisted of identifying two praiseworthy acts and praising the students for emitting those behaviors during recess. Mr. Harwood continued his observation of the target students at recess to determine whether they were praising others.

After a couple of weeks, Mr. Harwood noted that the students had learned to perform the praising skills in the training session, but had not generalized the skills to the playground. He decided to use the ten-step teaching interaction procedure and take advantage of teaching opportunities by assisting the students in using the skills during recess. The next day, Mr. Harwood saw Billy, one of his target students, watching another student perform a difficult trick with a soccer ball. This was a great opportunity for Billy to practice his praising skills, but Billy said nothing.

Mr. Harwood recognized this teaching opportunity, so he called Billy over and initiated the teaching interaction. "Billy, can I talk to you for a minute?" said Mr. Harwood. "You've been doing well in our social skills class, but I've noticed that sometimes you miss opportunities to use your praising skills during recess. For example, Joe just did an excellent trick with the soccer ball and you could have complimented him, but you just stood quietly and watched without saying anything. It would have been a great opportunity for you to compliment him. Let me show you what I mean. You pretend to be Joe and I'll be you, and I'll walk over and compliment you." Mr. Harwood looked Billy (now pretending to be Joe) in the eye, smiled, and in an appropriate tone of voice said, "Joe, that was a great trick you did with the soccer ball. Would you show me how to do that?" Mr. Harwood then asked Billy to do a role play, with Billy doing the praising. Mr. Harwood then complimented Billy on each correctly performed step in the praising skill. He ended the teaching interaction by asking Billy to look for another opportunity to use his praising skills during that recess period.

Exercise

1. List four types of role-play activities.
2. Describe four methods for enhancing the success of homework assignments.

Feedback

1. Four role-playing activities are (1) instructor role plays the social skill using a developed scenario with the student playing subordinate role, (2) student role plays the skill using a developed scenario with the instructor playing the subordinate role and assisting, (3) guided practice, and (4) student-initiated practice.
2. Four methods for enhancing the success of homework assignments include (a) using assignment cards for self-recording, (b) using student-initiated practice, (c) teaching behavioral rehearsal strategies, and (d) involving others in the activity.

FAST TRACK

REVIEW

Achieving social competence is an essential part of our growth and development. Many individuals acquire *social skills* as part of their natural development; others need assistance in developing the social skills necessary to successfully interact with others. A socially skilled person emits appropriate social behavior in a successful and positive manner during interpersonal interactions. Socially skilled persons also emit these social skills consistently over time and in the correct social context. Research has shown that all students can benefit from social skills instruction; students who are already socially competent may assist teachers in developing appropriate social behavior in other students.

A number of commercially available social skills curricula are available. Some of these programs are designed primarily for elementary students and others for secondary-aged students. While each of these programs is unique, all of them teach similar social skills and use similar instructional methods.

Successful instructional programs always include methods and procedures for assessing and evaluating student performance. Assessment and evaluation are important in social skills instruction as well. *Social skills checklists* and/or *sociometric ratings* are used in the initial screening process to identify students who can benefit from social skills instruction. *Direct observational methods* help document that students can emit the social skills correctly and in the natural environment. Three observational procedures are role-play tests, contrived situations, and naturalistic observations. Self-monitoring and self-evaluation procedures also provide a method for monitoring student progress after instruction has begun.

The best approach to teaching social skills is a direct instructional method using procedures such as role play and practice, coaching and prompting, positive reinforcement, behavioral rehearsal, and homework assignments. Social behaviors and all of their subcomponents should be clearly described, and students should be helped to understand the rationale for learning the social skill.

Exercises

1. List, describe, and give examples of the ten steps in a social skills teaching interaction.
2. Explain the procedure for conducting role-play and practice activities in the classroom.
3. Describe four basic procedures for achieving generalization of social skills behaviors from the classroom to community settings.

Feedback

1. The following ten steps should be included:
   a. *Positive approach*—Teacher makes an initial contact or opening statement in a nonpunitive manner.
   b. *Description of inappropriate behavior*—Teacher describes the inappropriate behavior.
   c. *Description of appropriate behavior*—Teacher describes the appropriate social behavior.
   d. *Rationale for the appropriate behavior*—Teacher describes the consequences, both good and bad, for emitting the appropriate and the inappropriate social behavior.
   e. *Modeling of desired behavior*—Teacher demonstrates the appropriate social skill.
   f. *Request for practice*—Teacher has student role play the correct social behavior.
   g. *Feedback during practice*—Teacher provides positive, constructive feedback.
   h. *Request for additional practice*—Teacher requests that the student role play additional situations.
   i. *Praise for accomplishments*—Teacher praises the student's performance during role-play and practice activities.
   j. *Homework practice assignment*—Teacher requests that the student attempt to use the new social skill in another situation that day.

2.　In conducting the role-play activities, the teacher would use guided practice, role-play situations, and student-initiated practice. With guided practice, the teacher role plays the student exhibiting the social skill, while the student watches or plays a subordinate role. Then the student takes over and role plays the social skill as the teacher provides whatever coaching and prompting is needed to help the student emit the appropriate social behavior. After the student has demonstrated mastery of the social skill, the teacher proceeds with additional student-initiated practice.

In student-initiated practice, the teacher has the student describe situations in which they might use the social skill and then constructs role-play situations to be similar to the naturalistic situation described by the student. Student-initiated practice is also useful in preparing for homework assignments.

3.　a.　Use of self-report of homework assignments is one method to achieve generalization. Homework requires students to emit the behavior in the community; their reports give the teacher feedback as to whether or not they are successfully performing the behavior in nontraining settings.

　　b.　Use of student-initiated practice during role-play times will help prepare students to successfully perform the homework assignments in community settings.

　　c.　Prepare the natural environment by informing other teachers, school personnel, peers, and parents that the student is learning the new social skill and ask them to assist in prompting and reinforcing the student so that she can successfully emit the new social behavior in the natural environment.

　　d.　Teach students self-management skills so that they can monitor and evaluate their own social behavior in the future.

TEN

Developing Instructional Programs Through Task Analysis

OBJECTIVES

After completing this chapter, you will be able to conduct a task analysis for a proposed or existing unit of instructional material. To do this you will learn to:

1. Formulate adequate behavioral objectives which include the desired performance, the conditions under which the performance will occur, and the criteria for adequate performance.
2. Specify the subskills and tasks of which the performance is composed, and place them in the correct order for instruction.
3. Specify and describe the prerequisite skills (entry behaviors) assumed by the instructional unit.

Task analysis is the process of determining the skills that must be taught if a student is to reach a specified instructional objective. A task analysis provides explicit guidance concerning the instructional materials which need to be designed. When task analysis is applied to an existing instructional program, the skills actually taught by the program are assessed. The analysis allows us to determine what the materials will actually teach and whether steps are missing in the material if it is to meet the desired teaching objectives.

Behavior analysis is a structured and explicit approach to teaching. Its assumptions imply that the teacher is responsible for what is learned and what is not. Behavior analysis suggests that the teacher has a responsibility, not only to provide students with an "opportunity" to learn, but rather to directly teach what the students are to learn. Task analysis clarifies what must be taught directly, the order in which it should be taught, and the results that should be obtained—all necessary steps in devising behavioral instruction.

Task analysis can be broken down into several steps. The first is the accurate formulation of the behavioral objective. The second, subskill analysis, is the sequential definition of the skills a learner must acquire to move from present skills (entry behaviors) to the behavioral objective. The third is the definition of the entry skills or behaviors it is assumed pupils will have upon beginning instruction. These three steps must be established for an instructional program as a whole and for each objective in the program.

There are several approaches to task analysis (Foshay, 1983). This chapter presents a behavioral perspective (Crandall, 1987; Solomon, 1976). Cognitive theory has generated approaches to task analysis that stress assumed "processing" of tasks more than overt behavior (Gardner, 1985). Although many like to believe that "cognitive" terms can be "translated" into behavioral terms, and vice versa, Hineline (1984) indicates the many pitfalls in these attempts.

This chapter emphasizes the application of task analysis to classroom settings (see, for example, Mechner, 1976). In business and industrial settings, the emphasis is more "work-oriented" (Sage & Rose, 1985; Kennedy, Esque, & Novack, 1983; Faris, 1983). Chase (1985) suggests the usefulness of task analysis (and other behavioral procedures) in the development of computer courseware; Crandall (1987) does much the same for the design of computer documentation.

FORMULATING OBJECTIVES

Objectives

A behavioral objective is a statement of what the learner will be able to do after successfully completing a unit of instruction. The objective for this chapter states that the learner "will be able to conduct a task analysis . . . ". The sum of all of the objectives of a program equals the goal of the instructional program. The sum of all of the objectives at the beginning of each chapter in this book equals the book's goal. If a learner can meet all of the objectives for each part of an instructional sequence, the learner has attained the goal of the instructor.

Subobjectives

Many objectives are easier to teach when broken down into smaller units, called **subobjectives.** On the first page of this chapter, the major objective is divided into three subobjectives. A learner who can perform the skills listed by the subobjectives has learned what is specified by the objective.

Components of Objectives

A behavioral objective has three major components: performance, conditions, and criteria.

Performance. A behavioral objective describes the new task or skill the student will have acquired at the completion of the course or course section. Because performance refers to behavior, it must be stated in objective, nonjudgmental terms. Performance defines the goals of teaching and is the first part of an adequate behavioral objective. The goals comprise the changes that the teacher hopes to produce.

Conditions. It is sometimes not enough merely to state the performance in formulating a behavioral objective. The overall situation in which the performance will occur—including the types of prompts, aids, and methods of testing—must be included. For instance, if the teacher wants students to be able to identify cases in which economic interests affected legislation, he must indicate whether he means that they will be able to write a paragraph about this relationship; whether they will be able to use source texts; whether, given a series of descriptive paragraphs, they will be able to identify those which reflect instances in which economic considerations influenced legislation; or whether they will be able to identify instances of economic factors' influencing legislation in the newspapers. Does being able to correctly name colors mean giving the color name for colored patches, naming all the colors in a drawing in a book, or being able to answer questions such as, "What color is an apple?" Each of these tasks is a different behavior, and failure to differentiate between the conditions is a common cause of failure to teach what is actually desired. These conditions often determine whether we say we want to teach recall, recognition, problem solving, and so forth.

The type of learning and the method of teaching required for performance vary widely under different conditions. To an extent, Gagne's (1970) eight levels of learning address this issue. According to Gagne, for instance, learning to match the names of presidents to political parties on a matching test is a different level of learning than relating the actions of presidents to their political parties; each requires a different type of teaching. A poorly worded objective stating that students will "know the political affiliations of presidents" might obscure these differences, lead to ambiguous teaching, and produce unreliable test results.

Correct specification of the conditions of performance will produce a behavioral objective that avoids these problems. It can also avoid trivial learning. Does the teacher really wish students merely to be able to list the major parts of a flower, or does she want them to be able to identify these parts on an actual flower? The performance under the former condition is relatively trivial from an educational point of view, while under the latter condition it might not be. One may be a first step toward teaching the other, however.

Criteria.   Once the performance and the conditions of an objective are adequately specified, the criteria for success must be stated. Is the objective met if the student can correctly spell 25 out of 40 words on a spelling list? Is the objective met only if the student correctly spells all of them? Is the objective met if, from a specified list of descriptions of legislation, the student can identify the influence of economic factors in half of them, or 80 percent of them—and within what time limit? These criteria must also be specified if the teacher is to be able to assess whether goals have been met.

The following example should help clarify the components of a behavioral objective and their relationship.

> *Performance.* At the completion of this teaching unit, the student will be able to correctly identify metaphors in poetry and write a brief sentence restating each metaphor in literal language.
>
> *Conditions.* Given the poetry anthology used as a text, during a one-hour class the student will select five poems not covered in class or homework, copy two metaphors from each poem, and write one to three sentences on each metaphor, stating the meaning in literal English.
>
> *Criteria.* At least nine of the student's selections will be metaphors, and at least seven of the descriptions will be correct, as determined by the teacher and the teacher's manual.

Here is another example for a similar task: "Given ten simple declarative sentences (third-grade reading level) consisting of a noun, a verb, a direct or indirect object, and various articles, adjectives, and adverbs, the student will be able to underline the subject of each sentence and circle the predicate verb in each sentence in ten minutes with no errors."

Stating the conditions and the criteria are critical for the instructional designer, as is all of task analysis (Reigeluth, 1983). For ease of communication, however, the performance alone, without the conditions or criteria, are often listed for audiences other than those who design educational materials.

Problems with Objectives

For objectives and subobjectives to be useful, they must be stated in objective terminology, lack superficiality, be instructional in nature, and refer to what the learner learns, not the content of the instruction.

Terminology.   Certain commonly used terms in education are open to interpretation, and this vagueness creates problems when these words are used in behavioral objectives.

VAGUE EDUCATIONAL TERMS

to know	to grasp the significance of
to understand	to enjoy
to appreciate	to believe

From *Preparing Instructional Objectives* by Robert F. Mager, copyright © 1984 by David S. Lake Publishers, Belmont, CA 94002.

What does a teacher mean when she states that she wants students to "know" the Bill of Rights? What performance does she expect? All of the following are possible interpretations:

1. The student has read the Bill of Rights.
2. The student has read the Bill of Rights and identified items from the Bill of Rights from a list of thirty possible rights.
3. The student correctly recites, verbally or in writing, the Bill of Rights in exact form.
4. The student paraphrases the Bill of Rights in paragraphs.
5. Given a hypothetical list of laws, the student marks those which violate the Bill of Rights and states what is violated.
6. Given the Bill of Rights, the student writes examples of actions violating the Bill of Rights.
7. Given a list of things a person might do, the student marks those protected and those not protected by the Bill of Rights.

Consider an objective which states that a student will "understand" addition "facts." Does this mean that he will be able to add two-digit numbers presented as problems on a worksheet, set up and add numbers from dictation ("How much is 7 and 5?"), or set up and solve word problems ("If you had 9 oranges and Jack gave you 4 more, how many would you have?")? Any or all of these may be desired, but it is necessary to define which of these the student is to do in order to demonstrate that he "knows" or "understands."

Superficial objectives. Packard (1975) points out that an objective may be technically correct, yet trivial. The following is an example:

> After reading pages 56 through 89, the student will be able to pass the multiple-choice test at the end of the chapter in a class period and obtain a score of 80 percent.

Assuming that the students know what a multiple-choice test is and can get the correct answers, the performance, conditions, and criteria are relatively well specified. The objectives are trivial, however, because they do not specify the skills actually learned by the student. Such statements are more useful in contingency contracts (see Chapter 9).

Noninstructional objectives. Objectives that do not meet the criteria for a behavioral objective may be useful for other purposes. The objective "Students will develop an appreciation and understanding of the arts" is relatively useless as a guide to instruction, but it may serve the purpose of helping a school to communicate to others its general goals and aims. Similarly, objectives that contain only a description of the performance may help a teacher communicate to parents. An example is, "Students will be able to correctly identify and give the meaning of poetic metaphors." Partial objectives of this sort are often called *goals*. Although goals are not suitable guides to instruction, they may be valuable for these other communication purposes.

Content as objectives. Most curriculum materials are described by their content. A list of content or topics is not the same as a list of behavioral objectives, however. A text or program may indicate that it covers "the Bill of Rights" without describing what students will learn. A teacher can use the same content to formulate and teach a wide range of objectives. Although a text may cover the Bill of Rights, it may not teach some of the teacher's objectives. It is highly improbable that one text alone will attain all of the objectives desired by a teacher. The teacher may have to modify or supplement the content of a curriculum, text, or program to meet particular objectives. Some of the behavioral objectives previously discussed with reference to the Bill of Rights would probably require that the teacher supplement most texts or provide additional input.

Classification of Objectives

Bloom and colleagues (1956) and Krathwohl, Bloom, and Masia (1964) have devised a taxonomy of educational objectives which classifies objectives in a systematic, theoretical way into three domains: the *cognitive, affective,* and *psychomotor*. A detailed breakdown of types of objectives within the first two domains has been published. The assumption is made that acquisition of skills related to objectives numbered lower in the taxonomy are prerequisites for higher skills. For example, taxonomic classification 1.24, "knowledge of criteria," is a prerequisite for category 1.25, "knowledge of methodology."

Bloom and Krathwohl assert that all adequately formulated behavioral objectives in education can be classified into one or another of their abstract taxonomic categories. Since these categories indicate which types of objectives are prerequisites for other objectives, their classifications should define for an educator the proper sequence in which to teach objectives. Consequently, by classifying the objectives into the categories in the taxonomy and comparing them with the theoretically ideal order, a teacher should be able to determine whether a set of objectives eliminates essential points.

Although this breakdown has a certain comprehensiveness, theoretical value, and clarity, it is usually not the most convenient classification for classroom use. Teachers usually find that the behaviors with which they are concerned are more conveniently grouped as *academic behaviors* (for example, learning math skills), *social-emotional behaviors* (learning certain ways of interacting with others), and *work skills* (staying on a task, attending, and using resources properly). Although this practical breakdown lacks some of the logical elegance and comprehensiveness of the Bloom and Krathwohl categorizations, it is very close to the everyday reality which teachers confront. Teaching academic skills, social-emotional skills, and work skills concern all teachers, and can form the basis for a task analysis and specific objectives for a class. In practice, task analysis is a difficult and arduous chore, and its use is realistically restricted to major objectives or problem areas.

In a third approach, some teachers find it more efficient to categorize classroom objectives in terms of the type of behavior considered. This approach groups objectives as *attending behaviors, transition behaviors,* or *academic behaviors.* Attending behaviors relate to a student's being "on task" or "off task." Obviously, students are usually attending to something, and being on or off task is usually defined in terms of the teacher's current plans for the class. Transition behaviors are the behaviors necessary for a student to move smoothly from one task to the next. They include putting away or taking out materials or walking from one room or location to another. Academic behaviors relate to the learning of specific subject-matter skills.

An analysis of classroom objectives from any of these three points of view should ultimately cover the same ground. While the latter two seem much more practical for the teacher, task analysis is applicable to objectives regardless of which approach is used.

EXAMPLE

In Figure 10-1, the major objective at the top is called the *terminal objective* and specifies a performance, conditions, and criteria. The subobjectives (labeled *intermediate skills* in Figure 10-1) become specific; many are actually subskills or tasks (see the next section). The subobjectives are sequenced so that prerequisites will be learned first. At the bottom are the assumed entry behaviors.

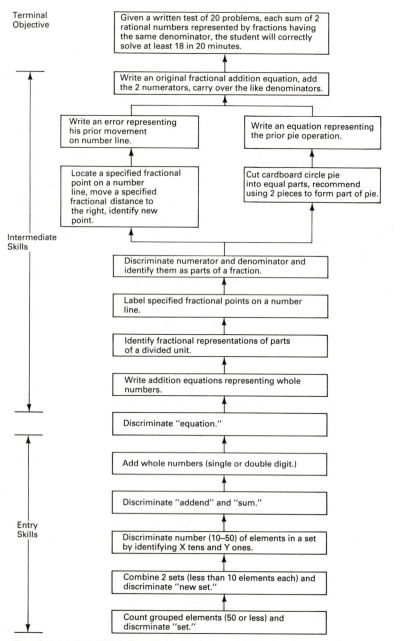

Terminal Objective

> Given a written test of 20 problems, each sum of 2 rational numbers represented by fractions having the same denominator, the student will correctly solve at least 18 in 20 minutes.

> Write an original fractional addition equation, add the 2 numerators, carry over the like denominators.

> Write an error representing his prior movement on number line.

> Write an equation representing the prior pie operation.

> Locate a specified fractional point on a number line, move a specified fractional distance to the right, identify new point.

> Cut cardboard circle pie into equal parts, recommend using 2 pieces to form part of pie.

Intermediate Skills

> Discriminate numerator and denominator and identify them as parts of a fraction.

> Label specified fractional points on a number line.

> Identify fractional representations of parts of a divided unit.

> Write addition equations representing whole numbers.

> Discriminate "equation."

> Add whole numbers (single or double digit.)

> Discriminate "addend" and "sum."

Entry Skills

> Discriminate number (10–50) of elements in a set by identifying X tens and Y ones.

> Combine 2 sets (less than 10 elements each) and discriminate "new set."

> Count grouped elements (50 or less) and discrminate "set."

From Packard, R. G. (1975). *Psychology of Learning and Instruction.* Columbus: Charles E. Merrill, 1975, p. 232. Used with permission.

FIGURE 10-1 An Example of a Simple Task Analysis

Exercise

Write an adequate behavioral objective containing two or more subobjectives related to some area of science. Include the essential components of an objective.

Feedback

Your subobjectives should list (a) a performance (b) the conditions under which it will occur, and (c) criteria for acceptable learning. The performance must use objective terminology and describe an actual skill. The performance should state what the student will *do*, not the *content* to be learned.

SUBSKILL ANALYSIS

After the behavioral objective and its subobjectives are formulated, the subskills necessary for each subobjective (skill) are analyzed. This is usually done by starting with the subobjective and asking "what must a student be able to do to meet this subobjective?" This leads to a list of subskills which, taken together, equal the subobjective. Each of these may assume earlier, prerequisite skills. This analysis is continued until a level of skills that should have been taught by some prior subobjective, or that it is assumed were learned elsewhere, is reached. These are the entry behaviors discussed in the final subobjective of this chapter. Carlisle (1983) makes these steps the core of task analysis.

Some objectives are so simple or unitary that they do not contain any subobjectives. In such a case, subskills for the objective are analyzed. Some subskills involve several steps and may require that the learner perform a number of tasks to complete them; it is then best to specify each task under the subskill. Each subskill or task usually becomes a discrete instructional unit in the final program and is usually taught in its entirety in a single instructional session.

The resulting list for each subobjective describes the subskills, perhaps further broken down into tasks, that must be taught. It is the beginning of a concrete guideline for designing instruction. Before starting instructional design, it is necessary to determine the order for teaching subskills and their associated tasks, if any. (For a detailed discussion of instructional design, see Engelmann & Carnine, 1982.)

Steps of Subskill Analysis

Subskill analysis includes three theoretical steps plus a fourth, practical step.

1. Specify all of the prerequisite behaviors a student must be able to perform to satisfactorily meet the behavioral subobjective or objective. These are often called *subskills*.

2. Ascertain the interdependencies among the subskills—that is, which subskills are prerequisites for other subskills and which depend upon prior skills.
3. Place the subskills in the order in which they should be learned, based mainly upon an analysis of interdependencies.
4. Develop some simple method to determine whether or not a student has mastered each subskill so he can progress to the next step. This is called *monitoring*.

These four steps must be followed for each behavioral objective.

Specifying subskills. A behavioral objective usually describes the final desired performance, but it does not indicate prerequisite learning. This is the purpose of subskill analysis. The student who is already competent (or the teacher) may overlook many of the components required for an adequate terminal performance. A person who has driven an automobile for many years frequently finds it difficult to specify all of the small steps that make driving appear "automatic" or "natural." For the beginner, each individual skill has to be learned. For example, the following are some of the earlier learned subskills required to divide a three-digit number by a single-digit number:

1. Identification of the dividend
2. Identification of the divisor
3. Determining whether the divisor is larger or smaller than the first digit in the dividend
4. If it is larger, determining whether it is larger or smaller than the first two digits in the dividend
5. Continuing the process in Steps 3 and 4 until the divisor is smaller than the first n digits
6. Determining the largest multiple of the divisor whose product is smaller than the first n digits in the dividend
7. Writing the multiple (multiplier) above the dividend with the columns correctly aligned
8. Correctly calculating the product
9. Writing this product beneath the first n digits in the dividend with the columns correctly aligned
10. And so forth.

Several things should be noted about this analysis of subskills.

1. There is more than one way to teach long division. The foregoing description presents a beginning analysis based upon one approach.
2. Students with different entering skills (see subobjective 3 of this chapter) may learn more effectively from one approach than from another.
3. Each subskill listed can be worded in a number of ways.
4. Most of the subskills listed have prerequisites which lead to additional subskills. For example, Step 4 requires a number of simpler skills related to discriminating whether numbers are the same or different and using the relations of "larger than" and "smaller than." Step 8 implies that the student has already acquired

a whole set of skills that must have already been learned before starting this program. Some of these subskills might also be better taught as several shorter tasks.

5. A final, very important point also needs to be made. The specification of subskills tells the instructor what to teach at each point. The previous analysis of long division, for example, indicates what must be learned at each stage and thus what must be taught. This is the only fact that justifies all this tedious work.

Unfortunately, there is no cut-and-dried formula for determining which subskills are required to perform a particular task. The best procedure is for the teacher to perform the task, carefully noting each step in the performance. This must be done with extreme care because the person who already possesses the skill tends to perform it so smoothly that he skips required steps or combines two steps into one.

For certain types of topics, defining objectives, subobjectives, and subskills can be rather complex. Figure 10–2 is an illustration from the math area.

Concepts.   Much academic learning involves the acquisition of concepts, as opposed to simple discrimination or the learning of a new motor skill. Task analysis helps clarify what must be taught in order for the student to learn a concept. Concept learning involves teaching a person to respond in one way to all things that have a specified defining characteristic and to respond in other ways to things that lack that characteristic. In addition, concepts must be generalized; that is, the learner must be able not only to respond on the basis of the defining characteristic, but also to make the response regardless of irrelevant characteristics.

One simple example is teaching a color concept. For a child to have the concept of "blue," he must be taught to respond only to the defining characteristic of light of a certain wavelength, which is the color blue. Thus, when blue is present, the child who has the concept will say "blue" when asked to name the color; when other colors are present, he will not say "blue," regardless of other characteristics. For the concept of blue, only color is relevant. When all color concepts for every color are learned—when the child can respond appropriately to all colors—it can be said that he "knows the colors."

A task analysis would break down the teaching of colors into several steps. To teach a specific color concept, the child must first learn to pick that color from sets of identical items that differ only in color. Thus, she might at first be presented with a number of blocks that are alike in all respects except color. She is taught to consistently point out the blue block and then to do this for a number of sets of items—balls and colored cloths as well as blocks. In each case she must name the blue item in the set. Then, in gradual progression, the student can be taught to discriminate the defining characteristic from a group of items whose members possess a variety of other differentiating characteristics, such as shape, size, and so on. When she is able

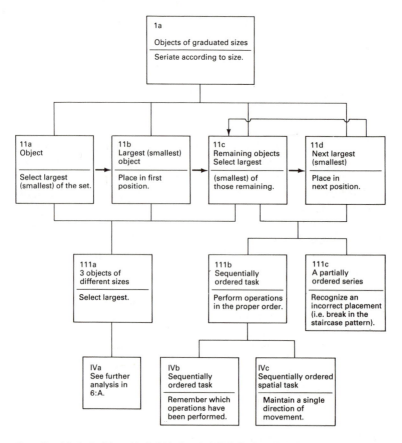

From Resnick, L. B., Wang, M. C. & Kaplan, J. (1973). Task analysis in curriculum design: a hierarchically sequenced introductory mathematics curriculum. *Journal of Applied Behavior Analysis, 6,* 679–709. Used with permission.

FIGURE 10–2   Example of Subskill Analysis.

in these circumstances to correctly identify the color being taught, she has also learned to generalize by responding only to the defining characteristic ("blueness") rather than to irrelevant characteristics.

At this point the teacher can move to teaching a second color concept, perhaps "red." When the child has mastered this concept, she would be given problems that require naming the color of both blue and red objects. This process would continue until she had learned all the color concepts and could respond correctly by naming the color of items in multicolored sets with a wide range of irrelevant characteristics.

Many concepts are more complex than color. The concept of "mammal" might be defined as a warm-blooded animal with mammary glands (previously taught concepts). Its size, shape, habitat, and food are irrelevant characteristics; both horses and whales are mammals because they share the defining characteristics of being warm-blooded and having mammary glands. It is irrelevant that one lives in the water and the other on land, that one has legs and the other fins, and so forth.

Some concepts depend on complex relationships or on other concepts for their defining characteristics. The concept "larger than" depends not on a specific defining attribute of a single object, but on the fact that if A occupies more space than B, then A is larger than B. John and Mary are cousins if they each have a parent who is a brother or sister of a parent of the other. These defining characteristics obviously depend on prior concepts. Similarly, the concept of a "molecule" assumes prior learning of the concept of "chemical characteristics."

Principles and *rules* are concepts that combine two or more previously learned concepts. For example, in Chapter 2 it was noted that the concept of "shaping" combines the concept of "selective reinforcement" and the concept of "successive approximations." Each of these is based on prior concept learning. Understanding the rule that a sentence must contain a noun and a verb also depends on already knowing the concepts "noun" and "verb."

Operations. **Operations** (Becker, Engelmann, & Thomas, 1975b) are complicated skills whose prompts are complex concepts. An example is teaching a student to balance a chemical equation. Actions based upon many previously learned concepts, such as "molecule" and "valence," and upon the relationships among them, must be performed. A task analysis of this skill would show that the concept of valence and suboperations based upon valence are prerequisites for the objective of balancing a chemical equation.

Understanding and knowledge. It is usually said that a person "understands" or "knows" something when she has acquired a particular set of concepts and operations concerning a topic. A child doesn't "understand" a sentence merely because he can sound it out fluently or define each word in it. However, when he can correctly perform complex operations, such as correctly responding to the instruction "tell me what happened," it is generally felt that he understands or comprehends the sentence. If a child can correctly multiply numbers presented on a piece of paper but cannot solve word problems, his learning is usually considered "rote"; it does not reflect "understanding" of multiplication. Understanding includes the operations of identifying a multiplication problem in a word problem, identifying the multiplier and the multiplicand, writing the multiplier and the multiplicand in the proper form (if necessary), and carrying out the multiplication. There may also be conceptual operations.

If the task analysis analyzes the objectives completely and specifies teaching relevant concepts and operations, the teacher may later be able to say she has taught the student to "understand." The result obtained will not depend upon the student or the teaching approach itself, but upon exactly what has been taught. The student learns what he is taught: If he is taught to "understand," he will learn that; if he is taught to perform "rotely," he will learn to do so. If the teacher realizes that *understanding* is not a mystical process, but refers to learning complex concepts and operations that can be analyzed, the results will be reflected in what the students learn.

Teaching and designing instruction for areas we call "knowledge" is not an easy task. The following example from Engelmann and Carnine (1982) illustrates a unit on "what a factory does" derived from an explicit analysis (Table 10–1).

TABLE 10–1

Teacher Does	Teacher Says and Does	Students Says
1. Present Figure 3.6 Touch A.	This chart shows what a factory does. Factory. Say it. (*Signal.*) A factory takes (*touch B*) raw material and changes it into (*touch C*) a product.	"Factory."
	Remember: (*follow arrow from B to A.*) Raw material goes into a factory. (*Follow arrow from A to C.*) A product comes out of the factory.	
2. Touch B.	First I'll tell you about some raw materials. Raw material. Say it. (*Signal.*)	"Raw material."
Touch iron, cotton, crude oil.	Remember: Raw material goes into a factory.	
3. Touch iron.	Iron. Say it. (*Signal.*) Iron is a raw material. Iron comes from iron mines.	"Iron."
4. Touch cotton.	Cotton. Say it. (*Signal.*) Cotton is a raw material. It grows on plants.	"Cotton."
5. Touch crude oil.	Crude oil. Say it. (*Signal.*) Crude oil is a raw material. It comes from under the ground.	"Crude oil."
6. Touch steel, cloth, gasoline.	A factory takes a raw material and changes it into a product. Product. Say it. (*Signal.*)	"Product."
	These are products. Remember: A product comes out of a factory.	
7. Touch D.	(*Follow arrow and touch each space as you say*) Iron is changed to steel. Say it. (*Signal.*) (*Follow arrow and touch each space as children respond.*)	"Iron is changed to steel."
	Steel is used to make many things—cars, lawn-mowers, cans, and hundreds of other products. Remember: iron is changed to steel.	
8. Touch E.	(*Follow arrow and touch each space as you say*) Cotton is changed to cloth. Say it. (*Signal.*) (*Touch each space as children respond.*)	"Cotton is changed to cloth."

From S. Engelmann & D. Carnine, *Theory of Instruction: Principles and Applications* (New York: Irvington, 1980), pp. 26–29.

Teacher Does	Teacher Says and Does	Students Says
	Some factories take the raw material cotton and change it into cotton cloth. Some shirts and blue jeans and sheets are made of cotton cloth. Remember: cotton is changed to cloth.	
9. Touch F.	(*Follow arrow and touch each space as you say*) Crude oil is changed to gasoline. Say it. (*Signal.*) (*Touch each space as children respond.*)	"Crude oil is changed to gasoline."
	Some factories take crude oil and boil it and put things in it. When they are done, they have changed the crude oil to gasoline. Crude oil also makes plastic and oil. But the big product is gasoline. Remember: crude oil is changed to gasoline.	
10. Touch A.	A factory needs things if it is to change raw material into products. Here are the things it needs.	
Touch G.	A factory needs transportation.	
Touch H.	It needs power.	
Touch I.	It needs labor, and	
Touch J.	It needs markets.	
11. Touch G.	A factory needs transportation. Needs transportation. Say it. (*Signal.*)	"Needs transportation."
	Transportation is what we do when we move something from one place to another. We need transportation to bring the raw material to the factory. We need transportation to move the product from the factory to some place where we can see it.	
Touch K.	Here are the big types of transportation used by factories: waterway, railway, highway. Waterway, railway, highway. Say it. (*Signal.*) (*Touch boat.*) A waterway is what boats use. A waterway is a river or a lake or an ocean. (*Touch train.*) A railway is what trains use. (*Touch truck.*) A highway is what trucks use. Remember: waterway for boats, railway for trains, highway for trucks.	"Waterway, railway, highway."
12. Touch H.	A factory needs power. Needs power. Say it. (*Signal.*) Some factories use steam power. They heat water with coal until the water turns into steam. Then the steam runs the machinery in the factory. Some factories use electric power. The electricity runs the machinery.	"Needs power."
	Remember: (*touch A*) a factory (*touch G*) needs transportation and (*touch H*) needs power.	

(*continued*)

TABLE 10-1 *(continued)*

Teacher Does	Teacher Says and Does	Students Says
13. Touch I.	A factory needs labor. Needs labor. Say it. *(Signal.)*	"Needs labor."
	Labor is another name for the workers who operate the machines in a factory. A lot of work is done by the machines, but some products need a lot of labor. Remember: *(touch A)* a factory *(touch G)* needs transportation and *(touch H)* needs power *(touch I)* and needs labor.	
14. Touch J.	The last thing a factory needs is a market. Needs market. Say it. *(Signal.)* A market is a place where the product is sold. The big markets are the big cities. The big cities are big markets because there are a lot of people in the big cities. Remember: a factory needs markets.	"Needs market."
15. Touch G.	Let's go over the needs of a factory one more time. Say it. *(Signal.)*	"Needs transportation.
Touch K.	What kinds of transportation are there? *(Signal.)*	"Waterway, railway, highway."
Touch H.	Say it. *(Signal.)*	"Needs power."
Touch I.	Say it. *(Signal.)*	"Needs labor."
Touch J.	Say it. *(Signal.)*	"Needs markets."
16.	Get ready to tell me all the facts about a factory.	
17. Touch the spaces in this order: (A,B,C,D, E,F,G-K, H,I,J.)	*(For each space, say)* Say it. *(Signal.)* *(Repeat until firm.)*	*(Children respond.)*
18. Remove Figure 3.6.		
19. Present Figure 3.7.	The spaces are empty on this chart. Get ready to tell me the exact words that go in each space.	
20. Touch the spaces in the order: A,B,C,D, E,F,G-K, H,I,J.)	*(For each space, say)* Say it. *(Signal.)*	*(Children respond.)*

From S. Engelmann & D. Carnine, (1980). *Theory of Instruction: Principles and Applications* (New York: Irvington Publishers, Inc.), pp. 26–28.

Subskill and Task Order

In this step, a determination is made as to which skills cannot be performed until others are performed, and which skills cannot be taught until others are taught. One skill can depend upon another for two reasons:

First, a student may not be able to learn one skill unless another has already been learned. For example, a student who does not know what a stimulus change is cannot be taught to discriminate whether or not a stimulus change was a presentation or a removal. A student who cannot add single-digit numbers cannot be taught carrying, because knowledge of how to add single-digit numbers is required to be able to carry. Because of such skill interdependency, certain skills cannot be taught until others are learned.

Second, one task in the final performance may be prompted by a previous task; that is, completion of one task may cue what should be done next. In the long-division example, the child cannot write and align the product until he has done the multiplication because this controls what he will write. In the final performance he must learn to do these operations in the correct order, each step prompted by the prior step. However, it is possible to teach skills in a different order than that in which they will eventually be used. For example, multiplication can be taught before dividends and divisors are taught; in fact, it is desirable to do so. In solving a division problem, however, a child will identify divisors before performing multiplication. Some operations may have to be carried out before others in the final performance, but they do not necessarily have to be learned in that order. Hoffman and Medsker (1983) stress the importance of this difference, noting that "instructional analysis" is the "missing link" that addresses this issue.

There are three guides to deciding the order in which to teach skills: (1) skills used in performing more complex skills must be identified and taught first; (2) the student must learn the correct order of tasks in the final performance of chained skills, and the cues that control this order, but this sequencing can be taught after the skills themselves have been acquired; (3) when no skills are prerequisite for other skills, the order of teaching is usually the same as the order of performance.

If subskills are interdependent—that is, if some subskills are prerequisites for others—allowing a child who has not mastered one skill to progress to the next will eventually lead to failure. One way to avoid this is to monitor student progress by designing brief assessments to measure whether or not a child has mastered each subskill. If the child performs satisfactorily, he should be allowed to progress to the next part of the program. If the child fails such a check, he sould repeat that part of the program, or some alternate remedial procedure should be used to teach the same skill.

EXAMPLE

Sulzer-Azaroff and Mayer (1977) present a wonderful example of sequencing subskills by Gustafson, Hotte, and Carsky. The sequence, which lists subskills in the order of performance, clearly indicates interdependencies; hair cannot be rinsed until it has been soaped, either in performance or in teaching.

Exercise

Break one of your subobjectives from the previous exercise into subskills and tasks. Put them in teaching order.

Feedback

Your list of subskills and tasks should

a. list objective behaviors
b. add up to the subobjective when combined
c. not teach a skill that requires already having learned a skill that appears later in the list
d. be worded so that you could test whether a student has learned each subskill or task before going on to the next

DETERMINING ENTRY BEHAVIORS

Entry Behaviors

Entry behaviors are prerequisite skills the student should already have learned before starting a program. Some entry skills, whether they involve reading and writing, attending, the ability to hold a pencil, or last year's math or English, are always assumed.

The analysis of subskills could conceivably go on forever. For most subobjectives or objectives, subskill analysis stops at the point at which it is safe to assume that nearly all children will already possess the skills in question. The skills may have been taught by earlier objectives or in other classes. The skills assumed to have already been learned are the required entry behaviors for the current instruction.

Successful use of task analysis depends on the creation of procedures to diagnose the actual, as opposed to assumed, entry behaviors of children. Individualized prescriptions based upon this diagnosis can be formulated to meet individual needs. Although diagnosis and prescriptions are not a part of task analysis, they are closely related to it. If diagnosis reveals that a student lacks the entry behaviors to begin working toward an objective, remedial instruction must be prescribed to develop these skills. If diagnosis indicates that a child already possesses skills included in the task analysis, these sections of instruction can be omitted and a modified accelerated program can be prescribed. By relating diagnosis and prescription to task analysis, the teacher can ensure that each child will move at a maximum rate without failure. Individualized instruction depends on assigning a child to an appropriate location in an appropriate program. If this is done correctly, individual needs can be met regardless of whether a one-to-one, small-group, or large-group approach is used.

Testing, even though it may reveal a student's strengths and weaknesses, is diagnostic only when it describes where a student is with respect to some specific instructional program or existing options. When this is true, diagnosis is also prescriptive, because it tells what to do next with the child and where to place him.

Occasionally, the analytic, diagnostic, and prescriptive tasks are done for the teacher (at least in part) by those who prepared the instructional materials. For example, most of the best math programs are based upon a careful analysis of the behavioral goals in teaching mathematics, the sequence of skills required, and the appropriate procedures for teaching. These programs include built-in measures to determine whether or not the program is appropriate for a particular student and, if so, where in the program to start the student. Although there are some excellent programs covering many subjects, teachers usually find that they have to use materials that do not do all these chores for them. Teachers must therefore be able to do these tasks.

The role of diagnosis.   Before instruction is begun, academic testing is conducted to determine whether each child possesses the assumed entry behaviors. Testing should also assess whether each child already has some or all of the skills taught by each unit of instruction. A child who lacks entry behaviors will be unable to benefit from instruction that assumes the presence of these skills, while a child who is taught skills he has already acquired will become bored and will not progress at maximal speed. Diagnosis should directly focus on determing the presence or absence of these skills; global instruments that measure broad indicators, like a student's grade level, are not usually useful for planning instruction. Unfortunately, if instruction is not based on task analysis, then these skills are not explicitly specified, and accurate diagnosis is impossible.

The role of prescription.   Prescription based on diagnostic information serves to individualize each student's instruction. Each student has the skills required to enter the program at the selected place. However, a child should not enter the program at a point at which time will be spent learning things she already knows.

In the sample task analysis presented earlier in Figure 10–1, children who are able to add whole numbers might enter the program at the point at which they will be taught about equations. A child who lacks only the ability to add double digits might be taught this quickly and then join the group that is learning to define equations. A child who lacked most entry skills might be placed in a remedial basic math program. A child who could perform the terminal objective or subobjective would not have this unit at all. Diagnosis, prescription, and task analysis work together to provide maximally individualized instruction.

Some commercially available programs have "automated" this entire procedure. Such programs have placement tests that tell the teacher whether the child is ready for the program at all, where in the program to enter the child, or whether the program is unnecessary for the child.

EXAMPLE

In Figure 10-1, Packard (1975) presents a task analysis whose objective relates to adding fractions. Note that several entry skills are specified; each of these assumes basic skills related to math concepts, reading, number discrimination, and so forth.

Exercise

List some entry skills for teaching students to count objects.

Feedback

There are various responses for this exercise, depending on the students being taught and on what is covered or not covered in the instructional program. Some responses include the following:

a. reciting the numbers 1 through 100 in order
b. discriminating one object from another
c. pointing to objects in order without skipping or repeating

---

FAST TRACK

REVIEW

The *goal* of an instructional program is broken down into a series of *objectives*. Each objective specifies a major skill that a student will be able to perform on completing the program. The goal comprises the combination of all of these objectives. Each objective, unless it is rather unitary and simple, is broken down into smaller units, called *subobjectives*. When a student has learned all of the subobjectives, the objective itself has been learned.

Various classification schemes have been developed for objectives. Some are theoretical, some are classroom-oriented, and some are pragmatic. To aid in the design of instruction, each objective or subobjective has three parts. One part defines the actual performance that the learner will acquire. The second part describes the conditions under which this performance will take place and the aids or supports assumed available. The third part defines the criterion level to be expected—how "good" the performance should be if the objective or subobjective is to be considered accomplished.

Many objectives are inadequately formulated, even though they contain all three components. The performance may not be stated in objective terms. The objective may be superficial or worded so as to emphasize something other than instruction. Poorly worded objectives or subobjectives often list the content of the material or state that the learner will "know" the material, rather than formulating what the learner will be able to do after instruction.

For purposes of designing instruction and teaching, subobjectives are broken down into the *subskills* that must be taught. Subskills may be further divided into a series of *tasks*; a task, or a subobjective not divided into tasks, is usually taught in a single lesson.

A determination must be made of which subskills must be taught before others, what the actual order of the final performance will be, and what will prompt the performer to move from one subskill or task to the next. During teaching, some method of ensuring mastery of one subskill before teaching the next must be developed.

One of the major challenges to designing quality instruction is clearly specifying complex objectives. Objectives or subobjectives that relate to concepts, operations, and the development of "understanding" or knowledge emphasize complex subskill analysis.

Behaviors or skills that are not taught by an instructional program, but are instead assumed to have already been learned, are called *entry behaviors*. Task analysis requires that the assumptions made by an instructional program about entry behaviors be made explicit. Assessing whether or not students possess the assumed entry behaviors is a major task of academic *diagnosis*; placing students appropriately on the basis of diagnostic information is the task of academic *prescription*.

Students learn what they are taught, and good objectives and subobjectives can be a great help to successful teaching. If the teacher supplements these objectives with a complete task analysis, including an analysis of subskills and a determination of the entry behaviors of students, he will be better able to meet the needs of both the group and individuals within the group. However, formulating objectives and completing a comprehensive task analysis are arduous tasks. Most teachers simply don't have enough time to do this adequately and also teach skillfully. Other staff have similar time constraints. As a practical matter, teachers should request materials, texts, and programs that specify objectives, provide evaluation data, and are based on a careful task analysis. Where such materials do not exist, teachers themselves may have to formulate objectives and complete the task analysis; they will probably be more successful if they request help from the administration or the school district.

The individual teacher can play an important role in the selection of school materials, for decisions on curriculum and texts or programs are sometimes based on insufficient data. By collecting data indicating that inadequate results are being obtained with currently used materials, the teacher can provide a powerful argument for program revision. Such data can provide a great service to teachers themselves, their students, and the entire school system.

CUMULATIVE EXERCISES

1. List the three major steps in task analysis.
2. What is the value of task analysis to a teacher?

3. Name and define each of the three components of a behavioral objective.
4. Each of the following objectives has one grossly defective component. Name the most defective component in each objective.
   a. During a 30-minute class, students will be able to pass a 50-item written test consisting of 10 randomly ordered problems, each presented 5 times, of the "9" multiplication table. Each problem will appear in the form $9 \times 1 = ?$, $9 \times 6 = ?$, and so on.
   b. In an oral test with no time limit, students will be able to correctly tell the exact time for every 5-minute interval from the hour to 5 minutes before the hour in the form "minutes after the hour" for times after 1:00, 5:00, 9:00, and 12:00 with at least 80 percent accuracy.
   c. On a 30-minute exam consisting of 5 brief essay questions, students will indicate that they know and understand the concepts of shaping, reinforcement, extinction, modeling, and prompting, with no errors.

Feedback

1. The three major steps in task analysis are as follows:
   a. formulating behavioral objectives
   b. analyzing subtasks and sequences
   c. determining assumed entry behaviors
2. Task analysis provides the teacher with the following: more precise definition of goals; more effective choice of skills and behaviors to be taught and the order in which they should be taught; more accurate measurement of learner progress; the ability to design a program that allows students to enter at their own skill levels; and the ability to analyze existing programs for problem areas.
3. The three components of a behavioral objective are
   a. performance
   b. conditions
   c. criteria
4. The most defective components of the behavioral objectives are as follows:
   a. criteria
   b. conditions
   c. performance

ELEVEN

Organizing Your Classroom

OBJECTIVES

After completing this chapter, you will be able to organize your classroom to maximize teaching effectiveness. To do this you will learn to:

1. Conduct teacher-directed activities.
2. Structure independent activities for students.
3. Schedule activities and transitions.
4. Arrange the physical structure of your classroom.

Teachers must organize their classrooms to ensure effective teaching. Classroom organization includes choosing, designing, and conducting appropriate teacher-directed activities for large-group, small-group, and one-to-one instruction, and for independent activities. Teachers will find that in most classes they must explicitly teach students to work independently.

Once formats are selected and procedures designed, the teacher must decide on a schedule. The schedule must take into account concurrent activities, such as independent work by some students while the teacher conducts a group. In addition to the schedule, the teacher must arrange the classroom so the physical location of equipment and work areas promotes effective teaching.

TEACHER-DIRECTED ACTIVITIES

Most classroom learning activities are teacher-directed; that is, they are designed by the teacher. The teacher provides students with the materials needed to complete activities, the teacher schedules activities, and the teacher, at least in part, formulates educational goals and objectives. However, it is convenient to call **teacher-directed** those activities in which instruction is physically initiated and conducted by the teacher, and to call activities that call for students to work under less supervision **independent activities**. Teacher-directed activities require explicit selection of the most appropriate format and careful planning of procedures.

Formats

Generally, teacher direction may be provided in one of three formats: large group, small group, and one-to-one. Each format should be used under different circumstances, and each requires a different situation.

The **large-group format** is the presentation of materials and learning activities to an entire class or large group. The materials and activities usually are not differentiated according to students' skills, interests, or learning rates. This may be appropriate for noncumulative subject matter with groups that are fairly homogeneous in learning rate and entry skills. However, large-group instruction is often misused; no attempt is made to accommodate programs to different skill levels, learning rates, or interests of students.

One procedure for increasing the probability that a large group of students will possess the prerequisite behaviors for a subject is to design and administer a pretest which they must pass at a given level of competency before being placed in the group. If students don't pass, they should be placed in an instructional setting that will teach those prerequisite skills. Another, more traditional, approach is to require students to pass a prerequisite class to enter a second. This technique requires careful integration of the classes in question with well-designed monitoring and mastery criteria.

To help accommodate a wider range of learning skills in a single large group, additional instructional sessions or experiences can be provided. Supplemental or remedial lectures, extra question-discussion groups, or supplemental materials at a more basic level than those presented in class can be used with slower students.

The **small-group format** allows for greater flexibility within the framework and limitations of the classroom. Through the use of small groups, teachers can individualize instruction for skill level, learning rate, and interest. After skill levels have been determined, the students are placed for instruction in a given subject with other students who are functioning at approximately the same level. In this manner a class may be divided for instruction into several small groups, each containing three to ten students, depending on the subject to be taught, the size of the class, and the skill level of the group. More advanced math groups may be relatively large, for example, while a group of students with many skill deficits will typically be kept quite small. As instruction proceeds, the teacher regroups the students as he observes differences in learning rates.

Small groups can also be formed on the basis of interest. These groupings usually do not take into consideration skill level and learning rate. They are usually fairly transitory, formed and disbanded at the request of students and/or teachers.

The small-group format has many advantages. It is useful for teaching basic skills in any subject. Mastery is essential to the learning of basic skills, and the intensive feedback and assistance this requires is much easier to provide in a small group than a large one. The small-group format allows the teacher to make ongoing diagnoses and prescriptions for academic and social behaviors, and it also allows the teacher to provide a high rate of reinforcement. Finally, the small-group approach also gives the students a social setting in which they can get to know each other quickly and learn productive patterns of working and interacting together.

The exclusive use of the **one-to-one format** is inefficient in a regular self-contained classroom, due to the number of students involved. It is effective in several special situations, however, particularly when it is necessary to reteach a skill the student has failed to grasp during group or independent study. It may also be the only effective instructional method with some slower learners, because it permits optimal feedback, reinforcement, monitoring, and error correction. The one-to-one format is more common in remedial or special-education classes; as a result, such classes usually have a much higher staff-to-pupil ratio than regular-education classes.

One-to-one instruction should not be confused with the ongoing individual interactions that every teacher must have with students in order to teach successfully. Normal one-to-one contact occurs when the teacher is performing mastery checks, during individual conferences, and when providing reinforcement and feedback.

Procedures

A number of procedures used with teacher-directed activities can help ensure success. These include explicitly teaching good attending behavior, using choral responding, adequately pacing instruction, using a standard routine, using error-correction procedures, and using reinforcement. Some of these procedures are better adapted to small-group instruction than to large-group format.

Attending. One important prerequisite skill for learning is attending. **Attending** is listening to the teacher's instructions, following directions, or responding to questions and commenting appropriately.

Effective listening is a major component of attending. Instruction in listening should begin with the teacher's first verbal statement to a class. The following are some general guidelines for listening instruction:

1. *Get their attention.* When making a verbal statement, the teacher should be sure that the "audience" is aware that he is about to speak and then wait for them to finish what they are doing and become quiet. He can do this by making an introductory statement such as, "May I please have your attention?" and praising students who then become quiet. The teacher should not continue until everyone is quiet and attentive.
2. *Teach in small units.* Once the group is quiet, the teacher can start speaking. If the material is long or complicated, frequent requests for questions can be used to break the presentation into smaller, more palatable units to avoid boredom.
3. *Keep it short.* While the teacher should make his statements clear, he should speak as little as possible. The longer a teacher speaks, particularly if he digresses, the less likely it is that students will attend (listen) to him.
4. *Get responses.* If the students do not have any questions, the teacher might ask some questions related to the presentation or ask students at random (rather than requesting volunteers) to paraphrase what has been said in order to make sure they have heard and attended. Behavior indicating that students have attended, such as answering correctly, should be reinforced.
5. *Reinforce good attending.* The teacher should repeat instructions as necessary but reinforce only those students who listen (attend) the first time an instruction is given. It is important, however, to distinguish not listening the first time from not understanding; the type of errors students make usually indicate which is the case.

Following verbal directions is a skill related to listening. Effective listening is a prerequisite to following verbal directions; however, students may not follow directions even when they have heard them. To teach students to follow directions, these steps are useful:

1. Give the minimal directions that will make it possible for the desired behavior to be emitted.
2. State the directions in a clear and concise manner.
3. Ask students to repeat what they have been asked to do.
4. Establish and enforce clear contingencies for following directions.

Once students have learned to listen and follow directions, effective instruction can begin.

Choral responding.   Choral responding, which has been used extensively in direct-teaching models, has been shown to be very effective. The United States Office of Education Follow-Through Program indicated that the direct-instruction program produced the largest gains in basic skills, as well as in cognitive and affective areas. This model utilized a small-group instructional format with a heavy emphasis on choral responding during instruction in these basic skills areas (Stebbins et al., 1977).

In the choral-responding procedure, the teacher directs all students in the group to respond orally together on signal. The signal may be spoken, gestured, or both. Responding on signal is essential because it prevents students from "parroting" each other and ensures that each is responding independently. Research by Carnine and Fink (1978) suggests that signaling increases the occurrence of attending and responding and thus correlates with improved academic performance.

One reason for the effectiveness of choral responding is that it allows every student to respond to every trial, thus increasing the total number of trials possible for each student during an instructional period. This is particularly important in basic-skills instruction, for which repetitions are usually necessary for mastery; examples are learning sound-symbol relationships, reading sounds in words, and memorizing certain mathematical facts.

Choral responding has been used effectively in small groups, but it may be less effective in large groups. One reason for this is that the teacher must carefully monitor the group to see that each student responds on signal and to check for incorrect responses; this is difficult to do with more than eight to ten students in a group. In addition, choral responding must be taught using modeling, approximations, and reinforcement, which is also more difficult in a large group.

Pacing.   Pacing—the rate at which instruction is presented—affects the amount of material covered in a certain period of time, the number of student responses in that time, and the rate of reinforcement students receive during instruction. The more frequently students respond during a presentation, the more frequently the teacher can reinforce them for answering correctly, listening carefully, and giving well thought-out responses.

Well-paced instruction allows students to master material but not become bored. The pacing of the teacher's presentation to a small group greatly affects the amount of students' on-task behavior. Carnine (1976) found that rapid presentation rates decreased students' off-task behavior. West and Sloane (1986) found that when the teacher controlled the pacing of seatwork in a small group, rapid pacing was associated with less off-task behavior and more correct academic responses per unit time. Brisk, but not frenetic, presentations, interspersed with frequent questions and requests for student responses, tend to maintain a high rate of on-task behavior.

Standard routines.   Teacher-directed instruction proceeds better when lessons follow a standard format. The general instructional paradigm for such a lesson involves three steps: (1) brief review of recently learned material, followed by presentation and practice of new information and tasks in isolation, (2) practice of new tasks in context, and (3) mastery check. (This paradigm may also be followed in designing lessons for self-instructional materials.)

Before the presentation, some formal or informal task analysis of the skills to be learned is required. The identified individual subskills are taught in isolation during the first step. During this initial presentation, the teacher calls for many practices of the subskills, making certain that every student has correctly responded before going on to the next step. In the second step, the subskills are practiced in a context similar to that specified by the conditions of the objective to which the skill is related. During this practice, the teacher ensures that every student has completed the practice of the subskills in context before going on to the third step, the mastery check.

Some examples may help to clarify the use of this paradigm. In a ballet class, the teacher begins each instructional period with a quick review of movements learned in the previous sessions (Step 1). This review usually covers movements that are particularly difficult to master. She then models a new movement for the class. The class practices the new movement (as a group) while the teacher watches, corrects, reinforces, briefly dances along with the students, stops the class, models the step again, and asks them to continue practicing. When she is satisfied that every student in the class has reached the minimal level of mastery, she demonstrates the movement in a "combination," a series of movements combined and danced to music or rhythm; this is Step 2, when the students practice the movement they learned in isolation in a meaningful context. Step 3, the mastery check, is done by watching each student perform the combination.

Similarly, in a reading lesson, (1) recently learned sounds and new sounds can be taught in isolation, then (2) read in words (context), and, finally, (3) each student can be tested on the sounds. Or, in a math lesson, (1) new multiplication facts can be presented, then (2) used in solving problems, and (3) checked in a quiz using the same facts in different problems.

Error correction.   Error correction is an important teaching procedure. The use of reinforcement has been discussed at great length in this book, but little has been said about what to do when students make errors. Some teachers prefer to ignore errors, but errors that are ignored usually tend to be strengthened via reinforcement for behaviors following the error, or through the reinforcers which progress itself provides. This is why monitoring student responses is important. All students will make errors on new material, and error correction should be a nonpunitive and matter-of-fact part of any instruction.

Error correction is a teaching procedure consisting of providing feedback about the incorrectness of a response, reteaching, and then providing the practice necessary for the student to emit the correct response. This combination of feedback, reteaching, and practice is an effective behavior-change device, particularly if it is provided immediately.

The steps in error correction are as follows:

1. Acknowledge the error, using a standard signal like "stop." Any verbal signal should be stated in a pleasant tone of voice.
2. Reinforce the student for stopping as soon as she hears the signal. This saves time and prevents the student from repeating the incorrect response.
3. Reteach the correct response.
4. Ask the student to practice the correct response several times.
5. Review the task on which the error was made later in the lesson if possible.

Reinforcement. All of these procedures use the reinforcement procedures described in previous chapters to maintain and strengthen appropriate behavior. In typical classrooms, most of this reinforcement will be social, and high rates of contingent social praise characterize good teaching. Most teachers recognize that lack of reinforcement will produce lack of results. However, many teachers "forget" what they have learned about effective reinforcement when first confronted with the reality of the classroom.

Excessive use of noncontingent praise, often for purposes of establishing "rapport," can destroy teaching as much as insufficient reinforcement. In effect, noncontingent praise makes social reinforcement ineffective. Teachers who indiscriminately praise all behavior in the beginning of the school year, especially if this is coupled with "allowing" undersirable behavior to occur for purposes of establishing rapport, usually regret it before the term is half over.

EXAMPLE

In her second-grade class, Ms. Stevens used teacher-directed activities in a number of areas. Her four reading groups were arranged in small-group format: a remedial group, an advanced group, and two "on grade level" groups, one slower and one faster. Ms. Stevens also had three teacher-directed math groups. In large-group format, she presented material designed to interest students in reading and math and asked questions at various levels so members of all groups could answer. To ensure that all students had opportunities to answer appropriate questions, she did not let students volunteer answers, but called on pupils systematically from a card listing group membership for each subject. One student received several hours a week of one-on-one reading instruction, and two received one-on-one remedial math instruction from an aide.

Other subjects were taught in a large-group format, supplemented by individualized help when necessary. Few prerequisite skills were required in these subjects (other than attending skills). Ms. Stevens used rapid pacing, with pauses for questions every 4 to 5 minutes.

During the first ten school days, the entire class had been formally taught how to listen and follow instructions. For this instruction, Ms. Stevens had used frequent social reinforcement, as well as a group contingency involving access to preferred activities when the entire class met standards of listening and following directions.

Finally, in small-group instruction, Ms. Stevens was careful to monitor every student and to correct all errors when they first occurred. She was particularly painstaking with the slower groups in ensuring that all students had attained mastery before proceeding.

Exercise

1. Describe some discoveries you might make about a particular subject matter with a particular group of children that would clearly indicate that you should use a small-group format rather than a large-group format.
2. List some important points in teaching effective listening.
3. Describe how to teach pupils to follow verbal instructions.
4. What are the advantages of choral responding?
5. How does rapid pacing improve a class?
6. What are the three parts of the general instructional paradigm for a teacher-directed lesson?
7. Describe the steps in error-correction procedures.
8. How should praise be used during the first week of school?

Feedback

1. The following indicate the use of a small-group format: children vary in skills, learning rate, and interests; subject matter is cumulative; extra remedial help is not available; the subject is beginning basic skills; children lack skills in following directions, listening, or working independently.
2. Do not talk until you have all of the students' attention. Speak briefly. Stop frequently and ask questions. Reinforce answers that indicate listening. Only reinforce listening the first time.
3. State instructions clearly and concisely. Have children repeat instructions back to you at first. Provide differential consequences for following and not following instructions. Give few instructions.
4. Choral responding allows all students to respond frequently and to be reinforced frequently but, when done correctly, requires each to respond independently and be monitored independently.
5. When rapid pacing is used, less off-task behavior occurs, students are reinforced more often, and the rate of correct responses is higher.
6. The three parts of a general instructional paradigm for a teacher-directed lesson are as follows:
   a. Review recent material and present new material in isolation.
   b. Practice new material in context.
   c. Check mastery.

7. The steps in error-correction procedures are as follows:
   a. Acknowledge the error by stopping at once; reinforce stopping.
   b. Reteach.
   c. Practice.
   d. Review and check later.
8. During the first week of school, praise should be used contingently and frequently.

INDEPENDENT ACTIVITIES

Independent, student-initiated activities are an essential component of instruction. Their successful use depends on how well the activities and materials are designed, how they are coordinated and integrated with the educational goals of the subjects taught, and how students are taught to perform them independently of the teacher.

The ability to initiate and complete work independently is important because students have to work independently while the teacher is with others, and because students outnumber staff. Independent work skills are essential if a teacher is to conduct small-group instruction. Otherwise, the instructional time is wasted for all students with whom the teacher is not directly working. Students who work independently allow the teacher to conduct small groups without being interrupted. If students cannot work independently, the total effective instructional time per day is greatly reduced.

Characteristics of Well-Designed Independent Activities

Independent activities may be used as a major teaching format or as reinforcers. Like any other method of instruction, independent activities designed to teach content or skills should be based on a good task analysis leading to (1) specific objectives, (2) analysis of entry behaviors, and (3) sequencing of concrete subskills to be learned. Materials and tasks must be designed to meet these requirements. Activities that are provided mainly to reinforce other behavior rather than to teach skills should meet two basic requirements: (1) they should be based on an analysis of what is reinforcing to students, not what the teacher thinks should be reinforcing; and (2) they should be contingent upon some specified behavior.

All activities, regardless of their purpose, should be well organized. Materials should be placed where students can get to them easily. The activities should contain easily followed directions, or the teacher should explain activities before releasing the students for independent work.

Teaching Independent Work Skills

Working independently involves several subskills which may be taught directly, although the specific skills may vary with the work. Examples include following the general rules of the class, listening to the teacher's instructions, following oral and written directions, determining which activity to begin, finding materials, setting them up, beginning work, completing work, correcting work or handing it in, and initiating the next activity.

These skills must be taught systematically, in the same way that other skills are taught. Once students have these skills, independent work can be assigned by simply organizing instruction and providing activities and materials.

Prerequisites. Before independent activities are implemented, students should be skilled in listening and following instructions. Classroom rules should be established on the first day of school. Research on rules suggests that although rules alone are ineffective in maintaining behavior, rules combined with effective consequences contribute significantly to appropriate classroom behavior (Greenwood et al., 1974a; Lovitt & Curtiss, 1969; Madsen, Madsen, et al., 1968; O'Leary et al., 1969). In his "human engineering model," Gilbert (1978) suggests that a major way to create incompetence is to "hide from people what is expected of them" (p. 87). Follow these general guidelines for using rules:

1. On the first day or two of school, talk with students about the need to establish a few rules which everyone must follow. Ask for their suggestions.
2. Make a list of suggesions, including your own.
3. Go over the list, deleting repetitions and nonessential rules.
4. Try to keep the list to five or six rules. If too many rules are listed, it will be more difficult to enforce them consistently.
5. Make a chart of the rules, including a description of the consequences for breaking each rule, and post it where it is clearly visible.
6. Begin enforcement immediately.

If the rules are reasonable and are enforced consistently, it should take only one or two weeks for students to begin following them. Listening, following directions, and following the rules should be taught during the first two to four weeks of school. Concurrently, the teacher should work with the students in as many teacher-directed activities as possible. This teaching provides diagnostic information needed to plan and implement independent activities.

Gradual introduction. Only one independent activity should be introduced to a class at a time. The initial activity should be well structured and directly related to some teacher-directed activity. That is, the first independent activity should be something that has already been done as a teacher-directed activity and can be carried out independently as a self-initiated task. For example, if students have chorally named the parts of a cell from a chart, they may then label in writing the parts of a cell from a handout. Students should be taught the steps necessary to complete the activity and then be given the opportunity to perform it. Feedback should be given, and the activity should be repeated by each student until she has completed it correctly, performing the appropriate accompanying social behaviors.

Independent activities should initially be relatively short and should provide for immediate teacher feedback on accuracy and quality. The activities may gradually be made longer, students may work on them for longer periods of time, and teacher feedback may be more delayed.

As students learn to perform the independent activities for one subject, activities can be introduced for another subject or as reinforcement, until all desired independent activities have been implemented. This gradual introduction of student-initiated activities helps to avoid the confusion, time wasting, off-task behavior, and lack of learning that may occur if students are expected to self-initiate activities but have not been formally taught to do so.

Teaching the steps of an independent activity. All independent activities require a series of necessary steps for completion. For example, doing an art project involves deciding on the project, working on the project without interfering with other students' work, putting materials away at the end of the work period, cleaning up, and turning in or displaying the project. Most students will not be able to perform these tasks with a simple verbal instruction from the teacher; the tasks must be formally taught.

When the tasks for an independent activity have been identified, they should be written and posted. The teacher should read the list with the students and then give each student opportunity to practice these tasks under teacher direction.

Most independent study skills consist of a sequence of small steps. The **lockstep procedure** allows the teacher to teach the entire group or class to carry out these steps while monitoring each student to make sure individual performance is correct. In a lockstep procedure, the behaviors required to perform a certain task are broken down into discrete steps, and the students role play each of the steps while the teacher monitors. When possible, the role playing is done by all students at the same time.

The teacher gives an instruction for the first step, models it if necessary, and then tells the students to do it. When all students have done it and have been checked, the teacher does the same for each step in the sequence, until the students have completed practice on the entire activity. During practice, the teacher corrects incorrect responses, prompts students with verbal or physical cues when they need help, and reinforces correct responses. The students are gradually asked to perform the steps with fewer and fewer prompts until they can perform the task completely on their own.

In a fifth grade, the steps for studying spelling were taught by using a lockstep procedure. Each student had a spelling list, a sheet of lined paper, and a pencil. The following steps were taught:

1. On the top of a piece of lined paper, write your name, the date, and the spelling lesson number.
2. Fold the paper lengthwise into three columns.
3. Cover the first word on the spelling list with the paper.
4. Pull the paper down and read the word.
5. Re-cover the word and write it in the first column.
6. Uncover the word on the list.
7. Spell the word on the list either aloud or in a whisper.
8. Spell the word on the lined paper.
9. If the spelling on the paper and the list agree, go to next word.
10. If the word is incorrect, put a check by it and write it correctly two times in the columns to the right of the word. Then go to the next word.

Initially, all students were taught each step in isolation, with instructions, student response, monitoring, correction, and reinforcement. After all steps were learned, steps were combined and instructions faded until each child could work independently without help or prompting.

Use of Records and Feedback

In core subjects like math, reading, history, science, and social studies, independent activities may provide a substantial part of learning. It is therefore important to have a method of assessing how much work students accomplish during independent work periods, the quality of the work accomplished, and the learning that has taken place as a result of the activities. In order to do this, the teacher needs some kind of record-keeping and feedback system.

Students may do at least part of the record-keeping in a folder they keep themselves. They can record dates, work completed, and the period or date during which it was completed. Completed work can then be handed in to the teacher, corrected, and recorded. The teacher and students then have a kind of cross-file record of completed work. Students have also been taught to graph such data as errors made on assignments (Fink & Carnine, 1975), with a resulting decrease in errors. If graphing is used, it must be taught formally, perhaps through a lockstep procedure. Teachers should also keep a record of mastery checks, including written and oral quizzes and exams. These are always corrected by the teacher, as opposed to practice activities, which students may correct.

Teachers should hold frequent conferences with students, during which record keeping is reviewed and feedback is given on both the work accomplished during independent work periods and the accuracy of record keeping. These conferences may be held less frequently as students demonstrate the ability to work responsibly. It is also important to provide ongoing feedback to students' parents. Short, written progress reports containing information on academic performance and social adjustment can periodically be sent home to parents.

Reinforcement and Maintenance of Independent Work

If independent learning activities and materials are well-designed and interesting, they will provide intrinsic reinforcement for independent work. Teaching independent work skills carefully and providing opportunities to work independently will stress the significance of this work. Intermittent consequences contingent upon appropriate independent work are the final ingredient needed to free the teacher from the need to constantly supervise each student.

Social reinforcement for desired independent work behavior should be given at a high rate when first teaching students to work independently. Praise should specify behaviors like self-initiating, getting started quickly, finishing on time, and producing high-quality work. In an interesting study by Marholin and Steinman (1977), it was found that when the teacher was absent from the room, students were less disruptive and more on task, and attempted to complete more problems when reinforcement was contingent on accuracy and rate of work completed than when reinforcement depended on "on-task" behavior. When contingencies are provided "for the products of a child's classroom activities, rather than for being on task, the child will become more independent of the teacher's presence, and more under the control of the academic materials" (p. 465). Ayllon and Roberts (1974) also found that when relevant academic skills were reinforced, on-task behavior increased.

It is also important to reinforce appropriate social behaviors, like helping others and waiting one's turn, that occur during independent activities. Care should be taken, however, not to praise behavior that discourages work completion. Teachers often wonder how it is possible to praise independent work activities while involved in an activity in some other area of the room. With careful classroom management, the teacher will periodically be able to stop, look around the room, and praise groups or individuals who are on task. This reinforces students' working independently and provides the group or individual with whom the teacher is presently working with a model for desired independent work behavior.

If token reinforcement is used, the token-dispensing system must allow the teacher to give points or tokens to students who are working independently, even while he is conducting small-group instruction.

Problems

Some children listen carefully to instructions and are generally well behaved, but still do not work independently. Sloane (1976) suggests that a child who is always unable to perform or who stays on task but accomplishes little may lack the academic skills required to complete the task, rather than work skills or motivation. A child who does well only sometimes, who works poorly when there are competing activities, or who will work for personal attention or some other powerful incentive but not otherwise probably has a problem that is not mainly academic. These symptoms suggest that reinforcers for independent work are ineffective. When an academic skill deficit is even suspected, it must be checked out. Academic diagnosis must determine whether there is a need for remedial work. If so, it must be provided before independent work skills can be developed.

Many children are skilled at shaping teachers to reinforce them for not completing work. These children may be reinforced by receiving attention, not receiving additional assignments, or being allowed to engage in other activities. The teacher is shaped to respond this way by negative reinforcement: The child is quiet and not bothersome when demands are not placed on him. The best way to avoid this is to make sure it does not start in the first place.

EXAMPLE

Ms. Stevens also used independent work in her classroom. She had explicitly taught independent work skills during the first weeks of school, when she also used lockstep procedures to teach listening and following directions.

All reading and math groups received independent work assignments keyed to their group progress. These assignments were from a "library" of well-designed activities prescribed for specific skills, developed from various sources by the second-grade teachers. Some assignments were scored by the students in the beginning of small-group period, and the results were given to Ms. Stevens. She or her aide periodically checked assignments for grading accuracy and gave mastery checks on material. Students who were having trouble were seen individually. While teaching the small groups, Ms. Stevens would periodically reinforce the independent workers. She placed red checks in her presentation books for groups to remind her to reinforce independent work.

One student never worked well independently as evidenced by assignments completed and mastery checks. After observation, the child was tested and found to be at a level below his classmates in math and reading. After various due process procedures had been carried out, the child was referred for individualized remedial work.

Exercise

1. What should be taught before independent work skills?
2. When should rules be started?
3. What is necessary to make rules effective?
4. How should independent activity skills be introduced?
5. Describe the lockstep procedure.
6. Name some ways students can help with, or add to, record keeping.
7. How and when does a teacher reinforce independent work?
8. Name two common problems related to independent work.

Feedback

1. Effective listening and following directions should be taught before independent work skills.
2. Rules should be started on the first day of class.
3. Consequences for following or not following rules are necessary if rules are to be effective.
4. Independent activity skills should be introduced one at a time, gradually, in steps.
5. The lockstep procedure breaks skills down into steps. Each step is initially taught alone. The teacher has all students role play the step together, monitors, corrects, and does not proceed until all have mastered the step. The next task in the sequence is then taught the same way. When all of the tasks have been learned, they are performed in the same way, but with fewer prompts and with more steps combined.
6. Students can help by recording completed work, graphing their work, and keeping folders of their work.
7. The teacher can reinforce independent work by periodically stopping, looking around, and praising groups or individuals who are on task.
8. Independent work can be hampered by students who lack academic skills, students who shape teachers up to reinforce not working.

SCHEDULING ACTIVITIES AND TRANSITIONS

Proper use of time is an important aspect of teaching. Research suggests that the amount of time used in instruction is strongly related to how much students learn (Rosenshine, 1976; Frederick & Walberg, 1980; Stallings, 1977). W. C. Becker has indicated that a high correlation exists between time spent on instruction and measured academic gains in DISTAR reading. Other research has attributed standardized achievement test scores to teaching (Becker, 1978; Becker & Gersten, 1982; Brophy, 1979) and thus, it would appear, to time spent teaching.

Time spent handling behavior problems, making transitions, handing out materials, and concentrating on other activities that do not contribute to student advancement subtracts from the time available for formal or informal instruction. Obviously, one factor that contributes to effective teaching is reducing the nonfunctional use of time by preventing behavior problems, scheduling efficiently, making transitions smooth and rapid, and using efficient logistical routines. Scheduling and transitions are discussed in this section.

Scheduling Activities

When planning the class schedule, teachers should try, whenever possible, to schedule desirable activities contingent upon completion of less-desired activities. Also, activities that are more difficult and less reinforcing should be scheduled early in the day. Students (and teachers) are often worn out by afternoon, and activities that are less mentally and physically strenuous will suffer less. However, a short, enjoyable activity might be scheduled for first thing in the morning in order to reinforce attendance.

Teachers often have trouble scheduling teacher-directed and student-initiated activities because of certain inaccurate assumptions. If certain assumptions are disregarded, scheduling becomes easier and more flexible:

1. The schedule does not have to be the same every day. It can repeat once a week or once every other week; or Monday, Wednesday, and Friday can be the same, and Tuesday and Thursday can be the same.
2. As long as they integrate with other class periods, all periods do not have to be of equal duration. Some subjects may be better taught in 90-minute periods; others are better suited to 30-minute periods. To facilitate scheduling, however, periods should be multiples of each other; for example, all periods should be 15, 30, 60, or 90 minutes long.
3. All pupils do not require the same amount of time for equivalent instruction. In a third grade, for instance, slower readers may need a total of an hour of reading a day, comprising 30 minutes of teacher-directed instruction and 30 minutes of independent work. More advanced students may need only 2 sessions a week of teacher-directed instruction and 5 sessions a week of independent work.

Steps in scheduling. During the initial two weeks of school, the teacher should take notes on her observations and suggestions for instruction for individual students and for groups. Once she has gathered enough information about the student population, she should plan a tentative schedule of teacher-directed and student-initiated activities. The following steps are helpful in scheduling:

1. Make a list of the subjects that must be taught, separately listing various levels of the same subject, including teacher-directed subjects and student-initiated activities.
2. List the students who have been tentatively placed in each subject and level.
3. Assign each subject an instructional format or formats (large group, small group, one-to-one).
4. Decide on the length of each activity and the weekly frequency with which it will occur.
5. Devise a master schedule indicating the time blocks for all of the activities. This tends to be a trial-and-error task, and activities may have to be reordered several times to accommodate each student's schedule.
6. For each time block, make sure each student is accounted for, each student is assigned only one activity, and the teacher is directing only one activity.
7. If students' schedules are quite different, write individual schedules for each student. The teacher should have a copy of the master schedule and of each student's schedule.
8. When the schedule is implemented, warn the students that it will probably be changed a few times to iron out flaws.
9. Make changes as necessary.

Classroom schedules can be organized in several ways. The following illustrate some possibilities.

Self-contained elementary. Ms. Hansen's second-grade class contained 27 students. The school in which she taught used a graded, self-contained model in which teachers were permitted to use any educational approach. The students were in Ms. Hansen's classroom all day except during morning and afternoon recess, lunch, and one period in the afternoon when they received instruction in physical education three times a week and music twice a week.

Ms. Hansen developed the following schedule (Figure 11–1) based on test data; reports from first grade; initial instruction on rules, attending, and independent work skills; observation; placement tests; and conferences.

When Ms. Hansen first implemented the three-group math and reading instruction schedule, she also began assigning structured independent activities for students to complete when they were not with her in instruction. The following figure shows a sample individual schedule of independent activities. John's schedule shows both the activities he worked on independently and the teacher-directed activities. Because he was in the lowest reading group and the middle math group, he spent somewhat more time in teacher-directed activities than did those students who were placed in higher math and reading groups. In January the teacher "regrouped" John into the middle reading group because of the progress he had made during the first part of the year. She then revised his individual schedule to include more independent work and less teacher-directed work. (See Figure 11–2.)

Junior high algebra. Assuming that all of the students had the prerequisite entry behaviors for algebra, Ms. Adams began the year teaching in a large-group format. After the first test she discovered that there was a wide range of skill levels in the class, so she decided to divide the class into three groups.

The class period was 50 minutes long, of which approximately 5 minutes were needed to record attendance and begin activities. Ms. Adams divided the remaining time into two blocks, one 20 minutes long, the other 25 minutes long. During the block of 25 minutes, the lowest group participated in teacher-directed activities; they spent the next 20 minutes in independent activities.

Ms. Adams felt that the advanced group of students could work for relatively long periods of time without teacher direction because the materials used were carefully programmed and contained exercises with self-correcting pages and recycling exercises. Ms. Adams taught the advanced group how to do the exercises, correct them, and complete the necessary recycling exercises. The teacher-directed time with this group was spent introducing new concepts and administering mastery quizzes.

The middle group worked quite well independently but needed some teacher direction during the introduction of new concepts. Ms. Adams worked with this group in three 20-minute blocks of time each week. During

	M	T	W	Th	F
			(x = repeat)		
8:30			Attendance and Opening		
8:45	Reading A	x	x	x	x
9:00	Reading A	x	x	x	x
9:15	Reading A	x	x	x	x
9:30	Math C	x	x	x	x
9:45	Monitor Ind. Work	x	x	x	x
10:00			Recess		
10:15	Reading B	x	x	x	x
10:30	Reading B	x	x	x	x
10:45	Math A	x	x	x	x
11:00	Math A	x	x	x	x
11:15	Math A	x	x	x	x
11:30			Lunch		
12:15	Monitor Ind. Work	x	x	x	x
12:30	Math B	x	x	x	x
12:45	Math B	x	x	x	x
1:00			Recess		
1:15	Social Studies	Writing	Social Studies	Writing	Social Studies
1:30	Social Studies	Writing	Social Studies	Writing	Social Studies
1:45	Reading C	Writing	Reading C	Writing	Reading C
2:00	Reading C	Monitor Ind. Work	Reading C	Monitor Ind. Work	Reading C
2:15	P.E.	Music	P.E.	Music	P.E.
2:30	P.E.	Music	P.E.	Music	P.E.

FIGURE 11-1 Weekly schedule, teacher directed activities.

	M	T	W	Th	F
			(x = repeat)		
Name:	John M.				
	M	T	W	Th	F
8:30	Attendance and Opening				
8:45	Reading A	x	x	x	x
9:00	Reading A	x	x	x	x
9:15	Reading A	x	x	x	x
9:30	Art	x	x	x	x
9:45	Art	x	x	x	x
10:00	Recess				
10:15	Spelling	x	x	x	x
10:30	Spelling	x	x	x	x
10:45	Math Home-work	x	x	x	x
11:00	Math Games	x	x	x	x
11:15	Free Choice	x	x	x	x
11:30	Lunch				
12:15	Social Studies	x	x	x	x
12:30	Math B	x	x	x	x
12:45	Math B	x	x	x	x
1:00	Recess				
1:15	Social Studies	Writing	Social Studies	Writing	Social Studies
1:30	Social Studies	Writing	Social Studies	Writing	Social Studies
1:45	Read along Tapes	Writing	Social Studies	Writing	Read along Tapes
2:00	Read along Tapes	Free Choice	Social Studies	Free Choice	Read along Tapes
2:15	P.E.	Music	P.E.	Music	P.E.
2:30	P.E.	Music	P.E.	Music	P.E.

FIGURE 11-2 Individual student schedule of independent activities.

the remainder of the time, they worked on the same programmed materials as the advanced group.

Ms. Adams' Schedule for Algebra

10:50–10:55	Opening Monday–Friday		
	Group A	Group B	Group C
10:55–11:15	Independent study M–F	Teacher-directed	Teacher-directed
		Independent Study T–Th	Independent Study M–W–F
11:15–11:40	Teacher-directed M–F	Independent study M–F	Independent study M–F
	Group A—Low Group B—Middle Group C—Accelerated		

The students within each group worked on the same exercises, despite the fact that the program was designed to be self-paced. Ms. Adams had found that working on the same exercises in small groups seemed to motivate the students to work harder; it also made it possible for her to keep track of each student's progress. Each group moved as fast as the students in the group could master the skills.

Handling Transitions

The pacing of transition periods from one activity to another is also important in maintaining on-task behavior. If transitions are long and allow students to waste much time, it will be more difficult to get the next activity under way. Transitions should be accomplished as quickly as possible; this is more likely to happen if the teacher prepares ahead of time for each of the day's activities and if students formally practice desired transition behavior.

Paine and colleagues (1983) suggest that transitions may average 8 minutes each and occur ten times a day in a typical classroom; the total transition time thus equals about 20 percent of the school day (p. 84); transitions that are slightly longer can seriously cut into useful time. Most teachers should easily be able to reduce total transition time to 40 minutes a day.

Sloane (1976, p. 117) suggests that transitions ("work routines") usually relate to starting or stopping activities, passing out or collecting materials, and moving from one location to another. Like independent activities, then, they can be taught. First, the tasks must be specified, rewritten as rules, and posted where students can see them. Again, the rules should be brief, concrete, and minimal. For example:

Materials

1. Start promptly when asked to pass things, take things out, or put things away.
2. Pass things without touching other students or their belongings.
3. Speak in a quiet voice so you can hear the teacher's instructions.

Provide social consequences when students handle transitions well, and try to start new activities with something interesting. Paine and coworkers (1983) suggest timing work under certain conditions; timing transitions and providing explicit consequences for meeting limits seems another obvious tactic.

EXAMPLE 1

Team-teaching schedule. Jackson Elementary was run on a traditional, self-contained basis. Several teachers wanted to try some innovative organizational approaches on a probationary basis in order to evaluate their effect on student learning. The principal agreed to allow the three fifth-grade teachers to implement team teaching in their three classrooms.

The three teachers, Mr. Dunlap, Ms. Aspen, and Mr. Brent, had a total of 81 fifth graders. In the past, each teacher had taught all students assigned to his or her classroom and had prepared for all of the required subjects in the curriculum, including math, reading, spelling, writing, grammar, science, music, social studies, art, and physical education (PE). All three of the teachers agreed that the excessive preparation left them with little or no time for individualizing the instruction within each of these subject areas.

Their first step in team teaching was to decide how they would share preparation and teaching for the ten subjects required in the curriculum. Ms. Aspen decided to teach all three levels of reading. This decision was made based on personal preference, training, and background. When possible, all teaching assignments were made on this basis. The teaching assignments are shown in the table which follows. The numbers following the subjects refer not to the level of the class, but to the period in which that class is offered. The letters refer to the days on which the class is taught. Enrollment in reading and math classes was based on data obtained from testing on the first day of school. The teachers assigned students to these two classes according to entry skill levels. For all other classes, assignments were based on attempts at equalizing teaching load for teachers and providing students with classes with many different students.

Teaching Assignments

Mr. Dunlap	Ms. Aspen	Mr. Brent
Math 1,3,5:M–F	Art 1,3,7:MWF	PE 1,2,4:TTh
Science 2,4,6:MWF	Spelling 1,3,7:TTh	
Writing/Grammar 1,2,4:TTh		
Music 2,4,6:TTh	Reading 2,4,6:M–F	Social Studies 5,6,7:M–F
Preparation 7:M–F	Preparation 5:M–F	Preparation 3:M–F

FIGURE 11-3 Master Schedule

Period	Time	Monday			Tuesday			Wednesday			Thursday			Friday		
		Mr. D	Ms. A	Mr. B	Mr. D	Ms. A	Mr. B	Mr. D	Ms. A	Mr. B	Mr. D	Ms. A	Mr. B	Mr. D	Ms. A	Mr. B
1	8:30 9:15	Math 1	Art 1	P.E. 1	Math 1	Spell 1	WR/GR1	Math 1	Art 1	P.E. 1	Math 1	Spell 1	WR/GR1	Math 1	Art 1	P.E. 1
2	9:20 10:05	Sc. 2	Read 2	P.E. 2	Music 2	Read 2	WR/GR2	Sc. 2	Read 2	P.E. 2	Music 2	Read 2	WR/GR2	Sc. 2	Read 2	P.E. 2
	10:10 10:25								Recess							
3	10:30 11:15	Math 3	Art 3	Prep	Math 3	Spell 3	Prep	Math 3	Art 3	Prep	Math 3	Spell 3	Prep	Math 3	Art 3	Prep
4	11:20 12:05	Sc. 4	Read 4	P.E. 4	Music 4	Read 4	WR/GR4	Sc. 4	Read 4	P.E. 4	Music 4	Read 4	WR/GR4	Sc. 4	Read 4	P.E. 4
	12:10 12:55								Lunch							
5	1:00 1:45	Math 5	Prep	Soc. St. 5	Math 5	Prep	Soc. St. 5	Math 5	Prep	Soc. St. 5	Math 5	Prep	Soc. St. 5	Math 5	Prep	Soc. St. 5
6	1:50 2:35	Sc. 6	Read 6	Soc. St. 6	Music 6	Read 6	Soc. St. 6	Sc. 6	Read 6	Soc. St. 6	Music 6	Read 6	Soc. St. 6	Sc. 6	Read 6	Soc. St. 6
	2:40 2:55								Recess							
7	3:00 3:45	Prep	Art 7	Soc. St. 7	Prep	Spell 7	Soc. St. 7	Prep	Art 7	Soc. St. 7	Prep	Spell 7	Soc. St. 7	Prep	Art. 7	Soc. St. 7

Figure 11–3 is a copy of the master schedule which shows the time, days, and teacher for each subject. Note that none of the reading and math classes overlap. They are all offered at different periods during the day, so that students can be placed without scheduling conflicts.

Each teacher had one period for "preparation" during the day. This time was spent in preparing lesson plans and materials, but when necessary, the teachers also used it to call students out of classes for individual conferences. This procedure might have caused conflict if the teachers had not been team teaching; however, they all agreed it was an important part of their program and encouraged its use. Team planning took place after school, in the half hour during which teachers were expected to remain at school.

The next table shows a student class schedule. Jane was put in second-period math (the "middle" math group) and fourth-period reading (the "low" reading group). The rest of her schedule worked around these classes. She was registered for six periods of required classes and had one elective. Elective activities included tutoring in one of the lower grades or in the school's unit for severely retarded children, helping the janitor, helping the kitchen staff, taking a study hall, or working as a teacher's aide. Students could sign up for one of these activities or a combination of several. If a student was falling behind in a subject, the teacher could request that the student temporarily suspend elective activities to use the time in a study hall or tutorial session.

Student Class Schedule

Name _____

Period	M	T	W	Th	F
1	PE	Wr/Gr	PE	Wr/Gr	PE
2	Math	x	x	x	x
3	Art	Spell	Art	Spell	Art
4	Read	x	x	x	x
5	Elect*	x	x	x	x
6	Sc	Mu	Sc	Mu	Sc
7	Soc	x	x	x	x

*Tutoring
Janitorial
Study hall
Teacher's assistant
Help in lunch room
Available for consultation

PE—Physical Education
Wr—Writing
Gr—Grammar
Sc—Science
Mu—Music
Soc St—Social Studies
X—Repeat

EXAMPLE 2

Transitions.　Ms. Stevens usually had no problems with transitions. After she changed the schedule at midterm, however, she had several groups of students moving to different locations and groups at the same time after her MWF 10:00–10:40 period. She designed a large chart listing the "Moving" rules and posted it at 9:55 each Monday, Wednesday, and Friday morning. The chart stated the following:

1. When the teacher tells you to go to your 10:45 activity, first move to the closest outside wall of the classroom and face the teacher.
2. Move to your right, staying a bit behind the person in front of you.
3. Keep moving until you are opposite your new work location.
4. Move to your new location and sit down (unless it is the toolbench).
5. If you talk, whisper or use a normal voice.
6. Do not walk so slowly or rapidly that you bump into anyone else.

When Ms. Stevens first established the new schedule, she posted the rule chart and reviewed it with the children. All started at their 10:00–10:30 location. She had them move in unison and corrected the few who were uncertain of "right" or of when they were "opposite" their new location. The first time Ms. Stevens tried this, she told the students, in separate steps, to "stand; move to the closest wall; move to the right, keeping a small space between you and your neighbor; stop opposite your new location (several needed help with this); and go to your new location." The second time, she told the students to "stand up, go to the wall, and move to your new location." On the third practice, she told the students only to move to the new location.

Exercise

Design a schedule for the following small third-grade class.

Student	Reading Group	Math Group
Sam	A	B
Mary	A	A
Jane	B	A
Alan	C	B
Carl	C	A
Jack	B	B
Eileen	B	B

You probably wish you could have a class this small—but this is only an exercise. The most advanced group for both subjects is designated A. Reading group C needs 5 hours of teacher-directed reading a week and 2 hours of independent work. Reading group B needs 3 hours of teacher-directed reading a week and 2 hours of independent work. Reading group A needs 1 hour of teacher-directed reading and 3 hours of independent reading a week. Both math groups need 3 teacher-directed and 2 independent hours of math a week. Alan also needs 1 hour of one-to-one math. All students need 3 hours a week of social studies (half large-group format, half independent activity), 3 hours a week of science (2 hours of independent work and 1 of large-group format), 3 hours a week of additional language arts, 1½ hours of PE (all large group taught by the PE teacher), 1 hour of music, and 1 hour of art (each also a large group taught by a specialist). Each day contains two 30-minute recesses and a lunch period from 11:45 to 12:30. Children arrive at school at 8:30 and leave at 2:45. There is only one teacher.

Feedback

Check your schedule for the following:

1. Is the teacher in only one place at a time?
2. Is each student in only one place at a time?
3. Is the schedule arranged so that switching to the activities most likely to be highly preferred can be used to reinforce completing those least preferred?
4. Are tedious activities excluded from the end of the day?

THE PHYSICAL STRUCTURE

The physical arrangement of the classroom directly affects student social and academic behavior (Weinstein, 1979), and obviously can affect the amount of work the teacher must do. The major factors are overall room arrangement and seating of specific students.

Room Arrangement

Any number of room arrangements will facilitate self-initiated activities. However, the area used for teacher-directed small-group activities must be located such that the teacher can see all other working areas from it. Clustered arrangements of small groups of desks or chairs at tables are easily monitored. Some teachers hesitate to seat students close together because socialization and other off-task behaviors are more likely to take place in such an arrangement than in the traditional "rows" arrangement. Although research supports the idea that closely clustered seating can promote disruptive behavior (Axelrod, Hall, & Tams, 1979), it is also true that with careful management procedures these off-task behaviors need not be a problem. "Distanced" or row seating might be best with an unruly class, and clustered seating might be preferable with a well-behaved (well-taught) class.

Students can learn a variety of social and work skills in the "cluster" seating arrangement and tend to like this kind of seating. As with any other skill, students must be taught appropriate study and social behavior for a cluster seating arrangement. They must learn to discriminate when it is appropriate to work absolutely silently (during tests), when it is acceptable to interact briefly, when they may study aloud together, and when they may socialize. All of these behaviors are appropriate at one time or another during the day, and students learn to discriminate through brief explanations, some teacher-directed role playing, and consistently provided consequences for appropriate social and study behaviors.

Materials areas and learning centers should be placed around the periphery of the classroom, where they don't interfere with physical movement. Tables for temporary group work and projects may be placed as necessary around the room. Teachers are often tempted to provide quiet, "private" areas in which students may study, read, or just be alone briefly. Two problems may occur with such areas, however. First, if a student were injured in one of these areas, a case could possibly be made that the teacher was not providing supervision, as the student was out of her sight. In addition, some students might abuse the privilege of a quiet area and use it to avoid work and supervision, especially without adequate independent skills training.

In designing the physical environment, an attempt should be made to reduce unnecessary movement and confusion. When an arrangement is being tentatively considered, the teacher should analyze the student and staff movements that will be required by going through one complete cycle of the classroom schedule. The arrangement should be planned with the schedule in mind, so that students can systematically move from one area to another without chaotic crossing and recrossing; the physical arrangement of the classroom should promote an orderly flow of traffic. In addition, the location and activity of the teacher during each part of the schedule should be such that she can easily monitor the entire room.

Individual Seating

Consideration must be given to the specific location of particular students. Slower students, disruptive students, and students with inadequate independent work skills should be seated where they can be more closely monitored. Adams (1969) and Adams and Biddle (1970) indicate that students seated near the center (from the teacher's viewpoint) interact more closely with the teacher. Thus, "problem" children should be seated front and center. This is rarely the case, however. Students usually seat themselves according to their own whims, or are seated by the teacher based on various social variables (Rist, 1970).

EXAMPLE

The year after she taught the small class, Ms. Stevens had a long, narrow classroom and a class containing 28 students, three of whom she believed would need a lot of individual academic attention and three of whom had "troublemaker" reputations. Other teachers had placed the teacher's desk at one of the long ends of the room and the aide's desk at the other. This was an obvious problem, as the aide was only present part of the time.

Ms. Stevens placed her desk in the middle of a long wall, near the windows, with a small cluster of group chairs and tables next to it. On the opposite wall she placed the aide's desk and a second small cluster of group chairs and tables. Thus, when she or the aide was conducting teacher-directed groups, they could monitor most of the room.

In the center section, facing the teacher, Ms. Stevens placed the troublemakers, separated from each other by the academically slower students, also in the center, and by more typical students. These students could easily be seen from any location in the room. The most advanced students were seated at the long ends of the classroom, except for one student who was academically bright but did not work well independently. Work areas and materials centers set up along the long walls, so no area was difficult to monitor.

A test run of movement through the schedule revealed no problems. Ms. Stevens assumed that as the year progressed and she got to know the students better, she might have to change the physical arrangement.

Exercise

How might you arrange a round classroom with 21 second-grade students in it? Partitions are available. Many students lack independent work skills, but all are, as far as is known, approximately on grade level. None are said to be behavior problems.

Feedback

It is tempting to put the teacher in the center. Alas, without a round teacher with eyes and ears on all sides or draconian electronic monitoring, such an arrangement would preclude effective monitoring. Fortunately, this class is not overly large, and it is effective to place the teacher's desk near one wall, facing the center. The least independent students can be placed close at hand and moved away as they "graduate" into independence.

It is also tempting to use the partitions to separate areas, but this will also prevent behavioral and safety monitoring. If there are no cupboards or closets, partitions might be used to hide stored materials. To facilitate movement, various teacher-directed small-group areas and work centers might be placed around the circumference or clustered in the center.

FAST TRACK

REVIEW

Classroom organization involves conducting teacher-directed and independent activities, scheduling and planning transitions, and arranging the physical classroom.

Teacher-directed activities take three formats: large group, small group, and one-to-one. The large-group format is most useful with noncumulative material or with students who are very similar in entry skills and learning rate. The small-group format is used with basic skills, cumulative subject matter, students who cannot work independently, and heterogeneous groups. In regular classrooms, constraints of time and numbers usually restrict the use of the one-to-one format to occasional remedial work.

Teacher-directed activities proceed more smoothly if students are explicitly trained in *attending* (listening and following verbal directions). *Choral responding* is especially useful with the small-group format. When used correctly, it has the effectiveness of one-to-one instruction and the efficiency of large-group instruction.

Rapid pacing of teacher-directed instruction reduces off-task behavior and maintains high academic gains, unless the pacing becomes frenetic. Specific work routines should be established and practiced. These will vary with each class, but might include routines for moving from one class location to another, for handing out (or in) materials, and for cleaning up.

Teacher-directed activities should include specific *error-correction procedures* to ensure mastery. Error correction includes stopping at the error, correcting it, briefly reteaching the correct response, and quickly reinforcing the correct behavior when it occurs. In general, teacher-directed activities require frequent reinforcement, which, in the context of the typical classroom and class, will consist of contingent social praise and attention.

Independent activities must also be directly taught. In a large class, especially in the lower elementary grades, much independent activity will occur while other students are involved in small-group instruction. Listening and following verbal directions should be taught before independent work skills. Independent skills should be taught in a step-by-step manner, perhaps using lockstep procedures. Additional independent work should be introduced gradually.

Frequent reinforcement should be provided for independent work. This requires teachers to periodically monitor the class, even while conducting a small group, giving one-to-one instruction, or doing paperwork. Some children seem to find it very difficult to learn to work independently. Some of these are children who lack the academic skills required to do the work; others are children who have learned to shape adults into reinforcing them for being nonindependent.

Effective scheduling and use of time during transitions is important, as research suggests that instructional time is a major determinant of academic gains. Scheduling must ensure that teachers and students need not be in more than one place at a time. Transitions should probably average 5 minutes each or less. Teaching of specific transition behaviors and posting of rules reduces transition times.

The classroom should be arranged so the teacher can monitor all students at all times. Although close "cluster" seating does increase disruption and may be unwise (if temporarily) with some classes, good behavior management procedures can overcome this problem. Cluster seating simplifies monitoring. The teacher's desk and other teaching locations should be placed so that the teacher can view all students at all times. This is obviously simpler with more than one staff member, but it is always necessary.

The overall arrangement should facilitate transitions. When considering physical arrangements, the teacher should visualize the entire schedule to ensure that the arrangement minimizes disruption. "Problem" students should be placed in front of the teacher's usual location and in the center. Independent, well-behaved, and advanced students should be placed at the periphery.

CUMULATIVE EXERCISE

You have a class of 25 fifth graders and a full-time aide. A few students are a year advanced in basic skills; some are as many as 2.5 years behind. Design teacher-directed and independent activity periods, specifying various teaching formats, a schedule, special procedures for the initial weeks of school, and a physical classroom structure. You may add any details you want. Try to approach an ideal within the limis of staff, space, and students.

Feedback

Your design should take into account the following factors:

1. Initial teaching of attending, independent work skills, and transitions. You may need a diagnostic period.
2. Selection of teacher-directed and independent activities based upon the subject characteristics, the current skills of the students, and the degree to which this is a basic skill area. This may change after you teach independent work skills.
3. Assignment of teacher-directed activities to small-group, large-group, or one-to-one formats based on student heterogeneity.
4. Use of good pacing, choral responding, routines, careful error correction and mastery monitoring, and reinforcement in teacher-directed activities.
5. Determination of prerequisite skills, gradual teaching, lockstep procedures, records, feedback, and reinforcement for independent work, and academic diagnosis and assessment of reinforcement for students who have difficulty with independent work skills.
6. A working schedule and planned transitions.
7. A room arranged so that all students can be monitored, space is provided for all activities, and troublesome students are seated in front and center locations.

TWELVE

Effective Teaching Strategies

OBJECTIVE

After completing this chapter, you should be able to analyze educational programs and identify effective teaching strategies. To do this, you will learn to

1. Describe and analyze three approaches to establishing individualized instructional programs.
2. Analyze educational evaluation procedures and describe how mastery criteria that include both accuracy and fluency standards, along with direct and frequent measurement of student performance, facilitate instructional decision making.
3. Analyze several educational programs and describe in each the teaching tactics that maximize student learning.

The National Commission on Excellence in Education (1983) has stated that, educationally, "our nation is at risk." The report states that "the educational foundations of our society are presently being eroded by a *rising tide of mediocrity* (italics added) that threatens our very future as a nation and a people (p. 5)." The commission lists several indicators of the risk:

1. Some 23 million American adults are functionally illiterate by the simplest test of everyday reading, writing, and comprehension.
2. About 13 percent of all 17-year-olds in the United States can be considered functionally illiterate. Functional illiteracy among minority youth may run as high as 40 percent.
3. Average achievement of high school students on most standardized tests is now lower than it was 26 years ago.
4. Over half the population of gifted students do not match their tested ability with comparable achievement in school. (pp. 8–9)

The "nation at risk" report set off an alarm, the responses to which were many and varied. A multitude of reports and editorials followed, some condemning education and others defending it, but most challenging the field of education to somehow halt the decline of quality education in America. These challenges to the educational system have awakened the public to a need for educational reform.

"A Nation at Risk" did provide some recommendations to assist in accomplishing the educational reform. However, one critical need—perhaps the most critical—is missing from that list of recommendations. Skinner (1984) comments on the recommendations of the report and that omission:

> We are said to need better teachers, and to get them we should pay them more, possibly according to merit. They should be certified to teach the subjects they teach. Scholarship standards should be raised to get better students. The school day should be extended from six to seven hours, more time should be spent on homework, and the school year should be lengthened from 180 to 200 or even 220 days. We should change what we are teaching. Social studies are all very well, but they should not take time away from basics (especially mathematics).
>
> As many of us have learned to expect, there is a curious omission from this list: It contains no suggestion that teaching be improved. Pedagogy is a dirty word. (p. 947)

This chapter focuses on pedagogy—those methods of teaching that have been demonstrated through empirical research to be effective. The methods discussed here are not based on a single educational program, but are procedures derived from several very successful behavioral approaches to education. Direct Instruction, Precision Teaching, Mastery Learning, Personalized System of Instruction (PSI), the Exemplary Center for Reading Instruction (ECRI) approach to reading and language arts, and the Classwide Peer Tutoring approaches have been selected for examination.

Nine characteristics of effective educational programs have been identified based on behavioral theory; all are demonstrated by these effective educational programs. These characteristics are discussed in this chapter and identified in the successful approaches. Table 12-1 summarizes these characteristics, grouped according to the three chapter subobjectives. Research has not provided all the answers for improving the quality of education; however, behavioral research has provided us with a teaching technology that works. Now we must apply the technology.

ESTABLISHING INDIVIDUALIZED INSTRUCTIONAL PROGRAMS

Importance of Individualized Education

In its report, the National Commission on Excellence in Education (1983) defined the term *excellence* and suggested a commitment to achieving that excellence with each individual. Their statement sets the stage for the establishment of high standards in education and also for an individualized approach to meeting students' needs.

TABLE 12-1   Characteristics of Effective Educational Programs

1. Teachers establish individualized instructional programs.
   a. Teachers accept a philosophy of teaching that states that most, if not all, students are capable of learning.
   b. Teachers accept the philosophy that it is their responsibility as teachers to find the right instructional strategies and materials to facilitate student learning.
   c. Teachers know the curriculum they are assigned to teach well enough to identify and sequence specific instructional objectives and to design or obtain appropriate curriculum materials.
   d. Teachers develop an instructional system that allows students to progress at their own pace. Teachers do not move students on to the next sequenced objective until they have mastered the current objective.
2. Teachers use ongoing educational evaluation procedures and instructional decision-making strategies to facilitate student learning.
   a. Teachers establish mastery criteria that specify both accurate and fluent performance.
   b. Teachers adopt evaluation strategies that directly and regularly (preferably daily) measure the behavior being taught.
   c. Teachers examine student performance data regularly (at least every six days) and employ decision-making strategies to determine how the student is progressing and what to do next (options include moving to a new objective, changing teaching tactics, or continuing the current program).
3. Teachers employ teaching tactics that maximize student performance.
   a. Teachers structure class activities to maximize academic engaged time and increase students' opportunities to respond.
   b. Teachers identify and utilize available resources (peer tutors, volunteers) to assist their implementation of instruction tactics.

We define "excellence" to mean several related things. At the level of the individual learner, it means performing on the boundary of individual ability in ways that test and push back personal limits in school and in the work place. Excellence characterizes a school or college that sets high expectations and goals for all learners, and tries in every way possible to help students reach them . . .

We do not believe that a public commitment to excellence in educational reform must be made at the expense of a strong public commitment to the equitable treatment of our diverse population. The twin goals of equity and high-quality schooling have profound and practical meaning for our economy and society, and we cannot permit one to yield to the other either in principle or in practice. To do so would deny young people their chance to learn and live according to their aspirations and abilities. It would lead to generalized accommodation to mediocrity in our society on one hand or the creation of an undemocratic elitism on the other.

Our goal must be to develop the talents of all to their fullest. Attaining that goal requires that we expect and assist all students to work to the limits of their capabilities. (pp. 12–13)

Skinner (1984) also emphasizes the importance of an individualized approach to education, stating that we must "stop making all students advance at essentially the same rate" (p. 947). He goes on to say,

Students are still expected to move from kindergarten through high school in twelve years. We all know what's wrong: Those who could move faster are held back, and those who need more time fall further and further behind. We could double the efficiency of education with one change alone—by letting each student move at his or her own pace. (p. 947)

An individualized approach benefits all students. If the gifted students are held back and forced to move along with their slower peers, they will not have an opportunity to use their talents and abilities. On the other hand, if the slow students are moved along at a pace faster than they can master the information being taught, they will not learn the concepts and skills and will become progressively more confused, as they do not have the prerequisites necessary for higher skills and knowledge. It is essential that each student be allowed to master each objective in the curriculum and then move on to the next skill; only in this way can each student reach her own potential.

Inherent in the commitment to individualized instruction is a unique philosophical approach to teaching. Teachers who individualize their instructional programs adhere to the philosophy that most, if not all, students can learn, given enough time, materials at the right level presented in manageable learning steps, and reinforcement for learning.

Carroll (1963) proposed a model based on the assumption that learning in school is a function of the amount of time spent by the student in proportion to the amount of time needed by the student to learn a particular skill. Based on this assumption, Bloom (1976) developed the Mastery Learning model. One of the underlying fundamentals of the Mastery Learning model is that nearly all students can learn the basic school curriculum, but some take longer than others. Bloom (1976) claimed that most students could learn if they were given enough instructional time.

The same underlying assumption is the basis for the Exemplary Center for Reading Instruction approach (ECRI). Reid (1986) states, "The center is built upon the belief that most, if not all, students can learn to read and write successfully if they are properly taught to do so." Likewise, two of the basic assumptions of the Direct Instruction approach are (1) that all students can be taught and (2) that teachers are responsible for student learning.

The philosophical assumption that all children can learn is sometimes difficult for school personnel to accept. When the student has difficulty learning, some teachers want to find excuses: "The student is handicapped," "She comes from a disadvantaged home," "He is unmotivated." The philosophy of individualized instruction suggests that, rather than looking for excuses, teachers should look for solutions. A teacher might ask questions like the following: How can I change my method of teaching to help the student learn? Are there stronger motivating factors that I can use to help encourage the student? Does the student lack prerequisite skills that I should go back and teach? Do I need to spend more time with this student and provide further assistance and practice in order for him to master this skill? The philosophy that all students can learn if teachers find the right way to teach them encourages teachers to search for ways to help students rather than finding excuses for the students' failure to learn.

Three Approaches to Individualization

Individualization does not necessarily mean that each student is working individually, separate from all other students, although programmed instruction makes this possible. The key principle is to use a method of instruction that ensures that each student masters each objective before progressing through the curriculum. There are various ways to meet the individual needs of students and ensure mastery. Three methods are discussed here: (1) task assignment grouping, (2) homogeneous grouping, and (3) the Personalized System of Instruction.

Task assignment grouping.   Task assignment grouping simply groups students together because they all need to learn the same task and they have all mastered the necessary prerequisite skills. When any student masters the skill the group is working on, she is assigned to a new group that is working on the next task in the sequence. Similarly, new students are added to a group as they master prerequisites. Teachers have the advantage of working with groups of students, as opposed to using one-to-one instruction, but students are always working on an appropriate instructional objective and don't move on until they have mastered the objective. Mastery Learning suggests that teachers with large classes use task assignment grouping.

Rubin and Spady (1984), in describing a math program that uses task assignment grouping, compare the system to ski schools:

This mathematics program closely parallels the system of instruction found in most ski schools. Typically, ski schools organize each of their instructional groups according to two criteria: (1) everyone in an instructional group shares a common need to learn the same thing at the same time, and the group is formed around that specific skill, objective, or outcome (for instance, everyone needs to learn snow-plow turns); (2) everyone in an instructional group has already mastered the objective that is prerequisite to learning this new objective (snow-plow stops). Skiers in one class may vary in age, ability, previous experience, socio-economic level, motivation, and the rate at which they are likely to learn the skill in question, but they are assigned to the same class because they **all need to learn the same new task at the same time.** When one of them learns this task, that person is reassigned to a new class on a new slope to learn the next step to effective skiing. Similarly, new students move into the class as they master its prerequisites. (p. 39)

Rubin and Spady point out that task assignment grouping is efficient because instruction is focused on specific objectives and the students in the group are ready to learn because they all have the prerequisite skills. Gifted students move through curricula quickly, master more tasks, and are thus unlikely to become bored. Handicapped students are unlikely to become frustrated because they have not been pushed along without achieving mastery.

Homogeneous grouping. Homogeneous grouping is similar to task assignment grouping in that both form small groups for instruction. To establish homogeneous groups, teachers pretest students and group those with similar skills together. All students may not have exactly the same prerequisite skills, but their skill *levels* are similar. Students move through the curriculum as a group. The teacher should ensure that each student in the group masters each instructional objective. Groups advance at different rates. A group of students with advanced skills can progress quickly; groups with less advanced skills may need more practice. Since students learn at different rates, teachers should expect to regroup them at intervals. However, students would not be regrouped as often as they would with the task assignment grouping method, in which students are regrouped for every task.

The Direct Instruction approach (Carnine & Silbert, 1979) and the ECRI approach (Reid, 1983) use small group instruction with homogeneous grouping. Carnine and Silbert (1979) explain how this approach provides students with individualized reading instruction and describe the advantages of this method.

Small groups are recommended for beginning reading instruction because of their efficiency. Beginning reading instruction requires frequent oral responding, which in turn calls for teacher feedback. This feedback can be most economically provided through small group instruction. Although students would benefit from extended periods of individual attention from a teacher every day, most schools cannot afford one-to-one teaching. While some special classrooms may have enough adults to provide intensive one-to-one reading instruction, most classrooms do not have the resources. Therefore, teachers must arrange their schedules to provide for small group instruction. By working with groups of five to ten students at a time for half an hour, the teacher provides students with much more teacher instruction on reading every day than would be available if the teacher worked with individuals. (p. 18)

A key part of the small group instruction provided in the ECRI and Direct Instruction programs is choral responding or unison oral responding. This procedure, which is designed to elicit many students responses, was introduced in Chapter 11 and will be discussed in more detail later in this chapter. The ECRI and the Direct Instruction programs use individualized practice activities and individual mastery tests in connection with the small-group instruction approach.

PSI. The Personalized System of Instruction, or PSI (Keller, 1968), is structured to allow students to work individually. PSI divides the curriculum into teaching units in which students read, learn the material, and pass mastery tests at their own pace. PSI is designed to encourage mastery learning by allowing the students to repeatedly take different versions of mastery tests until they have met the criteria specified by the teacher. Once students have mastered the material for a particular teaching unit, they proceed to the next unit, progressing through the curriculum at their own pace. The teacher, with the help of tutors or proctors, assists students with the material with which they need help in order to achieve mastery. PSI has been successfully used in a variety of settings, including elementary schools (Darcy-Frederick et al., 1981), secondary schools (Read, Archer, & Friedman, 1977), and colleges (Born, Gledhill, & Davis, 1972). Dineen, Clark, and Risley (1977) used a PSI approach with the addition of peer tutors in a spelling program with elementary school students. Their program demonstrated that the combination of the personalized system of instruction and peer tutoring can produce excellent results and improve spelling performance.

PSI has five defining characteristics: (1) self-pacing, (2) unit mastery, (3) a stress on written materials, (4) use of student proctors or tutors, and (5) the use of lectures to motivate rather than to supply essential information (Keller, 1968; Sherman, 1982). Self-pacing allows students to proceed at their own pace. Unit mastery requires students to reach the performance standards set by the teacher. The process of repeated testing should result in error remediation and reward final accomplishment. Stress on written materials requires clearly specified objectives and sequenced small steps, leading the student to mastery. As mentioned in Table 12–1, this requires that teachers have a comprehensive knowledge of the curriculum they are teaching. Proctors, or tutors, assist with testing, scoring, and tutoring, and enhance the personal-social aspect of the educational process (Keller, 1968). Lectures and demonstrations are used as vehicles of motivation; written materials and tutors supply much of the critical information.

The three approaches to individualization discussed here are advocating not "individualized instruction" that relies on unsupervised independent seatwork, but rather methods that promote student mastery of objectives before advancing through the curriculum. Teachers must play an active role in managing learning activities, instructing students, and providing positive and corrective feedback.

An individualized approach to education, focusing on student mastery, is a critical part of improving educational programs for students. Individualization may be challenging and require effort, time, training, and experience on the part of the teacher, but programs can be individualized to allow students to progress at their own pace and ensure that each student is mastering each concept in a curriculum before advancing. As outlined in Table 12–1, individualization also requires a philosophical commitment to mastery and teacher responsibility. A mastery learning approach is necessary both to allow gifted students to advance rapidly through a program and reach their potential and to permit learning disabled or slower students to learn prerequisite skills that are required for mastery of more advanced skills. While individualization requires effort on the part of teachers, most teachers find the effort rewarding as they watch students progress and become excited about learning.

EXAMPLE

Commercially available direct instruction programs provide teachers with directions for pretesting, grouping, and testing for mastery. An example is provided here on how to individualize instruction using the PSI method.

Klishis, Hursh, and Klishis (1980) utilized the PSI method to individualize a spelling program for fifth- and sixth-grade students. The students had a daily, half-hour spelling period in which they studied their spelling words and exercises and took spelling quizzes. The materials used included the school district–approved spelling text, a file box containing mimeographed answer sheets, student progress charts, and a file folder for each student. Students were required to pass a spelling quiz with 100 percent accuracy before they could advance from one unit to the next. Students who failed to master a quiz with a score of 100 percent were required to retake the quiz until they met criterion. The spelling quizzes consisted of having students spell and write each word from a spelling list and then write a sentence using the word. The students were required to pass 36 spelling units during the course of the school year. They were allowed to progress through the spelling units at their own pace. To help avoid procrastination, each student was given a progress chart with the proposed time schedule for unit completion. If students progressed ahead of schedule, they were given bonus recess time. If they fell behind, they were penalized by a loss of recess time.

Student proctors or peer tutors assisted in the quizzing process. Students who were ahead of schedule functioned as course managers. They handed out quizzes and answer sheets, kept student files in order, and kept the teacher informed of class progress. The final component of the program was active student responding, with an emphasis on permanent written products which could be used to objectively evaluate whether each student had mastered the unit. The results of this program clearly evidenced that the PSI method resulted in more effective learning of spelling in the elementary classroom. The students learned the material well and progressed through the units at a pace faster than the traditional one-unit-a-week method. Students also reported that they enjoyed the PSI method and liked serving as proctors.

Exercises

1. List and explain three strategies for individualizing instruction.
2. Select one of the three strategies and explain how you would use the strategy to individualize a math program for elementary students.

Feedback

1. Three methods of individualizing instruction are task assignment grouping, homogeneous grouping, and the Personalized System of Instruction (PSI). Task assignment grouping organizes students around each specific task. Those who have mastered the prerequisite tasks and now need to learn a particular skill are grouped together for instruction. As students master the task, they may leave that group and be placed in another group. No student progresses to a new skill or to a different group until they have mastered the skill currently being taught.

   Homogeneous grouping organizes students according to their ability and the objectives being taught. Although the groups may change, they probably will not change for every task. The group would remain together and progress through the curriculum together as long as some students did not progress ahead of or fall too far behind most of the group. In a homogeneous group, the members are brought together because they are on the same level and progress at approximately the same rate. The students within the group must master each skill being taught if the group is to progress or if they are to remain members of that particular group.

   PSI does not group students, but rather develops the curriculum materials so that each student can work through the curriculum individually. The curriculum is divided into small units, each of which has a mastery test. When students pass the mastery test, they move on to the next objective in the curriculum. No student is allowed to progress through the curriculum without mastering each step along the way.

2. The description of the individualized math program should be based on the four characteristics stated in the first part of Table 12–1 and should include the following:
   1. The selection of an individual or group procedure
   2. An explanation of how the procedure should work
   3. A method for monitoring and ensuring that each student will master each objective before progressing to the next step in the curriculum
   4. An explanation of how the procedure allows students to progress through the curriculum at different rates.

EVALUATION PROCEDURES AND INSTRUCTIONAL
DECISION-MAKING STRATEGIES

Evaluation and Mastery Learning

If teachers are going to be responsible for student learning, they must measure and evaluate each student's performance on a regular basis. Teachers should assess students and compare their performance level with the criterion set for mastery of the objective they are working on. A common but frustrating practice in education today is moving students as a group through a predetermined curriculum based on a predetermined time schedule, as opposed to evaluating each student's mastery of tasks and concepts. Many teachers harbor the misconception that they should move through a curriculum at a pace that enables them to cover an entire reading book or math book in a school year, regardless of whether or not the students have learned the material. To that end, such teachers cover a certain lesson each day and then move on. Some teachers test students on concepts as they go, but failure of some students to master all of the reading concepts, spelling words, or math problems does not deter the teacher from continuing on schedule through the curriculum. This is detrimental to learning because it slows the gifted student and rushes the slower student.

Table 12-1 outlines three characteristics of evaluation of student performance: (1) mastery criteria that include both accuracy and fluency standards, (2) direct and frequent measurement of student performance, and (3) the use of student performance data in making instructional decisions that promote student learning. These procedures are discussed here, followed by a discussion of *precision teaching*, an instructional approach that incorporates all three of these characteristics.

Accuracy and Fluency Standards

Some teachers do assess the accuracy of students' responses and continue to work with students, reassessing their performance until they achieve some accuracy criterion. However, educational research has demonstrated that accuracy of responding is not a sufficient criterion for determining mastery of most academic materials; it is necessary that students achieve *fluent* performance as well (Young & West, 1985). **Accuracy** is defined as correctly performing the academic skill being tested. **Fluency** refers to performing a skill or responding smoothly, quickly, and with ease. When both accurate and fluent responding have been achieved, the student has achieved **proficiency.**

Carnine and Silbert (1979) emphasize the importance of fluency in reading. They describe how a student first responds accurately but slowly and then progresses to fluent reading. Samuels (1976) speaks of moving from accuracy to fluent "automatic" reading. Dahl (1979) demonstrated a positive relationship between fluency and reading comprehension. Speer and Lamb (1976) reported a significant correlation between fluency and first-grade reading achievement. Research has demonstrated that hearing-impaired students learn math and reading skills faster (West & Young, 1983) and retain the skills better and longer (Young, West, & Crawford, 1985) when fluency is required as part of the criteria for mastery. Baer (1981) points out that teachers should continue teaching until a child can perform reading, math, or other skills fluently in order to have natural reinforcers take over and support the academic skills. Only when academic performance is fluent are skills likely to be retained and used in nonteaching situations (reading for enjoyment is an example).

It is important, then, to teach a child beyond mere acquisition of knowledge and assist the child in achieving fluent responding. Direct Instruction (Carnine & Silbert, 1979), ECRI (Reid, 1986), and Precision Teaching (White, 1986) are effective instructional approaches that emphasize both accuracy and fluency. These programs also stress measuring student responding to ensure both accuracy and fluency before advancing in the curriculum.

Direct and Frequent Student Evaluations

Discussing the purpose of measurement in education and the need for direct and frequent measurement of student performance, Young and West (1985) state:

> The purpose of measurement in education should be to provide an empirical basis for making decisions about how to educate students. Assessment data are used to place students in programs, curriculum, and ability groups (within classes). Data are used to decide whether to promote or retain a student. Determining students' academic grades is the most common use of evaluation data. Potentially, the most powerful use of information is for instructional decisions about students' individual daily performance and what we can do as educators to help them learn. Direct and frequent measurement and regular data analysis promotes ongoing decisions, instructional modifications, and may enhance the rate of educational progress. (p. 1)

Direct and frequent measurement refers to assessing specific behaviors and evaluating performance daily, or at least weekly. **Indirect measurement** refers to testing behaviors that may be related to, but are not specifically, the ones being taught. Assessing a student once or twice a year, as with standardized tests, is considered infrequent. Education has relied heavily on standardized tests. These tests are designed to sample a broad range of skills and to compare students to a normative sample. They are not designed to provide direct, repeated measures of specific behaviors which are the focus of instruction.

Student performance should be measured directly and regularly—daily if possible. West (1984) illustrates the importance of frequently measuring student performance by comparing the learning process to motion pictures. Each frame of the motion picture is an assessment of one small bit of a student's overall performance. The amount of information each frame provides is limited and is of little value in evaluating the student's ability to perform a task or his progress toward the mastery of an objective. The measurement of learning requires more than examination of a single response. In fact, the more responses we observe, the more accurate and representative will be our interpretation of what the student has learned and how well he is performing the task.

> If we can study many frames from our motion picture, we will know much more and have a much better idea of the continuous process the motion picture represents. However, just as one frame in a motion picture differs little from frames that are adjacent to it, we don't need to measure "knowing" constantly in order to detect significant changes in what is "known." But, just as it is difficult to determine the story reflected in a motion picture if we see only the first and last frames, measurement must be frequent enough to permit an inspection of the process of "coming to know" or learning. Therefore, measurement of learning should be frequent enough to detect changes in "knowing," and it should relate to specific skills the instructor considers to be important, presumably those which are the objects of instruction. (West, 1984, p. 1208)

Using evaluation data in making instructional decisions. Measuring student performance is of little value unless the teacher uses the peformance data to help the student. The purpose of collecting student data is to evaluate the student's learning and, in turn, the teacher's instructional procedures. The data should signal that the student is learning (responding more accurately and fluently) or not learning (not improving or declining in performance). If learning is satisfactory, the teacher can decide that his procedures are adequate and continue the instructional program. If learning is not satisfactory, the teacher should change his approach and modify the instructional program to meet the student's needs. Precision teaching is probably the best-developed system for evaluating accurate and fluent responding and using performance data to make instructional decisions that help students learn.

Precision Teaching

As mentioned in Chapter 5, Precision Teaching is primarily a measurement system for individualized instruction that can be used in connection with almost any teaching approach. Precision teachers believe that it is important that students achieve high levels of mastery or meet proficiency standards before advancing in a curriculum. Therefore, they measure both the accuracy and the fluency of responding. Precision teachers often use individualized curriculum probe sheets to monitor a student's progress through a curriculum. The probe sheets (see Figure 12–1) are arranged to provide students with multiple response opportunities (e.g., writing the answers to math problems, reading words from a reading list). The back of the probe sheet provides answers for student scoring (Figure 12–2).

The probe sheets are usually used each day as part of a timed activity. Typically, teachers allow students one minute to complete the sheet, making

FIGURE 12-1 Example of a probe sheet.

NAME _____ DATE _____ COUNT: CORRECT _____ ERROR _____

SEE TO WRITE: Double-Digit Addition with Regrouping

16+46	18+23	38+16	16+18	23+18	29+18	48+38	17+38	18+68	78+15	19+18	36+15	16+18	25+78	(28)
16+75	14+16	29+72	17+18	48+14	17+14	15+29	68+19	28+18	13+29	19+19	53+18	13+28	78+13	(56)
68+64	39+19	49+33	19+18	64+17	15+39	16+49	17+57	43+18	15+16	69+16	18+69	17+43	77+15	(84)
48+39	55+18	54+19	17+68	69+19	19+55	17+54	38+42	17+15	49+26	18+23	15+17	76+17	18+49	(112)
46+15	79+18	37+14	14+36	39+19	17+79	14+37	38+25	19+17	19+18	15+48	42+19	18+19	26+19	(140)
75+17	29+76	11+19	18+53	57+16	15+29	19+11	19+16	38+19	18+17	19+64	64+17	18+38	16+18	(168)
48+38	48+17	18+77	75+18	15+68	18+48	33+18	25+78	55+15	18+16	57+68	27+16	19+55	72+18	(196)

342

FIGURE 12-2 Example of a probe sheet with answers.

NAME _____ DATE _____ COUNT: CORRECT _____ ERROR _____

SEE TO WRITE: Double-Digit Addition with Regrouping

														Count
16+46=62	18+23=41	38+16=54	16+18=34	23+18=41	29+18=47	48+38=86	17+38=55	18+68=86	78+15=93	19+18=37	36+15=51	16+18=34	25+78=103	(28)
16+75=91	14+16=30	29+72=101	17+18=35	48+14=62	17+14=31	15+29=44	68+19=87	28+18=46	13+29=42	19+19=38	53+18=71	13+28=41	78+13=91	(56)
68+64=132	39+19=58	49+33=42	19+18=37	64+17=81	15+39=54	16+49=65	17+57=74	43+18=61	15+16=31	69+16=75	18+69=87	17+43=60	77+15=92	(84)
48+39=87	55+18=73	54+19=73	17+68=75	69+19=87	19+55=74	17+54=71	38+42=80	17+15=32	49+26=75	18+23=41	15+17=32	76+17=93	18+49=67	(112)
46+15=61	79+18=97	37+14=51	14+36=50	39+19=58	17+79=96	14+37=51	38+25=63	19+17=36	19+18=37	15+48=63	42+19=61	18+19=37	26+19=45	(140)
75+17=92	29+76=105	11+19=30	18+53=71	57+16=73	15+29=44	19+11=30	19+16=35	38+19=57	18+17=35	19+64=83	64+17=81	18+38=56	16+18=34	(168)
48+38=86	48+17=65	18+77=95	75+18=93	15+68=83	18+48=66	33+18=51	25+78=103	55+15=70	18+16=34	57+68=125	27+16=43	19+55=74	72+18=90	(196)

as many correct responses as possible. Students are taught that there are always more potential response opportunities available to them during the time period than they can possibly complete; therefore, they should respond quickly but never expect to complete the probe sheets. Students are usually given two or three 1-minute probe activities and then allowed to select their best score as an indication of their daily progress toward their goal. This procedure minimizes student frustration or anxiety over having to perform both quickly and accurately. Since all the activities are individualized and students progress at their own pace, students rarely become frustrated over having to respond rapidly.

This precision assessment procedure usually takes only 5 to 10 minutes of the total instructional time, thus allowing teachers time for instructional activities designed to assist the student in learning the skills and becoming fluent in the use of the skills. Teachers may use small-group instruction, such as the ECRI approach or Direct Instruction, in the instructional period. They may also opt to provide individualized practice opportunties as part of the PSI approach or the Classwide Peer Tutoring System. One of the strengths of the Precision Teaching approach is that it is an assessment and instructional decision-making technology that can be applied with most educational approaches.

It is important to note that the use of 1-minute timed probes is only one application of the Precision Teaching technology. Academic responding may be assessed while the student is responding from a textbook or other materials, and the time period may vary from a few seconds to 60 minutes to 24 hours. Inappropriate and appropriate social behavior may also be measured and evaluated using Precision Teaching strategies.

Some unique features of the Precision Teaching approach include the following: focus on directly observable behavior, use of time-based measurement (primarily frequency or rate data, although other temporal measures, such as duration, are also appropriate), the use of the Standard Behavior Chart, and data-based decision rules for evaluating student progress. White (1986) describes Precision Teaching as a four-step process: pinpoint, count, chart, and evaluate. *Pinpointing* is defining the target behavior so that the rate of a student's responding can be *counted* and *recorded* on the Standard Behavior Chart. The data are then analyzed, performance and teaching procedures *evaluated*, and instructional decisions made. The process is cyclical and is repeatable as the student learns.

The Standard Behavior Chart (Figure 12–3) is referred to as a semilog chart because the vertical lines are equally distanced but the horizontal lines unequally distanced. The horizontal lines are on a logarithmic scale. The vertical lines represent days; 140 successive calendar days are included on one chart. Every seventh line is thick or heavy, representing Sunday. The light, thin lines represent the other days of the week. The horizontal lines represent the frequency of the behaviors that are being recorded. The top three cycles of the chart represent whole numbers from 1 through 1,000; the three cycles include 1 through 10, 10 through 100, and 100 through 1,000.

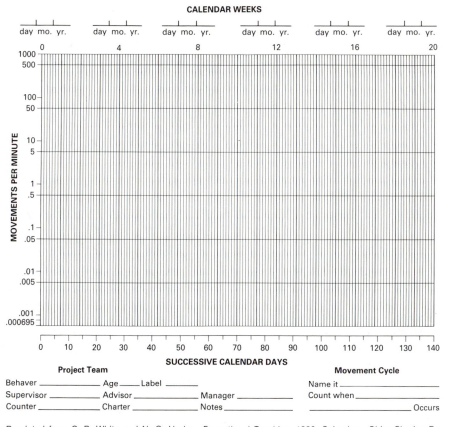

CALENDAR WEEKS

Reprinted from O. R. White and N. G. Haring, *Exceptional Teaching*, 1980. Columbus, Ohio; Charles E. Merrill.

FIGURE 12-3 Standard Behavior Chart.

The bottom three cycles of the chart represent behaviors that occur less than once per minute and range from 0.9 to 0.000695 (1 behavior in 24 hours).

Advantages of the Standard Behavior Chart. In academic programs in which teachers use the Precision Teaching 1-minute-timing method of assessment, daily rate scores are collected. The number of correct responses per minute and the number of error responses per minute are charted on a Standard Behavior Chart. This chart has several advantages over a traditional equal-interval chart. One advantage is that many different behaviors can be recorded on the same chart. For example, academic responses, such as math problems worked correctly or words read correctly, disruptive behaviors, fights, chores completed, praises, shares, arguments, or laps run, could be recorded on the chart without chart modifications.

The Standard Behavior Chart permits a wide range of rates of behaviors to be recorded on the same chart, from one behavior in 24 hours to 1,000 behaviors a minute. Behaviors that occur as infrequently as once or twice in a 6-hour school day, as well as a behavior such as reading 250 words a minute could be included on the same chart. The use of traditional equal-interval charts for the same range of behaviors would require a sheet of paper several blocks long. Many days' worth of data can be recorded on the chart; a single chart has 140 days. Two charts are all that are required to keep track of a child's behavior (in a particular subject area) for an entire school year.

The chart is standardized, which is an important advantage over traditional charts or graphs; teachers all over the country can use the same chart and the same charting conventions, and can easily and clearly interpret the data recorded on the chart, regardless of who entered it. One of the most important features of the chart is that teachers can draw trend lines on the chart that make it possible to accurately predict the behavior of a child for several days or weeks into the future. This ability to predict where the behavior is going is important; teachers are able to look at how fast a child is learning (as depicted by trend lines) and how many days, weeks, months, or years it might take a child to master a certain skill if they continue to improve at the same rate. If learning is occurring but the learning rate is too slow, teachers can modify instructional procedures and increase the rate of learning. White (1986) suggests that the results of each assessment should be charted as soon as possible. Plotting data on the chart is a quick and simple process which, with practice, should take only a few seconds to complete.

Standard charting conventions are used to make the chart easy to interpret. A few of those conventions, outlined by White (1986), are illustrated in Figure 12–4. For a more detailed descriptions of the chart, see White and Haring (1980). White (1986) discusses the Precision Teaching evaluation process:

> Simply "dropping dots on the chart" will not fulfill the purpose of Precision Teaching. One must carefully evaluate the pupil's progress daily, determine whether progress is satisfactory, and, if not, devise changes in the program to facilitate continued learning. Originally, only two decision rules were specified in precision teaching: If the pupil is progressing in the right direction, leave the program alone; if the pupil is essentially "flat" or going the wrong way, then change the program. In many cases, those rules are adequate for making appropriate decisions. Over the past decade, however, a number of Precision Teachers have developed much more formal guidelines to assist them in deciding precisely when and how a program should be changed (Albrecht, 1982a, 1982b; Liberty, 1972; Liberty, Haring, & White, 1980; West & Young, 1983; White & Haring, 1980, 1982; White & Liberty, 1976). (p. 528)

Computers are also being used to assist teachers in managing Precision Teaching programs (Hasselbring & Hamlett, 1983; West & Young, 1985). AC•CEL is a microcomputer program designed to assist teachers in individualizing their instructional programs and is used in connection with the

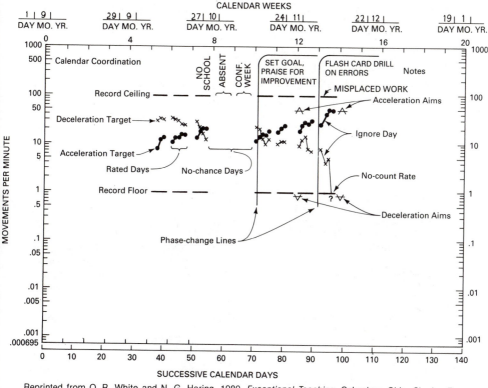

Reprinted from O. R. White and N. G. Haring, 1980, *Exceptional Teaching*. Columbus, Ohio: Charles E. Merrill.

FIGURE 12-4 Basic charting conventions.

Precision Teaching approach (West et al., 1985). Teachers use Precision Teaching probes to assess students' fluency on the particular academic skill being taught and then enter the students' performance scores into the microcomputer program for analysis. AC•CEL analyzes the students' performance over a 5- or 6-day period and provides the teacher and student with feedback regarding the student's progress toward a goal or aim. If the student is making satisfactory progress, the computer suggests that the teacher provide reinforcement and continue the program as it's currently being operated. If performance is not improving or is worsening, the computer suggests 1 of 22 instructional alternatives to guide the teacher in making instructional changes designed to improve the student's performance. Research indicates that if the teacher implements the computer-suggested change, the student's performance will improve during the next 6-day learning period (Calmes, 1984). AC•CEL provides teachers with a variety of reports that can be used to monitor students' progress, individualize the curriculum, and/or group students for instruction. This program and other CMI (Computer Managed Instruction) programs appear to be an excellent resource for teachers in the management of an individualized approach to education.

Research studies have documented the positive effects of Precision Teaching in facilitating learning in regular- and special-education programs (Beck, 1979a, 1979b, 1981a, 1981b; Haring, Liberty, & White, 1980; Young et al., 1986). Teachers must be trained in using Precision Teaching techniques, but the payoffs for students are great. An added benefit is that the techniques can be used with almost any curriculum.

EXAMPLE

The Precision Teaching program described here was used with CAP *(The Computational Arithmetic Program,* Smith & Lovitt, 1982) by a third-grade teacher. CAP is an arithmetic program designed to be used with groups or individuals in grades 1 through 6 who need to learn and become proficient in the basic computational skills of addition, subtraction, multiplication, and division. CAP includes 314 sequenced worksheets for FACTS (basic problems for all four computational areas), ADDITION (with and without carrying), SUBTRACTION (with and without borrowing), MULTIPLICATION (with and without carrying), and DIVISION (with and without remainders).

The teacher used the placement tests to place students in the CAP program. A filing system containing copies of the 314 worksheets was established. When students reached the mastery criterion, they moved to the next sheet in the sequence. Each student had a folder containing his currently assigned worksheet, an acetate sheet, and a copy of the Standard Behavior Chart. Students were also provided with a water-soluble pen (for use on the acetate sheet) and a small, damp sponge (for cleaning the acetate sheet).

The daily 15-minute routine consisted of the following activities: 5 minutes for students to review and practice their math skills, 5 minutes to take and correct two 1-minute timed probes, and 5 minutes to record the results of the probe on the Standard Behavior Chart, analyze the data, and make an instructional decision. Students were taught to work through the routine unassisted; they practiced independently, took the timed probes with the assistance of an audiocassette timing tape, wrote their answers on the acetate sheet which was placed over a worksheet, corrected their own work with answer keys, erased their acetate sheets, recorded their performance on the chart, analyzed their performance with the assistance of a posted decision-making flow chart, recorded their points, and confirmed their decisions with the teacher. The teacher circulated among the students and provided assistance as needed. The 15-minute Precision Teaching/computational session preceded a 40-minute math session using a basal math textbook. In the course of the year, the students learned to perform all of the computational skills accurately and fluently.

Exercises

1. Why is it important to evaluate student performance regularly?
2. Why should educators assess fluency of performance as well as accuracy?
3. Describe the unique features of Precision Teaching and the steps for implementation.

Feedback

1. It is necessary to evaluate student performance on a regular basis to ensure that the students are progressing toward meeting the criterion established for the objective. If progress is not occurring, the teacher should modify the student's instructional program to facilitate progress.
2. Research has shown that teaching students to respond fluently is related to academic achievement, retention of knowledge and skills, and the ability to use the academic skills in nonteaching situations.
3. Precision teachers pinpoint specific observable behaviors, collect data on the rate at which these behaviors occur, record the rate data on the Standard Behavior Chart, and make data-based instructional decisions to help students learn.

TEACHING TACTICS THAT MAXIMIZE LEARNING

Programs that Increase Academic Engaged Time and Opportunities to Respond

The National Commission on Excellence in Education reported three disturbing facts about the use of time in schools: (1) compared to other nations, American students spend much less time on school work, (2) time spent in a classroom and on homework is often used ineffectively, and (3) schools are not doing enough to help students develop either the study skills required to use time well or the willingness to spend more time on homework. The time spent in school, in and of itself, is not the major concern. What is important is actual academic engaged time or, in other words, the time students actually spend reading, writing, or engaging in other academic activities. Rosenshine and Berliner (1978) point out that the time spent on academic responding is correlated with achievement; the more opportunities to respond, the higher the achievement. In another study, Rosenshine (1979) reported that in some classrooms in which little student improvement was noted over the course of the year, only a few minutes of actual instruction occurred per day.

Greenwood, Delquadri, and Hall (1984) investigated academic engaged time and types of student responses during various classroom activities. Their data have some important implications for teachers:

... while 75 percent of the day was devoted to instruction in academic subjects, only 25 percent of the day was spent in active academic responding (Hall et al., 1982). Writing composed 16 percent of the day, while talking and reading silently composed only 4 percent and 3 percent, respectively. Reading aloud, answering questions, asking questions, and reciting each occurred less than 1 percent of the day. Passive attention to the teacher occupied the majority of instructional time, as much as 45 percent of the instructional day. (pp. 62–63)

In this study, students spent more time watching than they did responding. The students most in need of practice were seldom given the opportunity. Frequently, explanations of student failures place the blame with the child, not the learning environment. This study, and others, suggests that teachers may be able to prevent learning failure by increasing academic engaged time and opportunities to respond.

Direct Instruction and the ECRI approaches were designed to maximize the use of instructional time and increase student responding. Many of the teaching tactics used in these two programs were discussed in Chapter 11. The tactics are presented again here in the context of these two educational programs. Classwide Peer Tutoring (Greenwood, Delquadri, & Hall, 1984) also promotes student responding; this method will be discussed in the next section on identifying and utilizing resources.

Direct instruction.   Two distinct lines of instructional research use the term *direct instruction*. Rosenshine (1976) used the term to describe effective teaching practices that are correlated with student achievement. Bereiter and Engelmann (1966) developed a follow-through model program that became known as the "Oregon Direct Instruction" program (Stallings & Stipek, 1986). This second direct instruction program was further developed by Engelmann, Becker, Carnine, and their associates (Becker, in press). Both lines of research show promise; however, this chapter focuses on the latter direct instruction program. The Oregon Direct Instruction approach increases academic engaged time and opportunities to respond through organization of instruction and teaching tactics. The philosophy of direct instruction is "Teach more in less time, ... reduce wasted time and hasten the teaching of given objectives" (Becker, in press). Students should not be given academic work that is too easy or too difficult. Instructional materials should be appropriate to the student's level of functioning. Adequate time should be scheduled to ensure learning. Time should be well used, allowing students the opportunity to make many correct academic responses.

Teachers should organize their classrooms and materials to maximize learning. Carnine and Silbert (1979) state that "in addition to adequate instructional time, organized instruction involves arranging the physical setting and the instructional materials." Student materials should be arranged so they can be distributed quickly. Brophy and Evertson (1976), suggest that students should know (1) what the assignment is, (2) how to get help from the teacher or some designated person when needed, and (3) that they are accountable for completing the assignment appropriately and that it will be checked. Academic exercises to be completed independently may be placed in folders and given to students in advance of the independent study time. Additional independent work should be easily and quickly obtainable for students who finish their work early. All of these efforts are designed to facilitate efficient, economic, effective teaching.

The second component, and one of the most unique aspects of Direct Instruction, is the theory of instructional program design used in developing curriculum materials (Englemann & Carnine, 1982). Engelmann (1982) and Paine and Anderson-Inman (1985) describe most available curriculum materials as inadequate; their criticisms of the materials include (1) lack of clarity in introducing concepts, (2) insufficient examples, (3) inadequate review of material, and (4) failure to integrate new material with that which has been previously taught. Direct Instruction materials (1) state objectives as specific observable behaviors, (2) sequence skills to be taught in an optimal order to reduce student errors, (3) select and use appropriate and sufficient examples and nonexamples to assist students in learning to discriminate, (4) teach problem-solving strategies rather than memorization when possible, and (5) provide sufficient practice for students to learn to respond both accurately and fluently (Carnine & Silbert, 1979). Table 12–2 lists some commercially available curriculum materials that were developed using this theory of instruction.

The third component of Direct Instruction is the presentation techniques: small-group instruction, unison oral responding, signaling, pacing, monitoring, diagnosis and correction, and motivation (that is, the use of positive reinforcement and classroom behavior management procedures) (Carnine & Silbert, 1979).

The Direct Instruction model stresses small-group instruction as a method of individualizing instruction through homogeneous grouping and increasing students' opportunities to respond. Five to ten students work with the teacher for about a half hour of group instruction. Students sit close to the teacher so that he can closely monitor their attention and responses. The teacher uses signals and positive reinforcement to maintain their attention and response level.

A critical feature of small-group instruction is the use of unison responding. **Unison responding** is a technique by which students are taught to respond at the same time on the teacher's cue. The advantage of unison responding is that all students have an opportunity to frequently practice the skill they are working on throughout the instructional period. When the teacher calls only on individual students, some students may have the opportunity to respond only once or twice during a lesson. When unison responding (also referred to as choral responding) is used, students are able to respond often (perhaps hundreds of times) and can still be called upon by the teacher for some individual responses.

In order to maintain control of the group and have students respond only on cue, the teacher uses signals. A *signal* is a cue given by the teacher to tell the students when to respond. In direct instruction, the teacher ex-

TABLE 12-2   Reading Mastery*

A basal reading series intended for grades 1 through 6.

Program	Population	Overview	Publishers
Reading Mastery I Distar Reading	Preschool and primary students	Teaches basic decoding and comprehension skills. Students learn how to read letters, words, and stories, both aloud and silently. Students also answer literal comprehension questions about their readings. (160 lessons)	SRA
Reading Mastery II Distar Reading	Primary students who read at about a 2.0 level	Expands basic reading skills. Students learn strategies for decoding difficult words and for answering interpretive comprehension questions. Also teaches basic reasoning skills, such as using rules and completing deductions. (160 lessons)	SRA
Teach Your Child to Read in 100 Easy Lessons	Parents teaching average preschool and primary students (first-grade level)	A slightly accelerated version of Reading Mastery I. (100, rather than 160, lessons)	Simon & Schuster
Reading Mastery Fast Cycle I & II	Preschool and primary students of average or above average ability (first- and second-grade level)	Accelerates material presented in Reading Mastery I and II. (170 lessons)	SRA
Reading Mastery III	Primary students who read at about 3.0 level	Emphasizes reasoning and reference skills. Students apply rules in a wide variety of contexts and learn how to interpret maps, graphs, and time lines. Also teaches new vocabulary and complex sentence forms. (140 lessons)	SRA
Reading Mastery IV	Intermediate students who read at about a 4.0 level	Emphasizes problem-solving and reading in the content areas. Students evaluate prob-	SRA

Program	Population	Overview	Publishers
		lems and solutions, learn facts about the world, and complete research projects. Continues to introduce new vocabulary and sentence forms. (140 lessons)	
Reading Mastery V	Intermediate students who read at about a 5.0 level	Emphasizes literary skills. Students read novels, short stories, biographies, and poetry, as well as expository selections. Students analyze characters, settings, plots, and themes. Students also learn how to infer the main idea and how to predict word meaning from context. (120 lessons)	SRA
Reading Mastery VI	Intermediate students who read at about a 6.0 level	Teaches a wide range of literary, reasoning, and writing skills. Students interpret figurative language, analyze arguments, and complete writing assignments. The readings include a number of classic novels, stories, and poems. (120 lessons)	SRA
Reading Mastery I Spelling Book	Students in Reading Mastery I who have reached lesson 50	Emphasizes writing sounds, short phonetic words, a few short irregular words, and short sentences. (110 lessons)	SRA
Reading Mastery II Spelling Book	Students in Reading Mastery II between lessons 1 and 85	Emphasizes spelling common sound combinations such as *ar, al, sh, th,* and *wh,* phonetic words, some irregular words, and simple sentences. (79 lessons)	SRA

*The descriptions of these direct instructions materials were taken from the publishers catalogs (SRA, Simon & Schuster, C. C. Publications). The information in Table 12.2 was compiled by Patty Willis, Department of Special Education, Utah State University.

Direct Instruction Spelling Programs

Program	Population	Overview	Publisher
Reading Mastery I Spelling Book	Students in Reading Mastery I who have reached lesson 50	Emphasizes writing sounds, short phonetic words, a few short irregular words, and short sentences. (110 lessons)	SRA
Reading Mastery II Spelling Book	Students in Reading Mastery II between lessons 1 and 85	Emphasizes spelling common sound combinations such as *ar, al, sh, th,* and *wh,* phonetic words, some irregular words, and simple sentences. (79 lessons)	SRA
Spelling Mastery Level A	Second-grade or older students	Emphasizes a basic *phonemic* spelling strategy and the memorization of a set of high-utility *irregular words.* (60 lessons)	SRA
Spelling Mastery Level B	Third-grade or older students	Teaches advanced *phonemic* spelling strategies, high-utility *irregular words,* and the integration of all spelling skills into related language arts activities, with emphasis on writing skills. (140 lessons)	SRA
Spelling Mastery Level C	Fourth-grade or older students	Teaches a few hundred morphographs, a small set of useful structural spelling rules, and the integration of these spelling skills in a variety of writing and proofreading activities. (140 lessons)	SRA
Spelling Mastery Level D	Fifth-grade or older students	Teaches *advanced morphographs* and spelling rules, substantially increases ability to perform independently, and broadens the association of spelling and other lan-	SRA

Program	Population	Overview	Publisher
		guage arts, especially writing skills and word meanings. (140 lessons)	
Spelling Mastery Level E	Sixth-grade student–adults	Emphasizes *advanced morphographs* and spelling rules, substantially increases ability to perform independently, and broadens the association of spelling and other language arts, especially writing skills and word meanings. (140 lessons)	SRA
Corrective Spelling Through Morphographs	Fourth-grade students–adults	Teaches 650 morphographs and the principles for combining them, thereby enabling students to spell thousands of words, including most words on the complete Dolch word list and most commonly misspelled high school and college words. (140 lessons)	SRA

Direct Instruction Language Arts Programs

Distar Language: A basal language series for preschool through grade 3.

Program	Population	Overview	Publisher
Distar Language I	Preschool and primary	Teaches the language of instruction used in school along with word knowledge, the foundations for logical thinking, and oral language skills. (160 lessons)	SRA
Distar Language II	Primary students	Teaches the language foundation for reading	SRA

(*continued*)

Direct Instruction Language Arts Programs (*continued*)

Program	Population	Overview	Publisher
		comprehension, with emphasis on reasoning skills, following directions, and the meanings of words and sentences. (160 lessons)	
Distar Language III	Primary students	Focuses on the analysis of sentences, both spoken and written. Includes consideration of information communicated and mechanics, consolidated in writing exercises. (160 lessons)	SRA
Expressive Writing I	Elementary or secondary students who write 20 words per minute and read at middle third grade level or above	Teaches sentence-writing skills, paragraph-writing skills, and editing techniques. (50 lessons)	C.C. Publications
Expressive Writing II	Students who have completed Expressive Writing I or read at a fourth-grade level, can write in cursive, and can write and punctuate simple declarative sentences.	Teaches the student to write, punctuate, and edit compound sentences, sentences with dependent clauses, direct quotes in dialogue form, and sentences that list things. (45 lessons)	C.C. Publications
Cursive Writing Program	Third- and fourth-grade students or older students who are poor in cursive skills	Teaches the student who has already mastered manuscript writing how to form letters, create words, write sentences, and write faster and more accurately. (140 lessons)	C.C. Publications
Your World of Facts I	Third- through fifth-grade students or reme-	Teaches the facts and relationships taught in science and social	C.C. Publications

Program	Population	Overview	Publisher
	dial students with beginning third-grade reading skills	studies programs. Using the facts learned, the student can better understand their texts. Level I teaches 10–20 facts and relationships on 25 topics. (40 lessons)	
Your World of Facts II	Third- through fifth-grade students with beginning third-grade reading skills	Level II teaches hundreds of facts and relationships of climate and vertebrates. (45 lessons)	C.C. Publications

Corrective Reading

A remedial reading series for students in grades 4 through 12 and for adults who have not mastered decoding and comprehension skills.

DECODING STRAND

Program	Population	Overview	Publisher
Corrective Reading: Decoding A (Word-attack Basics)	Fourth-grade students–adults	Emphasizes basic skills: identifying sounds, rhyming, sounding out, and word and sentence reading. (60 lessons)	SRA
Corrective Reading: Decoding B (Decoding Strategies)	Fourth-grade students–adults	Emphasizes critical letter and word discriminations, letter combinations, and story reading with comprehension questions. (140 lessons)	SRA
Corrective Reading: Decoding C (Skill Applications)	Fourth-grade students–adults	Emphasizes advanced decoding skills: word buildups, affixes, vocabulary, story reading with comprehension questions, and outside reading applications. (140 lessons)	SRA

(continued)

COMPREHENSION STRAND

Program	Population	Overview	Publisher
Corrective Reading: Comprehension A (Thinking Basics)	Fourth-grade students–adults	Emphasizes oral language skills: deductions, inductions, analogies, vocabulary building, and inferences. (60 lessons)	SRA
Corrective Reading: Comprehension B (Comprehension Skills)	Fourth-grade students–adults	Emphasizes literal and inferential skills, reading for information, writing skills, following sequenced instructions, analyzing contradictions, and learning information. (140 lessons)	SRA
Corrective Reading: Comprehension C (Concept Applications)	Fourth-grade students–adults	Emphasizes advanced comprehension applications: survival skills, reading for information, analyzing arguments, and reasoning. (140 lessons)	SRA
Mathematics Modules: Basic Fractions	Fourth- through twelfth-grade students	Teaches addition, subtraction, and multiplication of fractions and whole numbers, writing mixed numbers for fractions, and finding equivalent fractions. (55 lessons)	SRA
Mathematics Modules: Fractions, Decimals, and Percents	Fourth- through twelfth-grade students	Teaches addition, subtraction, multiplication, and division of fractions, mixed numbers, and decimals. Also teaches reducing improper fractions, writing decimals or percents for fractions, writing fractions or percents for decimals, and writing fractions or decimals for percents. (70 lessons)	SRA
Mathematics Modules: Ratios and Equations	Fourth- through twelfth-grade students	Teaches ratios, rate and distance problems, logical simple analysis, and story problems. (60 lessons)	SRA

Direct Instruction Mathematics Programs

Distar Arithmetic
A basal arithmetic series for preschool through grade 2.

Program	Population	Overview	Publisher
Distar Arithmetic I	Preschool and primary students	Emphasizes beginning problem-solving strategies for addition, subtraction, and stories. (160 lessons)	SRA
Distar Arithmetic II	Primary students	Emphasizes advanced problem-solving strategies for addition with carrying, multiplication, fractions, column subtraction, and complex story problems. (160 lessons)	SRA

Corrective Mathematics:
A remedial series in basic mathematics for grades 3 through 12 and adults who have not mastered basic skills.

Program	Population	Overview	Publisher
Corrective Mathematics: Addition	Third- through twelfth-grade students	Teaches basic facts, addition of two or more numbers with and without carrying, and story problems. (65 lessons)	SRA
Corrective Mathematics: Subtraction	Third- through twelfth-grade students	Teaches basic facts, subtraction with and without borrowing, and story problems. (65 lessons)	SRA
Corrective Mathematics: Multiplication	Third- through twelfth-grade students	Teaches basic facts, multiplication with and without carrying, and story problems. (65 lessons)	SRA
Corrective Mathematics: Division	Third- through twelfth-grade students	Teaches basic facts, long division with and without remainders, and story problems. (65 lessons)	SRA

plains to the students that sometimes she will make the response, sometimes she will ask for individual responses, and sometimes she will signal for the group to respond in unison.

Appropriate **pacing** is another key feature of direct instruction. Research has demonstrated that students respond better, are more attentive and on task, and exhibit fewer behavior problems with fast-paced instruction as opposed to slow-paced instruction (Carnine, 1976; West, 1981; West & Sloane, 1986).

Teachers must monitor student performance closely during the group session, listening carefully to responses while watching students' eyes and mouths to detect whether all students are responding. By watching the students' lips and tongues, the teacher can determine whether students are responding correctly. With older students, the teacher can rely on written assignments as a method of monitoring learning. Direct instruction also uses individual student tests to check the accuracy and rate of responding before moving students through the curriculum.

Although direct instruction procedures are effective, they are not without the potential for error. All students make some errors in the process of learning. Direct instruction deals with these errors through the use of correction procedures. Teachers learn to diagnose specific errors or error patterns and correct them. Direct instruction teaches the use of a six-step correction procedure for small-group instruction. The first step involves having the teacher praise a student who responds correctly. Next, the teacher models the correct response and, third, leads the student through a correct response. Leading involves providing a model as the student responds. Fourth, the teacher does an immediate, informal test by asking the student to make an individual response to determine if he now can respond correctly. The fifth step involves further testing by having the student respond on alternating examples of previous correct responses and repeating the corrected previous error response. The last step in the correction procedure is for the teacher to provide a delayed test later in the instructional session.

Teachers who use direct instruction also learn to use appropriate classroom behavior management procedures. Teachers learn to provide high rates of praise and other social reinforcers for correct responding. As necessary, teachers may also use other types of reinforcers to motivate students to attend and respond correctly.

The effectiveness of direct instruction is well documented (Gersten, Carnine, & White, 1984). The direct instruction follow-through model was originally validated through one of the largest and most extensive social experiments ever conducted (McDaniels, 1975). The follow-through experiments examine the effectiveness of 22 intervention models; the Direct Instruction model produced the highest student achievement (Gersten, Carnine, & White, 1984). While the Direct Instruction model is most effective with instructional materials developed according to the Engelmann and Carnine theory of instruction, the presentation techniques or teaching tactics that are used in direct instruction can be adapted for use with any curriculum materials. The teaching tactics can themselves facilitate increased opportunities to respond and more accurate, fluent responding.

ECRI approach. The Exemplary Center for Reading Instruction (ECRI) approach is similar in many ways to the Direct Instruction model. The major difference in the two programs is that the ECRI model has been developed for use with existing curriculum materials and emphasizes pedagogy, or appropriate principles of instruction, whereas the Direct Instruction model emphasizes materials based on the Engelmann and Carnine (1982) theory of instruction as well as effective teaching strategies. The ECRI approach is designed to guarantee high levels of mastery and instructs teachers to use the following effective teaching strategies (Reid, 1983):*

1. *Elicit rapid overt responses from students* during instruction and as they practice. (Students learn by "doing" and "saying.") The overt responses requested of students in skills groups are most often in unison. Unison and group responses offer security to the unresponsive students as they learn to respond with others and motivate all students to respond more enthusiastically and rapidly.

2. *Keep every student on task.* Prevent students from procrastinating in offering responses. Supervise their practice time (time to master) and monitor their responses during instruction.

3. *Increase the rate of responses of all students,* but especially those who have been least rapid; expect pupils who respond more slowly to complete a task in less time than faster students.

4. *Expect every pupil to achieve mastery at high (83 to 100 percent) levels of accuracy,* with rate as another criterion. Allow students to move on in skill sequences as rapidly as they achieve mastery.

5. *Model for students during instruction* so that they make fewer errors as they learn, and hence are able to discriminate fine differences in their work when compared to others; prompt students as they learn and practice. Then gradually fade the prompts until students respond correctly without assistance. Move from a model-match level of learning to a memory-match level, and then to a recall level.

6. *Diagnose and prescribe instantly* when incorrect responses, or no responses, occur.

7. *Reinforce correct responses and reteach* if students respond incorrectly or do not respond. Ignore inappropriate behavior. Employ only those techniques that build self-esteem. Eliminate sarcasm and criticism in teaching; never demean. Use the behavior management techniques that most effectively extinguish incorrect responses, reinforce correct responses, and maintain them at the rate and mastery levels established.

8. *Correlate language skills activities* to increase the number and types of student responses. (For example, write and spell that which the pupil reads.) Emphasize the development of the skills of expressing ideas (speaking and writing) as well as those of understanding ideas (listening and reading). Teach reading as a means

*From E. R. Reid, *Teaching Scheduling and Recordkeeping* (Salt Lake City: Cove Publishers, 1983).

and not an end—as a way to learn to speak and write more effectively and to serve personal and other needs. (pp. 7–8)

For further description of the implementation of the ECRI approach, see Reid (1986).

IDENTIFYING AND UTILIZING AVAILABLE RESOURCES

The challenge of individualizing instruction, assisting students in achieving accurate and fluent responding, and maximizing opportunities to respond demands much time and attention. Effective teachers learn to identify and use available resources to assist them in accomplishing these tasks. The use of microcomputers, is an example of a time-saving resource. Other examples include using aides, volunteers, parents, and students (peers). Peer tutoring is an efficient, effective instructional strategy.

Classwide peer tutoring.   Greenwood, Delquadri, and Hall (1984) developed a Classwide Tutoring system to individualize instruction and increase students' opportunities to respond. The characteristics of this program included the following:

1. All children in the classroom had the opportunity to engage in the academic behavior.
2. Error correction was immediate and efficient, and resulted in the emission of correct responses.
3. Sufficient response opportunities were provided and correct responses obtained from the student to indicate mastery of the instructional objectives.
4. The response required during instruction had a direct bearing on the response to be tested for mastery (for example, writing of spelling words in practice as opposed to writing words in the testing situation).
5. The teacher used the procedures on a regular, daily basis.
6. Student satisfaction with the procedures was an element that enabled their frequent, continued use. (p. 72)

The Classwide Peer Tutoring System has been tested on a large number of students and in a variety of curriculum areas (including math, reading, and spelling) and has been found to be very successful in improving student learning (Cheney, Likins, & Landeen, 1986; Delquadri et al., 1983; Greenwood, Dinwiddie, Terry, Wade, Stanley, Thibadeau, & Delquadri, 1984). Delquadri and colleagues (1986) describe the basic procedures of the tutoring program, which is in a game format. Tutoring periods usually require 30 minutes, 10 minutes of which can be planned for each student to serve as a tutor, 10 minutes to be tutored, and 5 to 10 minutes to add and post individual and team points. Students are randomly assigned to one of two teams each week.

Restructuring weekly teams ensures that all children are eventually on a winning team.

The teacher signals the beginning of the tutoring period and students move to their partners. The tutee responds to the material—he might, for example, read sentences in the assigned passage—and earns points for his team. The tutor observes the reading awards points, and corrects errors. The tutor gives the tutee 2 points for correctly reading a sentence or 1 point for successfully correcting an error identified by the tutor. To correct the error, the tutor pronounces the correct word and the tutee rereads the sentence until it is correct. In spelling and math, points are based on saying and writing the correct response.

The teacher supervises the tutoring, moving among the students to provide assistance and award bonus points to tutors for correct tutoring behaviors. After the first 10-minute period, the tutor and tutee switch roles and the tutoring continues. After the second tutoring session has ended, individual points are summed and reported aloud to the teacher. Students' points are posted on a team chart. The winning team is applauded for winning, as is the losing team for making a good effort. No other rewards are given for the points. The procedures are easy to implement and are enjoyed by the students.

EXAMPLE

Two first-grade teachers used Classwide Peer Tutoring, Precision Teaching, and a feedback system to improve their students' mastery of reading and spelling skills. The tutoring program used a game format (Carta, Dinwiddie, Kohler, Delquadri, & Greenwood, 1984). Each week the students in the class were divided into two groups; the students within each group were paired so that each student was assigned to work with one other student. Each student took his turn tutoring and being tutored. When acting as a tutor, the student would listen to the tutee read, ask her comprehension questions, and give her spelling words (from the basal reader). The student would listen to the tutee respond and record reading, comprehension, or spelling errors. The tutor would award the tutee points for reading, correctly answering comprehension questions, and correctly spelling words. When the tutee made an error, the tutor corrected the error by modeling the correct answer, awarding a point to the tuttee for practicing the correct response, and requesting assistance from the teacher when necessary.

The peer tutors also gave the tutees 1-minute timed precision teaching probes on reading and recorded the number of words read correctly per minute. The tutor gave the reading rate to the tutee, who posted it on his Standard Behavior Chart. The tutor gave the tutee 5 additional points if the student met the daily goal that had been set by the teacher. Each tutor would record his tutee's individual score and their team score on posted charts.

After about 15 minutes, the tutor and tutee switched roles and the same steps were repeated. The students earned points for appropriate behavior (being a "good sport," speaking quietly, paying attention, and working hard), as well as for correct academic responses and tutoring behaviors. The students were also taught to praise the students they worked with and encourage them to do their best. The tutoring procedures, coupled with the Precision Teaching probes, the point system, and the public posting of scores, allowed the teacher to individualize the curriculum and have the students engage in many correct academic responses every day. The program was highly successful in that all students made excellent reading and spelling gains, learned the positive social interaction skills of praising and complimenting others, and enjoyed the peer tutoring activities.

Exercises

1. Explain the importance of students' having many opportunities to make correct academic responses.
2. Explain the similarities and differences between the Oregon Direct Instruction program and the ECRI approach.

Feedback

1. Making correct responses and practicing these responses repeatedly is important because academic responding is highly correlated with achievement. Research has demonstrated that students typically spend most of their school day in nonacademic activities or in passive academic activities; that is, they may be listening to the teacher speak or listening to other students respond, but they actually spend very little time responding themselves. Students need many opportunities each day to read, write answers, compute problems, or perform other kinds of academic tasks. The teacher must select instructional strategies that facilitate opportunities for the student to make academic responses.
2. Both Direct Instruction and ECRI (1) stress teaching students in small groups, (2) utilize unison responding, (3) stress that students should master objectives in a curriculum by demonstrating that they can perform tasks both accurately and fluently, and (4) attempt to improve education by maximizing instructional time and avoiding time-wasting activities. The primary difference between ECRI and Direct Instruction is that the ECRI approach is designed to be used with any curriculum materials, while the Direct Instruction program has been used primarily with instructional materials developed in accordance with the Engelmann and Carnine (1982) theory of instruction. However, some teachers have used the principles of Direct Instruction with other curriculum materials; therefore, the two approaches are probably much more similar than they are different.

FAST TRACK

REVIEW

This chapter focuses on characteristics of effective instructional programs. Several educational approaches to teaching academic skills are discussed because no one method is comprehensive enough to meet the needs of all teachers and students. Emphasis is placed on a philosophy of teaching that states that most, if not all, students are capable of learning and that teachers must accept the responsibility of finding the right instructional strategies and materials to facilitate learning. Teachers must know the curriculum they are teaching well enough to be able to identify and sequence specific instructional objectives and design or obtain appropriate curriculum materials for teaching these objectives. Once teachers know precisely what they are going to teach, then they should develop an instructional system that allows students to progress through the curriculum at their own pace. Moving all students through a curriculum at the same rate slows gifted students and moves too fast for those who are having academic difficulties.

All students should be given the time and instructional assistance to meet both accuracy and fluency mastery criteria. Research has demonstrated that it is important for students to learn to perform academic skills not only accurately, but also with fluency and ease.

The Precision Teaching approach, a measurement system that can be used with any curriculum, assists teachers in measuring both accuracy and fluency of student responding. The Precision Teaching approach encourages the use of direct, daily measurement of student performance. In academic programs, students are typically given short, 1- and 2-minute timed drills at the end of each instructional period. These timed drills serve to measure student learning. Student performance data are charted on the Standard Behavior Chart and student progress is monitored. Data are analyzed and instructional decisions are made about what instructional strategies should be used to best facilitate student learning.

Teachers should use instructional strategies that maximize student performance and increase students' opportunity to respond. Research has demonstrated that academic engaged time or increasing the number of response opportunities is directly correlated with student achievement. Three instructional approaches were reviewed to provide teachers with examples of different ways to teach students effectively and increase their response opportunities.

The Direct Instruction program organizes the educational program and schedules activities in a way to maximize students' academic engaged time. Direct instruction utilizes small group instruction with unison responding as a technique to individualize learning and allow students an opportunity to make many academic responses in a relatively short amount of time. Direct Instruction presentation techniques include the use of small groups, unison responding, signals, pacing, monitoring, and positive reinforcement. Direct Instruction's programs also utilize the theory of instruction developed by Engelmann and Carnine (1982) in the development of curriculum materials.

The ECRI approach is similar to Direct Instruction but is designed to be used with any curriculum materials. The basic principles of the ECRI approach include maximizing the amount of instructional time; using positive reinforcement; eliciting overt, accurate, rapid responses; establishing high expectations for mastery of materials; and increasing the rate of teaching behaviors through the use of instructional directives. Research suggests that both the ECRI approach and Direct Instruction are effective instructional strategies for improving student achievement.

Classwide Peer Tutoring was designed specifically for increasing students' opportunities to respond. Classwide Peer Tutoring is based on the principles of positive reinforcement for correct responding, peer-mediated contingencies, and the principles of systematic feedback. All students in the class are paired together in a tutee–tutor relationship. One student tutors the other for about 10 minutes; the roles then change and the tutee becomes the tutor. The system facilitates many academic responses during the tutoring sessions. Research has demonstrated that Classwide Peer Tutoring is effective with a variety of students, in both regular- and special-education programs, and with a variety of curriculum areas: reading, math, and spelling.

The programs discussed in this chapter may be used by teachers as they have been developed and are commercially available or published in professional journals. However, the instructional strategies that are incorporated within these approaches can often be used with different materials and in combination to maximize learning. Regardless of which instructional programs or strategies teachers select, it is important that they assume the responsibility for student learning.

References

ACHENBACH, T. M. (1978). The child behavior profile I: boys aged 6–11. *Journal of Consulting and Clinical Psychology, 46,* 478–488.

ACHENBACH, T. M., & EDELBROCK, C. S. (1978). The child behavior profile II: boys aged 12–16 and girls 6–11 and 12–16. *Journal of Consulting and Clinical Psychology, 47,* 223–33.

ADAMS, R. (1969). Location as a feature of instructional interaction. *Merrill Palmer Quarterly, 15,* 309–22.

ADAMS, R., & BIDDLE, B. J. (1970). *Realities of teaching: Explorations with videotape.* New York: Holt, Rinehart & Winston.

ALBRECHT, P. (March 1982a). *Data decision rules.* Paper presented at the Second Annual Precision Teaching Conference, Orlando, Fla.

ALBRECHT, P. (March 1982b). Data-based decision rules. Paper presented at a symposium, Second Annual Precision Teaching Conference, Orlando, Fla.

ALEXANDER, R. N., CORBETT, T. F., & SMIGEL, J. (1976). The effects of individual and group consequences on school attendance and curfew violations with predelinquent adolescents. *Journal of Applied Behavior Analysis, 9,* 221–26.

ALLEN, K. E., HENKE, L. B., HARRIS, F. R., BAER, D. M., & REYNOLDS, N. J. (1967). Control of hyperactivity by social reinforcement of attending behavior. *Journal of Educational Psychology, 58,* 231–37.

ALTHAUSER, R. P., & HERBERLEIN, T. A. (1970). Validity and the multitrait–multimethod matrix. In H. L. Costner (ed.), *Sociological methodology.* San Francisco: Jossey-Bass.

ANDREWS, G., & INGHAM, R. J. (1972). Stuttering: An evaluation of follow-up procedures for syllable timed speech/token system therapy. *Journal of Communication Disorders, 5,* 307–19.

ASHER, S. R., & HYMEL, S. (1981). Children's social competence in peer relations: Sociometric and behavioral assessment. In J. D. Wine & M. D. Smye (eds.), *Social competence.* New York: Guilford.

ASHER, S. R., & RENSHAW, P. D. (1981). Children without friends: Social knowledge and social skill training. In S. R. Asher & J. M. Gottman (eds.), *The development of children's friendships.* New York: Cambridge University Press.

AXELROD, S., HALL, R. V., & TAMS, A. (1979). Comparison of two common classroom seating arrangements. *Academic Therapy, 15*(1), 29–36.

AYLLON, T., & AZRIN, N. H. (1968). *The token economy: A motivational system for therapy and rehabilitation.* New York: Appleton-Century-Crofts.

AYLLON, T., & HAUGHTON, E. (1962). Control of the behavior of schizophrenic patients by food. *Journal of the Experimental Analysis of Behavior, 5,* 324–34.

AYLLON, T., & McKITTRICK, S. M. (1982). *How to set up a token economy.* Lawrence, Kansas: H & H Enterprises.

AYLLON, T., & MICHAEL, J. (1959). The psychiatric nurse as a behavioral engineer. *Journal of the Experimental Analysis of Behavior, 2,* 324–34.

AYLLON, T., & ROBERTS, M. D. (1974). Eliminating discipline problems by strengthening academic performance. *Journal of Applied Behavior Analysis, 7,* 71–76.

AZRIN, N. H., & FOXX, R. M. (1971). A rapid method of toilet training the institutionalized retarded. *Journal of Applied Behavior Analysis, 7,* 71–76.

AZRIN, N. H., & HOLZ, W. C. (1966). Punishment. In W. Honig (ed.), *Operant behavior: Areas of research and application.* New York: Appleton-Century-Crofts.

AZRIN, N. H., & POWERS, M. A. (1975). Eliminating classroom disturbances of emotionally disturbed children by positive practice procedures. *Behavior Therapy, 6,* 525–34.

AZRIN, N. H., & WESOLOWSKI, M. D. (1974). Theft reversal: An overcorrection procedure for eliminating stealing by retarded persons. *Journal of Applied Behavior Analysis, 7,* 557–81.

BAER, D. M. (1977). Reviewer's comment: Just because it's reliable doesn't mean that you can use it. *Journal of Applied Behavior Analysis, 10,* 117–19.

BAER, D. M. (1981). *How to plan for generalization.* Austin, Tex.: Pro-Ed.

BAER, D. M., & WOLF, M. M. (1970). The entry into natural communities of reinforcement. In R. Ulrich, T. Stachnik, & J. Mabry, *Control of human behavior, 2.* Glenview, Ill.: Scott, Foresman.

BAILEY, S. L. (1983). Extraneous aversives. In S. Axelrod & J. Apsche (eds.), *The effects of punishment on human behavior.* San Diego: Academic Press.

BAILEY, J. S., WOLD, M. M., & PHILLIPS, E. L. (1970). Home-based reinforcement and the modification of pre-delinquent classroom behavior. *Journal of Applied Behavior Analysis, 3,* 223–33.

BANDURA, A. (1969). *Principles of behavior modification.* New York: Holt, Rinehart & Winston.

BARKLEY, J. (1966). Interest patterns associated with measures of desirability. *Personality Guidance Journal, 45,* 56–60.

BARKLEY, R., COPELAND, A., & SIVAGE, C. A. (1980). A self-control classroom for hyperactive children. *Journal of Autism and Developmental Disorders, 10,* 75–89.

BARRETT, R. P., & SHAPIRO, E. S. (1980). Treatment of stereotyped hair-pulling with overcorrection. *Journal of Behavior Therapy and Experimental Psychiatry, 11,* 317–20.

BARRISH, H. H., SAUNDERS, M., & WOLF, M. M. (1969). Good behavior game: Effects of individual contingencies for group contingencies on disruptive behavior in a classroom. *Journal of Applied Behavior Analysis, 2,* 119–24.

BARTON, E. S. & OSBORNE, J. G. (1978). The development of classroom sharing by a teacher using positive practice. *Behavior Modification, 2,* 231–50.

BECK, R. (1981a). *Curriculum management through a database-Validation report for ESEA Title IV.* Great Falls, Mont.

BECK, R. (1979b). *Great Falls public schools report for the Office of Education joint dissemination review panel, special education.* Precision Teaching Project, Great Falls, Mont.

BECK, R. (1981b). *High school basic skills improvement project.* Validation report for Innovation Grant, ESEA Title IV-C, Great Falls, Mont.

BECK, R. (1979a). *Report for the Office of Education joint dissemination review panel, regular education.* Great Falls, Mont: Precision Teaching Project.

BECK, S. (1983). Overview of methods. In J. L. Matson & S. E. Breuning (Eds.) *Assessing the mentally retarded* (pp. 3–26). New York: Grune & Stratton.

BECKER, W. C. (1978). The national evaluation of Follow Through: Behavior-theory-based programs come out on top. *Education and Urban Society, 10,* 431–58.

BECKER, W. C. (1971). *Parents are teachers.* Champaign, Ill: Research Press.

BECKER, W. C. (in press). Direct Instruction: A twenty-year review. In L. A. Hamerlynck & R. P. West (Eds.), *Designs for excellence in education: The legacy of B. F. Skinner.* Hillsdale, N.J.: Erlbaum.

BECKER, W. C., CARNINE, D. & THOMAS, D. R. (1969). *Reducing behavior problems: An operant conditioning guide for teachers.* Urbana, Ill: Educational Resources Information Center.

BECKER, W. C., ENGELMANN, S., & THOMAS, D. R. (1975a). *Teaching 1: Classroom management.* Chicago: Science Research Associates.

BECKER, W. C., ENGELMANN, S., & THOMAS, D. R. (1975b). *Cognitive learning and instruction.* Chicago: Science Research Associates.

BECKER, W. C., & GERSTEN, R. (1982). A follow-up of Follow-Through: The later effects of the direct instruction model on children in fifth and sixth grades. *American Educational Research Journal, 19,* 75–92.

BECKER, W. C., MADSEN, C. H., ARNOLD, C. R., & THOMAS, D. R. (1967). The contingent use of teacher attention and praise in reducing classroom behavior problems. *Journal of Special Education, 1,* 287–307.

BELLACK, A. S., & HERSEN, M. (1977). *Behavior modification: An introductory textbook.* Baltimore: Williams & Wilkins.

BEREITER, C., & ENGELMANN, S. (1966). *Teaching disadvantaged children in the preschool.* Englewood Cliffs, N.J.: Prentice-Hall.

BERLER, E. S., GROSS, A. M., & DRABMAN, R. S. (1982). Social skills training with children: Proceed with caution. *Journal of Applied Behavior Analysis, 15,* 41–53.

BESALEL-AZRIN, V., AZRIN, N. H., & ARMSTRONG, P. M. (1977). The student-oriented classroom: A method of improving student conduct and satisfaction. *Behavior Therapy, 8,* 193–204.

BIJOU, S. W. (1970). What psychology has to offer to education—now. *Journal of Applied Behavior Analysis, 3,* 65–71.

BIJOU, S. W., & BAER, D. M. (1963). Some methodological contributions from a functional analysis of child development. In L. P. Lipsett & C. S. Spiker (eds.), *Advances in child development and behavior,* Vol. 1. New York: Academic Press.

BIJOU, S. W., BIRNBRAUER, J. S., KIDDER, J. D., & TAGUE, C. (1966). Programmed instruction as an approach to teaching of reading, writing, and arithmetic to retarded children. *Psychological Record, 16,* 505–22.

BIJOU, S. W., & PETERSON, R. (1971). The psychological assessment of children: A functional analysis. In P. McReynolds (ed.), *Advances in psychological assessment.* Palo Alto, Calif.: Science and Behavior Books.

BIJOU, S. W., PETERSON, R. F., & AULT, N. H. (1968). A method to integrate description and experimental field studies at the level of data and empirical concepts. *Journal of Applied Behavior Analysis, 1,* 175–91.

BIRNBRAUER, J. S., WOLF, M. M., KIDDER, J. D., & TAGUE, C. (1965). Classroom behavior of retarded pupils with token reinforcement. *Journal of Experimental Child Psychology, 2,* 219–35.

BLECHMAN, E. A. (1986). *Solving child behavior problems at home and school.* Champaign, Ill.: Research Press.

BLESSINGER, B. (1974). Modification of sobbing behavior. In R. Ulrich, T. Stachnik, & J. Mabry, *Control of human behavior, 3,* Glenview, Ill.: Scott, Foresman and Co.

BLOOM, B. (1976). *Human characteristics and school learning.* New York: McGraw-Hill.

BLOOM, B. S., ENGLEHART, M. D., FURST, E. J., HILL, W. H., & KRATHWOHL, D. R. (1956). *A taxonomy of educational objectives. Handbook I: The cognitive domain.* New York: Longman.

BOLSTAD, O., & JOHNSON, S. (1972). Self-regulation in the modification of disruptive classroom behavior. *Journal of Applied Behavior Analysis, 5,* 443–54.

BORN, D. G., GLEDHILL, S. M., & DAVIS, M. L. (1972). Examination performance in lecture-discussion and personalized instruction courses. *Journal of Applied Behavior Analysis, 5,* 33–43.

BORNSTEIN, P. H., HAMILTON, S. B., & QUEVILLON, R. P. (1977). Behavior modification by long distance: Demonstration of functional control over disruptive behavior in a rural classroom setting. *Behavior Modification, 1,* 369–80.

BOSTOW, D. E., & BAILEY, J. B. (1969). Modification of severe disruptive and aggressive behavior using brief timeout and reinforcement procedures. *Journal of Applied Behavior Analysis, 2,* 31–37.

BRANTNER, J. R., & DOHERTY, M. A. (1983). A review of timeout: A conceptual and methodological analysis. In S. Axelrod & J. Apsche (eds.), *The Effects of Punishment on Human Behavior.* New York: Academic Press.

BRIGHAM, T. A., HOPPER, C., HILL, B., DE ARMAS, A., & NEWSOM, P. (1985). A self-management program for disruptive adolescents in the school: A clinical replication analysis. *Behavior Therapy, 16,* 99–115.

BRISTOL, M. M., & SLOANE, H. N. (1974). Effects of contingency contracting on study rate and test performance. *Journal of Applied Behavior Analysis, 7,* 271–85.

BRODEN, M., BRUCE, C., MITCHELL, M. A., CARTER, V., & HALL, R. V. (1970). Effects of teacher attention on attending behavior of two boys in adjacent desks. *Journal of Applied Behavior Analysis, 3,* 199–203.

BRODEN, M. R., HALL, V. R., & MITTS, B. (1971). The effect of self-recording on the classroom behavior of two eighth-grade students. *Journal of Applied Behavior Analysis, 4,* 191–200.

BROPHY, J. E. (1983). If only it were true: A response to Geer. *Educational Researcher, 12,* 10–13.

BROPHY, J., & EVERTSON, C. (1976). *Learning from teaching: A developmental perspective.* Boston: Allyn & Bacon.

BROWN, W. E. (May 1972). Praise–criticism ratio: Do teachers take advantage of it? *Behaviorally Speaking.*

BUEHLER, R. E., PATTERSON, G. R., & FURINESS, J. M. (1966). The reinforcement of behavior in an institutional setting. *Behavior Research and Therapy, 4,* 157–167.

BURGIO, L. D., WHITMAN, T. L., & JOHNSON, M. R. (1980). A self-instructional package for increasing attending behavior in educable mentally retarded children. *Journal of Applied Behavior Analysis, 13,* 443–59.

BURLEIGH, R. A., & MARHOLIN, D. (1977). Don't shoot until you see the whites of his eyes: Analysis of the adverse side effects of verbal prompts. *Behavior Modification, 1,* 109–22.

BURRON, D., & BUCHER, B. (1978). Self-instructions as discriminative cues for rule-breaking or rule-following. *Journal of Experimental Child Psychology, 26,* 46–57.

Bushell, D. (1978). An engineering approach to the elementary classroom: The Behavior Analysis Follow-Through program. In A. C. Catantia and T. A. Brigham (eds.), *Handbook of applied behavior analysis*. New York: Irvington Publishers.

Butler, C., & Lahey, B. B. (1979). *Use of preschool peer therapists to increase appropriate interaction in socially deficient preschool children*. Unpublished manuscript.

Calmes, L. J. (1984). *The effects of a microcomputer decision-making program on the self-management of student academic performance*. Unpublished masters thesis, Utah State University.

Cannon, D., Sloane, H. N., Agosto, R., DeRisi, W., Donovan, J., Ralph, J., & Della Piana, G. (1971). *The Fred C. Nelles School for Boys rehabilitation system*. Salt Lake City, Utah: Behavior Systems Corporation.

Canter, L., & Canter, M. (1982). *Assertive discipline*. Los Angeles: Lee Canter & Associates.

Cantrell, R. P., Cantrell, M. L., Huddleston, C. M., & Woolridge, R. L. (1969). Contingency contracting with school problems. *Journal of Applied Behavior Analysis, 2,* 215–20.

Carlisle, K. E. (1983). The process of task analysis. *Journal of Instructional Development, 6,* 31–35.

Carmines, E. G., & Zeller, R. A. (1979). Reliability and validity. *Quantitative Applications in Social Sciences,* 17 (serial no. 07-017).

Carnine, D. W. (1976). Effects of two teacher presentation rates on off-task behavior, answering correctly, and participation. *Journal of Applied Behavior Analysis, 9,* 199–206.

Carnine, D. W., & Fink, W. T. (1978). Increasing the rate of presentation and use of signals in elementary classroom teachers. *Journal of Applied Behavior Analysis, 11,* 35–46.

Carnine, D. & Silbert, J. (1979). *Direct instruction reading*. Columbus, Ohio: Chas E. Merrill.

Carr, E. G., & Lovaas, O. I. (1983). Contingent electric shock as a treatment for severe behavior problems. In S. Axelrod & J. Apsche (eds.), *The effects of punishment on human behavior*. New York: Academic Press.

Carr, E. G., Newsom, C. D., & Binkoff, J. A. (1980). Escape as a factor in the aggressive behavior of two retarded children. *Journal of Applied Behavior Analysis, 13,* 101–17.

Carroll, J. (1963). A model of school learning. *Teachers College Record, 64,* 723–33.

Carta, J., Dinwiddie, G., Kohler, F., Delquadri, J., & Greenwood, C. R. (1984, Sept). *The Juniper Gardens classwide peer tutoring programs for spelling, reading and math-teacher's manual*. Juniper Gardens Children's Project, Bureau of Child Research, University of Kansas.

Cartledge, G., & Milburn, J. F. (1980). *Teaching social skills to children*. Elmsford, N.Y.: Pergamon Press.

Casella, M. A. (1971). *The effect of of contracting specific high probability behavior as reinforcement of the study behavior of college students*. Master's thesis, University of Utah.

Cautela, J. R., Cautela, J., & Esonis, S. (1982). *Forms for behavior analysis with children*. Champaign, Il.: Research Press.

Chase, P. N. (1985). Designing courseware: Prompts from behavioral instruction. *The Behavior Analyst, 8,* 65–76.

Cheney, D., Likins, M., & Landeen, J. (1986, May). *The effect of academic peer tutoring on social interactions and sociometric status in elementary students*. Paper presented at the twelfth annual convention of the Association for Behavior Analysis, Milwaukee, Wis.

Cheney, D., Morgan, D. P., & Young, K. R. (1984). *Assertiveness skills for adolescents*. Logan, Utah: Utah State University.

Clark, H. B., Northrop, J., & Wood, R. (1980). *Social skills development: Applications of individual and group training*. Las Vegas, Nev.: Children's Behavior Services, Mental Health Center.

Cohen, H. L., & Filipczak, J. A. (1971). *New learning environment*. San Francisco: Jossey-Bass.

Coie, J. D., & Dodge, K. A. (1983). Continuities and changes in children's social status: A five-year longitudinal study. *Merrill-Palmer Quarterly, 29,* 261–82.

Cole, P. (1978). Personal communication.

Coleman, R. A. (1970). A conditioning technique applicable to elementary school classrooms. *Journal of Applied Behavior Analysis, 3,* 293–97.

Combs, M. L., & Slaby, D. A. (1977). Social skills training with children. In B. B. Lahey & A. E. Kazdin (Eds.), *Advances in clinical child psychology*. (Vol. 1) New York: Plenum.

Conley, O. S., & Wolery, M. R. (1980). Treatment by overcorrection of self-injurious eye-gouging in preschool blind children. *Journal of Behavior Therapy and Experimental Psychiatry, 11,* 121–25.

Conners, C. K. (1969). A teacher rating scale for use in drug studies with children. *American Journal of Psychiatry, 126,* 884–88.

Cooley, C. H. (1902). *Human nature and the social order*. New York: Scribner's.

Cowart, J., Carnine, D., & Becker, W. C. (1973). *The effects of signals on attending, responding, and following diet instructions*. Unpublished manuscript, University of Oregon.

COWEN, E. L., PEDERSON, A., BABIGIAN, H., IZZO, L. D., & TROST, M. A. (1973). Long-term follow-up of early detected vulnerable children. *Journal of Consulting and Clinical Psychology, 41*, 438–46.

CRAIGHEAD, W. E., KAZDIN, A. E., & MAHONEY, M. J. (1976). *Behavior modification: Principles, issues, and applications.* Boston: Houghton Mifflin.

CRANDALL, J. A. (in press). *Instructional design in computer documentation (tentative title).* Englewood Cliffs, N.J.: Prentice-Hall.

CRONBACH, L. J. (1970). *Essentials of psychological testing.* New York: Harper & Row, Pub.

CROUCH, P. L., GRESHAM, F. M., & WRIGHT, W. R. (1985). Interdependent and independent group contingencies with immediate and delayed reinforcement for controlling classroom behavior. *Journal of School Psychology, 23*, 177–87.

DAHL, P. (1979). An experimental program for teaching high-speed word recognition and comprehension skills. In T. C. Lovitt (ed.), *Communications research in learning disabilities and mental retardation.* Baltimore, Md.: University Park Press.

DARCY-FREDRICK, L., LITTLE, N. M., SWANSON-WILLIAMS, J., DEITZ, S. M., & KELLER, F. S. (1981). PSI in the elementary school. *Journal of Personalized Instruction, 5.*

DELLA-PIANA, G. M. (1971). *The development of a model for the systematic writing of poetry.* Salt Lake City, Utah: Bureau of Educational Research, University of Utah.

DELQUADRI, J., GREENWOOD, C. R., WHORTON, D., CARTA, J. J., & HALL, R. V. (1986). Classwide Peer Tutoring. *Exceptional Children, 52*(6), 535–42.

DELQUADRI, J., WHORTON, D., ELLIOTT, M., & GREENWOOD, C. R. (1983). *Training school consultants as mediators for home and school tutoring: Outcomes and effects.* Kansas City, Kans.: Juniper Gardens Children's Project, Bureau of Child Research, University of Kansas.

DeMYER, M. K., HINGTEN, J. N., & JACKSON, K. (1981). Infantile autism reviewed: A decade of research. *Schizophrenia Bulletin, 7*, 388–451.

DeRISI, W. J., & BUTZ, G. (1975). *Writing behavioral contracts: A case simulation practice manual.* Champaign, Ill.: Research Press.

DINEEN, J. P., CLARK, H. B., & RISLEY, T. R. (1977). Peer tutoring among elementary students: Educational benefits to the tutor. *Journal of Applied Behavior Analysis, 10*, 231–38.

DOLEYS, D. M. (1977). Behaviour treatments for nocturnal enuresis in children: A review of the recent literature. *Psychological Bulletin, 84*, 30–54.

DOLEYS, D. M., WELLS, K. S., HOBBS, S. A., ROBERTS, M. W., & CARTELLI, L. M. (1976). The effects of social punishment on noncompliance: A comparison with timeout and positive practice. *Journal of Applied Behavior Analysis, 9*, 471–82.

DOUGLAS, V. I., PARRY, P., MARTON, P., & GARSON, C. (1976). Assessment of a cognitive training program for hyperactive children. *Journal of Abnormal Child Psychology, 4*, 389–410.

DRABMAN, R. S., SPITALNIK, R., & O'LEARY, K. D. (1973). Teaching self-control to disruptive children. *Journal of Abnormal Psychology, 82*, 10–16.

Education joint dissemination review panel, regular education. Precision Teaching Project, Great Falls, Mont.

ELAM, D., & SULZER-AZAROFF, B. (1972). Group versus individual reinforcement modifying problem behaviors in a trainable mentally handicapped classroom. Master's thesis, Southern Illinois University.

ENDO, G. T., & SLOANE, H. N. (1982). Generalization of a semantic-syntactic structure. *Behavior Modification, 6*, 349–406.

ENGELMANN, S. (1982). A study of 4th–6th grade basal reading series. *Direct Instruction News, 1*(3), 1, 4, 19.

FOSTER, S. L., & RITCHEY, W. L. (1979). Issues in the assessment of social competence in children. *Journal of Applied Behavior Analysis, 12*, 625–38.

ENGELMANN, S., & CARNINE, D. (1982). *Theory of instruction: Principles and application.* New York: Irvington Publishers.

EPSTEIN, L. H., DOKE, L. A., SAJAWAJ, T. E., SORRELL, S., & RIMMER, B. (1974). Generality and side effects of overcorrection. *Journal of Applied Behavior Analysis, 7*, 385.

ERKEN, N., & HENDERSON, H. (1976). *Practice skills mastery program.* Logan, Utah: Mastery Programs, Ltd.

EVANS, G. W., & OSWALT, G. L. (1968). Acceleration of academic progress through the manipulation of peer influence. *Behavior Research and Therapy, 6*, 189–95.

FARIS, J. P. (1983). Employee training: The state of the practice. *Training and Development Journal, 37*, 85–93.

FARNUM, M., & BRIGHAM, T. (1978). The use and evaluation of study guides with middle school students. *Journal of Applied Behavior Analysis, 11*, 137–44.

FATANE, B., & VARLEY, J. (1970). *The unresponsive bystander.* New York: Appleton-Century-Crofts.

FERSTER, C. B., & DeMYER, M. K. (1962). A method for the experimental analysis of the behavior of autistic children. *American Journal of Orthopsychiatry, 32*, 89–98.

2

2

FINK, W. T., & CARNINE, D. W. (1975). Control of arithmetic errors by informational feedback. *Journal of Applied Behavior Analysis*, 8, 461.

FIRESTONE, P. (1976). The effects and side effects of timeout on an aggressive nursery school child. *Journal of Behavior Therapy and Experimental Psychiatry*, 7, 79–81.

FIXSEN, D. L., PHILLIPS, E. L., & WOLF, M. (1973). Achievement place: Experiments in self-government with pre-delinquents. *Journal of Applied Behavior Analysis*, 6, 31–47.

FOSHAY, W. R. (1983). Alternative methods of task analysis. *Journal of Instructional Development*, 6, 2–9.

FOXX, R. M. (1977). Attention training: The use of overcorrection avoidance to increase the eye contact of autistic and retarded children. *Journal of Applied Behavior Analysis*, 10, 489–99.

FOXX, R. M., & AZRIN, N. H. (1972). Restitution: A method of eliminating aggressive-disruptive behaviors of retarded and brain damaged patients. *Behavior Research and Therapy*, 10, 15–27.

FOXX, R. M., & AZRIN, N. H. (1973). The elimination of autistic self-stimulatory behavior by overcorrection. *Journal of Applied Behavior Analysis*, 6, 1–14.

FOXX, R. M., & BECHTEL, D. R. (1983). Overcorrection: A review and analysis. In S. Axelrod & J. Apsche (eds.), *The effects of punishment on human behavior*. San Diego: Academic Press.

FREDERICK, W. C., & WALBERG, H. J. (1980). Learning as a function of time. *Journal of Educational Research*, 73, 183–194.

FRENCH, D. C., & TYNE, T. F. (1982). The identification and treatment of children with peer-relationship difficulties. In J. P. Curren & P. M. Monti (eds.), *Social skills training: A practical handbook for assessment and treatment*. New York: Guilford Press.

GAGNE, R. M. (1970). *The conditions of learning* (2d ed.). New York: Holt, Rinehart & Winston.

GAMBRILL, E. D. (1975). *Behavior modification: Handbook of assessment, intervention, and evaluation*. San Francisco: Jossey-Bass.

GARDNER, M. (1985). Cognitive psychological approaches to instructional task analysis. In E. W. Gordon (ed.), *Review of Research in Education*, pp. 157–195. Washington, D.C.: American Educational Research Association.

GEER, R. D. (1982). Countercontrols for the American Educational Research Association. *The Behavior Analyst*, 5, 65–76.

GELFAND, D. M. (1962). The influence of self-esteem on rate of verbal conditioning and social matching behavior. *Journal of Abnormal and Social Psychology*, 65, 259–265.

GELFAND, D. M., GELFAND, S., & DOBSON, W. R. (1967). Unprogrammed reinforcement of patient's behavior in a mental hospital. *Behavior Research and Therapy*, 5, 201–207.

GELFAND, D. M., & HARTMANN, D. P. (1984). *Child behavior analysis and therapy*. Elmsford, N.Y.: Pergamon Press.

GELFAND, D. M., JENSON, W. R., & DREW, C. J. (1981). *Understanding childhood behavior disorders*. New York: Holt, Rinehart & Winston.

GERSTEN, R., CARNINE, D., & WHITE, W. A. T. (1984). The pursuit of clarity: Direct Instruction and applied behavior analysis. In W. L. Heward, T. E. Heron, D. S. Hill, & J. Trap-Porter (eds), *Focus on behavior analysis in education*. Columbus, Ohio: Chas E. Merrill.

GIBBS, J. W., & LUYBEN, P. D. (1985). Treatment of self-injurious behavior: Contingent versus noncontingent positive practice overcorrection. *Behavior Modification*, 9, 3–21.

GILBERT, T. F. (1978). *Human Competence: Engineering Worthy Performance*. New York: McGraw-Hill.

GITTELMAN-KLEIN, R. (1980). The role of test for differential diagnosis in child psychiatry. *Journal of the American Academy of Child Psychiatry*, 19, 413–438.

GLOVER, J., & GRAY, A. L. (1976). Procedures to increase some aspect of creativity. *Journal of Applied Behavior Analysis*, 9, 79–84.

GLOVER, J. A., ZIMMER, J. W., FILBECK, R. W., & PLAKE, B. S. (1980). Effects of training students to identify the semantic base of prose materials. *Journal of Applied Behavior Analysis*, 13, 655–67.

GLYNN, E. L., THOMAS, J. D., & SHEE, S. M. (1973). Behavioral self-control of on-task behavior in an elementary classroom. *Journal of Applied Behavior Analysis*, 6, 105–13.

GOFFMAN, E. (1959). *The presentation of self in everyday life*. New York: Doubleday.

GOLDSTEIN, A. P. (1981). *Psychological skills training*. New York: Pergamon Press.

GOTTMAN, J. M., & McFALL, R. M. (1972). Self-monitoring effects in a program for potential high school dropouts: A time-series analysis. *Journal of Consulting and Clinical Psychology*, 39, 273–81.

GRAUBARD, P., & ROSENBERG, H. (1974). *Classrooms that work*. New York: Dutton.

GREENBERG, D. J., & MEAGHERS, R. B. (1977). The courts and the token economy: An empirical approach to the problem. *Behavior Therapy*, 8, 377–82.

GREENE, B. F., BAILEY, J. S., & BARBER, F. (1981). An analysis and reduction of disruptive behavior on school buses. *Journal of Applied Behavior Analysis*, 14, 177–92.

GREENWOOD, C. R., DELQUADRI, J. C., & HALL, R. V. (1984). Opportunity to respond and student academic performance. In W. L. Heward, T. E. Heron, D. S. Hill, & J. Trap-Porter (eds.), *Focus on behavior analysis in education.* Columbus, Ohio: Chas E. Merrill.

GREENWOOD, C. R., DINWIDDIE, G., TERRY, B., WADE, L., STANLEY, S., THIBADEAU, S., & DELQUADRI, J. C. (1984). Teacher- versus peer-mediated instruction: An ecobehavioral analysis of achievement outcomes. *Journal of Applied Behavior Analysis, 17,* 521–38.

GREENWOOD, C., HOPS, H., DELQUADRI, J., & GUILD, J. (1974). Group contingencies for group consequences in classroom management: A further analysis. *Journal of Applied Behavior Analysis, 7,* 413–25.

GREENWOOD, C. R., SLOANE, H. N., & BASKIN, A. (1974). Training elementary-aged peer-behavior managers to control small group programmed mathematics. *Journal of Applied Behavior Analysis, 7,* 103–14.

GREER, R. D. (1983). Contingencies of the science and technology of teaching and prebehavioristic research practices in education. *Educational Researcher, 12,* 3–14.

GRESHAM, F. M. (1981). Assessment of children's social skills. *Journal of School Psychology, 19,* 120–33.

GRESHAM, F. M., & GRESHAM, G. N. (1982). Interdependent, dependent, and independent group contingencies for controlling disruptive behavior. *Journal of Special Education, 16,* 101–10.

GRIFFITH, R. G. (1983). The administrative issues: An ethical and legal perspective. In S. Axelrod & J. Apsche (eds.), *The effects of punishment on human behavior.* New York: Academic Press.

GRONLUND, N. D. (1959). *Sociometry in the classroom.* New York: Harper & Brothers.

GRONLUND, N. E. (1971). *Measurement and evaluation in teaching* (2d ed.). New York: Macmillan.

GRONLUND, N. E. (1973). *Preparing criterion-referenced tests for classroom instruction.* New York: Macmillan.

GRONLUND, N. E. (1974). *Improving marking and reporting in classrooms.* New York: Macmillan.

GRONLUND, N. E., & ANDERSON, L. (1963). Personality characteristics of socially accepted, socially neglected, and socially rejected junior high school pupils. In J. M. Seidman (ed.), *Educating for mental health.* New York: Thomas Y. Crowell.

GUESS, D., SAILOR, W., RUTHERFORD, G., & BAER, D. M. (1968). An experimental analysis of linguistic development: The productive use of the plural morpheme. *Journal of Applied Behavior Analysis, 4,* 297–306.

GUSTAFSON, C., HOTTE, E., & CARSKY, M. (1976). *Everyday living skills.* Unpublished manuscript, Mansfield Training School, Mansfield Depot, Conn.

GUTHRIE, E. R. (1935). *The psychology of learning.* New York: Harper & Row, Pub.

HALL, R. V., DELQUADRI, J., GREENWOOD, C. R., & THURSTON, L. (1982). The importance of opportunity to respond in children's academic success. In E. B. Edgar, N. G. Haring, J. R. Jenkins, and C. G. Pions (eds.), *Mentally handicapped children: Education and training.* Baltimore: University Park Press.

HALL, R. V., FOX, R., WILLARD, D., GOLDSMITH, L., EMERSON, M., OWEN, M., DAVIS, F., & PORCIA, E. (1971). The teacher as observer and experimenter in the modification of disputing and talking out behavior. *Journal of Applied Behavior Analysis, 4,* 141–49.

HALL, R. V., LUND, D., & JACKSON, D. (1968). Effects of teacher attention on study behavior. *Journal of Applied Behavior Analysis, 1,* 12.

HALLMAN, R. S. (1974). Extinction of ruminations: A case study. *Behavior Therapy, 5,* 565–68.

HAMBLIN, R., HATHAWAY, C., & WODARSKI, J. (1971). Group contingencies, peer tutoring, and accelerating academic achievement. In E. A. Ramp and B. L. Hopkins (eds.), *A new direction for education.* Lawrence: University of Kansas Press.

HALLAM, R. S. (1974). Extinction of ruminations: A case study. *Behavior Therapy, 5,* 565–68.

HARING, N. G., LIBERTY, K. A., & WHITE, O. R. (1980). *Field-initiated research studies of phases of learning and facilitating instructional events for the severely and profoundly handicapped.* (Available from the U.S. Office of Special Education, Project No. 443 CH 60397A, Grant No. G007500593.)

HARRIS, F. R., WOLF, M. M., & BAER, D. M. (1964). Effects of adult social reinforcement on child behavior. *Young Children, 10,* 8–17.

HARRIS, V. M., & SHERMAN, J. A. (1973). Effects of peer tutoring and consequences on the math performance of elementary classroom students. *Journal of Applied Behavior Analysis, 6,* 587–97.

HARRIS, V. M., & SHERMAN, J. A. (1973). Use and analysis of the "Good Behavior Game" to reduce disruptive classroom behavior. *Journal of Applied Behavior Analysis, 6,* 405–17.

HARRIS, V. M., SHERMAN, J. A., HENDERSEN, D. G., & HARRIS, M. S. (1972). Effects of peer tutoring on the spelling performance of elementary students. In G. Semb (ed.), *Behavior analysis and education.* Lawrence: The University of Kansas Support and Development Center for Follow Through.

HART, B. M., REYNOLDS, N. J., BAER, D. M., BRWAWLEY, E. R., & HARRIS, F. R. (1968). Effect of contingent and non-contingent social attention on the cooperative play of a pre-school child. *Journal of Applied Behavior Analysis, 1,* 73–76.

HARTMANN, D. P. (1977). Considerations in the choice of interobserver reliability measures. *Journal of Applied Behavior Analysis, 10,* 103–16.

HARTMANN, D. P., ROPER, B. L., & BRADFORD, D. C. (1979). Some relationships between behavioral and traditional assessment. *Journal of Behavioral Assessment, 1*, 3–21.

HASSELBRING, T., & HAMLETT, C. (1983). *Aimstar: A computer software program.* Portland, Oreg.: ASIEP Education Co.

HAWKINS, R. P. (1982). Developing a behavior code. In D. P. Hartmann (ed.), *Using observers to study behaviors: New directions for methodology of social and behavioral science.* San Francisco: Jossey-Bass.

HAYNES, S. N. (1978). *Principles of behavioral assessment.* New York: Gardner Press.

HENDERSEN, H. S., ERKEN, N. F., & JENSON, W. R. (1986). Variable interval reinforcement as a practical means of increasing and maintaining on-task behavior in classrooms. *Techniques.*

HENDERSEN, H. S., JENSON, W. R., & BINGELL, N. (1982). Management of the behavior of emotionally disturbed children through peer social reinforcement. Unpublished manuscript.

HERBERT, E. W. (1973). *Computation guide for interobserver reliabilities.* Salt Lake City: Bureau of Educational Research, University of Utah.

HERSEN, M., & EISLER, R. M. (1976). Social skills training. In W. E. Craighead, A. E. Kazdin, & M. J. Mahoney (Eds.), *Behavior modification: Principles, issues, and applications.* Boston: Houghton Mifflin.

HERSEN, M., & BARLOW, D. H. (1976). *Single-case experimental designs: Strategies for studying behavior change.* Elmsford, N.Y.: Pergamon Press.

HINELINE, P. N. (1984). Can a statement in cognitive terms be a behavior-analytic interpretation? *The Behavior Analyst, 7,* 97–100.

HOBBS, T. R., & HOLT, M. M. (1976). The effects of token reinforcement on the behavior of delinquents in cottage settings. *Journal of Applied Behavior Analysis, 9,* 189–98.

HOFFMAN, C. K., & MEDSKER, K. L. (1983). Instructional analysis: The missing link between task analysis and objectives. *Journal of Instructional Development, 6,* 17–23.

HOMME, L. E., CSANYI, A. P., GONZALES, M. A., & RECHS, J. R. (1970). *How to use contingency contracting in the classroom.* Champaign, Ill.: Research Press.

HOPKINS, B. L., & HERMANN, J. A. (1977). Evaluating interobserver reliability of interval data. *Journal of Applied Behavior Analysis, 10,* 121–26.

HOPKINS, B. L., SCHUTTE, R. C., & GARTON, K. L. (1971). The effects of access to a playroom on the rate and quality of printing and writing of first and second grade students. *Journal of Applied Behavior Analysis, 4,* 77–87.

HORNE, B. A. (1977). Behavioral treatment of trichotillomania. *Behaviour Research and Therapy, 10,* 125–29.

HORNER, R. D., & KEILITZ, I. (1975). Training mentally retarded adolescents to brush their teeth. *Journal of Applied Behavior Analysis, 8,* 301–309.

HULL, C. L. (1948). *Principles of behavior.* New York: Appleton-Century-Crofts.

HULL, C. L. (1951). *Essentials of behavior.* New Haven, Conn.: Yale University Press.

HULL, C. L. (1952). *A behavior system.* New Haven, Conn.: Yale University Press.

HUNDERT, J., & BUCHER, B. (1978). Pupils' self-scored arithmetic performance: A practical procedure for maintaining accuracy. *Journal of Applied Behavior Analysis, 11,* 304.

HYMEL, S., & ASCHER, S. R. (1977). *Assessment and training of isolated children's social skills.* Paper presented at the biennial meeting of the Society for Research in Child Development, New Orleans (ERIC Documentation Reproduction Service, No. ED 136-930).

JACKSON, D. A., DELLA-PIANA, G. M., & SLOANE, H. N. (1975). *How to Establish a Behavior Observation System.* Englewood Cliffs, N.J.: Educational Technology Publications.

JENKINS, J. R., MAYHALL, W. F., PESCHKA, C. M., & JENKINS, L. M. (1974). Comparing small group and tutorial instruction in resource rooms. *Exceptional Children, 40,* 245–50.

JENNE, T., YOUNG, K. R., WEST, R. P., & MORGAN, D. P. (May 1986). *Teaching social skills and self-management strategies to behaviorally disordered adolescents: Skill acquisition and generalization.* Paper presented at Association for Behavior Analysis, Twelfth Annual Convention, Milwaukee, Wis.

JENSON, W. R., NEVILLE, M. H., SLOANE, H. N., & MORGAN, D. (1982). Spinners and chart moves. *Child and Family Behavior Therapy, 4,* 81–85.

JENSON, W. R., PAOLETTI, P. & PETERSEN, P. B. (1984). Self-monitoring plus a contingency to reduce a chronic throat-clearing tic in a child. *The Behavior Therapist, 7,* 192.

JENSON, W. R., & SLOANE, H. N. (1979). Chart moves and grab bags: A simple contingency management system. *Journal of Applied Behavior Analysis, 12,* 334.

JOHNSON, M., & BAILEY, J. S. (1974). Cross-age tutoring: Fifth graders as arithmetic tutors for kindergarten. *Journal of Applied Behavior Analysis, 7,* 223–32.

JONES, F. H., & MILLER, W. H. (1974). The effective use of negative attention for reducing group disruption in special elementary school classrooms. *The Psychological Record, 24,* 435–48.

KALFUS, G. R. (1984). Peer-mediated intervention: A critical review. *Child and Family Behavior Therapy, 6,* 17–43.

KAZDIN, A. E. (1977). Artifact, bias, and complexity of assessment: The ABCs of reliability. *Journal of Applied Behavior Analysis, 10*, 141–50.

KAZDIN, A. E. (1977). *The token economy: A review and evaluation.* New York: Plenum.

KAZDIN, A. E. (1982). The token economy: A decade later. *Journal of Applied Behavior Analysis, 15*, 431–45.

KAZDIN, A. E. (1984). *Behavior modification in applied settings.* Homewood, Ill.: Dorsey Press.

KAZDIN, A. E., & BOOTZIN, R. R. (1972). The token economy: An evaluative review. *Journal of Applied Behavior Analysis, 5*, 343–72.

KAZDIN, A. E., & KLACK, J. (1973). The effect of nonverbal teacher approval on student attentive behavior. *Journal of Applied Behavior Analysis, 6*, 643–54.

KAZDIN, A. E., & MASCITELLI, S. (1980). The opportunity to earn oneself off a token system as a reinforcer for attentive behavior. *Behavior Therapy, 11*, 68–78.

KELEMAN, L. S., WEST, M. E., & YOUNG, K. R. (1975). Social reinforcement manual. In K. R. Young & L. S. Keleman, *Classroom management systems.* Salt Lake City: BEI.

KELLER, F. S. (1968). Good-bye, teacher . . . . " *Journal of Applied Behavior Analysis, 1*, 79–89.

KELLY, J. A. (1982). *Social skills training: A practical guide for interventions.* New York: Springer, 1982.

KENNEDY, P., ESQUE, T., & NOVAK, J. (1983). A functional analysis of task analysis procedures for instructional design. *Journal of Instructional Development, 6*, 10–16.

KIRIGIN, K., PHILLIPS, E. L., FIXSEN, D., & WOLF, M. (1972). *Modifications of the homework behavior and academic performance of pre-delinquents with home-based reinforcement.* Presented at the meetings of the American Psychological Association, Honolulu.

KLISHIS, M. J., HURSH, D. E., & KLISHIS, L. A. (1980). Individualized spelling: An application and evaluation of PSI in the elementary school. *Journal of Personalized Instruction, 4*, 3.

KRATHWOHL, D. R., BLOOM, B. S., & MASIA, B. P. (1964). Taxonomy of objectives. *Handbook 2: Affective domain.* New York: D. McKay.

KRATOCHWILL, T. R., & WETZEL, R. J. (1977). Observer agreement, credibility, and judgement: Some considerations in presenting observer agreement data. *Journal of Applied Behavior Analysis, 10*, 133–39.

KRUG, D. A., ARICK, J. R., & ALMOND, P. J. (1980). *Autism screening instrument for educational planning.* Portland, Oreg.: ASIEP Publishers.

KUNZELMAN, H. P., COHEN, M. A., HULTON, W. J., MARTIN, C. L., & MINGO, A. R. (1970). *Precision teaching.* Seattle, Wash.: Special Child Publications.

KUYPER, D. S., BECKER, W. C., & O'LEARY, K. D. (1968). How to make a token system fail. *Exceptional Children, 35*, 101–109.

LADD, G. W., & ASHER, S. R. (1985). Social skill training and children's peer relations. In L. L'Abate & M. A. Milan (eds.), *Handbook of social skills training and research.* New York: John Wiley.

LAHEY, B. B., MCNEES, M. P., & MCNEES, M. C. (1973). Control of an obscene "verbal tic" through timeout in an elementary school classroom. *Journal of Applied Behavior Analysis, 6*, 101–104.

LANCIONI, G. E. (1982). Normal children as tutors to teach social responses to mentally withdrawn schoolmates: Training, maintenance, and generalization. *Journal of Applied Behavior Analysis, 15*, 17–40.

LANG, P. J., & MALAMED, B. G. (1969). Case report: Avoidance conditioning therapy of an infant with chronic ruminative vomiting. *Journal of Abnormal Psychology, 74*, 1–8.

LeBLANC, J. M., BUSBY, K. H., & THOMSON, C. L. (1974). The functions of time-out for changing the aggressive behaviors of a preschool child: A multiple-baseline analysis. In R. Ulrich, T. Stachnik, and J. Mabry, *Control of human behavior,* Vol. 3 Glenview, Ill.: Scott, Foresman.

LIBERTY, K. A. (1972). *Decide for progress: Dynamic aims and data decisions.* Working paper, Regional Resource Center for Handicapped Children, University of Oregon, Eugene.

LIBERTY, K. A., HARING, N. G., & WHITE, O. R. (1980). Rules for data-based strategy decisions in instructional programs: Current research and instructional implications. In W. Sailor, B. Wilcox, & L. Brown (eds.), *Methods of instruction for severely handicapped students.* Baltimore, Md.: Paul H. Brookes.

LIDZ, C. S. (1981). *Improving assessment of school children.* San Francisco: Jossey-Bass.

LIKINS, M., MORGAN, D. P., & YOUNG, K. R. (1984). *Being positive and making friends.* Logan, Utah: Department of Special Education, Utah State University.

LITOW, L., & PUMROY, V. (1975). A brief review of classroom group-oriented contingencies. *Journal of Applied Behavior Analysis, 8*, 341–47.

LOVAAS, O. I., & SIMMONS, J. Q. (1969). Manipulation of self-destruction in three retarded children. *Journal of Applied Behavior Analysis, 2*, 143–57.

LOVITT, T. C. (1969). *Self-management projects with children.* Unpublished manuscript, University of Washington.

LOVITT, T. C. (1973). Self-management projects with children with behavioral disabilities. *Journal of Learning Disabilities, 6*, 15–28.

LOVITT, T. C., & CURTISS, K. (1969). Academic response rate as a function of teacher and self-imposed contingencies. *Journal of Applied Behavior Analysis, 2,* 49–53.

LUDWIG, P. J., & MAEHR, M. L. (1967). Changes in self-concepts in stated behavioral preferences. *Child Development, 38,* 453–69.

MADSEN, C. H., BECKER, W. C., & THOMAS, D. R. (1968). Rules, praise, and ignoring elements of elementary classroom control. *Journal of Applied Behavior Analysis, 1,* 139–50.

MADSEN, C. H., BECKER, W. C., THOMAS, D. R., KOSER, L., & PLAGER, E. (1968). An analysis of the reinforcing function of "sit down" commands. In R. K. Parker (ed.), *Readings in educational psychology.* Boston: Allyn & Bacon.

MADSEN, C. H., MADSEN, C. K., SAUDARGUS, R. A., HAMMOND, W. R., & EDGAR, D. E. (1970). *Classroom RAID (Rules, Approval, Ignore, Disapproval): A cooperative approach for professionals and volunteers.* Unpublished manuscript, University of Florida.

MAGER, R. F. (1962). *Preparing instructional objectives.* Palo Alto, Calif.: Fearon Publishers.

MAGER, R. F., & PIPE, P. (1965). *Analyzing performance problems.* Belmont, Calif.: Fearon Publishers.

MAIN, G. C., & MUNRO, B. C. (1977). A token reinforcement program in a public junior-high school. *Journal of Applied Behavior Analysis, 10,* 93–94.

MALYN, D., & JENSON, W. R. (1986). *The use of chartmoves and spinners to improve homework compliance.* Paper presented at the Association for Behavior Analysis, Milwaukee, Wis.

MANIS, J. G., & MELTZER, B. N. (1972). *Symbolic interaction.* Boston: Allyn & Bacon, 1972.

MARHOLIN, D., II, & STEINMAN, W. M. (1977). Stimulus control in the classroom as a function of the behavior reinforced. *Journal of Applied Behavior Analysis, 10,* 465–78.

MARTIN, G., & PEAR, J. (1983). *Behavior modification: What it is and how to do it.* Englewood Cliffs, N.J.: Prentice-Hall.

MARTIN, P. L. (1978, March). *Behavior change techniques: Overcorrection and other treatments.* Paper presented at the meeting of the California Behavior Analysis Conference II, Stockton, Calif.

MARTIN, R. (1975). *Legal challenges to behavior modification.* Champaign, Ill.: Research Press.

MARTIN, R. (1977). *Workshop materials: Educational rights of handicapped children.* Champaign, Ill.: Research Press.

MAYER, G. R., ROHEN, T. H., & WHITLEY, A. D. (1969). Group counseling with children: A cognitive behavioral approach. *Journal of Counseling Psychology, 16,* 142–49.

MCCONNELL, S. R., STRAIN, P. S., KERR, M. M., STAGG, V., LENKNER, D. A., & LAMBERT, D. L. (1984). An empirical definition of school adjustment. *Behavior Modification, 8,* 451–73.

MCDANIELS, G. L. (1975). The evaluation of follow-through. *Educational Researcher, 4,* 7–11.

MCREYNOLDS, V. (1969). Application of timeout from positive reinforcement for increasing the efficiency of speech training. *Journal of Applied Behavior Analysis, 2,* 199–205.

MECHNER, F. (1976). Writing terminal objectives for curricula: Science, education, and behavioral technology. In J. G. Holland, C. Solomon, J. Doran, & D. E. Frezza (eds.), *The analysis of behavior in planning instruction.* Reading, Mass.: Addison-Wesley.

MEDLAND, M. B., & STACHNICK, T. J. (1972). The good behavior game: A replication and systematic analysis. *Journal of Applied Behavior Analysis, 5,* 45–51.

MEICHENBAUM, D. H., & GOODMAN, J. (1971). Training impulsive children to talk to themselves: A means of developing self-control. *Journal of Abnormal Psychology, 77,* 115–26.

MILLENSON, J. R. (1967). *Principles of behavioral analysis.* New York: Macmillan.

MILLENSON, J. R., & LESLIE, J. C. (1979). *Principles of behavioral analysis.* New York: Macmillan.

MILLER, L. K., & FEALLOCK, R. A. (1975). A behavior system for group living. In E. Ramp and G. Semb (eds.), *Behavior analysis: Areas of research and application.* Englewood Cliffs, N.J.: Prentice-Hall.

MINUCHIN, S., CHAMBERLIN, P., & GRAUBARD, P. (1967). A project to teach learning skills to disturbed children. *American Journal of Orthopsychiatry, 37,* 558–67.

MOFFAT, J. M. (1972). *Contingency contracting with money for college students predicted to fail.* Master's thesis. University of Utah.

MOFFAT, S. W. (1972). *Contingency contracting with study behavior using activity reinforcers.* Master's thesis, University of Utah.

MORENO, J. L. (1934). *Who shall survive? A new approach to the problem of human interrelations.* Washington, D.C.: Nervous and Mental Disease Publishing Co.

MORGAN, D. P., & YOUNG, K. R. (1984). *Teaching social skills: Assessment procedures, instructional methods, and behavior management techniques.* Logan: Utah State University.

MOSTOFSKY, D. I., & BALASCHAK, B. A. (1977). Psychobiological control of seizures. *Psychological Bulletin, 84,* 723–50.

MYERS, E. B., & JENSON, W. R. (1985). *An introduction to legal issues in the use of behavior management in the schools.* Paper presented at the Council for Exceptional Children, Anaheim, Calif.

National Commission on Excellence in Education (1983, April). *A nation at risk: The imperatives for educational reform.* Washington, D.C.: U.S. Department of Education.

NEISWORTH, J. T., & MOORE, F. (1972). Operant treatment of asthmatic responding with the parents as therapist. *Behavior Therapy, 3,* 257–62.

NELSON, R. O. (1977). Methodological issues in assessment via self-monitoring. In J. D. Cone & R. P. Hawkins (eds.), *Behavioral assessment: New directions in clinical psychology.* New York: Brunner/Mazel.

NEWSOM, C., FAVELL, J. E., & RINCOVER, A. (1983). In S. Axelrod & J. Apsche (eds.), *The effects of punishment on human behavior.* New York: Academic Press.

NORDQUIST, V. M. (1971). The modification of a child's enuresis: Some response–response relationships. *Journal of Applied Behavior Analysis, 4,* 241–47.

NUNNALLY, J. (1978). *Psychometric theory.* New York: McGraw-Hill.

O'LEARY, K. D. (1972). Behavior modification in the classroom: A rejoinder to Winett and Winkler. *Journal of Applied Behavior Analysis, 5,* 505–11.

O'LEARY, K. D. (1978). The operant and social psychology of token systems. In A. C. Catantia and T. A. Brigham (eds.), *Handbook of applied behavior analysis.* New York: Irvington Publishers.

O'LEARY, K. D., & BECKER, W. C. (1967). Behavior modification of an adjustment class: A token reinforcement program. *Exceptional Children, 33,* 637–42.

O'LEARY, K. D., & BECKER, W. C., EVANS, M. B., & SAUDERGRAS, R. A. (1969). A token reinforcement system in a public school: A replication and systematic analysis. *Journal of Applied Behavior Analysis, 2,* 3–13.

O'LEARY, K. D., & DRABMAN, R. (1971). *Token reinforcement programs in the classroom: A review. Psychological Bulletin, 75,* 379–98.

O'LEARY, K. D., KAUFMAN, K. F., KASS, R. E., & DRABMAN, R. S. (1970). The effects of loud and soft reprimands on the behavior of disruptive students. *Exceptional Children, 37,* 145–55.

O'LEARY, K. D., POULOS, R. W., & DEVINE, V. T. (1972). Tangible reinforcers: Bonuses or bribes? *Journal of Clinical and Consulting Psychology, 38,* 1–8.

O'LEARY, K. D., ROMANCZYK, R. G., KASS, R. E., DIETZ, A., & SANTAGROSSI, D. (1971). Procedures for classroom observation of teachers and children. Unpublished document, University of New York at Stony Brook.

O'LEARY, S. G., & DUBEY, D. R. (1979). Applications of self-control procedures by children: A review. *Journal of Applied Behavior Analysis, 12,* 449–65.

OLIVER, S. D., WEST, R. C., & SLOANE, H. N. (1974). Some effects on human behavior of aversive events. *Behavior Therapy, 5,* 481–93.

PACKARD, R. G. (1975). *Psychology of learning and instruction: A performance-based course.* Columbus, Ohio.: Chas E. Merrill.

PAINE, S. C., RADICCHI, J., ROSELLINI, L. C., DEUTCHMAN, L., & DARCH, C. B. (1983). *Structuring your classroom for academic success.* Champaign, Ill.: Research Press.

PARSONS, L. R., & HEWARD, W. L. (1979). Training peers to tutor: Evaluation of a tutor training package for primary learning-disabled students. *Journal of Applied Behavior Analysis, 12,* 309–10.

PATTERSON, G. R. (1965). An application of conditioning techniques to the control of a hyperactive child. In L. P. Ullman and L. Krasner (eds.), *Case studies in behavior modification.* New York: Holt, Rinehart & Winston.

PATTERSON, G. R. (1971). Behavioral intervention procedures in the classroom and in the home. In A. E. Bergin & S. L. Garfield (eds.), *Handbook of psychotherapy and behavior change: An empirical analysis.* New York: John Wiley.

PATTERSON, G. R. (1982). *Coercive family process.* Eugene, Or.: Castalia Publishing Co.

PATTERSON, G. R., SHAW, D. A., & EBNER, M. J. (1969). Teachers, peers, and parents as agents of change in the classroom. In F.A.M. Benson (ed.), *Modifying deviant social behavior in various classroom settings.* Monograph No. 1. Eugene: Department of Special Education, College of Education, University of Oregon Press.

PAVLOV, I. P. (1927). *Conditioned reflexes.* New York: Dover Publications.

PAZULINEC, R., MEYEROSE, M. & SAJWAJ, T. (1983). Punishment via response cost. In S. Axelrod & J. Apsche (eds.), *The effects of punishment on human behavior.* New York: Academic Press.

PETERS, R., & DAVIES, K. (1981). Effects of self-instructional training on cognitive impulsivity of mentally retarded adolescents. *American Journal of Mental Deficiency, 85,* 377–82.

PHILLIPS, E. L. (1968). Achievement place: Token reinforcement procedures in a home-style rehabilitation setting for "pre-delinquent" boys. *Journal of Applied Behavior Analysis, 1,* 213–23.

PHILLIPS, E. L., PHILLIPS, E. A., WOLF, M. M., & FIXSEN, D. L. (1971). Achievement place: Modification of the behaviors of pre-delinquent boys within a token economy. *Journal of Applied Behavior Analysis, 4,* 45–59.

PHILLIPS, E. L., PHILLIPS, E. A., WOLF, M. M., & FIXSEN, D. L. (1973). Achievement place: Development of the elected manager system. *Journal of Applied Behavior Analysis, 6,* 541–61.

PORTERFIELD, J. K., HERBERT-JACKSON, E., & RISLEY, T. R. (1976). Contingency observation: An effective and acceptable procedure for reducing disruptive behavior of young children in a group setting. *Journal of Applied Behavior Analysis, 9,* 55–64.

PREMACK, D. (1959). Toward empirical behavior laws: I: Positive reinforcement. *Psychological Review, 66,* 219–33.

PURKEY, S. C., & SMITH, M. S. (1983). Effective schools: A review. *Elementary School Journal, 83,* 427–52.

QUAY, H. C., & PETERSON, D. R. (1975). *Manual for the problem behavior checklist.* Unpublished paper.

RAMP, E. A., & HOPKINS, B. L. (eds.) (1971). *A new direction for education: Behavior analysis, 1,* Lawrence, KS: Department of Human Development, The University of Kansas.

REID, E. R. (1986). Practicing effective instruction: The Exemplary Center for Reading Instruction approach. *Exceptional Children, 52*(6), 510–19.

REID, E. R. (1983). *Teaching scheduling and record keeping.* Salt Lake City, Utah: Cove Publishers.

REID, J. B. (1978). *A social learning approach to family intervention: 2: Observation in home settings.* Eugene, Oreg.: Castalia Publications.

REID, H. P., ARCHER, M. B., FRIEDMAN, R. M. (1977). Using the personalized system of instruction with low-reading-ability middle school students: Problems and results. *Journal of Personalized Instruction, 2,* 4.

REIGELUTH, C. M. (1983). Current trends in task analysis. *Journal of Instructional Development, 6,* 24–30.

REPP, A. C., DEITZ, D. E., BOLES, S. M., DEITZ, S. M., & REPP, C. F. (1976). Differences among common methods for calculating interobserver agreement. *Journal of Applied Behavior Analysis, 9,* 109–13.

REPP, A. C., ROBERTS, D. M., SLACK, D. J., REPP, C. F., & BERKLER, M. S. (1976). A comparison of frequency, interval, and time-sampling methods of data collection. *Journal of Applied Behavior Analysis, 13,* 501–508.

RESNICK, L. B., WANG, M. C., & KAPLAN, J. (1973). Task analysis in curriculum design. A hierarchically sequenced introductory mathematics curriculum. *Journal of Applied Behavior Analysis, 6,* 679–709.

RHODE, G., MORGAN, D. P., & YOUNG, K. R. (1983). Generalization and maintenance of treatment gains of behaviorally handicapped students from resource rooms to regular classrooms using self-evaluation procedures. *Journal of Applied Behavior Analysis, 16,* 171–88.

RICHARDS, C. S. (1975). Behavior modification of studying through study skills advisement and self-control procedures. *Journal of Counseling Psychology, 22,* 431–36.

RINN, R. C., & MARKLE, A. (1979). Modification of social skills deficits in children. In A. S. Bellack, & M. Hersen (eds.), *Research and practice in social skills training.* New York: Plenum.

RISELY, T. R., & CATALDO, M. F. (1973). *Planned activity check: Materials for training observers.* Lawrence: Center for Applied Behavior Analysis, University of Kansas.

RISELY, T., & WOLF, M. (1967). Establishing functional speech in echolalic children. *Behavior Research and Therapy, 5,* 73–88.

RIST, R. C. (1970). Student social class and teacher expectations: The self-fulfilling prophecy in ghetto education. *Harvard Educational Review, 40,* 411–51.

ROBERTSON, S. J., SIMON, S. J., PACHMAN, J. S., & DRABMAN, R. D. (1979). Self-control and generalization procedures in a classroom of disruptive retarded children. *Child Behavior Therapy, 4,* 347–62.

ROBIN, A. L., ARMEL, S., & O'LEARY, K. D. (1985). The effects of self-instruction on writing deficiencies. *Behavior Therapy, 6,* 178–87.

ROBINS, L. N. (1966). *Deviant children grow up: A sociological and psychiatric study of sociopathic personality.* Baltimore: Williams & Wilkins.

ROFF, M., SELLS, S. B., & GOLDEN, M. M. (1972). *Social adjustment and personality development in children.* Minneapolis: The University of Minnesota Press.

ROISTACHER, R. C. (1974). A microeconomic model of sociometric choice. *Sociometry, 37,* 219–38.

ROLLINGS, J. P., BAUMEISTER, A., & BAUMEISTER, A. (1977). The use of overcorrection procedures to eliminate the stereotyped behaviors of retarded individuals. *Behavior Modification, 1,* 29–46.

ROSEN, H. S., & ROSEN, L. A. (1983). Eliminating stealing: Use of stimulus control with an elementary student. *Behavior Modification, 7,* 56–63.

ROSENBAUM, M. S., & DRABMAN, R. S. (1979). Self-control training in the classroom: A review and critique. *Journal of Applied Behavior Analysis, 12,* 467–85.

ROSENSHINE, B. V. (1976). Classroom instruction. In N. G. Gage (ed.), *The psychology of teaching methods:*

The 77th yearbook of the National Society for the Study of Education. Chicago: University of Chicago Press.

ROSENSHINE, B. V. (1979). Content, time, and direct instruction. In P. Peterson and H. Walberg (eds.), *Research on teaching: Concepts, findings, and implications.* Berkeley, Calif.: McCuteham.

ROSENSHINE, B. V., & BERLINER, D. C. (1978). Academic engaged time. *British Journal of Teacher Education, 4,* 3–16.

ROSS, D. M., & ROSS, S. A. (1982). *Hyperactivity: Current issues, research, and theory.* New York: John Wiley.

RUBIN, S. E., & SPADY, W. G. (1984). Achieving excellence through outcome-based instructional delivery. *Educational Leadership,* May, 37–44.

RUSCH, F., CLOSE, D., HOPS, H., & AGOSTA, J. (1976). Overcorrection: Generalization and maintenance. *Journal of Applied Behavior Analysis, 9,* 498.

RUTTER, M., MAUGHAN, B., MORTIMORE, P., OUSTON, J. (1979). *Fifteen thousand hours: Secondary schools and their effects on children.* Cambridge: Harvard University Press.

SAGE, J. E., & ROSE, V. A. (1985). Analyzing work behaviors. In H. Birnbrauer (ed.), *The ASTD Handbook for Technical and Skills Training* (pp. 33–46). Alexandria Va.: American Society for Training and Development.

SAMUELS, S. J. (1976). Automatic decoding and reading comprehension. *Language Arts, 53,* 323–25.

SCHAEFER, H. H., & MARTIN, P. L. (1966). Behavioral therapy for "apathy" of hospitalized schizophrenics. *Psychological Reports, 19,* 1147–58.

SCHMIDT, G. W., & ULRICH, R. E. (1969). Effects of group contingent events upon classroom noise. *Journal of Applied Behavior Analysis, 2,* 171–79.

SCHWITZGEBEL, R. L., & SCHWITZGEBEL, R. K. (1980). *Law and psychological practice.* New York: John Wiley.

SHAPIRO, E. S. (1979). Restitution and positive practice overcorrection in reducing aggressive-disruptive behavior: A long term follow up. *Journal of Behavior Therapy and Experimental Psychiatry, 10,* 131–34.

SHAPIRO, E. S., ALBRIGHT, T. S., & AGER, C. L. (1986). Group versus individual contingencies in modifying two disruptive adolescents' behavior. *Professional School Psychology, 1,* 105–16.

SHAPIRO, E. S., BARRETT, R. P., & OLLENDICK, T. H. (1980). A comparison of physical restraint and positive practice overcorrection in treating stereotypic behavior. *Behavior Therapy, 11,* 227–33.

SHERMAN, J. G. (1982). Logistics. In F. S. Keller & J. G. Sherman (eds.), *The PSI handbook: Essays on personalized instruction.* Lawrence, Kans.: TRI Publications.

SHERRINGTON, C. S. (1906). *The integrative action of the nervous system.* New Haven: Yale University Press.

SIDMAN, M., KIRK, B., & WILLSON-MORRIS, M. (1985). Six-member stimulus classes generated by conditional-discrimination procedures. *Journal of the Experimental Analysis of Behavior, 43,* 21–42.

SIDMAN, M., & TAILBY, W. (1982). Conditional discrimination vs. matching to sample: An expansion of the testing paradigm. *Journal of the Experimental Analysis of Behavior, 37,* 5–22.

SIEGEL, G. M., LENSKE, J., & BROEN, P. (1969). Suppression of normal speech disfluencies through response cost. *Journal of Applied Behavior Analysis, 2,* 265–76.

SINGLETON, L. C., & ASHER, S. R. (1977). Peer preferences and social interaction among third-grade children in an integrated school district. *Journal of Educational Psychology, 69,* 330–36.

SKINNER, B. F. (1938). *The behavior of organisms.* New York: Appleton-Century-Crofts.

SKINNER, B. F. (1948). *Walden two.* New York: Macmillan.

SKINNER, B. F. (1953). *Science and human behavior.* New York: Macmillan.

SKINNER, B. F. (1954). The science of learning and the art of teaching. *Harvard Educational Review, 24,* 86–97.

SKINNER, B. F. (1984). The shame of American education. *American Psychologist, 39,* 947–54.

SLOANE, H. N. (1976). *Classroom management: Remediation and prevention.* New York: John Wiley.

SLOANE, H. N., & JACKSON, D. A. (1974). *A guide to motivating learners.* Englewood Cliffs, N.J.: Educational Technology Publications.

SLOANE, H. N., YOUNG, K. R., & MARCUSEN, T. (1977). Response cost and human aggressive behavior. In B. C. Etzel, J. M. LeBlanc, & D. M. Baer (eds.), *New developments in behavioral research, theory, method and application, in honor of Sidney W. Bijou.* Hillsdale, N.J.: Erlbaum.

SLOGGETT, B. B. (1971). Use of group activities and team rewards to increase classroom productivity. *Teaching Exceptional Children, 3,* 54–66.

SMITH, D. D., & LOVITT, T. C. (1982). *CAP: The computational arithmetic program.* Austin: Pro-Ed.

SMITH, D., YOUNG, K. R., KURESA, S., MORGAN, D. P., & WEST, R. P. (1986). *Teaching self-management skills to high school students.* Paper presented at the Ninth Annual Intervention Procedures for Exceptional Children conference, Logan, Utah.

Smith, S., & Guthrie, E. R. (1921). *General psychology in terms of behavior.* New York: Appleton-Century-Crofts.

Solnick, J. V., Rincover, A., & Peterson, C. R. (1977). Some determinants of the reinforcing and punishing effects of timeout. *Journal of Applied Behavior Analysis, 10,* 415–424.

Solomon, C. (1976). Preparing behavioral objectives. In J. G. Holland, C. Solomon, J. Doran, & D. E. Frezza (eds.), *The analysis of behavior in planning instruction.* Reading, Mass: Addison-Wesley.

Solomon, R. W., & Wahler, R. G. (1973). Peer reinforcement control of classroom problem behaviors. *Journal of Applied Behavior Analysis, 6,* 49–56.

Speer, O. B., & Lamb, G. S. (1976). First grade reading ability and fluency in naming verbal symbols. *Reading Teacher, 29,* 572–76.

Spradlin, J. E., & Girardeau, F. L. (1966). The behavior modification of severely retarded persons. In N. R. Ellis (ed.), *International review of research in mental retardation, 1,* New York: Academic Press.

Staats, A. W. (1973). Behavior analysis and token reinforcement in educational and curriculum research. In *Behavior modification in education: The 72d yearbook of the National Society for the Study of Education.* Chicago: University of Chicago Press.

Staats, A. W., Minke, K. A., Finley, J. R., Wolf, M., & Brooks, L. O. (1964). A reinforcer system and experimental procedure for the laboratory study of reading acquisition. *Child Development, 35,* 209–31.

Stallings, J. (1977). How instructional processes relate to child outcomes. In G. D. Borich (ed.), *The appraisal of teaching: Concepts and process* (pp. 104–113). Reading, Mass.: Addison-Wesley.

Stallings, J. A., & Stipek, D. (1986). Research on early childhood and elementary school teaching programs. In M. C. Wittrock (ed.), *Handbook of research on teaching programs.* New York: Macmillan.

Stebbins, L. B., St. Pierre, R. G., Proper, E. D., Anderson, R. B., & Cerva, R. T. (1977). *Education as experimentation: A planned variation model.* Washington, D.C.: U.S. Office of Education.

Stengel, E. (1971). *Suicide and attempted suicide.* Middlesex, England: Penguin.

Sulzer, B., Hunt, S., Ashby, E., Koniarski, C., & Krams, M. (1971). Increasing rate and percentage correct in reading and spelling in a fifth-grade public school class of slow readers by means of a token economy. In E. Ramp and B. L. Hopkins (eds.), *A new direction for education: Behavior analysis.* Lawrence: University of Kansas Press.

Sulzer-Azaroff, B., & Mayer, R. G. (1986). *Achieving educational excellence: Using behavioral strategies.* New York: Holt, Rinehart & Winston.

Sulzer-Azaroff, B., & Mayer, G. R. (1977). *Applying behavior-analysis procedures with children and youth.* New York: Holt, Rinehart & Winston.

Taylor, L., & Sulzer, B. (1971). *The effects of group versus individual contingencies on resting behavior of preschool children using free time as a reinforcer.* Unpublished paper, Southern Illinois University.

Thomas, C., Sulzer-Azaroff, B., Lukeris, S., & Palmer, M. (1976). Teaching daily self-help skills for long-term maintenance. In B. Etzel, J. LeBlanc, and D. Baer (eds.), *New development in behavioral research: Theory, method, and application.* Hillsdale, N.J.: Lawrence Erlbaum Associates.

Thomas, J. D., Presland, I. E., Grant, M. D., & Glynn, T. L. (1978). Natural rates of teacher approval and disapproval in grade seven classrooms. *Journal of Applied Behavior Analysis, 11,* 94–94.

Thorndike, E. L. (1932). *The fundamentals of learning.* New York: Columbia University Press.

Thorndike, E. L. (1911). *Animal intelligence.* New York: Macmillan.

Thorndike, E. L. (1898). Animal intelligence: An experimental study of the associative processes in animals. *Psychological Review Monograph Supplement, 2* (Whole no. 8).

Timbers, G. D., Timbers, B. J., Fixen, D. L., Phillips, E. L., & Wolf, M. M. (1973). *Achievement Place for pre-delinquent girls: Modification of inappropriate emotional behaviors with token reinforcement and instructional procedures.* Paper read at the American Psychological Association, Montreal, Canada.

Tolman, E. C. (1938). The determiners of behavior at a choice point. *Psychological Review, 45,* 1–41.

Tolman, E. C. (1932). *Purposive behavior in animals and men.* New York: Appleton-Century-Crofts.

Ullman, C. A. (1957). Teachers, peers, and tests as predictors of adjustment. *Journal of Educational Psychology, 48,* 257–67.

Van Alstnyne, D., & Hattwick, L. A. (1939). A follow-up study of the behavior of nursery school children. *Child Development, 10,* 43–69.

Van Houten, R. (1984). Setting up feedback systems in the classroom. In W. L. Heward, T. E. Herson, D. S. Hill, & J. Trap-Porter (eds.), *Focus on behavior analysis in education.* Columbus, Ohio: Merrill.

Van Houten, R. (1983). Punishment: From the animal laboratory to the applied setting. In S. Axelrod & J. Apsche (eds.), *The effects of punishment on human behavior.* San Diego: Academic Press.

Van Houten, R. (1979). Social validation: The evolution of standards of competency for target behaviors. *Journal of Applied Behavior Analysis, 12,* 581–91.

VAN HOUTEN, R. & DOLEYS, D. M. (1983). Are social reprimands effective? In S. Axelrod & J. Apsche (Eds.), *The effects of punishment on human behavior.* San Diego: Academic Press.

VAN HOUTEN, R., & VAN HOUTEN, J. (1977). The performance feedback system in a special education classroom: An analysis of public posting and peer comments. *Behavior Therapy, 8,* 366–76.

VARGAS, J. S. (1977). *Behavioral psychology for teachers.* New York: Harper and Row.

WAHLER, R. G., (1969). Setting generality: Some specific and general effects of child behavior therapy. *Journal of Applied Behavior Analysis, 2,* 239–46.

WALDROP, M. F., & HALVERSON, C. F. (1975). Intensive and extensive peer behavior. Longitudinal and cross-sectional analyses. *Child Development, 46,* 19–26.

WALKER, H. M. & BUCKLEY, N. K. (1973). Teacher attention to appropriate and inappropriate classroom behavior: An individual case study. *Focus on Exceptional Children, 5,* 5–11.

WEINSTEIN, C. S. (1979). The physical environment of the school. *Review of Educational Research, 49,* 577–610.

WELLS, K. C., FOREHAND, R. H., and GREN, K. D. (1977). Effects of a procedure derived from the overcorrection principle on manipulated and nonmanipulated behaviors. *Journal of Applied Behavior Analysis, 10,* 679–87.

WEST, R. P. (1981). *The effects of two levels of teacher presentation rate and reinforcement on classroom disruptions, performance accuracy, and response rate.* Doctoral dissertation, University of Utah, Salt Lake City.

WEST, R. P. (1984). Quantifying learning through the use of direct and frequent performance measurement. In L. P. Grayton & J. M. Biedenbach (eds.), *1984 ASEE annual conference proceedings.* Washington, D.C.: American Society for Engineering Education.

WEST, R. P., & SLOANE, H. N. (1986). Teacher presentation rate and point delivery rate: Effects of classroom disruption, performance accuracy, and response rate. *Behavior Modification, 10* (3), 267–86.

WEST, R. P., & YOUNG, K. R. (March 1983). *The use of decision rules to assist normal and handicapped students to manage their own academic programs.* Paper presented at the Second Annual Precision Teaching Conference, Orlando, Fla.

WEST, R. P., & YOUNG, K. R. (1983). *Utah School for the Deaf: Precision teaching research project final report.* Logan: Utah State University.

WEST, R. P., & YOUNG, K. R. (1985). Precision teaching: The foundation for curriculum monitoring and computerized instructional decision making. In R. P. West & K. R. Young (eds.), *Precision teaching: Instructional decision making, curriculum and management, and research.* Proceedings from the National Precision Teaching Conference, Park City, Utah, April 1984. Logan: Utah State University.

WEST, R. P., YOUNG, K. R., WEST, W. J., JOHNSON, J. I., & FRESTON, C. W. (1985). *AC CEL: An expert system for student performance evaluation and instructional decision-making.* Great Falls, Mont.: Precision Teaching Materials and Associates.

WEXLER, D. (1973). Token and taboo: Behavior modification, token economies, and the law. *California Law Review, 61,* 81–109.

WHITE, M. H. (1975). Natural rates of teacher approval and disapproval in the classroom. *Journal of Applied Behavior Analysis, 8,* 367–72.

WHITE, M. J., & WHITE, K. G. (1977). Citation analysis of psychology journals. *American Psychologist, 32,* 301–305.

WHITE, O. R. (1986). Precision teaching–Precision learning. *Exceptional Children, 52*(6), 522–34.

WHITE, O. R., & HARING, N. G. (1976). *Exceptional Teacher.* Columbus, Ohio: Chas. E. Merrill.

WHITE, O. R., & HARING, N. G. (1980). *Exceptional Teaching* (2d ed.). Columbus, Ohio: Chas. E. Merrill.

WHITE, O. R., & HARING, N. G. (1982). Data-based program-change decisions. In M. Stevens-Dominguez & K. Stremel-Campbell (eds.), *Ongoing data collection for measuring child progress.* Seattle: Western States Technical Assistance Resource (WESTAR).

WHITE, O. R., & LIBERTY, K. A. (1976). Evaluation and measurement. In N. G. Haring & R. Schiefelbusch (eds.), *Teaching special children.* New York: McGraw-Hill.

WHITE-BLACKBURN, G., SEMB, S., & SEMB, G. (1977). The effects of a good behavior contract on the classroom behavior of sixth-grade students. *Journal of Applied Behavior Analysis, 10,* 312.

WHITLEY, A. D., & SULZER, B. (1970). Reducing disruptive behavior through consultation. *The Personnel and Guidance Journal, 38,* 836–41.

WILLIAMS, C. D. (1959). The elimination of tantrum behavior by extinction procedures. *Journal of Abnormal and Social Psychology, 59,* 269.

WILLIAMS, C. D., (1965). The elimination of tantrum behavior by extinction procedures. In L. P. Ullmann and L. Krasner (eds.), *Case studies in behavior modification.* New York: Holt, Rinehart & Winston.

WINETT, R. A., & WINKLER, R. C. (1972). Current behavior modification in the classroom: Be still, be quiet, be docile. *Journal of Applied Behavior Analysis, 5,* 499–504.

WINKLER, R. C. (1970). Management of chronic psychiatric patients by a token reinforcement system. *Journal of Applied Behavior Analysis, 3,* 47–55.

WITRYOL, S. L., & FISCHER, W. F. (1960). Scaling children's incentives by the method of paired comparisons. *Psychological Reports, 7,* 471–74.

WOLF, M. M., BIRNBRAUER, J. S., WILLIAMS, T., and LAWLER, J. (1965). A note on apparent extinction of the vomiting behavior of a retarded child. In L. P. Ullmann and R. Krasner (eds.), *Case studies in behavior modification.* New York: Holt, Rinehart and Winston.

WOLF, M. M., GILES, D. K., & HALL, R. V., (1968). Experiments with token reinforcement in a remedial classroom. *Behavior Research and Therapy, 6*(1), 51–64.

WOLF, M. M., RISLEY, T. R., & MEES, H. L. (1964). Application of operant conditioning procedures to the behavior problems of an autistic child. *Behavior Research and Therapy, 1,* 305–12.

YELTON, A. R., WILDMAN, B. G., & ERICKSON, M. T. (1977). A probability-based formula for calculating interobserver agreement. *Journal of Applied Behavior Analysis.*

YOUNG, J. A., & WINCZE, J. P. (1974). The effects of the reinforcement of compatible and incompatible alternative behaviors on the self-injurious and related behaviors of a profoundly retarded female adult. *Behavior Therapy, 5,* 614–23.

YOUNG, K. R., & WEST, R. P. (1984). *Parent training: Social skills manual.* Logan: Utah State University.

YOUNG, K. R., & WEST R. P. (1985). *Precision teaching: Strategies for instructional decision-making.* Logan, Utah: Behavioral and Educational Training Associates.

YOUNG, K. R., WEST, R. P., & CRAWFORD, A. (1985). The acquisition and maintenance of reading skills by intellectually handicapped deaf students. *Journal of Precision Teaching, 5,* 73–85.

YOUNG, K. R., WEST, R. P., HOWARD, V. F., & WHITNEY, R. (1986). Acquisition, fluency training, generalization, and maintenance of dressing skills of two developmentally disabled children. *Education and Treatment of Children, 9*(1), 16–29.

YOUNG, K. R., WEST, R. P., & SMITH, D. (1984). *A cooperative parent/school program for teaching social skills to handicapped children.* Final Report. U.S. Office of Education, Office of Special Education.

ZIMMERMAN, B. J., & ROSENTHAL, T. L. (1974). Observational learning of rule-governed behavior by children. *Psychological Bulletin, 81,* 29–42.

ZIMMERMANN, E . H., & ZIMMERMANN, J. (1962). The alteration of behavior in a special classroom situation. *Journal of the Experimental Analysis of Behavior, 5,* 614–23.

ZIMMERMAN, E. H., & ZIMMERMAN, J. (1962). The alteration of behavior in a special classroom situation. *Journal of the Experimental Analysis of Behavior, 5,* 59–60.

Index

Behavioral interviewing, 144–45
Behavioral objective, 280–87
Behavioral rehearsal strategy, 271
Behavioral self-management, defined, 214
Behavioral self-management contracts, 213–23
  establishing goals, 215, 216
  evaluating performance, 215–19
  examples of, 222–23
  identifying target behaviors, 214–15
  reasons for, 213
  as transition strategy to self-management, 220–21
Behavior checklists, 145–46
Behavior management systems, peers as monitors or managers of, 245
Behavior of Organisms, The (Skinner), 26
Bellack, A. S., 92
Bereiter, C., 350
Berkler, M. S., 150
Berler, F. S., 275
Berliner, D. C., 349
Biddle, B. J., 326
Bijour, S. W., 9
Bingell, N., 245
Binkoff, J. A., 87
Birnbrauer, J. S., 87
Blechman, E. A., 171
Blessinger, B., 90
Bloom, B., 333, 334
Bloom, B. S., 284–85
Boles, S. M., 150
Bolstad, O., 217
Bootzin, R. R., 172
Born, D. G., 336
Bornstein, P. H., 93
Bostow, D. E., 100
Bradford, D. C., 139
Brantner, J. R., 98, 100
Bribery, token economies as form of, 171
Brigham, T. A., 213, 244
Broden, M. R., 151
Broen, P., 93
Brophy, J.E., 9, 315, 350
Brown, W. E., 76

Bucher, B., 220, 244
Buckley, N. K., 56, 171, 172, 236
Buehler, R. E., 229
Burgio, L. D., 220
Burleigh, R. A., 111
Burron, D., 220
Bushby, K. H., 100
Bushell, D., 172
Bus-riding behavior, 234–35
Butler, C., 245

C

Clames, I. J., 347
Cannon, D., 196
Canter, L., 64
Canter, M., 64
CAP (The Computational Arithmetic Program), 348
Carlisle, K. E., 287
Carmines, E. G., 140
Carnine, D., 287, 292, 294, 305, 312, 335, 339, 340, 350, 351, 360, 361, 364
Carr, E. G., 87, 110
Carroll, J., 333
Carta, J. J., 184, 362, 363
Cartelli, L. M., 112
Cartledge, G., 261
Case design, 158–59
Casella, M. A., 205
Cataldo, M. F., 150
Cautela, J. R., 68
Cerva, R. T., 305
Charting conventions, 346, 347
Chase, P. N., 280
Checklists
  behavior, 145–46
  for naturalistic observations, 264
  social skills, 258–59
Cheney, D., 362
Children
  participation in identification and selection of reinforcers, 68–69
  privacy rights of, 125
Choral responding (unison), 305, 351–60
Clarity of contingency contract, 205–6
Clark, H. B., 243, 245, 273, 274, 336

Parents (*cont.*)
  privacy rights of, 125
  social skills teaching and, 272–73
  time-out with isolation usage and,
    102
Parry, P., 220
Parsons, L. R., 243
Patterson, G. R., 75, 146, 229, 231
Pavlov, I. P., 6, 21
Pazulinec, R., 92
Pear, J., 220
Pedagogy. *See* Strategies, effective
    teaching
Pederson, A., 251
Peer(s)
  influence, group contingency use for,
    228, 229
  less formal use in classroom of, 242–
    47
  management system, 183
  reinforcement, 230–31, 233, 245, 246–
    47
  tutoring, 243–46, 362–65
Penalties in contingency contract, 200–
    201
Performance
  of behavioral self-management
    contract, evaluating, 215–19
  as component of behavioral objective,
    281, 282
  feedback systems in the classroom,
    164–67
Permanent products, 146
Personalized System of Instruction
    (PSI), 336, 337–38
Peschka, C. M., 243
Peters, R., 220
Petersen, P. B., 151
Peterson, C. R., 105
Peterson, D. R., 145
Phillips, E. A., 245, 273
Phillips, E. L., 172, 197, 245, 273
Physical arrangement of classroom,
    325–27
Physical descriptions, 20
Physical prompts, 117–20, 270
Physical punishment, 110–11, 113, 124–
    25, 129

Pinpointing behavior, 35–36, 47, 143,
    344
Plake, B. S., 44
Porcia, E., 88, 232
Porterfield, J. K., 99
Positive-practice overcorrection, 31, 47,
    117, 118, 121–22, 129–30
Positive reinforcement, 16, 25, 27, 47,
    53–82
  common objections to uses of, 73–75
  time-out from, 30–31, 47, 98–109, 129
  types of reinforcers, 54–62
    disadvantages and advantages of,
      62–67
    identifying potential, 67–73
Poulos, R. W., 171
Powers, M. A., 118
Practice
  phase of learning, 164–65
  for social skills, 269–70
Practice Skills Mastery Program, 184
Praising, lesson in, 268
Precision Teaching, 153–54, 341–49,
    363, 364
Prediction from Standard Behavior
    Chart, 346
Premack, D., 67
Premack principle, 67
Prerequisite learning, 288–289
Prerequisites for independent activities,
    310
Prerequisite skills, 304
Prescription based on entry skills, 297–
    98
Presentation techniques, Direct
    Instruction, 351–60
Presland, I. E., 56
Priming, 188
Principles, 291
Privacy rights, 125
Privileges, 123
Probe sheets, 341–44
Proficiency, 339
Program evaluation, 136
Prompting, 42
  modeling, 43, 45, 47–48, 76, 269
  physical, 117–20, 270
  of social skills, 270–71

Understanding, subskill analysis and, 291–94
Unison responding, 351–60
United States Office of Education Follow-Through Program, 305
Unit mastery, 336
Unresponsive child in token economy, 187–88
Utility of measurement technique, 141–42

V

Validity, 140, 143
Van Alstnyne, D., 251
Van Houten, J., 231
Van Houten, R., 109, 113, 164, 166
Vargas, J. S., 171
Varley, J., 230
Verbal prompts, 270
Verbal reprimands, 111–13
Voluntary behavior, 21, 22

W

Wade, L., 243, 362
Wahler, R. G., 228, 229, 245
Walberg, H. J., 315
Waldrop, M. F., 251
Walker, H. M., 56, 146, 171, 172, 236, 255
Walker, J., 255
Wang, M. C., 290
Watch-and-see strategy, 67–68
Watson, J., 6, 21
Weinstein, C. S., 325
Wells, K. C., 117
Wells, K. S., 112
Wesolowski, M. D., 117
West, M. E., 60
West, R. C., 96, 114
West, R. P., 215, 252, 254, 260, 264, 272, 305, 339, 340, 346, 347, 360
West, W. J., 347
Wexler, D., 188

White, K. G., 9
White, M. H., 56, 77
White, M. J., 9
White, O. R., 154, 340, 344, 345, 346, 348
White, W. A. T., 360
White-Balckburn, G., 196
Whitley, A. D., 74, 269
Whitman, T. L., 220
Whorton, D., 362
Willard, D., 88, 232
Williams, C. D., 74
Williams, T., 87
Willson-Morris, M., 44
Wincze, J. P., 110
Winkler, R. C., 93
Wodarski, J., 231, 233
Wolery, M. R., 117
Wolf, M. M., 87, 99, 111, 172, 184, 197, 233–34, 241, 245, 273
Wood, R., 273, 274
Work skills, 285
Wright, W. R., 242
Written contingency contract by negotiation, 201
Written materials, stress on, 336
Wyatt v. Stickney, 123, 125, 126, 188

X

X axis, 152

Y

Y axis, 152
Young, F. R., 96, 114
Young, J. A., 110
Young, K. R., 60, 190, 214, 215, 217, 252, 254, 255, 260, 264, 268, 269, 272, 274, 275, 339, 340, 346, 347

Z

Zeller, R. A., 140
Zimmer, J. W., 44